Negotiating Adolescence in Times of Social Change

The decline of the Socialist governments in Eastern and Central Europe and the resulting political and economic reorganizations of the 1990s provided a dramatic illustration of the far-reaching effects of social change. For those interested in the health and well-being of youth, such instances of social upheaval raise questions of how young people are affected socially and psychologically and whether their development is compromised or enhanced. If social change compromises development, the additional question arises as to what can be done to sustain healthy development in times of social change. The answers to these questions have important implications for our future in a global community because the youth of today are the adults of tomorrow.

This important volume considers the processes through which societal changes exert an impact on the course of adolescent development and on adolescents' social and psychological adjustment. Additionally, several chapters identify individual and contextual factors that can modify the impact of social change and enhance the likelihood of a successful transition to adulthood. Chapter authors include social scientists from Germany, the United Kingdom, and the United States.

Negotiating Adolescence in Times of Social Change

Edited by

LISA J. CROCKETT
University of Nebraska–Lincoln

RAINER K. SILBEREISEN
Friedrich-Schiller University of Jena

CAMBRIDGE
UNIVERSITY PRESS

Dedicated to the memory of John A. Clausen, whose work on the sociology of
adolescence helped shape the views represented in this volume

PUBLISHED BY THE PRESS SYNDICATE OF THE UNIVERSITY OF CAMBRIDGE
The Pitt Building, Trumpington Street, Cambridge, United Kingdom

CAMBRIDGE UNIVERSITY PRESS
The Edinburgh Building, Cambridge CB2 2RU, UK   http: //www.cup.cam.ac.uk
40 West 20th Street, New York, NY 10011-4211, USA   http: //www.cup.org
10 Stamford Road, Oakleigh, Melbourne 3166, Australia
Ruiz de Alarcón 13, 28014 Madrid, Spain

First published 2000

Printed in the United States of America

Typeface Times Roman 10.25/13 pt. and Helvetica   *System* LaTeX 2_ε [TB]

A catalog record for this book is available from
the British Library.

Library of Congress Cataloging in Publication Data

Negotiating adolescence in times of social change / edited by Lisa J.
  Crockett, Rainer K. Silbereisen.
      p.   cm.
    Includes indexes.
    ISBN 0-521-62389-8 (hc.)
    1. Adolescence.   2. Adolescent psychology.   3. Social change.
  I. Crockett, Lisa J.   II. Silbereisen, Rainer K.
  HQ796.N415   1999
  305.235 – dc21   99-10716
                                                      CIP

ISBN 0 521 62389 8   hardback

Contents

Contributors

Jerald G. Bachman
Institute for Social Research
University of Michigan
Ann Arbor, Michigan, USA

Hans Bertram
Humboldt University of Berlin
Department of Sociology
Berlin, Germany

Klaus Boehnke
Department of Sociology
Chemnitz University of Technology
Chemnitz, Germany

Jeanne Brooks-Gunn
Child Development and Education
Teachers College
Columbia University
New York, New York, USA

John Bynner
Centre for Longitudinal Studies
Institute of Education
University of London
London, England

Katherine Jewsbury Conger
Institute for Social and Behavioral
    Research
Iowa State University
Ames, Iowa, USA

Rand D. Conger
Institute for Social and Behavioral
    Research
Iowa State University
Ames, Iowa, USA

Lisa J. Crockett
Department of Psychology
University of Nebraska–Lincoln
Lincoln, Nebraska, USA

Glen H. Elder, Jr.
Carolina Population Center
University of North Carolina
Chapel Hill, North Carolina, USA

Constance A. Flanagan
Agricultural and Extension
    Education
The Pennsylvania State University
University Park, Pennsylvania,
    USA

Mary Agnes Hamilton
Human Development
Cornell University
Ithaca, New York, USA

Stephen F. Hamilton
Human Development
Cornell University
Ithaca, New York, USA

Janet Hardy
School of Medicine
Johns Hopkins University
Baltimore, MD, USA

Kathryn E. Hood
Human Development and Family
    Studies
The Pennsylvania State University
University Park, Pennsylvania, USA

Lloyd D. Johnston
Institute for Social Research
University of Michigan
Ann Arbor, Michigan, USA

Peter Noack
Department of Developmental
    Psychology
Friedrich-Schiller University of Jena
Jena, Germany

Patrick M. O'Malley
Institute for Social Research
University of Michigan
Ann Arbor, Michigan, USA

Anne C. Petersen
W. K. Kellogg Foundation
Battle Creek, Michigan, USA

Martha A. Rueter
Institute for Social and Behavioral
    Research
Iowa State University
Ames, Iowa, USA

Stephen T. Russell
Department of Human
    and Community Development
University of California
Davis, California, USA

Robert J. Sampson
Department of Sociology
University of Chicago
Chicago, Illinois, USA

Alice Schlegel
Department of Anthropology
University of Arizona
Tucson, Arizona, USA

Sara Schley
Center for Young Children and
    Families
Teachers College
Columbia University
New York, New York, USA

John Schulenberg
Institute for Social Research, and
Department of Psychology
University of Michigan
Ann Arbor, Michigan, USA

Michael J. Shanahan
Human Development and Family
    Studies
The Pennsylvania State University
University Park, Pennsylvania, USA

Rainer K. Silbereisen
Department of Developmental
    Psychology
Friedrich-Schiller University of Jena
Jena, Germany

Ruby Takanishi
Foundation for Child Development
New York, New York, USA

Gisela Trommsdorff
Psychology Department
University of Konstanz
Konstanz, Germany

Preface

The decline of the Socialist governments in Eastern and Central Europe and the resulting political and economic reorganizations of the 1990s provided a dramatic illustration of the far-reaching effects of social change. For social scientists interested in the health and well-being of youth, such instances of social upheaval raise questions of how young people are affected socially and psychologically by societal changes, and whether their development is compromised or enhanced. Further, if social change compromises development, the additional question arises as to what can be done to sustain healthy development in times of social change. The answers to these questions have important implications for our future in a global community because the youth of today are the adults of tomorrow. As we stand on the brink of a new century and take stock of the old one, addressing these questions seems especially timely. This was the impetus for the present volume.

In February 1996, a diverse group of social scientists (psychologists, sociologists, and anthropologists) from Germany, the United Kingdom, and the United States convened at the Pennsylvania State University to discuss the ways in which social change may affect adolescent development, the likely consequences for adolescent functioning and well-being, and the kinds of social interventions needed to support healthy development in a changing society. Entitled "Negotiating Adolescence in Times of Social Change," the conference was organized to consider the abrupt and more gradual social changes affecting Western industrialized countries. Drawing on the ecological and life course perspectives, we were especially interested in the processes through which societal changes exert an impact on (1) the course of adolescent development and (2) adolescents' social and psychological adjustment. Additionally, we sought to identify individual and contextual factors that can modify the impact of social change and enhance the likelihood of a successful transition to adulthood. The conference presentations formed the basis of the present volume, and we have retained the conference format in which some presenters focused on their own research and others provided integrative commentaries. The original presentations have been revised, however, in the light of discussions and exchanges that occurred during and following the conference.

Many people contributed to planning the conference and preparing this volume. The conference was initiated as part of an ongoing exchange program between the Department of Human Development and Family Studies of the Pennsylvania State University (United States) and the Department of Developmental Psychology of the Friedrich-Schiller University of Jena (Germany). The two departments fund the exchange program, and we are greatly indebted to them for their support of the program and the conference. We would also like to thank the German Research Council for its generous support of the German presenters, all of whom were participating in a Council-funded research initiative titled "Childhood and Adolescence in Germany Before and After Unification." Finally, we would like to acknowledge the contributions of several individuals who played an important role in the conference and the resulting volume. We are indebted to Leann Birch, who was instrumental in funding the conference and the exchange program; to Fred Vondracek for his help in identifying an excellent group of presenters; and to Sheila Bickle, who kept track of numerous organizational and logistical details in preparation for the conference. We also wish to thank Annett Weise, Katrin Mueller, Verona Christmas, and Jennifer Wyatt for their valuable help in preparing for the conference and editing the book. Most of all, we are indebted to the authors of the chapters for their exciting insights and ideas, their openness to feedback, and their contributions to lively discussions at the conference.

Lisa J. Crockett and Rainer K. Silbereisen

1   Social Change and Adolescent Development: Issues and Challenges

Lisa J. Crockett and Rainer K. Silbereisen

Like other phases of the life span, adolescence is shaped by the sociocultural context in which it occurs. The skills young people are expected to master, the kinds of choices they must make, and the settings they negotiate during the adolescent years are prescribed by social institutions (e.g., the educational system) and by shared expectations concerning the requirements for success in adulthood (Crockett, 1997). Social change, which entails large-scale alterations in ideological, technological, and economic systems within societies, has significant implications for adolescent development. For example, social change can affect the structure and dynamics of social contexts that adolescents experience on a daily basis such as family, school, and youth groups. It can also alter the social institutions and cultural belief systems that organize the adolescent period.

Social change has diverse origins. In some cases, change is spurred by pivotal historical events that can abruptly alter the opportunity matrix for young people's development. Examples include political revolutions such as the break-up of the former Eastern bloc, ethnic conflicts as exemplified in the Balkans, immigration, religious movements such as the fundamentalist upsurge in several Islamic countries, and technological breakthroughs that reorient large segments of the economy. In other cases, changes in social organization occur more gradually as with the post–World War II increase in women's labor force participation, the recent rise in divorce, and the growing proportion of elderly in many industrialized countries.

Determining the consequences of such societal-level changes for adolescent development presents formidable challenges. Social change on one or more dimensions must be documented, the complex processes through which social change may affect adolescents must be identified, and the hypothesized causal processes must be linked empirically to adolescent outcomes. In this chapter, we discuss these challenges and the conceptual issues they raise. We begin with one example of social change and use it as a springboard for discussing four questions:

1. What kinds of contextual changes are produced by social change?
2. How (through what mediating processes) do these changes affect adolescent development and well-being?

1

3. What individual and contextual factors appear to moderate these processes and their outcomes?
4. What are the implications of social change for adolescent adjustment?

Finally, we outline the organization of the present volume as it relates to these issues.

The Great Depression: An Example of Social Change

The myriad pathways through which social change affects adolescent development are illustrated in Elder's studies of the Great Depression (Elder, 1974). During the 1930s, the economic downturn created financial strains for many families in the United States. To cope with hardships such as decreased earnings and loss of credit, families had to reduce expenses and find ways to generate additional income. In response to this need, adolescent boys initiated income-earning activities earlier than usual by finding work outside the home. Adolescent girls contributed to the family economy by helping their mothers produce goods for the family's use. These two kinds of work brought differential rewards. As a consequence of working for pay, boys gained independence from parental supervision, exhibited more autonomous behavior, and developed higher self-esteem. In contrast, the work of girls was unpaid, and thus they had no personal earnings to buy goods (e.g., nice clothes) that would have increased their status in the peer group. Moreover, rather than increasing their independence, girls' work tied them firmly to home. Thus, girls did not experience the benefits of working that accrued to boys. Although boys and girls both had to adapt to family hardship resulting from the economic downturn, the roles available to boys and girls differed, fostering different experiences.

The long-term consequences of early economic disadvantage also differed for adolescent boys and girls. Most of the boys served in World War II and profited from postwar educational benefits (the GI Bill). As a result, many had career achievements comparable to peers whose families had not suffered economically during the Depression. In contrast, economically disadvantaged girls tended to marry early and devote themselves to raising children. Many girls entered the labor force during World War II but were subsequently laid off to provide jobs for returning veterans. Although their lives were in keeping with the prevailing social norms of the 1950s, these women exhibited psychological disadvantage relative to peers as reflected in poorer self-esteem and mental health (Elder, 1974). Thus, adult opportunity structures, which differed for males and females, interacted with adolescent experiences to shape the lives and adjustment of Depression-era adolescents.

Apart from altering adolescents' economic roles within the family, financial pressures during the Depression often disrupted family relationships and parenting. Strains related to job loss, bankruptcy, and depleted savings frequently led to marital disputes. Marital clashes, in turn, resulted in a deterioration in family climate and parental socialization efforts. Not surprisingly, such repercussions were associated with lower psychological well-being in the children. Notably, marital clashes and disputes were exacerbated if the father showed explosive tendencies initially or had a difficult temperament. The financial crisis accentuated these personality attributes, increasing the hostility experienced by the children (Caspi & Bem, 1990; Elder & Caspi, 1990). Thus, although family functioning mediated some of the effects of economic pressures on adolescent adjustment, the personality of key players (particularly the accentuation of negative dispositions) was an important moderator of these effects.

This example shows that social change operates at multiple levels, from the immediate social contexts adolescents experience to national alterations in opportunities for employment, military service, and education. These effects, often moderated by the behavior of parents, may alter adolescent development in myriad ways, for example, by affecting family roles and relationships, by delaying or accelerating entry into adult work and family roles, or by influencing psychological well-being. In turn, adolescents' experiences affect their subsequent development by interacting with the array of opportunities and risks present in a given historical era to influence adult attainments.

Elder's work also underscored the point that social change can affect people differentially on the basis of such individual characteristics as gender and age. The differential impact of family economic hardship for adolescent girls and boys has already been described. Additionally, age was found to interact with gender. Whereas adolescent girls were more vulnerable than boys to negative outcomes of family economic hardship, among younger children, boys were the more vulnerable gender (Elder, 1974; see also Werner & Smith, 1982). Other individual characteristics also proved important for Depression-era adolescents; for example, physically unattractive girls were especially likely to experience paternal rejection under conditions of financial hardship (Elder, Nguyen, & Caspi, 1985).

In sum, the impact of social change is far from uniform. Economic or political crises such as the Depression do not reach all members of a population equally: Some people are more closely linked to the crisis and more likely to experience its effects. Furthermore, the consequences of an event vary according to age, gender, and other characteristics of the person and social context. Thus, some processes (e.g., family financial pressure) may have differential effects for distinct subgroups of adolescents. Indeed, different processes or mechanisms may be active for such subgroups.

Contextual Changes Produced by Social Change

Identifying the mechanisms linking social change to adolescent development at a given time and place requires an understanding of the sociocultural context and how it is changing. The ecological and life course perspectives provide insights into the social environment and the elements that may change under conditions of social upheaval. The ecological perspective affords a differentiated view of the environment by dividing it into multiple levels that influence each other (Bronfenbrenner, 1979, 1989). The life course perspective identifies the constraints on development imposed by social norms and institutions and elucidates the ways in which individuals negotiate their life course in the context of these social constraints (Elder, 1998; Mayer, 1986). Both perspectives posit a dynamic interplay between individual and social context that shapes the course of development.

From an ecological perspective (Bronfenbrenner, 1979, 1989), adolescent development takes place within the immediate social contexts of everyday life: the family, the peer group, the school, and, increasingly, the adolescent workplace. The roles and relationships within these "microsystems" form the basis of daily interactions between the adolescent and the social environment which, over time, shape individual development. Furthermore, these contexts are embedded in a multilevel environmental structure in which "overarching cultural and social belief systems . . . cut across and impinge on multiple microsystems" (Wachs, 1996, p. 796). This suggests that changes in cultural and institutional patterns can influence adolescent development in multiple ways.

First, such changes can alter the structure and dynamics of particular microsystems, as when economic recessions modify family roles and dynamics (Elder, 1974), or when prevailing attitudes about alcohol and other drug use influence norms within the peer group (e.g., Johnston, O'Malley, & Bachman, 1994).

Second, changing institutional patterns may alter the relationships between microsystems involved in child socialization. For example, the collapse of the Socialist political system in the former East Germany changed the relationship between families and schools. Under the Socialist regime, schools were responsible for socializing children to be good citizens and were required to instill values reflecting a "socialist personality." With unification, the task of fostering personality development became the exclusive province of the family, and the role of schools was limited to teaching cognitive skills. This change in the function of schools was accompanied by a reduction in school-based extracurricular activities, which had been a primary source of afterschool child care. The reduction left many families overwhelmed by the need to organize child supervision and take over unfamiliar socialization activities. Researchers have warned that this breakdown in the coordination between microsystems could produce a "socialization vacuum" (Trommsdorff, Chakkarath, & Heller, 1996).

Third, distal (i.e., macrosystem) forces such as the status of the job market may also affect adolescents directly. The potential for proximal and distal effects of social change is illustrated by the rise in divorce rates in the United States in the 1960s and 1970s and the related increase in single-parent families (e.g., Hernandez, 1997). On one level, parental divorce alters the family microsystem because the removal of a parent necessarily alters roles and relationships within the family (Hetherington & Clingempeel, 1992). On another level, the increased number of single-parent families can lead to macrosystem changes that affect adolescents. For example, new child support policies in the United States have been initiated to ensure that nonresident parents contribute to the economic support of their children. In sum, an ecological analysis suggests that social change may operate at multiple levels of the adolescent's social context and that alterations at one level may stimulate changes at other levels. Changes at each level can have direct or indirect effects on adolescent adjustment and development.

The life course perspective offers a complementary framework that emphasizes the importance of social norms and institutions in shaping developmental paths. At a very general level, societies provide "rough scripts and casts of characters whose interactions tend to shape individual lives" (Clausen, 1991, p. 805). More concretely, institutions such as the educational system provide fairly well-articulated paths for individuals to follow; for example, the progression from elementary school through secondary school to college. Furthermore, the contingencies operating between institutions support an implicit sequencing of role transitions (i.e., school completion, job entry, marriage, and parenthood) during the transition to adulthood (Hogan & Astone, 1986). If these contingencies change suddenly in the wake of political or economic events, traditional pathways and timetables may be disrupted, leaving young people to negotiate the transition to adulthood with few institutional supports.

The life course perspective also emphasizes the connection between distinct periods of the life span. Adolescence is viewed as a staging ground for adulthood, a period when young people make decisions (knowingly or unknowingly) that have important implications for their subsequent development (Crockett & Crouter, 1995). The choices adolescents make (e.g., to attend college or not) affect the opportunities and obstacles they encounter in their adult lives.

The utility of combining the ecological and life course perspectives is evident in cases of radical alterations in political or economic systems. For example, the reunification of Germany, an instance of macrosystem change, produced a marked shift in institutional arrangements in the former Eastern bloc countries. Institutional supports that had guaranteed employment, financial security, health care, and child care collapsed, creating a situation in which traditional routines no longer brought the expected results (Heinz, 1996). Thus, reunification affected the dynamics of such microsystems as family and the workplace, and these effects had implications for individual functioning.

Reunification also affected optimal strategies for managing the transition to adulthood. In the former East Germany, preparing for a profession was institutionalized as an integrated sequence of training experiences, apprenticeships, and employment opportunities. Once young people chose a profession (with strong guidance from parents and teachers), they could slip into an institutional mold and be carried toward a career without the risk of unexpected changes along the way. Moreover, a secure, full-time job was virtually guaranteed. In this context, early vocational choice and commitment were instrumental and brought rewards. In contrast, people in West Germany had more vocational options but without the guarantee of secure, full-time jobs; also, technological change was in progress. Under these circumstances, greater flexibility regarding vocational choice was beneficial; it was better to remain open to new information and alert to emerging options than to adhere to firm vocational commitments (Kerpelman, Pittman, & Lamke, 1997). With unification, adolescents in the former East Germany are now confronting this unfamiliar scenario and will need to adjust their strategies and timetables concerning vocational identity.

In summary, the ecological and life course perspectives provide complementary frameworks for analyzing the impact of social change. Social change can alter the structure and dynamics of everyday contexts such as the family or the relations between these contexts. Moreover, social change can alter the institutions that support particular choices and life paths. Presumably, these changes affect adolescents' development by altering their goals, strategies, and choices.

Mediating Processes: Perceptions, Goals, and Plans

With age, children become increasingly able to select and shape their environments in ways that influence their development (e.g., Lerner, 1982). Increased capacity in this regard is a hallmark of adolescence; compared with children, adolescents have greater cognitive and behavioral capabilities that enable them to influence their environments. Moreover, in Westernized nations, adolescents are granted increased autonomy to make decisions with long-term consequences (e.g., dropping out of high school, attending college, getting married). Thus, adolescents have considerable opportunity to set goals and plan their future, although there is tremendous variability in how much goal-setting and planning actually occurs. Individuals can use several cognitive mechanisms to shape their development actively, including personal goals, identity, efficacy beliefs, and planful competence (e.g., Brandtstädter, 1997; Clausen, 1991). These processes may mediate the effects of social change on adolescent development.

Personal Goals

Adolescents set goals that guide their actions and influence their subsequent development. In recent psychological research, concepts such as personal tasks (Little, 1993), life tasks (Cantor, 1994), and personal goals (Nurmi, 1993) have been used to characterize such efforts. These concepts have a problem-solving metaphor in common: adolescents are thought to perceive social expectations and to define tasks for themselves based on these expectations. For example, Nurmi (e.g., 1989) has shown that adolescents' (and adults') personal goals reflect culturally based developmental tasks associated with their phase of life. How adolescents translate these expectations into personal striving is a product of their individual interests, perceptions of viable options, and capacity for strategic planning. Social change may alter young people's goals (e.g., by changing the available options, the value placed on particular goals, or the capabilities and credentials required for accomplishing particular goals).

Identity

The development of personal goals is related to the broader process of identity formation. By many accounts (Erikson, 1968; Havighurst, 1948/1972), forming an identity is the overarching task of adolescence, subsuming more circumscribed tasks such as pursuing one's education, choosing a vocation, or establishing mature relationships with peers. Following Erikson (1968) and more recent work by Marcia (1980) and Waterman (1982), the development of a coherent, integrated sense of self is linked to finding one's niche in society and acquiring a sense of self as existing through time. Young people who have formed an identity know who they are, where they came from, and where they are headed. An identity provides a framework linking personal goals and choices to the life course as a whole.

Some kinds of social change may interfere with the usual process of identity formation. For example, the array of available occupations may change, delaying the formation of a vocational identity. Additionally, some people may experience a disjuncture in their personal biography if past achievements that are central to their identity become irrelevant in the new social order. As an example, the transformation to market economies in former European Socialist countries shifted the nature of the personal and social skills needed for success. Characteristics such as impression management, communication skills, and willingness to take risks and show responsibility became more important than before for both blue and white collar workers (Baethge, Andretta, Naevecke, Rossbach, & Trier, 1996; Koehler, 1996). Presumably, adolescents perceived these new requirements and reoriented their goals accordingly. By inducing new personal goals, social change affected identity formation and other aspects of development.

Self-Efficacy

Control or efficacy beliefs (Bandura, 1995) represent a third important mechanism of self-produced development. Without the belief that one is able to arrange things in a way that facilitates achievement of one's goals and enhances life satisfaction, the motivation for goal-directed action would be lost (Silbereisen & Eyferth, 1986). Adolescents who lack such beliefs might withdraw from the challenge of shaping their futures or pursue their goals less energetically or in less cognitively sophisticated ways. Most important, only those convinced of their efficacy will seek out and explore new settings that further stimulate their developmental progress.

Recent experiences in former Eastern bloc countries suggest that social change can influence adolescents' efficacy-related beliefs. Grob et al. (1996) compared adolescents from seven Western and seven former Eastern bloc countries in terms of perceived control. They found higher scores among Eastern bloc youth and speculated that the rapid expansion of individual freedom had stimulated an increase in perceptions of personal autonomy and efficacy.

Planful Competence

Individuals also shape their development through planning. Strategic planning entails more than formulating and pursuing goals; it requires a clear mental representation of a course of action in terms of strategies, sequencing of activities, and so forth. Clausen (1991) reported important differences among adolescents in "planful competence," which is defined as a combination of dependability, intellectual investment, and self-confidence.

Societal change can alter the extent to which planful competence plays a role in young people's future-oriented choices. In a recent study, Shanahan and his colleagues (Shanahan, Elder, & Miech, 1997) compared two cohorts of gifted men. One cohort faced the poor job prospects of the Depression era; the other encountered the boom economy of the post–World War II period. The different economic milieus were associated with differential effects of planful competence. Men of the older cohort tended to stay in school regardless of their level of planful competence, apparently waiting for better times. In contrast, planfully competent men in the later cohort received more education than their less planful peers. Evidently, the limited employment opportunities of the Depression constrained behavioral choices, reducing the role of planful competence in men's educational decisions.

The foregoing suggests a general model of the processes mediating social change effects. Social change entails alterations in cultural beliefs, social institutions, or both. Changes at this more distal level affect operations within immediate social contexts (microsystems) as well as the beliefs espoused by parents, peers, and the media. In turn, altered roles, relationships and practices within proximal social contexts, in conjunction with perceptions of economic opportunities and vocational options, are likely to influence adolescents' personal goals, strategies for attaining their goals, identity, self-efficacy beliefs, and planful competence. These perceptions are then translated into actions and choices that shape subsequent development.

Moderators of Social Change Effects

As noted earlier, the effects of social change do not apply uniformly to an entire population. Rather, effects vary as a function of the individual's age or developmental status at the time of the social transformation. A contemporary example comes from research on values in East and West Germany after unification. The difference in collectivist values was small in 1991, but even smaller by 1996, reflecting the effects of unification (Reitzle & Silbereisen, 1997). However, the decrease in collectivist values among former East Germans was not uniform. Rather, those who were adolescents at the time of unification (and had spent their adolescent "impressionable" years under East German conditions) showed less change in attitudes than those who were younger at the time of unification.[1] More broadly, personal characteristics such as gender, ethnicity, temperament, and other "developmentally instigative" characteristics (Bronfenbrenner, 1989) condition how people respond to an individual and how the individual engages the social world. These characteristics moderate the effects of social change on development.

For example, psychological characteristics such as self-efficacy and locus of control alter the impact of social change. Among former East Germans, individuals who exhibited higher internal control beliefs were generally more successful following unification than their peers, particularly regarding employment (Diewald, Huinink, & Heckhausen, 1996). Thus, an internal locus of control served a protective function in the wake of social upheaval.

Implications for Adolescent Adjustment

Social change is expected to have implications for adolescent development and adjustment. Although some degree of social change is characteristic of modern industrialized societies, changes that alter the organization of social life are presumed to present major adaptive challenges that can overburden the coping capacities of some young people. This should be especially true when young people are also attempting to cope with the normative changes of adolescence or with nonnormative life events such as parental death (e.g., Petersen, 1987). Certainly, the degree of challenge depends on the scale, rate, and pervasiveness of change: Large-scale political reorganizations that permeate all levels of society may have greater effects than more circumscribed changes that primarily affect a single microsystem. Where change is more gradual and limited, most people can find a balance between what worked in the past and what the new situation requires. Thus, the danger lies not in change per se but in rapid, pervasive change.

Further, as is true for most crises, social change implies both risks and opportunities. The balance between these two sides of the coin is not the same across phases of the life span or for individuals who held different social positions before the change. We might expect a less orderly progression to adulthood for many youth during periods of rapid social change and a greater chance of failure en route for those unable to adapt to new demands and take advantage of new opportunities. At the same time, for youth whose projected life course before the change would have been rigidly prescribed and economically limited, the disruption in normative patterns opens up new avenues for achievement and personal satisfaction. As noted earlier, the impact of such societal changes will also depend in part on characteristics of the individual (temperamental, social, cognitive) that affect the ways in which adolescents negotiate the changing social, political, and economic landscape.

In summary, social change can be studied as a natural experiment in which the social parameters that sustain normative developmental patterns are in flux. By examining these changes and assessing their impact on adolescent development, we can learn which parameters comprise critical social supports. Furthermore, because rapid, large-scale social change is presumably stressful (disrupting institutional contingencies and creating uncertainty about optimal courses of action), the study of social change enables a look at the impact of stress on adolescent functioning and the identification of factors that may enhance resilience.

Organization of the Present Volume

The implications of social change for adolescent development and the processes through which effects of social change occur are the subject of the present volume. Currently, we know little about the diverse ways in which social change affects adolescence, the mechanisms involved, and the impact of distinct kinds of social change (e.g., limited or pervasive). Equally important, there is limited information on the role of individual characteristics in determining adolescents' responses to social change, although some research has begun to address this issue with adults (Bandura, 1995). Thus, we do not know which characteristics may be most beneficial in helping young people cope successfully.

This volume is organized around several themes emerging from the preceding discussion: models of social change effects, implications of social change for the nature and timing of adolescent transitions, impact of social change on immediate contexts (family, peer group, and neighborhood), the relation of social change to adolescent health and well-being, and implications for social intervention. In the first section, Elder and Russell offer a multilevel model of the intersection of social change and individual lives; they provide a "road map" of the points at which social change affects individual development. The chapter by Brooks-Gunn and colleagues examines social change through the lens of intergenerational differences in teenage childbearing. The commentary chapter by Trommsdorff offers a complementary model of social change effects that emphasizes the role of the individual's subjective experience.

The second section addresses the implications of social change for the nature and timing of adolescents' developmental transitions. Schlegel focuses on adolescents' ability to borrow cultural forms (e.g., traditions) from other societies and incorporate them into their own developmental transitions, thereby participating in the production of social change. Bynner shows that the nature and timing of adolescents' developmental transitions are altered as a side effect of social change, and that these alterations have differential consequences for adolescents who occupy distinct positions in the social structure. The chapter by Silbereisen compares the timing of developmental transitions in former East and West Germany after unification and shows that East–West differences in individual timetables reflect the distinct institutional patterns that existed before unification. The commentary chapter by Shanahan and Hood focuses on human agency and its role in adolescents' responses to social change.

The third section tackles the impact of social change on particular social contexts. Noack examines the role of unification on adolescent peer groups and norms and notes that similar cultural practices can yield different outcomes in different settings. Bertram shows that the distribution of family types (singles, married couples, widows) has changed over the 20th century and that this has potential implications for adolescent development. Sampson discusses the changing neighborhood patterns affecting some U.S. cities and their implications for the control of adolescents and neighborhood crime. The commentary chapter by Flanagan highlights the active role of adolescents as agents of social change.

The fourth section addresses the issue of adolescent health. Conger and colleagues summarize their tests of a path model linking family economic pressure to marital distress, parent–child interaction, and adolescent emotional well-being. Schulenberg and colleagues examine adolescent well-being across multiple U.S. cohorts and find that post–high school changes in psychological well-being and substance use are largely similar for cohorts who graduated between the mid-1970s and mid-1990s. In his commentary, Boehnke discusses the challenge of capturing social change through the study of cohorts.

The fifth section applies our emerging knowledge of social change to the design and implementation of interventions aimed at fostering healthy adolescent development. The dilemma is how to prepare youth for adulthood when ongoing social change makes the future difficult to predict. Hamilton and Hamilton argue for better coordination among the various institutions that adolescents must navigate, especially the school-to-work-transition. Takanishi focuses on "basic survival skills" needed to make a successful transition to adulthood and identifies general strategies for social intervention. In her commentary chapter, Petersen identifies the challenge of preparing youth for a future that cannot be fully divined and emphasizes the importance of family and community in supporting a successful transition to adulthood in times of social change.

References

Alwin, D. F. (1994). Aging, personality, and social change: The stability of individual differences over the adult life span. In D. L. Featherman, R. M. Lerner, & M. Perlmutter (Eds.), *Life-span development and behavior, Vol. 12* (pp. 135–185). Hillsdale, NJ: Erlbaum.

Baethge, M., Andretta, G., Naevecke, S., Rossbach, U., & Trier, M. (1996). *Die berufliche Transformation in den neuen Bundesländern* [The transformation of occupational demands in the new federal states]. Münster: Waxmann.

Bandura, A. (1995). Exercise of personal and collective efficacy in changing societies. In A. Bandura (Ed.), *Self-efficacy in changing societies* (pp. 1–45). Cambridge, England: Cambridge University Press.

Brandtstädter, J. (1997). Action perspectives on human development. In W. Damon (Ed.), *Handbook of child psychology: Vol. 1. Theoretical models of human development* (5th ed. pp. 807–863). New York: Wiley.

Bronfenbrenner, U. (1979). *The ecology of human development: Experiments by nature and design.* Cambridge, MA: Harvard University Press.

Bronfenbrenner, U. (1989, April). *The developing ecology of human development: Paradigm lost or paradigm regained?* Paper presented at the biennial meeting of the Society for Research in Child Development, Kansas City, MO.

Cantor, N. (1994). Life task problem solving: Situational affordances and personal needs. *Personality and Social Psychology Bulletin, 20,* 235–243.

Caspi, A., & Bem, D. (1990). Personality continuity and change across the life course. In L. Pervin (Ed.), *Handbook of personality* (pp. 549–575). New York: Guilford Press.

Clausen, J. S. (1991). Adolescent competence and the shaping of the life course. *American Journal of Sociology, 96,* 805–842.

Crockett, L. J. (1997). Cultural, historical, and subcultural contexts of adolescence: Implications for health and development. In J. Schulenberg, J. L. Maggs, & K. Hurrelmann (Eds.), *Health risks and development during adolescence* (pp. 23–53). Cambridge, England: Cambridge University Press.

Crockett, L. J., & Crouter, A. C. (1995). Pathways through adolescence: An overview. In L. J. Crockett & A. C. Crouter (Eds.), *Pathways through adolescence: Individual developmental in relation to social contexts* (pp. 1–12). Mahwah, NJ: Lawrence Erlbaum Associates.

Diewald, M., Huinink, J., & Heckhausen, J. (1996). Lebensverläufe und Persönlichkeitsentwicklung im gesellschaftlichen Umbruch. Kohortenschicksale und Kontrollverhalten in Ostdeutschland nach der Wende [Life histories and developmental control in times of macrosocial ruptures: The case of different birth cohorts in the transformation process in Eastern Germany]. *Kölner Zeitschrift für Soziologie und Sozialpsychologie, 48,* 219–248.

Elder, G. H., Jr. (1974). *Children of the Great Depression: Social change in life experience.* Chicago: University of Chicago Press.

Elder, G. H., Jr. (1998). The life course and human development. In W. Damon (Series Ed.) & R. Lerner (Vol. Ed.), *Handbook of child psychology: Vol. 1. Theoretical models of human development* (5th ed., pp. 939–991). New York: Wiley.

Elder, G. H., Jr., & Caspi, A. (1990). Studying lives in a changing society: Sociological and personological explorations. In A. I. Rabin., R. A. Zucker, & S. Frank (Eds.), *Studying persons and lives* (pp. 201–247). New York: Springer-Verlag.

Elder, G. H., Jr., Nguyen, T. V., & Caspi, A. (1985). Linking family hardship to children's lives. *Child Development, 56,* 361–375.

Erikson (1968). *Identity: Youth and crisis.* New York: Norton.

Grob, A., Little, T. D., Wanner, B., & Wearing, A. J. (1996). Adolescents' well-being and perceived control across 14 sociocultural contexts. *Journal of Personality and Social Psychology, 71,* 785–795.

Havighurst, R. J. (1948/72). *Developmental tasks and education* (3rd ed.). New York: McKay.

Heinz, W. (1996). Berufsverläufe im Transformationsprozess [Occupational trajectories during the social and political transformations]. In S. E. Hormuth, W. R. Heinz, H.-J. Kornadt, H. Sydow, & G. Trommsdorff (Eds.), *Individuelle Entwicklung, Bildung und Berufsverläufe* (pp. 273–358). Opladen, Germany: Leske & Budrich.

Hernandez, D. J. (1997). Child development and the social demography of childhood. *Child Development, 68,* 149–169.

Hetherington, E. M., & Clingempeel, W. G. (1992). Coping with marital transitions. *Monographs of the Society for Research in Child Development, 57* (Serial No. 227).

Hogan, D. P., & Astone, N. M. (1986). The transition to adulthood. *Annual Review of Sociology, 12,* 109–130.

Johnston, L. D., O'Malley, P. M., & Bachman, J. G. (1994). *Drug use among American high school students: National trends through 1993.* Rockville, MD: National Institute of Drug Abuse.

Kerpelman, J. L., Pittman, J. F., & Lamke, L. K. (1997). Toward a microprocess perspective on adolescent identity development: An identity control theory approach. *Journal of Adolescent Research, 12,* 325–346.

Koehler, T. (1996). Managementkultur Ost und West: Zur personalen Situation des leitenden Managements in der Region Ostthüringen [Management culture East and West: The personal situation of upper level managers in the eastern Thuringia region]. In W. Frindte, T. Fahrig, & T. Koehler, *Deutsch-deutsche Spiele.* Münster, Germany: Lit.

Lerner, R. M. (1982). Children and adolescents as producers of their own development. *Developmental Review, 2,* 342–370.

Little, B. R. (1993). Personal projects and the distributed self: Aspects of a conative psychology. In J. Suls (Ed.), *Psychological perspectives on the self* (pp. 157–185). Hillsdale, NJ: Erlbaum.

Marcia, J. (1980). Identity in adolescence. In J. Adelson (Ed.), *Handbook of adolescent psychology* (pp. 159–187). New York: Wiley.

Mayer, K. U. (1986). Structural constraints on the life course. *Human Development, 29*(3), 163–170.

Nurmi, J. E. (1989). Development of orientation to the future during early adolescence: A four-year longitudinal study and two cross-sectional comparisons. *International Journal of Psychology, 24,* 195–214.

Nurmi, J. E. (1993). Adolescent development in an age-graded context: The role of personal beliefs, goals, and strategies in the tackling of developmental tasks and standards. *International Journal of Behavioral Development, 16,* 169–189.

Petersen, A. C. (1987). The nature of biological-psychosocial interactions: The sample case of early adolescence. In R. M. Lerner & T. T. Foch (Eds.), *Biological-psychosocial interactions in early adolescence* (pp. 35–61). Hillsdale, NJ: Lawrence Erlbaum Associates.

Reitzle, M., & Silbereisen, R. K. (1997, April). *Adapting to social change: Adolescents' values in Eastern and Western Germany.* Paper presented at the Biennial Meeting of the Society for Research in Child Development, Washington, DC.

Shanahan, M. J., Elder, G. H., & Miech, R. A., (1997). History and agency in men's lives: Pathways to achievement in cohort perspective. *Sociology of Education, 70,* 54–67.

Silbereisen, R. K., & Eyferth, K. (1986). Development as action in context. In R. K. Silbereisen, K. Eyferth, & G. Rudinger (Eds.), *Development as action in context: Problem behavior and normal youth development* (pp. 3–16). New York: Springer-Verlag.

Trommsdorff, G., Chakkarath, P., & Heller, P. (1996). Kindheit im Transformationsprozess [Childhood during the process of social and political transformation]. In S. E. Hormuth, W. R. Heinz, H.-J. Kornadt, H. Sydow, & G. Trommsdorff (Eds.), *Individuelle Entwicklung, Bildung und Berufsverläufe* (pp. 11–78). Opladen, Germany: Leske & Budrich.

Wachs, T. D. (1996). Known and potential processes underlying developmental trajectories in childhood and adolescence. *Developmental Psychology, 32,* 697–801.

Waterman, A. (1982). Identity development from adolescent to adulthood: An extension of theory and a review of research. *Developmental Psychology, 18,* 341–358.

Werner, E. E., & Smith, R. (1982). *Vulnerable but invincible: A longitudinal study of children and youth.* New York: McGraw-Hill.

Part I

Models of Social Change Effects

2   Surmounting Life's Disadvantage

Glen H. Elder, Jr. and Stephen T. Russell

Children of disadvantage are seldom expected to do well in life. Childhood handicaps are known to cumulate, narrowing the range of options and the prospects for life success. Chronic disruptions of family life can undermine school achievement and occupational prospects; likewise, family instability makes friends more valuable and can enhance the risk of antisocial peers. These cycles of disadvantage are well known (Rutter & Madge, 1976). Less recognized, however, is the number of young people who manage to surmount life's disadvantage.

Thirty years ago Jean Macfarlane (1963) discovered that a good many study members in her Berkeley Guidance sample had risen above Depression hardships during the 1930s. They had fared better than staff predictions. She sought explanations for this turnaround in the psyche and proximal world of the individual, focusing on the maturation value of hardship experiences. "We have learned that no one becomes mature without living through the pains and confusions of maturing experiences" (1971, p. 341). She concluded that developmental gains may be associated with the departure from home and community; these changes often provide an opportunity to "work through early confusions and inhibitions" (p. 341). Pathways out of disadvantage identify human agency as a strategic perspective on adolescents who are growing up during times of social change.

Historical times shape the transition to adulthood and thus help to explain the disparity between a Depression childhood and adult achievement. Nearly three out of four of the Berkeley men were mobilized into the armed forces during World War II and the Korean conflict, and those who grew up in Depression hardship entered the military at the earliest possible time, right out of high school (Elder, 1986).

During the past several years support for this research has come from multiple sources, including the National Institute of Mental Health (MH00567, MH19734, MH43270, MH48165, MH51361), the National Institute on Drug Abuse (DA05347), the Bureau of Maternal and Child Health (MCJ-109572), the MacArthur Foundation Research Network on Successful Adolescent Development among Youth in High-Risk Settings, a contract with the U.S. Army Research Institute, the Iowa Agriculture and Home Economics Experiment Station (Project No. 3320), and a Research Scientist Award (MH 00567).

17

Between high school and the middle years, these men gained more self-confidence and occupational progress than other men in the service and sample. Some of this developmental change may have occurred through the stabilizing influence of a supportive marriage during the postwar years. Veterans' access to higher education also played a role in their life success.

This chapter argues that an understanding of social change in the lives of young people has much to do with the research questions we ask and their points of entry. The effect of this change is contingent on the personal history young people bring to the new situation, on their life stage at the time, and on the demands of the situation. In this sense, life history can be viewed in part as an expression of human agency and the construction of lives.

In life course theory, the principle of human agency states that "individuals construct their own life course through the choices and actions they take within the constraints and opportunities of history and social circumstances" (Elder, 1998). To explore the full implications of this principle, we draw upon three other principles of life course study: the location of individual lives in historical time and place, the differential timing of lives through events and experiences, and linked lives.

This chapter focuses briefly on two different historical periods in which adolescence was shaped by the agency of young people and their particular opportunities and constraints: the Great Depression of the 1930s, and, 50 years later, the Great Farm Crisis and rural decline of the 1980s and 1990s (Elder, 1995). The resulting portrait is documented by a longitudinal research program on lives in changing times over three decades.[1] Studies of "children of the Great Depression" were launched in the mid-1960s by the senior author, Glen H. Elder, at the Institute of Human Development, University of California, Berkeley. The project on rural Midwestern youth was modeled after the Depression research and began in 1988–89.

Within these historical eras, we view the agency of youth in terms defined by specific historical times and places. World War II played a major role in structuring pathways out of Depression disadvantage. Some 50 years later, migration to urban areas of economic prosperity provided a general escape route for youth in the disadvantaged rural Midwest of the United States. In each era, societal changes left their mark on the expression of human agency in youth's "negotiation of adolescence."

Changing Times in Lives: Asking the Research Question

Differing birth years in a changing society expose the young to different historical worlds with their distinctive priorities, constraints, and options. People who share the same birth years are said to be members of a birth cohort. Historical influences are expressed as cohort effects when social change differentiates the life course of successive cohorts. Historical influences also take the form of a period effect when the impact is relatively uniform across successive birth cohorts. In both cases, birth year and cohort membership are merely a proxy for exposure to a particular type of historical change.

To know whether individual lives reflect historical change we must move beyond specific cohorts and their historical context to the direct study of changing environments. The research question should focus on the social change in question and its life course implications, as in the analysis of Depression hardship and its effects on young adolescents (Elder, 1974). What is the process by which the economy's collapse altered the childhood and adolescence of the young? Five mechanisms in life course theory are helpful in charting this process. The concept of *life stage* at the time of change indicates that a changing environment has different implications for people who differ in age and social role at the time. A drastic decline in the economy affects adult workers through a declining employment and commercial market, whereas young children are influenced by the resulting changes in family life and economic support.

A second mechanism is known as the *situational imperatives* in which adaptations are governed by the behavioral requirements of the new situation. New job opportunities entail new behavioral imperatives and thus invite personal change toward different objectives. A third mechanism, the *accentuation principle*, states that requirements of the new situation interact with the individual's life history and acquired dispositions to produce behavioral adaptations. Stressful situations, for example, accentuate irritable tendencies. A fourth mechanism refers to the *equilibrating process of losing and regaining control* in life transitions. Social change entails some loss of personal control, which prompts efforts to regain control, such as the entry of more family members into the labor market during periods of family economic distress. Lastly, social change of any kind can alter the life prospects of youth through people who are significant in their lives. The mechanism of *interdependent lives* refers to these multiple channels of influence.

When the objective is to understand social change in young lives, inquiry ideally explores the particular change and its behavioral implications. The developmental consequences of social change extend across life domains, such as work and family, and across stages of the life course. In *Children of the Great Depression* (Elder, 1974), the effects of family income loss during the 1930s were expressed through family adaptations to children's values, psychology, and achievement. The same linking process applies to contemporary children who are growing up in disadvantaged inner-city neighborhoods and rural areas (Elder, 1995). Impoverished neighborhoods and communities limit the resources and options of families and thus affect the development of children.

This point of departure represents the "framing statement" of the study and is usually specified in the general research question (See Figure 1). What is the impact of an economic downturn, for example, on family and child? How are nationwide changes in educational requirements expressed in the lives of a new generation? General framing statements do not rule out other secondary points of entry and

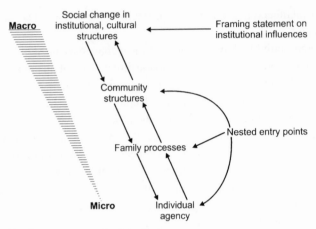

Figure 1. Framing statements and points of entry.

their research questions. For example, the biological constraints of pubertal status were important for understanding the self-consciousness of "children of the Great Depression" (Elder, 1974) in a time of economic hardship. The study also explored sources of self-esteem.

Large, complex studies generally have multiple levels; social change and individual development, for example, may be linked through community structure and family-level processes. The objective for a study that is framed in terms of social change is to nest developmental analyses within these social contexts. Cairns and Cairns (1991, p. 250) listed five levels of analysis that are relevant to a study of aggression, extending from the individual and interindividual levels to social networks that link people, connections between networks, and the larger cultural–ecological system. Change in the latter system might be traced through social networks to the individual child. This causal sequence could depend in part on the relation between family and school or family and peers, the internetwork domain. The complexity of taking note of all levels might seem unwieldy and impractical, yet recognition of this conceptual map constitutes the first step toward making informed, simplifying research decisions.

The most important decision involves the *entry point that frames the study, the framing statement*; it spans multiple levels of individual and social life. At the macroanalytic level, the influences of social change establish developmental constraints for choices and individual agency at the microanalytic level. Framing statements place individuals in the broad context of social change; however, the choices that people make and their efficacy depend on the changing society and the developing individual.

Adolescence is a particularly important phase of life for the study of social change. Free of adult roles and responsibilities, youth have the possibility of developing novel responses to changes that occur in their lives and communities. Clausen

(1993) argued that it is the planful adolescent who is most likely to make wise decisions in shaping the life course; it is the planfulness of adolescence that shapes the life course from young adulthood through later life. Planful adolescents are better prepared "for adult roles and will select, and be selected for, opportunities that give them a head start" (p. 21). However, planfulness counts for much less when options are few. For example, during the Chinese Cultural Revolution (1966–76), the residential, work, and marital decisions of urban youth were made in large measure by their work units (Elder, Wu, & Jihui, 1993).

In the United States, hard times and war have structured options for families and youth and have done so in large part according to the age of the individual. Older children in Depression hard times went to work to help the family and benefited from the skills and esteem produced by such work, whereas younger children spent the majority of their earliest years in hard-pressed households, often suffering from family disruption and conflict (Elder, 1981). In addition to life stage, the choices of Depression young people had much to do with significant others, their family, and friends. Economic hardships, for example, undermined parental nurturance through strained marital relationships (Conger & Elder, 1994). The adverse effect of these hardships on children was minimized in families with strong emotional ties.

Up to this point, we have viewed youth's pathways to adulthood in terms of choices and actions in ecologies defined by historical time and place. Any effort to assess the impact of historical time requires research questions that relate specific social changes to individual experience. These questions and their entry points represent framing statements for the research when they specify the major objective of a study. As in *Children of the Great Depression* (Elder, 1974, enlarged edition, 1999), a framing statement for research, with its research question and point of entry (e.g., from the change event or process) is typically coupled with secondary research questions and entry points. To understand the full meaning of this point, we turn first to children who grew up in the Great Depression and then to a study of rural youth who face a limited future in the rural Midwest.

Children of the Great Depression

Two groups of California children entered the troubled decade of the 1930s at different ages: the Oakland Growth sample of 167 members (birth dates, 1920–21), and the Berkeley Guidance sample of 214 members (birth dates, 1928–29 — Elder, 1974/1999, 1981). Data on these cohorts were collected across the 1930s on an annual basis and during widely spaced follow-ups into the 1980s. After many years of study, we know that the cohort age disparity made a substantial difference in lives. People of unlike age bring disparate experiences and skills to changing times and occupy different roles and statuses. These differences shape the imprint of historical events on individual lives.

All members of the Oakland cohort were young children during the prosperity of the 1920s, a period of rapid growth in California. They were too old in the 1930s to be wholly dependent on deprived households, and they avoided the demoralization of an unreceptive labor market by entering college and jobs as the country mobilized for war. Most of the men served in the armed forces of World War II. By contrast, the Berkeley cohort followed a path that maximized developmental risks, especially among males. They encountered family hardships during the early dependency years of childhood and the developmental problems of adolescence during a period of mass mobilization in World War II. An essential perspective for understanding the Great Depression is the wide variation in family loss and well-being. Some families lost heavily, whereas others managed to avoid meaningful losses altogether in the middle and working class. Keeping this variation in mind, along with a one-fourth decline in cost of living, we identified nondeprived and deprived families; deprived families lost 34% or more of their 1929 income by 1933. This division proved to be equally appropriate for the Berkeley cohort.

Three family processes offered a way of thinking about the impact of the Depression economy on children. The economic collapse made a difference in children's lives through changes in their families. Changes were expressed in (1) the household economy, (2) family relationships, and (3) social and emotional strains. These changes occurred in both cohorts, but they had different implications for older and younger children. We begin with the older group, the Oakland cohort.

The first pathway in Figure 2 illustrates drastic income loss that shifts the household economy toward more labor-intensive operations. These shifts include the entry of mother and children into productive roles as earners, the involvement of children in household operations, and a reduction of expenditures. Changes of this kind had far-reaching implications for the older Oakland cohort. Boys from deprived homes contributed paid income to assist their parents, as did a smaller number of girls, whereas girls in hard-pressed families often took over more household tasks

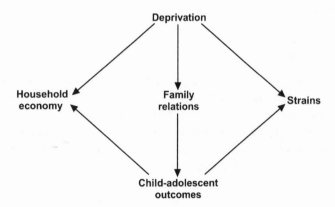

Figure 2. Family patterns as linkages.

when mother assumed a paid job. These household changes enable us to understand the precocious work orientation of boys who grew up in deprived families — their involvement in work and their management of money in later life.

Boys who acquired paid jobs during the 1930s became more socially independent between junior high and high school when compared with nonemployed youth, and these boys were judged to be more responsible in financial matters by their mothers. Staff observers judged boys with jobs to be more efficacious and energetic than the nonemployed on a set of rating scales. Efficacious youth may have sought work, but their mastery experience no doubt strengthened feelings of personal efficacy.

Oakland boys who took on the responsibilities of paid jobs and household chores were likely to have given more thought to the future and especially to their preferred form of work. Working boys were more apt as adults to have a crystallized sense of their work career when compared with other men. The working boys settled more quickly on a stable line of work and displayed less floundering during their 20s. This pattern of work had much to do with the occupational success of men who grew up in hard-pressed Oakland families during the 1930s.

A second microtheory of family processes focuses on a shift in family relationships: pathway 2 in Figure 2. The father's loss of earnings and resulting changes in family support increased the relative power of the mother, reduced the effectiveness and level of parental control, and diminished the father's attractiveness as a role model. The mother became a more central parental figure in the family on matters of affection, authority, and the division of labor. More important, such family changes in response to income loss accelerated the social independence of boys and enhanced the family dependence of girls. Although boys from deprived families often lost a significant male figure, the change in family pattern reinforced the domestic role of girls and their subordination to the mother. As a result, girls from deprived families acquired strong preferences for a conventional domestic way of life – an orientation they expressed in adulthood in values concerning family life, marriage, and children.

The third microtheory centers on social strains: pathway 3 in Figure 2. Drastic income losses magnified the likelihood of family discord, disorganization, and demoralization. Prolonged discord led to family disorganization, diminished family control over individual behavior, and increased the likelihood of erratic, unpredictable actions such as arbitrary discipline. Demoralization refers to the melancholy state of family climate and outlook. These conditions were especially prevalent in deprived working-class families, and it is among their offspring that we find the most enduring adverse effects of hard times in the 1930s. Their disadvantage in education and health by midlife were not observed among adults from the deprived middle class.

Adolescence entailed different meanings for girls and boys in the Oakland cohort, particularly within the working class. Compared with boys, girls were more exposed to the dynamics of conflictive families through their household responsibilities. Deprived girls were less well dressed in school than the nondeprived and more often felt excluded from groups and social activities of age mates. They were also more self-conscious and experienced more hurt feelings and mood swings. Consistent with these findings, other research has identified the transition to adolescence as a time of psychological vulnerability for girls, and self-image disturbances appear to be more common among girls than boys during this period (Simmons & Blyth, 1987; Werner & Smith, 1992). Family adaptations to income loss may have compounded these stage-specific developmental difficulties for girls.

In adulthood, Oakland women from deprived households did not fare as well as the men owing to the simultaneous stresses of Depression hardship and early adolescence. The Oakland women tended to marry at an earlier age, and they more frequently dropped out of the labor force after marriage or before the birth of a first child. At midlife, family, children, and homemaking distinguished the priorities of these women from those of the nondeprived regardless of education or current economic situation.

Seven to eight years younger than their Oakland counterparts, the Berkeley children encountered the economic crisis when they were more dependent on parental support and at risk of family instability and strain (Elder, 1981; Elder, Liker and Cross, 1984; Elder, Caspi, & Nguyen, 1986). In this situation, girls were protected from economic stress in large measure through a close relationship to their mothers, whereas boys were more exposed to conflicts and cross-pressures. Boys in deprived families were less likely to be hopeful, self-directed, and confident about their future in adolescence than youth who were spared such hardship. This outlook is one element of negative well-being that emerged in adolescence. Other features included passivity, withdrawal from adversity, and self-defeating behavior.

By comparison, the deprived Berkeley girls were not less goal-oriented than the nondeprived, and they were not less assertive and self-directed. Indeed, a deprived family environment seemed to provide greater family security for the young Berkeley girls, which perhaps reflects the warmth of mother–daughter ties under conditions of hardship. This female bond represents the strongest intergenerational tie among families in the Great Depression. A gender bias of this kind presumably contributed to the greater vulnerability of young boys (Berkeley cohort) to family stress, as observed. Boys tend to be more vulnerable to environmental insults during the first several years of life (Rutter, 1982). Early adolescence proved to be a period of greater risk for girls, as seen in the life experience of the Oakland cohort.

These cohort and gender differences faded as we followed the Oakland and Berkeley men and women up to the middle years of life. The Depression's impact also faded. The younger Berkeley men from hard-pressed families seemed to have little going for them during their wartime adolescence. They lacked self-confidence and direction in life, and many had experienced prolonged hardship in their families. Yet we find little evidence of an enduring socioeconomic disadvantage from their childhood misfortune. How did they manage to rise above their early disadvantage? What life transitions could change their lives around?

Entry into higher education, a supportive spouse, and military service came to mind as potential turning points (Elder & Caspi, 1988). We focused on military service for the men because of its historic link to opportunity for the disadvantaged since the 1930s. Early entry into the service brought access to higher education through the GI Bill. Nearly three fourths of all Berkeley men served in the military, extending from the end of World War II into the Korean conflict; all but a tenth of the Oakland males served in World War II.

Military service established greater opportunity for survivors by (1) severing men from backgrounds of disadvantage and failure, (2) establishing a time-out or moratorium in which to mature and think about the future, and (3) providing an expanded range of experiences and knowledge. Basic training fostered equality and comradeship among recruits by separating them from their pasts. The training made prior identities irrelevant, required uniform dress and appearance, and rewarded performance on the basis of cooperation and group achievement. Family background was less relevant, producing a sense of being on one's own in obligation to mates. An Oakland veteran recalled his experience as "instant maturity." A former marine in the Oakland cohort remembered entering this new world in terms of "sink or swim."

Military service pulled men out of their civilian careers and gave them a time-out from such pressures. They could work through their problems and consider the future without having to answer for lack of career progress. Stouffer and his associates (1949, vol. 2, p. 572) found that for many soldiers in World War II, "perhaps for a majority, the break caused by Army service [meant] a chance to evaluate where they had gotten and to reconsider where they were going." For young men with a deprived background, military service offered a legitimate time-out from work and educational options and thus an alternative to the course charted by their families.

Mobilization tended to increase the range of awareness through new experiences and people. Out of this experience might come greater awareness of self and others, an expanded range of social experiences and role models, and greater tolerance. A veteran interviewed just after World War II in Havighurst's study (Havighurst, Baughman, Burgess, & Eaton, 1951, p. 188) noted the incredible diversity of his acquaintances in the service and their influence on his life choices. As he put it, the experience "sort of opens up your horizons. . . . You start thinking in broader terms than you did before." Greater independence, a broader range of experience, and a time-out from career pressures do not represent all features of military service in World War II, but they define in combination a pathway that offered the promise of new opportunities for young men from the Depression, especially when they entered in the years after high school and before major adult obligations.

Most of the Oakland men had experiences of this kind, as did the Berkeley men. Military service was a successful way for many to sever ties to a disadvantaged past; however, it did not render childhood disadvantages irrelevant. As if the Berkeley men knew the service offered a way out of hardship, those who grew up in deprived homes were twice as likely as men from nondeprived households to enter the service "early," right out of high school. For young men of this period, socialized in experiences of the Great Depression and global war, military service represented a strategic path in achieving greater opportunity and mobility (Elder, 1986). The trajectory from Depression hardship to military service produced substantial gains in adult competence up to midlife.

Marriage was a more viable path of escape from hardship than military service for young women at the time. Moreover, the Depression experience tended to orient women to life accomplishment through marriage by increasing the importance of interpersonal ties and reducing the value of higher education for daughters who, as one father put it, "are only going to marry." Indeed, a middle-class mother from the Berkeley sample expressed aspirations for her daughter as "college, social popularity, and an early marriage." In both cohorts, young women tended to rise above the limitations of their Depression childhood through marriage mobility.

Overall, we find that war mobilization in the 1940s and 1950s played a critical role in establishing pathways out of disadvantage for the Oakland and Berkeley cohorts. Just as historians claim that World War II put an end to the economic doldrums in the United States, war mobilization pulled a large number of young men and women out of chronic hard times (Sampson & Laub, 1997). Most of the Oakland men were drawn into the military and generally married shortly before and during the Second World War. Most of the Oakland women worked on the home front. The younger Berkeley cohort attained adolescent age during the war years, and some men even managed to enter military service during the last years of conflict. Most of these men served after the war through the Korean conflict. The Berkeley women from hard-pressed families improved their lives through work, advanced education, and marriage.

The two cohorts have different stories to tell through Depression and War, but in both cases military service established access to new opportunities. Youth who sought these opportunities were able to alter the course of their lives, often over-coming their disadvantaged origins. Such pathways are less available to American youth in the post–Cold War era as budget pressures reduce the size of the military population.

By comparison, *escape routes from hard times in rural America* have changed little across the decades. An increasingly smaller number of young people aspire to farming as a plausible way of life. Most look to other places for a livelihood. The incentives of city life attract the displaced and jobless as well as youth who seek education and job training. In the mid-1980s, we launched a study of rural youth and their families in a troubled region of the Midwest (Conger & Elder, 1994). Land values had declined by more than 60% along with other economic indicators. This downturn proved to be the most severe economic decline since the Great Depression, and we turned to life course theory and the Depression studies for an analytic model. In the light of these changing conditions we asked, How do the rural youth of today work out their futures in a declining region? Just as some Depression youth managed to escape their misfortunes through the military, rural youth have generally looked to prospering urban centers for a future. Outmigration is the path many envision.

Rural Decline and Life Choices: The 1980s and 1990s

The agricultural crisis of the 1980s widened the gap between prospering urban centers of the Midwest and declining rural areas. This contrast can be seen in the premier farm state of Iowa, where the capital city of Des Moines flourished through the 1980s while wages dramatically fell in rural communities only 50 miles away. The Iowa Youth and Families Project was launched in 1989 by Rand Conger and a research team to assess the impact of this socioeconomic crisis and trend. In the north-central region of the state, we recruited 451 rural families that had a 7th grade child with a near sibling and two parents. Nearly a fifth of these families had strong ties to the land – they were either farming full-time or part-time. Data were collected on these family members on an annual basis up to 1992 and then in 1994 and 1995 as the focus child left high school and moved into young adulthood.

As noted, this study was designed with key features of the Depression project in mind. In both projects, we viewed family processes and adaptations as linkages between socioeconomic decline and life experiences for the younger generation. In addition, key distinctions in life course theory were employed, such as life stage, the agency of youth in constructing their lives, and linked or interdependent lives through family and community. We focus on the adolescents of these rural families, asking how they imagine their own futures. Will they stay in their local communities, despite the decline of wages and employment opportunities? Or will they look outward to the prospering urban centers of the region?

The Farm Crisis hit during these adolescents' early childhood years, and rural decline has continued up to the present. At the end of high school, we catch a glimpse of its impact on their lives and futures. To place their families within the agricultural economy, we distinguish between fathers who went into farming, those who managed only a part-time operation, and those who either lost their farm or stayed out of farming altogether. Farming places children in a more interdependent world oriented toward family priorities. With family as firm and firm as family, participation in the work of the farm was expected of all members of each farm family (Salamon, 1992): "an interdependence prevails between the farm and the farm families: business decisions are intimately connected with the life course of family members and household management" (p. 45).

Farm children, and especially boys, have more work to do according to their reports, and they are most likely to be involved with parents in this activity. In

1992, when they were in the 10th grade, a quarter of the boys from farming families reported that one half or more of the time they spent working was spent with their fathers. Only 6% of nonfarm boys, on the other hand, reported spending as much work time with their fathers. The story is different for girls, however; rural fathers work in different spheres from their daughters. Few girls, whether from a farm or nonfarm background, reported spending any work time with their fathers.

During early adolescence, farm boys and girls tend to spend more time with family and less time with age mates when compared with children in nonfarm families (Elder, King, & Conger, 1996). This difference applies to afterschool time, in particular, and reflects in some ways the dependency of farm children on the transportation provided by parents. Not surprisingly, the greater involvement of farm parents in the lives of their children extends to community-based activities such as 4-H and the Future Farmers of America; this is true for boys and girls, and for time spent with mothers and fathers. Joint activities promote a sense of significance that is most common among farm boys who plan to live in rural areas in the future. In fact, these youth report that their fathers seek their advice and opinions more often than farm youth who anticipate life in urban areas (Elder & Conger, in press).

Historically, the pull of distant places has been greatest among the most able youth. Outmigration is selective of the better educated. Are the more successful young people in our sample most likely to aspire to leaving home for distant places or are the forces leading youth away more diverse in motivation, ranging from dislike of parents to occupational plans? We turn first to the antecedents of life plans, such as the desire to settle near family or away from home. Life on a farm represents the most rural of preferences. Like military service following the Great Depression, the residential preferences of today's rural youth provide a window on their agency and their potential to overcome the disadvantages of a declining region. We ask whether and how family influences affect such preferences.

The desire to settle near family and in one's "hometown" must eventually be reconciled to the migration requirements of a preferred line of work (Hektner, 1994; Schonert-Reichl & Elliot, 1994). In the case of rural America, some youth have loosened their local attachments by the high school years so that they are free to make plans to live elsewhere. Others subordinate family to job considerations and, even while wishing to stay near family, realize that employment prospects will be more likely in urban centers. Still other youth have not faced the contradictory nature of job opportunity and local residence. Conflict between local attachments and the need to leave the area for employment may lead to depression and insecurity; indeed, Schonert-Reichl and Elliot (1994, p. 2) argued that pressures to resolve these tensions may jeopardize the emotional health of young adults. Hektner (1994) found evidence of this stress among rural youth.

We traced the local attachments and migration intentions of Iowa youth from 8th through the 11th grade (Elder, King, & Conger, 1996), considering attachments to parents, relatives, and life in the community. The study found an overall decline in preference for living near family from 8th to the 11th grade, a trend reflected in a declining significance of parents and religious ties to adolescents. As was true for Depression-era youth, gender is an important factor. Even in junior high school, girls were less likely to want to stay in their local communities than boys – in part because agricultural employment is less available for them. Girls were more aware than boys of the difficult economic climate; nevertheless, the potential for local employment also dropped in the perception of boys.

Generally, a weakening of attachments to family, relatives, and community is related to these youth's increasing awareness of the worsening economic situation and their desire for recreation and material comforts in a financially secure life. Having grown up during the Farm Crisis, many feel pushed to seek their fortunes elsewhere. When interviewed, some youth talked about having a life free of financial strains. The ideal life at age 30 for a 12th grade girl in Iowa centered on "a steady, good-paying job. That's the main thing. I want to have money. I don't want to be poor. I don't want to have to wonder where I'm going to get the money for the next bill."

To focus more on residential choice and life-style, we turned to the desire to live on a farm. In the eighth grade over 25% of the Iowa adolescents reported that it was important for them to live on a farm in the future. For many of them, life on a farm ensured a greater sense of family, more interaction between the generations, and shared work. Youth who had grown up on a farm were most likely to prefer life on a farm, but we also found a substantial number of youth who were headed away from the farm. Advanced education, good jobs, and the bright lights of the city were attractions to many. We assumed that youth who followed this path would have less in common with parents and especially with the father when compared with those who chose the life-style of farm parents. Four groups emerged when we compared life-style choices: farm youth who wanted to live on a farm and those who did not, and nonfarm adolescents who made the same choices.

Our measures of parent–youth relationships (1989–91) use reports by the adolescent and observer ratings based on videotaped family interaction (Conger & Elder, 1994). The survey questions were factor analyzed to produce scales. In each year of the study, youth reported on their identification with each parent (such as "When I grow up, I'd like to be like my mother"), monitoring (such as "In the course of a day, how often does your Dad know where you are?"), rejection (e.g., "Mother finds fault with me even when I don't deserve it"), hostility (e.g., "How often does your father get angry with you?"), warmth (such as "How often does your mother let you know she really cares about you?"), and harshness (e.g., "When you do something wrong, how often does your father lose his temper and yell at you?").

For the first 3 years of the study, families were videotaped in their homes, and their interactions were rated on scales by observers in a laboratory. Ratings for parental

Table 1. *Summary of variance results in parent–child relationship measures by farm ecology and youths' future residential preference.*

	Father–child relationship	Mother–child relationship
Farm youth farm preference	• Identification – high • Monitoring[a] – high • Rejection – low • Hostility[a] – low • Harsh fathering – low • Warmth – high • *Warmth – high*	• *Warmth – high* • *Encourages independence – high*
Nonfarm youth farm preference	• Rejection – high • Harsh fathering – high • *Warmth – low*	
Farm youth nonfarm preference	• Identification – low • Monitoring[a] – low	• Monitoring[a] – low
Nonfarm youth nonfarm preference		

Note: Data are based on adolescent reports (1989–1994). Observational reports (1989–1991) are in italics. On scales reported by adolescents, the following statistics were derived:
Identification – 4 items, average $\alpha = .83$
Monitoring – 6 items, average $\alpha = .75$ (fathers), .68 (mothers)
Rejection – 5 items, average $\alpha = .84$
Hostility – 12 items, average $\alpha = .90$
Harsh fathering – 4 items, average $\alpha = .73$
Warmth – 8 items, average $\alpha = .93$.
[a]Data available for 1989–1992.

warmth index each parent's expression of interest, care, concern, or encouragement toward the child. The parents' demonstrations of trust in, and encouragement of, the child's thoughts and actions were the basis of a rating on the encouragement of independence. For the purposes of this chapter, we do not report mean differences but rather condense the findings in a way that depicts relationship variations between parents and youth in each group defined by farm status and future preference.

Taken as a whole, the results show the centrality of the father in the lives of youth from farm families who desire life on a farm (See Table 1). The results indicate the strongest ties to the father across the four groups. These men tend to be very much involved in bringing up their children. They are more likely than other groups of parents to know where their children are. This close monitoring is not coupled with tension or conflict. We find little evidence of child rejection or hostility and harshness by fathers. In fact, paternal warmth is strongest among these adolescents. They report this difference, and so do outside observers.

Some adolescents from farms chose a different lifestyle, and their relationships with parents differ from those of farm youth who want to live on a farm. Their parents are less likely to know where they are, they spend less time with their fathers, and the father is less salient. The two generations are moving away from each other. From other analyses (Elder & Conger, in press), we find that mothers' disenchantment with farm life may be a primary source of this path out of farming for boys and girls. These women are most likely to wish they could leave farming for a life that provides more economic stability.

Family relationships also distinguish nonfarm youth who desire a life other than farming from those who favor this way of life. Youth from nonfarm families who claim to prefer life on a farm have little chance of farming as a career because their fathers do not farm, but they are attracted to it as a world in which they at least imagine success. They rate their fathers as more harsh and rejecting than other youth, and observers place the fathers low on warmth. These adolescents also rank lowest in academic performance and self-confidence (Elder & Conger, in press) and thus lack the resources for achievement outside the local community. The desire to live on a farm seems to represent an imagined "way out" for young people who do not measure up academically and experience troubled relations at home.

With few exceptions, relations with the mother do not vary by background and youth's choice of future. However, their dissatisfactions with farming are a factor in the lives of farm youth who prefer another life. Family farming in the American Midwest is a male enterprise, by and large, and relations with the father turn out to be primary in the lives of youth who choose the farm as a place in which to live. Close relations with the father are distinctive of farm boys *and* girls who favor life on a farm, whereas more paternal rejection and harshness are distinctive of nonfarm youth who also choose life on a farm, an option with little chance of becoming a reality.

This glimpse into the lives of rural youth is merely an initial report from the field in a long-term study of regional change, family adaptation, and the life course. Just as the military, marriage, and higher education established a bridge to opportunity for Depression youth, migration plans suggest similar pathways for rural youth in their troubled region. Their first step in this direction involves the decision either to settle at home or move away. Individual differences and family influences shape this step; so has youths' growing awareness of the economic decline of their local communities.

Conclusion

Historical time and place in youth's transition to adulthood is the central theme of this chapter, and we have explored two widely separated historical eras with this in mind using the analytic model of life course study: (1) Californians who were born at opposite ends of the 1920s, grew up in the Great Depression of the 1930s, and then encountered a world war followed by an extended period of prosperity (Elder, 1974, 1979, 1981); and (2) Iowans who were born during the mid-1970s in the rural north-central region, experienced the Great Farm Crisis as young children, and left high school in the mid-1990s at a time when life opportunities led to other places (Conger & Elder, 1994; Elder, 1992; Elder & Conger, in press). This study of the rural Midwest was designed to parallel and extend the earlier urban study of Depression youth in the San Francisco Bay area.

Historical time and place marked off different pathways to adulthood in the two settings. The depressed economy of Oakland, Berkeley, and the San Franciso Bay area was followed in the 1940s by mass mobilization for World War II. The rapid growth of industrial work and military service created pathways to adulthood for members of the Oakland cohort. Full employment also improved conditions for the younger Berkeley cohort. Half a century later, the booming urban economy of the 1980s and 1990s produced bittersweet options for rural Iowans who saw opportunities leading away to urban places and jobs. As it had over the century, outmigration and advanced education became the escape route for a large number of young Iowans just as military service had established paths out of the Great Depression some 50 years earlier.

The imprint of historical time and place on young lives represents a framing statement in this comparative study. We sought information on how some youth managed to rise above the limitations of economic disadvantage and declining opportunity. Within the opportunities and constraints of each historical era, marked by traditional gender roles, young people made plans and choices that gave distinctive form to their life course. Hard times in the Great Depression reinforced traditional sex-role patterns, placing young girls in domestic roles and limiting their advanced education. Boys in hard-pressed families sought jobs in the community and gained greater social independence as a result. In contemporary rural Iowa, still distinguished by its male-centered social system, "leaving home for opportunities elsewhere" continues to represent a central motif of growing up female. Girls were more likely than boys to seek opportunities away from the local community. On farms, boys were more engaged than girls in farm work, and they envisioned more opportunity in agricultural work than girls did. Clearly, gendered inequality represents a significant feature of the transition to adulthood across these widely separated historical contexts.

In both of these ecologies, family processes tell us something about the way historical change makes a difference in the lives of young people. Consider first the Great Depression. Changes in the household economy prompted mothers and children to move into productive roles outside the family. Particularly for boys, participation in the paid labor force in early adolescence helped to shape their goals, expectations, and values through adult life. Family relationships were also altered by the economic crisis; the stresses of increased work demands and financial strains often led to ineffective parenting and a decrease of child monitoring. Finally, social and economic strains brought on by the Depression created tension between parents, and their discipline in turn became more harsh and unpredictable. Changes in the household economy, social relationships, and social-emotional strains played an important role in the lives of Depression-era children.

In later life, war mobilization during the 1940s and 1950s helped to create pathways out of disadvantage for young men who grew up during hard times. Mobilization provided access to higher education through the educational funds of the GI Bill, and it functioned as a "matchmaker" by bringing young men and women together on or near military bases. Marriage established a pathway out of disadvantage for many women; most had been socialized to favor marriage and family as lifetime goals. In the case of men, military service broadened life opportunities and experiences through social contacts, travel, and skill training.

Like urban young people who came of age in the Great Depression, rural youth from Midwestern America, some 50 years later, were also engaged in productive roles. Especially on farms, the choices and options of boys and girls formed different life courses. Among boys, helping the family extended beyond household chores to the work of the farm itself. But shared time with parents was not limited to boys and farm work. Boys and girls in farm families spent more time in activities with parents, compared with other youth, and these activities included participation in school and community groups. Joint activities between the generations fostered ties to the family and region.

The agency of ambitious rural youth was expressed in migration plans, indicating a conscious effort to surmount the limitations of local communities that lacked jobs. Such plans were expressed more often by girls than by boys, by achievement-oriented youth, and by youth who were not attached to relatives and the local church. The father was usually significant as a parental figure among young people who planned to stay in the local community, whereas the mother emerged as the most salient parent among boys and girls who planned to leave home for advanced education and a good job. This contrast was especially pronounced among youth from farming families. Will these differences persist in the post–high school years? An answer to this question will come as we follow the cohort into the young adult years.

To explore the interplay of young lives with changing historical conditions, we have drawn upon core principles of life course theory beginning with the principle of historical time and place. This principle links historical change to life experience in particular ecologies (such as the San Francisco Bay area of the 1920s, 1930s, and 1940s and the rural agricultural world of young Iowans who were born in the mid-1930s). The principle of human agency underscores the active role of young people in making life choices within the constraints and options of a particular time and place. The timing of such choices and personal events plays an important role as well, such as the life stage when particular historical events are experienced. This principle of the timing of events and social roles acquires greater meaning when we note that all such changes are experienced through the lives of people who are significant to us – the principle of linked lives. The Depression and Iowa studies trace historical change through the linked lives of family members.

We have applied these life course principles to drastic economic decline and its developmental implications, but the same principles should also be useful in tracing out the effects of other types of change, whether gradual or abrupt, such as the impact of German reunification on family adaptations, schooling, and work experience in the Eastern region (see Noack, Hofer, & Youniss, 1995). In all times and places, the personal imprint of such change depends on numerous factors, including the life stage of young people at the time, their resourcefulness, the experiences they bring to the new situation, and the personal history and supportiveness of significant others. All of these distinctions have special relevance to the young adult transition, a strategic point at which to link history and lives.

References

Cairns, R. B., & Cairns., B. D. (1991). Social cognition and social networks: A developmental perspective. In D. J. Pepler & K. H. Rubin (Eds.), *The development and treatment of childhood aggression* (pp. 249–278). Hillsdale, NJ: Lawrence Erlbaum Associates.

Clausen, J. A. (1993). *American lives: Looking back at the children of the Great Depression.* New York: Free Press.

Conger, R. D., & Elder, G. H., Jr. (1994). *Families in troubled times: Adapting to change in rural America.* Hawthorne, NY: Aldine de Gruyter.

Elder, G. H., Jr. (1974). *Children of the Great Depression: Social change in life experience.* Chicago: University of Chicago Press (25th anniversary edition, enlarged, West View Press).

Elder, G. H., Jr. (1979). Historical change in life patterns and personality. In P. B. Baltes & O. G. Brim, Jr. (Eds.), *Life-span development and behavior, Vol. 2* (pp. 117–159). New York: Academic Press.

Elder, G. H., Jr. (1981). Social history and life experience. In D. H. Eichorn, J. A. Clausen, J. Haan, M. P. Honzik, & P. H. Mussen (Eds.), *Present and past in middle life* (pp. 3–21). New York: Academic Press.

Elder, G. H., Jr. (1986). Military times and turning points in men's lives. *Developmental Psychology, 22* (2), 233–245.

Elder, G. H., Jr. (1991). Lives and social change. In W. R. Heinz (Ed.), *Theoretical advances in life course research, Vol. 1* (pp. 58–86). Weinheim, Germany: Deutscher Studien Verlag.

Elder, G. H., Jr. (1992, March). *Children of the farm crisis.* Paper presented at the Society for Research on Adolescence, Washington, DC.

Elder, G. H., Jr. (1995). Life trajectories in changing societies. In A. Bandura (Ed.), *Self-efficacy in changing societies* (pp. 46–57). New York: Cambridge University Press.

Elder, G. H., Jr. (1998). The life course and human development. In W. Damon (Series Ed.) & R. M. Lerner (Vol. Ed.), *Handbook of child psychology: Vol. 1. Theoretical models of human development* (pp. 939–991). New York: Wiley.

Elder, G. H., Jr., & Caspi, A. (1988). Human development and social change: An emerging perspective on the life course. In N. Bolger, A. Caspi, G. Downey, & M. Moorehouse (Eds.), *Persons in context: Developmental processes* (pp. 77–113). Cambridge, England: Cambridge University Press.

Elder, G. H., Jr., Liker, J. K., & Cross, C. E. (1984). Parent-child behavior in the great depression: Life course and intergenerational influences. In P. B. Baltes & O. G. Brim, Jr. (Eds.), *Life-span development and behavior, Vol. 6* (pp. 109–158). New York: Academic Press.

Elder, G. H., Jr., & Conger, R. D. (Eds.). (in press). Children of the land: Adversity and success. Chicago: University of Chicago Press.

Elder, G. H., Jr., King, V., & Conger, R. D. (1996). Attachment to place and migration prospects: A developmental perspective. *Journal of Research on Adolescence, 6*(4), 397–425.

Elder, G. H., Jr., Caspi, A., & Nguyen, T. V. (1986). Resourceful and vulnerable children: Family influences in hard times. In R. K. Silbereisen, K. Eyferth, & G. Rudinger (Eds.), *Development as action in context: Problem behavior and normal youth development* (pp. 167–186). New York: Springer-Verlag.

Elder, G. H., Jr., Wu, W., & Jihui, Y. (1993). *State-initiated change and the life course in Shanghai, China.* Unpublished manuscript.

Havighurst, R. J., Baughman, J. W., Burgess, E. W., & Eaton. W. H. (1951). *The American veteran back home.* New York: Longmans, Green.

Hektner, J. (1994, April). *When moving up implies moving out: Rural adolescent conflict in the transition to adulthood.* Paper presented at the Annual Meeting of the American Educational Research Association, New Orleans, LA.

Macfarlane, J. W. (1963). From infancy to childhood. *Childhood Education, 39,* 336–342.

Macfarlane, J. W. (1971). Perspectives on personality consistency and change from the Guidance Study. In M. C. Jones, N. Bayley, J. W. Macfarlane, & M. P. Honzik (Eds.), *The course of human development. Selected papers from the longitudinal studies, Institute of Human Development, the University of California, Berkeley* (pp. 410–415). Maltham, MA: Xerox College Publishing.

Noack, P., Hofer, M., & Youniss, J. (Eds.). (1995). *Psychological responses to social change: Human development in changing environments.* Berlin: Walter de Gruyter.

Rutter, M. (1982). Epidemiological-longitudinal approaches to the study of development. In W. A. Collins (Ed.), *Minnesota symposia on child psychology: Vol. 15. The concept of development* (pp. 105–144). Hillsdale, NJ: Erlbaum.

Rutter, M., & Madge, N. (1976). *Cycles of disadvantage: A review of research.* London: Heinemann.

Salamon, S. (1992). *Prairie patrimony: Family, farming, & community in the midwest.* Chapel Hill, NC: University of North Carolina Press.

Sampson, R. J., & Laub J. H. (1997). A life course theory of cumulative disadvantage and the stability of delinquency. In T. P. Thornberry (Ed.), *Developmental theories of crime and delinquency: Advances in criminological theory, Vol. 7* (pp. 133–161). New Brunswick, NJ: Transaction Publishers.

Schonert-Reichl, K. A., & Elliott, J. P. (1994, February). *Rural pathways: Stability and change during the transition to young adulthood.* Paper presented at the Biennial Meeting of the Society for Research on Adolescence, San Diego, CA.

Simmons, R. G., & Blyth, D. A. (1987). *Moving into adolescence: The impact of pubertal change and school context.* New York: Aldine de Gruyter.

Stouffer, S. A., Lumsdaine, A. A., Lumsdaine, M. H., Williams, R. M., Jr., Smith, M. B., Janis, I. L., S. A., Star, & Cottrell, L. S., Jr. (1949). *The American soldier: Combat and its aftermath* (Vol. 2). Princeton, NJ: Princeton University Press.

Werner, E. E., & Smith, R. S. (1992). *Overcoming the odds: High risk children from birth to adulthood.* Ithaca, NY: Cornell University Press.

3   Marriage and the Baby Carriage: Historical Change and Intergenerational Continuity in Early Parenthood

Jeanne Brooks-Gunn, Sara Schley, and Janet Hardy

> Susie and Johnny sitting in a tree
> K. I. S. S. I. N. G.
> First comes love, then comes marriage
> Then comes Susie with a baby carriage
> (American jump rope rhyme)

Women have always become mothers during their teenage years. However, in most industrialized countries, marriage preceded the baby carriage. Few births to young women occurred in the absence of marriage. Even when an unmarried girl became pregnant, societal norms and parental sanctions usually resulted in a hasty marriage (what was termed a shotgun marriage because the man who got a young woman pregnant was forced to marry her). Consequently, when a young woman did become pregnant, marriage would precede (by a few months) or quickly follow the child's birth. The rhyme quoted above that young girls in the United States chant when jumping rope was almost a universal fact of life.

Over the past 40 years a dramatic change in the context of teenage childbearing has occurred. In 1960, 40% of girls were married by the age of 19 compared with 15% in 1986. In 1960, 15% of all teenage births were to unmarried girls. In 1995, 75% of teenage births occurred out of wedlock (Ventura, Martin, Curtin, & Matthews, 1997). An examination of the rates of unwed teenage births across different ethnicity and race categories in 1995 has revealed that, for Blacks, the

The writing of this chapter was supported by the National Institute of Child Health and Human Development's Research Network on Child and Family Well-Being. Additional support came from the Robert Wood Johnson Foundation, the Russell Sage Foundation, and the W.T. Grant Foundation. The two studies – the Baltimore Study of Teenage Motherhood and the Pathways to Adulthood Study – were possible through the generous support of a number of foundations and federal agencies. The Baltimore Study of Teenage Motherhood was funded by the Robert Wood Johnson Foundation, the W.T. Grant Foundation, and the Ford Foundation. The Pathways to Adulthood Study was funded by the Robert Wood Johnson Foundation, the W.T. Grant Foundation, and the Johns Hopkins University Population Center. The contributions of our colleagues are much appreciated; we would like to thank, in particular, Frank Furstenberg, Jr. and Sam Shapiro, our collaborators, as well as Tess Miller, Nan Astone, and Margaret Ensminger.

rate was 95%, whereas it was 68% for Whites and 67% for Latinos. Thus, the context of teenage childbearing has shifted from marital to nonmarital. At the same time, marriage and childbearing ages have increased over the past two decades for middle-class youth, although not for poorer youth (Cherlin, 1992; Rosenheim & Testa, 1992).

Age of first sexual activity has also changed historically. In the 1970s, one half of all girls were sexually active in their teenage years, but in the 1980s two thirds were (Coley & Chase-Lansdale, 1998). Between 1960 and 1990, more teenagers began having sex and were engaging in intercourse at earlier ages (Brooks-Gunn & Furstenberg, 1989). For example, 46% of women who turned 20 years old between 1958 and 1960 had had sexual intercourse by the age of 19, 53% of women who turned 20 between 1970 and 1972 had done so, and 66% of women who turned 20 between 1985 and 1987 had engaged in such activity (The Alan Guttmacher Institute, 1994). About three quarters of girls are sexually active by the age of 19. Increases were particularly strong among those who turned 20 between 1985 and 1987, for 41% of boys and 21% of girls reported having had sex by the time they turned 16 (The Alan Guttmacher Institute, 1994).

Youth in the United States are notorious (among the Western countries) for irregular contraceptive use. As a consequence, the United States has the highest teenage pregnancy and childbearing rates of all of the Western nations even though the rates of sexual activity are not dramatically different across nations such as the Netherlands, France, and Great Britain (Jones, Forrest, Goldman, Henshaw, Lincoln, Rosoff, Westoff, & Wulf, 1985; Jones, Forrest, Henshaw, Silverman, & Torres, 1988).

If precipitous marriages were still the norm, the high rates of teenage motherhood would perhaps not have become the focus of so much concern. However, the other change in the United States (and, to an extent, in other Western nations) has been the dramatic rise in out-of-wedlock births. One in three births today are to unmarried women. The proportion is highest for teenage mothers: 7 in 10 of all U.S. births to adolescent women under the age of 20 occur out of wedlock (The Alan Guttmacher Institute, 1994).

In brief, the expected sequence of first love, then marriage, and finally the baby carriage has undergone profound changes in the past 25 to 30 years. Although the timing of marriage and parenthood has become uncoupled for many women across the childbearing years, teenage mothers have been the leaders in this trend. In this chapter, we explore the developmental transition to parenthood in the context of historical change with a primary focus on adolescent mothers. We present results from two studies that consider the timing of parenthood from an intergenerational perspective: The Baltimore Study of Teenage Motherhood and the Pathways to Successful Adulthood Study.

The first study illustrates the similarities and differences among teenage mothers and their daughters who did and did not become adolescent parents in the late

1980s. Our main objective has been to chart the different circumstances in which girls became teenage mothers in the late 1980s and early 1990s compared with those in which their mothers gave birth as young women in the 1960s. The Baltimore Study of Teenage Motherhood is a 30-year follow-up of African American girls who gave birth in the late 1960s. These young women and their children were seen in the 1970s, 1980s, and 1990s, and this timespan allows us to examine the unfolding of the life courses of the original teenage mothers and their first-born children (Baydar, Brooks-Gunn, & Furstenberg, 1993; Brooks-Gunn, Guo, & Furstenberg, 1993; Furstenberg, Brooks-Gunn, & Morgan, 1987). Using the Baltimore Study data set, we examined the characteristics of teenage mothers in 1968 and 1988, looking at two generations within the same families. Our primary interest was to determine if the second generation of teenage mothers fared as well as their mothers at the same point in the life course or if they did less well. We speculated on the implications of such differences (or lack thereof) upon the life courses of the teenage mothers of 1988.

Intergenerational continuity in timing of childbearing was considered in the second study. The focus was broadened to timing of childbearing (rather than a specific focus on only teenage childbearing) and expanded to include the sons as well as daughters of a sample of women who gave birth, again in Baltimore, in the 1960s. The Pathways to Successful Adulthood study was a 30-year follow-up of the Johns Hopkins Collaborative Perinatal Study (JHCPS). These women and their children were seen at birth and 1, 4, 8, and 27–33 years after the birth (Hardy, Astone, Brooks-Gunn, Shapiro, & Miller, 1998; Hardy, Shapiro, Astone, Miller, Brooks-Gunn, & Hilton, 1997; Hardy, Shapiro, Mellits, Skinner, Astone, Ensminger, LaVeist, Baumgardner, & Starfield, 1997). Unlike the Baltimore Study of Teenage Motherhood, the Pathways Study included a random sample of inner-city women seeking care in the public obstetrical clinic of the Johns Hopkins Hospital from 1960 to 1964; consequently, the maternal age of childbearing ranged from 12 to 47 years of age. Additionally, African American and White women were included in the sample. Indeed, it is only coincidental that these two 30-year studies drew their samples from the same urban metropolitan area. Three research questions were investigated with the Pathways to Successful Adulthood data set, the first having to do with intergenerational continuity of age at first birth, the second with intergenerational timing of parenthood and the outcomes of the second generation, and the third with intergenerational timing of parenthood and the childhood characteristics of the second generation.

The Baltimore Study of Teenage Motherhood

The Circumstances of Teenage Mothers in 1968 and 1988

To examine historical changes in the context of teenage parenthood, we contrast the circumstances of the teenage mothers in 1968 with those of their daughters who

Table 1. *Design of the Baltimore Study of Teenage Motherhood.*

	Interview dates	Participants	Attempted interviews	Completed interviews	
				N	*%*
Time 1: during pregnancy	1966–1968	Adolescent mothers, their mothers	404 379	404 350	100 92
Time 2: 1 year after delivery	1968–1970	Adolescent mothers	404	382	95
Time 3: 3 years after delivery	1970	Adolescent mothers	404	363	90
Time 4: 5 years after delivery	1972	Adolescent mothers, their children	404 331	331 306 '	82 92
Time 5: 16–17 years after delivery	1983–1984	Adolescent mothers, their children	404 392	289 296	80 76

Source: Table adapted from Furstenberg, Brooks-Gunn, & Morgan, 1987, Table 1.2, p. 12.

became teenage mothers in the late 1980s. We also ask the question, How do the circumstances of the daughters who became young mothers differ from those of the girls who delayed childbearing in the late 1980s? These analyses are based on the Baltimore Study of Teenage Motherhood.

The Baltimore study was initiated as an evaluation of a comprehensive care program for 404 teenage mothers at Sinai Hospital in 1966 (see Table 1). These young women were followed during their pregnancy and when their first child was 1, 3, 5, and 16–17 years of age. The young women's mothers were also contacted at each of these time points, adding a multigenerational perspective. Between 76 and 95% of the respondents were interviewed at each follow-up time point.

Furstenberg, Levine, and Brooks-Gunn (1990) compared generational differences of mothers and daughters within two groups: those in which daughters had become early parents by the last follow-up time point (by the age of 16–17) and those in which daughters had avoided early childbearing. Table 2 summarizes the distribution of teenage mothers and their daughters who had a teenage birth and those who did not. Clear generational differences between the teenage mothers were found. A higher proportion of the mothers had been married at some point in their lives than the daughters (either those who had become parents or those who had not). Relationships between unmarried fathers and their children were weaker in the second-generation young mothers than in the first. Unmarried fathers in the first generation were more likely to have been furnishing economic support (41 vs. 21%) and more likely to have continued contact with their children than were the males in the second generation (38% of the first-generation fathers had no contact compared with 55% of the second-generation fathers).

Table 2. *Among mothers who had a teenage birth and their daughters, percentage in the Baltimore study with selected characteristics or attitudes at comparable points in their lives, by whether daughter had a teenage birth.*

	Daughter with teen birth		Daughter without teen birth	
	Mothers ($N = 42$)	Daughters ($N = 42$)	Mothers ($N = 72$)	Daughters ($N = 72$)
Graduated from high school	40	43	45	82[a]
Failed a grade	33	57[a]	17	28
Employed	36	29	44	67[a]
Public assistance	31	60[a]	32	3[a]
Ever married	60	14[a]	49	4[a]
Receives child support[b]	41	21	46	c
Wants to marry after age 25[d]	18	68[a]	24	67[a]

[a] Difference between mothers and daughters is significant at $p < .05$.
[b] Among the 22, 30, and 41 respondents of the 3 respective groups who were not living with the father of their child.
[c] Percentage not given because of small numbers.
[d] Among the 17, 36, 37, and 69 respondents of the 4 respective groups who had never married.
Source: Table adapted from Furstenberg, Levine, & Brooks-Gunn, 1990, Table 2, p. 58.

In addition, the daughters who had become teenage mothers were much more likely than their mothers to have failed a grade (57 vs. 33%) even though equal proportions had graduated from high school (40% in the first and 43% in the second generation of teenage mothers). Employment rates were similar for the two generations of teenage mothers (36% in the first and 29% in the second generation).

It seems as if the teenage mothers of the late 1980s were not faring as well as their mothers did when they became young mothers in the late 1960s. The former have a poor prognosis for exceeding their own mothers' educational accomplishments in later life. The daughters were almost twice as likely to have failed at least one grade in school as their mothers, which is a factor predictive of not completing education beyond the age of 20 years (Furstenberg, Brooks-Gunn, & Morgan, 1987; Guo, Brooks-Gunn, & Harris 1996). The daughters' rates of educational attainment were similar to those of their mothers at a comparable age, even though more urban African American women in general graduated from high school in the late 1980s than in the late 1960s.

Historical Context for Each Generation

The second generation of young mothers not only has lower marriage rates than in the first generation, but has lower rates of educational attainment. Several contextual features are noteworthy. The young mothers of 1968 did not have the option of a legal abortion. Clearly, their teenage daughters had the choice of ending the pregnancy, if they desired. The legislation brought forth by *Roe v. Wade* (1973) provided the second generation an option (depending on their religious and moral beliefs about abortion). Studies of teenage girls in the 1970s and 1980s suggest that those who chose abortion did better in school (less grade retention, higher achievement scores, greater expectations for high school graduation and post–secondary school training) (Furstenberg, Brooks-Gunn, & Chase-Lansdale, 1989; Hayes, 1987; Maynard, 1997).[1]

Another cohort change has to do with the regulations relating to high school attendance. In the late 1960s, pregnant girls were often asked not to return to their high schools (lest they set a bad example). Indeed, in the Baltimore Study, girls who remained in high school went to a special school for pregnant teenagers. The Poe School (its motto was "Never More") offered the opportunity to continue high school in a small, intimate, and by all accounts from that time, intellectually nurturing setting. In fact, when we examined the success of the first generation of women 17 years after the birth of their first child, the strongest predictor of years of completed schooling and work status was attendance at the Poe School (over 20 other characteristics and conditions were held constant; Furstenberg et al., 1987). In stark contrast, by 1988, girls in Baltimore (as elsewhere throughout the nation) did not have to leave their home high schools upon learning of impending birth. Rather, girls were (and are today) urged to stay in their schools. Additionally, little stigma associated with pregnancy is reported. Several recent media stories have presented cases of pregnant girls continuing in high-status elected positions in their high schools such as cheerleaders, class officers, and homecoming courts. This phenomenon is not limited to urban high schools but has been occurring in suburban and rural communities as well. From a civil rights perspective, the normalization of life activities for pregnant girls is laudatory. At the same time, without more attention (via smaller classes, less opportunities for male relationships), perhaps pregnant girls are at a disadvantage in large high schools. Our results from the Baltimore Study, although not proof positive, hint at such a possibility.

Another fascinating cohort difference is found when looking at paternal involvement in those cases where marriage did not take place. We might have expected similar rates once cohort differences in marriage were held constant. Why did the fathers in 1988 have less contact than their counterparts in 1968? If anything, one might predict the opposite. After all, pressure to marry a pregnant girlfriend had virtually disappeared by the late 1980s in urban African American communities, and paternal involvement after an unwed birth was (and is) common: About four fifths of all African American fathers who are not married go to the hospital immediately after the baby is born (Chase-Lansdale, Gordon, Coley, Wakschlag, & Brooks-Gunn, 1999; McLanahan, Garfinkel, Brooks-Gunn, & Zhao, 1998). Recent analysis of the National Longitudinal Study of Youth – Child Supplement (NLSY–CS) (Chase-Lansdale, Mott, Brooks-Gunn, & Phillips, 1991) suggests that in the late 1980s and early 1990s, about one fifth of unwed African American fathers were living with the mother at the time of birth and that a little less than half saw their infant weekly, one fifth monthly, and only about one tenth very infrequently (McLanahan et al., 1998; see also Bumpass & Sweet, 1989). Regrettably, little comparable data exist from the late 1960s or 1970s (to see whether a decline over time in father contact has occurred when looking at a nationally representative sample of unwed fathers).

We can speculate about the reasons for the cohort changes (if in fact they exist beyond our admittedly select and nonrepresentative sample of Baltimore families). It is possible that in the late 1960s teenage fathers were encouraged to assume some paternal responsibilities even in the absence of marriage; that is, fathers were expected by their family, the young mother's family, and others in the community to remain very involved in their children's lives. Indeed, some family sociologists believe that fatherhood is becoming more of an optional role than in earlier decades (Furstenberg, 1995; Garfinkel & McLanahan, 1995). Responsibilities are linked to having a relationship with the mother. When an intimate partnership ends, in many cases so does the father's relationship with the child.

Economists have argued that the paternal role has diminished because young fathers play little economic role in the family (Brien & Willis, 1997a). High unemployment, low wage rates, and the instability of job histories for those who have few marketable skills are often the plight of young fathers. In addition, young mothers are able to receive some support from the state (Aid for Families of Dependent Children [AFDC] or now Temporary Aid to Needy Families [TANF] as well as food stamps and Medicaid, Duncan & Brooks-Gunn, 1998), which perhaps reduces the value of poor young men's contributions (Currie, 1997; Moffitt, Reville, & Winkler, 1995). In the 20 years between 1968 and 1988, wage rates for unskilled and semiskilled labor and high school dropouts (and even high school graduates) fell in the United States, making it more likely that the economic contributions of young fathers would not be high (although non-resident fathers who have low education still are not providing the amount of child support of which they are capable, Brien & Willis, 1997b; Phillips & Garfinkel, 1993; Wilson, 1987; 1991). Although these conditions were true across race and ethnic groups, African American males suffered disproportionately from the changes. At the same time, however, the value of welfare stipends also dropped because AFDC payments did not keep pace with inflation (Ellwood & Bane, 1994; Chase-Lansdale & Brooks-Gunn, 1995). Many young mothers on welfare supplemented their stipends by part-time (and often off-the-books) employment (Brooks-Gunn, Smith, Berlin, & Lee, 1999; Edin & Lein, 1997).

Continuity Across Generations in Parenthood Timing

It is believed that intergenerational continuity exists for the occurrence of teenage motherhood. However, relatively few studies have examined this topic until recently

(Furstenberg et al., 1990; Kahn & Anderson, 1992; Manlove, 1997; Presser, 1978). In the Baltimore Study of Teenage Motherhood, it is possible to estimate the number of daughters of teenage mothers who went on to become young childbearers themselves: 36% of the first-born daughters of the original teenage mothers had become mothers themselves by age 19. This figure is similar to that generated from the National Longitudinal Study of Youth (NLSY) when examining the childbearing status of those African American youth who were offspring of mothers aged 14 to 17 (Furstenberg et al., 1990). In the NLSY, 33% of the daughters of young mothers became young childbearers themselves compared with only 21% of the daughters of mothers who were 20 years old or older at the time of first birth.

However, these studies have not examined congruence for delayed childbearing (for example, not having children until, at the earliest, the late 20s). Continuity for timing of childbearing between mothers and their sons also has not been explored. Both of these topics are addressed in the Pathways to Successful Adulthood Study. The Pathways Study population, database, methods, and potential biases have been described in detail in Hardy, Shapiro, Astone, et al. (1997) and Hardy, Shapiro, Mellits, et al. (1997). Table 3 summarizes the design of the Pathways Study (see appendix for additional information). Inner-city women (the first generation mothers, G1s) were initially enrolled in the study at their first prenatal visit ($n = 2,307$), and they and their children (the second-generation children, G2s; $n = 2,694$) were followed until their children reached the age of 8. From 1992 to 1994, respondents were contacted again, and retrospective data were collected on the G1s ($n = 1,552$) and the G2s ($n = 1,758$), including information on family and environmental circumstances and relationships, G2's childhood and adolescent health, behavior and schooling, and life events and circumstances during young adulthood such as fertility and childbearing.

Intergenerational Continuity of Age at First Birth. The first-generation women from the Pathways Study were grouped into three categories distinguishing women by their age when they first gave birth to a child: less than 20, between 20 and 24, and 25 years or older (this last category includes those with no children). If one compares the younger generation's adult outcomes of high school education, financial independence of public support, and teenage childbearing, children of older mothers were faring better than children of younger mothers (Hardy, Shapiro, Astone, et al., 1997, Table 2, p. 804).

To examine intergenerational patterns of age at first birth using chi-square tests of significance (see Figures 1a and 1b adapted from Hardy et al., 1998), we tested the association between the G1's age at first birth and their first-born children's age at first birth for their first-born girls and boys. Of the women who had their first child before the age of 20, 40% of their first-born daughters and 21% of their first-born sons also had a child before the age of 20. Only 9% of the first-born daughters of mothers who delayed childbearing became teenage childbearers, versus 12%

Table 3. *Design of the Pathways to Adulthood study.*

	Interview dates	Participants	Information collected	N
Enrollment: First prenatal care visit	1959–1964	Inner-city women		2,307
Time 1: pregnancy through child's first year	1960–1965	Mothers (G1s), their children (G2s)	Birth status information. Pediatric, neurologic, developmental observations every 4 months. Sociodemographic information.	2,307 2,694
Time 2: preschool	1963–1968	Children (G2s)	Language, hearing, speech at 36 months. Psychological tests, behavioral observations at 48 months.	2,694
Time 3: early school age	1967–1973	Children (G2s)	Psychological tests, behavioral observations, academic achievement tests at 84 months. Neurologic, pediatric observations at 90 months. Language, hearing, speech at 96 months. Sociodemographic information.	2,694
27–33 Year follow-up	1992–1994	Mothers (G1s), their children (G2s)	Retrospective information: Family relationships, childhood and adolescent behavior, school achievements and problems. Life history calendar: schooling, marital history, living arrangements, fertility, employment, welfare utilization. Information about any children of the G2s, including psychological tests, behavioral observations, academic achievement tests on those between 7 and 8 years of age.	1,552 1,758

Source: Table constructed from information in Hardy, Shapiro, Mellits, *et al.*, 1997.

of the first-born sons. The intergenerational effect was found for Black and White subsamples in the Pathways data set. Note that the sample size for the early-parent sons was quite small ($n = 45$), indicating that most first-born sons did not become parents in their teen years. The analysis was redone with the age distribution moved upwards by 2 years, and the results did not change substantively. Similar results were found in the Baltimore study (Furstenberg et al., 1987): one half as many sons as daughters reported becoming a teenage parent. However, in the present study delayed parenthood on the part of the mothers and their children was linked strongly for boys as well as for girls.

We also examined the intergenerational continuity using the G2 child as the reference. Table 4 presents these data. Here we looked at those G2 sons and daughters who were teenage parents and the percentage who had teenage mothers. These data provide a picture of what a health, welfare, or educational professional would see in an institutional setting (because such a professional would not be seeing all offspring of teenage parents but would be working with the current generation of adolescent parents). Of course, the percentages are much higher (given the change

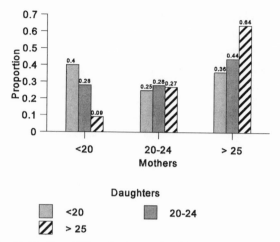

Figure 1a. Distribution of G1 mothers' age at first birth by G2 age at birth of first child. (Adapted from Hardy et al., 1998.)

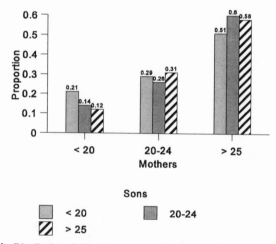

Figure 1b. Distribution of G1 mothers' age at first birth by G2 age at birth of first child. (Adapted from Hardy et al., 1998.)

in reference group): almost three quarters of all first-born G2 teenage mothers and fathers had a teenage mother; across all G2 offspring, the percentage was two thirds. Our point is that the links, although significant irrespective of which generation is the reference group, will be perceived as stronger when the focus is on a sample of current teenage parents. Indeed, this fact probably contributes to the widespread concerns of public health and education service providers and policymakers.

Intergenerational Timing of Parenthood and Outcomes in the Second Generation. We were interested in whether it is important to consider the intergenerational timing of parenthood when examining the outcomes of the second generation. In

Table 4. *With the G2 child as the reference, intergenerational patterns of age at first parenthood – percent distribution of G1 mother's age at delivery by G2 child's age at first parenthood.*

	G1 Age at first birth		
First born G2s: G2 age at first birth ($n = 524$)	<20 ($n = 167$)	20–24 ($n = 79$)	≥25 ($n = 22$)
Daughters			
<20	.73	.24	.02
20–24	.59	.32	.09
≥25	.55	.32	.13
		$p < .002$	
Sons	($n = 156$)	($n = 73$)	($n = 26$)
<20	.71	.22	.07
20–24	.63	.26	.11
≥25	.57	.32	.11
		$p < .132$	
All G2s: G2 age at first birth ($n = 1758$)	($n = 569$)	($n = 291$)	($n = 91$)
Daughters			
<20	.69	.25	.06
20–24	.58	.34	.08
≥25	.53	.33	.13
		$p < .001$	
Sons	($n = 489$)	($n = 237$)	($n = 79$)
<20	.66	.30	.04
20–24	.63	.29	.08
≥25	.58	.29	.13
		$p < .004$	

regression models that do not include the age of first birth for both generations, we often see relatively small (and often insignificant) effects of teenage motherhood upon children's outcomes. In part, of course, this is because early motherhood is associated with low maternal education, poverty, unemployment, and single parenthood (Brooks-Gunn & Chase-Lansdale, 1995; Coley & Chase-Lansdale, 1998; Furstenberg, Brooks-Gunn, & Chase-Lansdale, 1989).

Analyses suggest associations between the intergenerational pattern of age of first childbearing and self-sufficiency outcomes for G2 daughters and sons. We define self-sufficiency as completion of high school and the presence of a healthful lifestyle that includes no heavy alcohol or illicit drug use and no arrests or incarcerations during the year before the 27–33-year follow-up time point. Figure 2a presents the distribution of successful adult outcomes for G2 daughters by age at birth of first child and G1 mother's age at first birth. For G1 mothers who had their first child before the age of 20, 19% of their first-born daughters who had also had their first child before the age of 20 had graduated from high school, whereas 28%

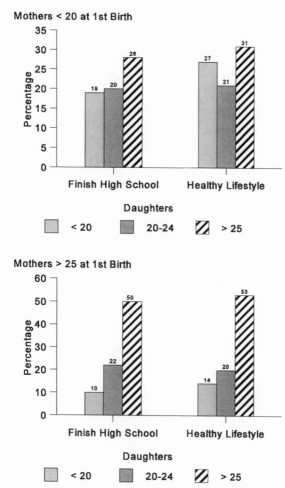

Figure 2a. Percent distribution of successful adult outcomes for G2 daughters by age at birth of first child and G1 mother's age at first birth. (Figures adapted from Hardy et al., 1998 Figure 1.)

of their daughters who delayed childbearing until at least the age of 25 had graduated from high school. For the early childbearing first-born daughters, 27% of them had a healthful lifestyle, versus 31% of the daughters who delayed childbearing. For G1 mothers who delayed childbearing until at least the age of 25, only 10% of their first-born early childbearing daughters had graduated from high school and 14% had a healthful lifestyle, whereas among their first-born delayed childbearing daughters, 50% had graduated from high school and 53% maintained a healthful lifestyle. The effect of daughters' timing of childbearing is most pronounced for girls whose mothers had delayed childbearing. That is, few daughters of teenage mothers completed high school and had a healthful lifestyle whether or not they delayed childbearing themselves. In contrast, outcomes for daughters of mothers who

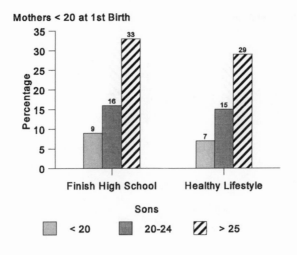

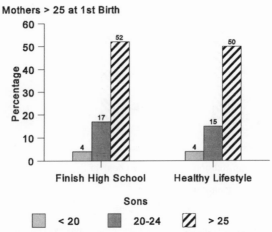

Figure 2b. Percent distribution of successful adult outcomes for G2 sons by age at birth of first child and G1 mother's age at first birth. (Figures adapted from Hardy et al., 1998 Figure 1.)

had delayed childbearing differed dramatically, depending on when they initiated childbearing.

For first-born sons, the picture is somewhat different. Figure 2b presents the distribution of successful adult outcomes for G2 sons by age at birth of first child and G1 mother's age at first birth. For G1 mothers who had their first child before the age of 20, 9% of their first-born sons who had also had their first child before the age of 20 had graduated from high school, whereas 33% of their sons who delayed childbearing until at least the age of 25 had graduated from high school. For the early childbearing firstborn sons, 7% of them had a healthful lifestyle, whereas 29% of the sons who delayed childbearing did. For G1 mothers who delayed childbearing until at least the age of 25, of their firstborn early childbearing sons only 4% had graduated from high school and 4% maintained a healthful lifestyle, whereas of their firstborn delayed childbearing sons, 52% had graduated from high school and 50% had a healthful lifestyle. Thus, the age of fatherhood of a son had a large effect irrespective of whether his mother had been a teenage mother. In contrast, early timing of mothers' childbearing had an important effect for girls, suppressing their rates of high school completion and incidence of healthful lifestyles whether or not they themselves became early childbearers.

Intergenerational Timing of Parenthood and Childhood Characteristics of the Second Generation. We also looked at associations between patterns of G1 and G2 age at first becoming a parent and certain G2 family and personal characteristics during childhood and adolescence. Taking the two groups that are likely to be the most disparate (G2 daughters of teenage G1 mothers who became teenage mothers themselves and G2 daughters of later childbearing G1 mothers who delayed their own childbearing until after the age of 25), we found clear differences: higher IQ scores at 4 and 7 years of age (odds are 2.2:1 and 2.57:1 respectively), smaller probability of repeating a grade in school (odds of repeating a grade are 0.49:1), delay until after the age of 16 in initiating sexual activity (odds 4.13 to 1), and avoidance of arrest during the teenage years (odds of being arrested are 0.18 to 1). The G2 teenage mothers were also more likely to come from more severely disadvantaged families, for their G1 mothers were more likely to have been single, poor, and less well-educated. If one compares the daughters of G1 teenage mothers, the later childbearing daughters were likelier to have more favorable characteristics than the teenage childbearing daughters (odds of higher IQ scores: 1.48:1 at age 4, 1.72:1 at age 7; odds of repeating a grade in school: 0.65:1; odds of being arrested: 0.44:1; odds of delaying sexual activity until at least 16 years of age: 3.92:1). Clearly, family circumstances matter. Also, the girls who became teenage mothers had not done as well in school during elementary school as had those who delayed childbearing. Perhaps their relatively poor school performance led to school disengagement in the junior high and high school years, increasing the likelihood of early sexual activity. No significant differences in the age of menarche for the groups of daughters were found; physically, the groups matured at similar rates (see Hardy et al., 1998).

These analyses fit with research done by Manlove (1997), who used a British cohort of women to examine congruence in timing of motherhood for mothers and daughters. The British National Child Development Study (NCDS) is a sample derived from a birth cohort of over 17,000 children born in 1958 and therefore is similar to the Pathways sample vis-à-vis historical time. In predicting the age at which the daughters had their first birth, the following factors were significant: maternal timing of childbirth, social class, maternal education, maternal single parenthood, and early sexual experience. The onset of menarche was not important in the British study either.

For sons in the Pathways study, a different pattern was seen. Although clear differences between sons of early and later childbearing G1 mothers were observed, sons who themselves became early parents and those who did not were quite similar. A positive association between sons of early and later childbearing G1 mothers was found such that boys whose mothers delayed childbearing had higher IQ scores at age 4 and at age 7 (odds are 1.77:1 at each age point), had a decreased likelihood of being arrested during their teen years (odds are 0.71:1), and were more likely to delay their first sexual experience until after the age of 16 years (odds are 3.15:1). However, in contrast to the analysis results for the daughters, no differences were seen between those sons who did and did not delay fatherhood (Hardy et al., 1998).

Although the distributions for the second-generation daughters and sons move positively (in general) with increasing age, the effect for the males is less strong than the effect for the females. This is true even though similar underlying factors seemed to be operating in the men and the women. At the same time, the negative effects of being and having an early parent may be seen somewhat earlier for the girls than the boys (i.e., the early childhood IQ scores).[2]

Conclusion

All role transitions have variability in timing as a central feature. Individual, family, and historical time are three characteristics relevant to the study of role transitions. Individual time refers to each family member's life course. Family time denotes the interweaving of individual members' life courses. Historical time focuses on the patterns in a societal and historical context (Elder, 1974; Hagestad, 1986). In the United States, becoming a parent during the teenage years is usually considered to be early or "off-time" vis-à-vis becoming a parent during young adulthood. In different historical periods and in nonindustrial societies, teenage parenthood was normative and would not have been perceived as off-time (Vinovskis, 1992). In Western nations, the age of childbearing has risen in the last century (with historical exceptions such as the post–World War II period). These trends are believed to have been influenced by lower fertility and infant mortality rates as well as increased proportions of young women completing high school and entering the work force (Modell, Furstenberg, & Herschberg, 1976; Modell & Goodman, 1990).

Furthermore, individual, family and historical trends in timing of a transition are not always synchronous. Consequently, members of the same family may perceive events such as teenage parenthood to be off-time, whereas others do not. And historical trends may vary within particular contexts. Variation in age of childbearing exists within historical periods and cohorts. Within particular contexts, young childbearing may have been more common and perhaps less likely to have been perceived as off-time. For example, teenage childbearing in the absence of marriage is more common for African American girls than for other racial or ethnic groups. In 1990, there were 84 nonmarital births per 1,000 black 15–17-year-old women, 65 for Latino 15–17 year olds, and 23 for White 15–17-year-old women (the Alan Guttmacher Institute, 1994, p. 54). Consequently, in some neighborhoods, teenage motherhood may not be seen as off-time (Burton, 1990). Rates of unwed young mothers have soared for all racial and ethnic groups over the past 15 years; perceptions of teenage motherhood as being off-time may now only exist in select middle-class suburban communities across all racial and ethnic groups (Brooks-Gunn & Chase-Lansdale, 1995). In brief, it is important to consider all three aspects of timing when studying a particular role transition. In this chapter, we used age of parenthood as an illustration of the ways in which historical, individual, and family timing interact.

The life course perspective looks at lives unfolding over time as well as the intersection between multiple lives. Multiple life courses are usually studied within the frame of the family. A few studies examined the unfolding of lives between spouses and partners, although few data sets include couple data and span several decades (Brooks-Gunn, Phelps, & Elder, 1991). The interplay among lives typically focuses on parents and children and less often on siblings. Looking at parents and children provides, if the time frame is long enough, the continuity among generations for any number of life events (see special section of *Developmental Psychology*, 1998). Often, questions are framed in terms of the persistence of various circumstances, such as poverty, teenage parenthood, or welfare receipt (Furstenberg et al., 1990; Duncan, Hill, & Hoffman, 1988; Gottschalk, 1996). In this chapter, the focus is on the persistence of teenage parenthood across two generations as well as the broader question of continuity in age of parenthood (teenage years, early 20s, or later).

Another, perhaps complementary approach to studying two generations over time is to look at sibling similarities and differences. Several scholars have used sibling models to examine the effects of early parenthood upon women's economic, educational, and fertility outcomes. For example, Geronimus and Korenman (1992) have suggested that teenage childbearing has fewer long-term consequences than previous research indicated (Furstenberg et al., 1987; Hayes, 1987). Comparing the outcomes of sisters, one of whom was a teenage mother and one of whom was not, reduces the possibility that any differences seen between younger and older childbearers are really due to unmeasured family characteristics. Presumably, such fixed-effects models account for some of the characteristics of families that are not easily measured (such as motivation, habits, and preferences). Several of the large nationally representative longitudinal data sets include siblings, such as the Panel Study of Income Dynamics and the National Longitudinal Study of Youth (Brooks-Gunn, Brown, Duncan, & Moore, 1995). Three analyses using the sibling approach report fewer differences between girls who became mothers as youth and their relatives (in some studies, cousins as well as sisters were included) who delayed childbearing. However, these analyses do not totally eliminate the long-term economic consequences (Hoffman, Foster, & Furstenberg, 1993; Moore et al.,

1993). Furthermore, these techniques do not control for possible differences between the sisters themselves. In an innovative study, Hotz and his colleagues (1996, 1997) compared the outcomes of sisters who were pregnant during adolescence but miscarried and sisters who had live births. The sisters who became adolescent mothers were less likely to complete high school but more likely to get a GED; no differences were found for welfare receipt in young adulthood. Sibling analyses can also be used to look at the similarity in outcomes such as age of parenthood, welfare receipt, economic outcomes, and timing (e.g., Are girls with sisters who got pregnant as teens at increased risk of teen pregnancy too?). Regrettably, the Baltimore Study of Teenage Motherhood and the Pathways to Successful Adulthood were not designed as sibling studies.

Across multiple intergenerational studies, including the British NCDS (Manlove, 1997), the Baltimore Study, and the Pathways to Adulthood study, effects of teenage parenthood are seen for cognitive and educational outcomes as well as in timing of fertility. This is true for sons and daughters, Blacks and Whites, and in the United States as well as in Britain. Mechanisms include factors such as low socioeconomic status (poverty, the stress of social disadvantage, and reliance on public sources of support). Child characteristics include IQ and the timing of initial sexual activity. Pathways include the link between low socioeconomic status in early childhood and poor school readiness, which in turn influences IQ, grade failure, and school achievement (Baydar, Brooks-Gunn, & Furstenberg, 1993; Brooks-Gunn & Duncan, 1997; Guo, Brooks-Gunn, & Harris, 1996; Smith, Brooks-Gunn, & Klebanov, 1997; Zhao, Brooks-Gunn, Singer, & McLanahan, in press). By high school, these indicators of educational problems are associated with more disengagement from school as well as an increased likelihood of engaging in risk-taking and risky behaviors, including early sexual behavior. No pathway is found through an earlier onset of menarche, as has been proposed in small-scale, nonrepresentative studies. In other studies, about one third of all girls who are teenage mothers drop out of school before the pregnancy, suggesting that many of these young women have very low educational engagement (Maynard,1995) and, perhaps, low intelligence as measured by IQ tests and academic achievement.

It is also important to note that substantial variation exists in the childhood circumstances of offspring of teenage mothers. Not only were daughters who delayed childbearing but had teenage mothers more likely to have grown up in poor households than those late childbearers without teenage parents, but they also were more likely to have low IQ scores and to have failed a grade in the elementary school years. By the adolescent years, they were more likely to have been arrested. How did these youth avoid adolescent parenthood? We look at those G2s who did and did not delay childbearing but had teenage mothers for a partial answer (see Hardy et al., 1998). Comparisons within the G1 teenage mother group suggest that the G2 girls who delayed childbearing had higher IQ scores and had mothers who were more likely to have graduated from high school and to be married than those G2 girls who were early childbearers. At the same time, equal proportions had had sexual intercourse early and had been held back a grade. It is likely that education was perceived as more important in these families (Furstenberg et al., 1987; Brooks-Gunn & Chase-Lansdale, 1995), and parental monitoring may have been more common given the greater likelihood of two parents in the home (McLanahan, 1997; McLanahan & Sandefur, 1994). Other potential "protective" factors (i.e., sociability, efficacy, social competence) may have been operating but were not measured in this study (Haggerty, Sherrod, Garmezy, & Rutter, 1994; Rutter, 1987; Werner & Smith, 1982).

The historical context has changed considerably from the early 1960s to the early 1990s (the starting and ending time points of data collection in the Pathways to Adulthood Study). The rate of adolescent childbearing in the United States is almost 2 times as high as Britain (which has the next highest rate of early parenthood). The U.S. rate is also 4 times as high as that of Sweden and Spain and 7 times that of the Netherlands and Denmark (Coley & Chase-Lansdale, 1998; United Nations, 1991). Rates are still much higher if we only look at the fertility rate of White girls in the United States. Thus, the high rates are not due to the ethnic diversity of the United States. In conclusion, considerable continuity in the timing of parenthood is seen across generations. Furthermore, this persistence is seen in the face of large cohort changes. These analyses yield evidence that historical time and family time provide a context for teenage childbearing.

Appendix

Potential Biases

In a 30-year longitudinal study, bias is a major concern. Those G2 children who, on the basis of family and personal characteristics (Appendix Tables 1 and 2), were least likely to become self-sufficient adults, were disproportionately lost to the study after age 8. The bias is to be in the direction of minimizing differences between successful and unsuccessful children. Recall bias, another potential problem, was minimized by emphasizing the collection of data pertaining to concrete, easily defined and remembered characteristics and events. Identical questions pertaining to the health, schooling, employment, family formation and environment of the G2 child between age 8 and 18 were asked of both mother and child. Concordance was generally high (Hardy, Shapiro, Mellits et al., 1997). In the G2 interview, use of the life history calendar appeared to minimize difficulty with recall. No serious discrepancies were noted on supernumeration. Bias due to missing data points was seldom a problem in analysis. There was generally little missing data ($< 1.0\%$). Analyses were routinely run with and without missing values; rarely were significant differences found, and they disappeared when a marker for missing values was entered into the equation. Possible bias of G2 outcome from the inclusion of siblings (14% of G1 mothers had more than one G2) was examined by use of

Table 1. *Final status of second generation children followed in the Johns Hopkins Collaborative Perinatal Study (at 8 years).*

	Total	%
Liveborn children (1959–1965)	4025	100.0
Died neonatal period	122	3.0
Died after neonatal period	65	1.6
Eligible for final 8-year exam	3838	95.4
Refused follow-up	115	2.9
Adopted – unable to follow-up	11	0.3
Moved out of area	210	5.2
Transferred to other CPP site	12	0.3
Not examined at 8 years	58	1.4
Whereabouts unknown	32	0.8
Received 8-year exam	3400	84.5

Table 2. *Final status of the G2 children selected for the Pathways to Adulthood study*

Final status of field effort	Total	%
Eligible G2 children	2694	100.0
Not located	474	17.6
Located	2220	82.4
Not fieldable		
Out of country/incapable	11	0.4
Deceased, no data	17	0.6
Fieldable	2192	81.4
Refused	135	5.0
Incomplete (in field)	157	5.8
Deceased with data	71	2.6
Interview with relative	71	2.6
Full interview	1758	65.3
Response rate (known outcome)	71.4	
Response rate (full interview)	65.3	

Liang-Zeger technique for effects of clustering (Liang & Zenger, 1986) and found to be non-significant. No age effects for the G2s (who ranged between ages 27 and 33 years) have been found in this sample (Hardy, Shapiro, Mellits et al., 1997).

How representative are the families in the Pathways to Adulthood Study to other urban families in the 1960s? In the early 1960s, approximately one third of births to black women living in Baltimore took place at the Johns Hopkins Hospital. Comparison between the black JHCPS enrollees and all black women delivering a baby in Baltimore in 1960 showed no substantial differences in age, education, parity or marital status or in rates of low birthweight and perinatal mortality. Furthermore, the black mothers enrolled in the JHCPS were similar to the black mothers enrolled in the project in Philadelphia, New York, Memphis and New Orleans. However, the white women enrolled in the JHCPS were very different from other white women having babies in Baltimore in 1960 and in the other urban CPP projects. They were younger and less well educated and had higher rates of low birthweight and perinatal mortality. In fact, they were more like the black women than white Baltimore women, in general. To our knowledge, no other longitudinal study has a population that includes groups of black and white families living in the same inner-city areas, under similar socioeconomic conditions.

References

The Alan Guttmacher Institute. (1994). *Sex and America's teenagers.* New York: Author.

Baydar, N., Brooks-Gunn, J., & Furstenberg, F. F., Jr. (1993). Early warning signs of functional illiteracy: Predictors in childhood and adolescence. *Child Development, 64*(3), 815–829.

Brien, M. J. & Willis, R. J. (1997a). Costs and consequences of early childbearing for fathers, the young mothers, and their children. In R. Maynard (Ed.), *Kids having kids: Economic costs and social consequences of teen pregnancy.* Washington, DC: Urban Institute Press.

Brien, M. J. & Willis, R. J. (1997b). The partners of welfare mothers: Potential earnings and child support. *The Future of Children, 7*(1), 65–73.

Brooks-Gunn, J., Brown, B., Duncan, G., & Moore, K. A. (1995). Child development in the context of family and community resources: An agenda for national data collection. In *Integrating federal statistics on children: Report of a workshop* (pp. 27–97). Washington, DC: National Academy Press.

Brooks-Gunn, J., & Chase-Lansdale, P. L. (1995). Adolescent parenthood. In M. Bornstein (Ed.), *Handbook of parenting: Vol. 3. Status and social conditions of parenting.* Mahwah, NJ: Lawrence Erlbaum Associates.

Brooks-Gunn, J., & Duncan, G. (1997). The effects of poverty on children. *The Future of Children, 7*(2), 55–71.

Brooks-Gunn, J., & Furstenberg, F. F., Jr. (1989). Adolescent sexual behavior. *American Psychologist, 44*(2), 249–257.

Brooks-Gunn, J., Guo, G., & Furstenberg, F. F., Jr. (1993). Who drops out of and who continues beyond high school?: A 20-year follow-up of black urban youth. *Journal of Research on Adolescence, 3*(3), 271–294.

Brooks-Gunn, J., Phelps, E., & Elder, G. H. (1991). Studying lives through time: Secondary data analyses in developmental psychology. *Developmental Psychology, 27*(6), 899–910.

Brooks-Gunn, J., Smith, J., Berlin, L., & Lee, K. (1999). Familywork: Welfare changes, parenting, and young children. In G. K. Brookins (Ed.), *Exits from poverty.* New York: Cambridge University Press.

Bumpass, L. L., & Sweet, J. A. (1989). Children's experiences in single-parent families: Implications of cohabitation and marital transitions. *Family Planning Perspectives, 21,* 256–260.

Burton, L. M. (1990). Teenage childbearing as an alternative life-course strategy in multigeneration black families. *Human Nature, 1*(2), 123–143.

Chase-Lansdale, P. L., & Brooks-Gunn, J. (1995). *Escape from poverty: What makes a difference for children?* New York: Cambridge University Press.

Chase-Lansdale, P. L., Gordon, R.A., Coley, R. L., Wakschlag, L. S., & Brooks-Gunn, J. (1999). Young African-American multigenerational families in poverty: The context, exchange, and processes of their lives. In E. M. Hetherington (Ed.), *Coping with divorce, single parenting, and remarriage: A risk and resilience perspective* (pp. 165–191). Mahwah, NJ: Lawrence Erlbaum Associates.

Chase-Lansdale, P. L., Mott, F. L., Brooks-Gunn, J., & Phillips, D. (1991). Children of the NLSY: A unique research opportunity. *Developmental Psychology, 27*(6), 918–931.

Cherlin, A. J. (1992). *Marriage, divorce, remarriage.* Cambridge, MA: Harvard University Press.

Coley, R. L., & Chase-Lansdale, P. L. (1998). Adolescent pregnancy and parenthood: Recent evidence and future directions. *American Psychologist, 53*(2), 152–166.

Currie, J. (1997). Choosing among alternative programs for poor children. *The Future of Children: Children and Poverty, 7*(2), 113–131.

Duncan, G. J., Hill, M. S., & Hoffman, S. D. (1988). Welfare dependence within and across generations. *Science, 1*, 467–471.

Edin, K., & Lein, L. (1997). *Making ends meet.* New York, NY: Russell Sage Foundation Press.

Elder, G. H., Jr. (1974). *Children of the Great Depression.* Chicago, IL: University of Chicago Press.

Ellwood, D. T., & Bane, M. (1994). *Welfare realities: From rhetoric to reform.* Cambridge, MA: Harvard University Press.

Furstenberg, F. F., Jr. (1995). Dealing with dads: The changing roles of fathers. In P. L. Chase-Lansdale & Brooks-Gunn (Eds.) *Escape from poverty: What makes a difference for children?* New York: Cambridge University Press.

Furstenberg, F. F., Jr., Brooks-Gunn, J., & Chase-Lansdale, P. L. (1989). Adolescent fertility and public policy. *American Psychologist, 44*(2), 313–320.

Furstenberg, F. F., Jr., Brooks-Gunn, J., & Morgan, S. P. (1987). *Adolescent mothers in later life.* New York: Cambridge University Press.

Furstenberg, F. F., Jr., Levine, J. A., & Brooks-Gunn, J. (1990). The daughters of teenage mothers: Patterns of early childbearing in two generations. *Family Planning Perspectives, 22*(2), 54–61.

Garfinkel, I., & McLanahan, S. (1995). The effects of child support reform on child well-being. In P. L. Chase-Lansdale & J. Brooks-Gunn (Eds.) *Escape from poverty: What makes a difference for children.* New York: Cambridge University Press.

Geronimus, A. T., & Korenman, S. (1992). The socioeconomic consequences of teen childbearing reconsidered. *Quarterly Journal of Economics, 107*(4), 1187–1214.

Gottschalk, P. (1996). Is the correlation in welfare participation across generations spurious? *Journal of Public Economics, 63*, 1–25.

Guo, G., Brooks-Gunn, J., & Harris, K. M. (1996). Parental labor-force attachment and grade retention among urban Black children. *Sociology of Education, 69*, 217–236.

Hagestad, G. O. (1986). Dimensions of time and the family. *American Behavioral Scientist, 29* (6), 679–694.

Haggerty, R. J., Sherrod, L. R., Garmezy, N., & Rutter, M. (1994). *Stress, risk, and resilience in children and adolescents: Processes, mechanisms, and interventions.* New York: Cambridge University Press.

Hardy, J. B., Astone, N. M., Brooks-Gunn, J., Shapiro, S., & Miller, T. L. (1998). Like mother, like child: Intergenerational patterns of age at first birth and their associations with adult outcomes in the second generation. *Developmental Psychology.*

Hardy, J. B., Shapiro, S., Astone, N. M., Miller, T. L., Brooks-Gunn, J., & Hilton, S. C. (1997). Adolescent childbearing revisited: The age of inner-city mothers at delivery is a determinant of their children's self-sufficiency at age 27 to 33. *Pediatrics, 100* (5), 802–809.

Hardy, J. B., Shapiro, S., Mellits, E. D., Skinner, E. A., Astone, N. M., Ensminger, M., LaVeist, T., Baumgardner, R. A., & Starfield, B. H. (1997). Self-sufficiency at ages 27 to 33 years: Factors present between birth and 18 years that predict educational attainment among children born to inner-city families. *Pediatrics, 99*(10), 80–87.

Hayes, C. D. (1987). *Risking the future: Adolescent sexuality, pregnancy, and childbearing.* Washington, DC: National Academy Press.

Hoffman, S. D., Foster, E. M., & Furstenberg, F. F. (1993). Re-evaluating the costs of teenage childbearing. *Demography, 30,* 1–13.

Hotz, J. V., McElroy, S. W., & Sanders, S. (1996). The costs and consequences of teenage childbearing for mothers. *Chicago Policy Review, 1*, 55–94.

Hotz, J. V., McElroy, S. W., & Sanders, S. (1997). The impacts of teenage childbearing on the mothers and the consequences of those impacts for government. In R. A. Maynard (Ed.), *Kids having kids: Economic costs and consequences of teen pregnancy* (pp. 55–94). Washington, DC: The Urban Institute Press.

Jones, E. F., Forrest, J. D., Goldman, N., Henshaw, S. K., Lincoln, R., Rosoff, J. I., Westoff, C. F., & Wulf, D. (1985). Teenage pregnancy in developed countries: Determinants and policy implications. *Family Planning Perspectives, 17*(2), 53–63.

Jones, E. F., Forrest, J. D., Henshaw, S. K., Silverman, J., & Torres, A. (1988). Unintended pregnancy, contraceptive practice and family planning services in developed countries. *Family Planning Perspectives, 20*(2), 53–67.

Kahn, J. R., & Anderson, E. (1992). Intergenerational patterns of teenage fertility. *Demography, 29,* 39–57.

Manlove, J. (1997). Early motherhood in an intergenerational perspective: The experiences of a British cohort. *Journal of Marriage and the Family, 59,* 263–279.

Maynard, R. (1995). Teenage childbearing and welfare reform: Lessons from a decade of demonstration and evaluation research. *Children and Youth Services Review, 17*(1), 309–332.

Maynard, R. (1997). *Kids having kids: Economic costs and social consequences of teen pregnancy.* Washington, DC: Urban Institute Press.

McLanahan, S. (1997). Poverty among children in single parent, divorced, and remarried families. In G. Duncan & J. Brooks-Gunn (Eds.), *Consequences of growing up poor.* New York, NY: Russell Sage Foundation Press.

McLanahan, S., Garfinkel, I., Brooks-Gunn, J., & Zhao, H. (1998, May). *Unwed parenthood: Antecedents and consequence.* Paper presented at the annual meeting of the Population Association of America, Chicago, IL.

McLanahan, S., & Sandefur, G. D. (1994). *Growing up with a single parent: What hurts, what helps?* Cambridge, MA: Harvard University Press.

Modell, J., & Goodman, M. (1990). Historical perspectives on adolescence and adolescents. In S. Feldman & G. Elliott (Eds.), *At the threshold: The developing adolescent.* Cambridge, MA: Harvard University Press.

Modell, J., Furstenberg, F. F. Jr., & Herschberg, T. (1976). Social changes and transitions to adulthood in historical perspective. *Journal of Social Issues, 1*(1), 67–86.

Moffitt, R. A., Reville, R., & Winkler, A. E. (1995). *Beyond single mother: Cohabitation, marriage, and the U.S. welfare system* (Institute for Research on Poverty Discussion Paper No. 1068-95). Madison: University of Wisconsin.

Moore, K. A., Myers, D. E., Morrison, D. R., Nord, C. W., Brown, B., & Edmonston, B. (1993). Age at first childbirth and later poverty. *Journal of Research on Adolescence, 3*(4), 393–422.

Phillips, E., & Garfinkel, I. (1993). Income growth among nonresident fathers: Evidence from Wisconsin. *Demography, 30*(2), 227–241.

Presser, H. B. (1978). Social factors affecting the timing of the first child. In W. B. Miller & L. F. Newman (Eds.), *The first child and family formation.* Chapel Hill, NC: Carolina Population Center.

Rosenheim, M. K., & Testa, M. F. (Eds.). (1992). *Early parenthood and coming of age in the 1990s.* New Brunswick, NJ: Rutgers University Press.

Rutter, M. (1987). Psychosocial resilience and protective mechanisms. *American Journal of Orthopsychiatry, 57,* 316–331.

Smith, J. R., Brooks-Gunn, J., & Klebanov, P. K. (1997). The consequences of living in poverty for young children's cognitive and verbal ability and early school achievement. In G. J. Duncan & J. Brooks-Gunn (Eds.), *Consequences of growing up poor* (pp. 132–189). New York, NY: Russell Sage Foundation Press.

United Nations. (1991). *Demographic yearbook.* New York: Author.

Ventura, S. J., Martin, J. A., Curtin, S. C., & Matthews, T. J. (1997). Report of final mortality statistics, 1995. *Monthly Vital Statistics Report, 45*(11) (Suppl. 2), 1.

Vinovskis, M. A. (1992). Historical perspectives on adolescent pregnancy. In M. K. Rosenheim & M. F. Testa (Eds.), *Early parenthood and coming of age in the 1990s* (pp.136–149). New Brunswick, NJ: Rutgers University Press.

Werner, E. E., & Smith, R. S. (1982). *Vulnerable but invincible: A longitudinal study of resilient children and youth.* New York: McGraw-Hill.

Wilson, W. J. (1987). *The truly disadvantaged: The inner city, the underclass, and public policy.* Chicago: University of Chicago Press.

Wilson, W. J. (1991). Public policy research and the truly disadvantaged. In C. Jencks & P. E. Peterson (Eds.), *The urban underclass.* Washington, DC: The Brookings Institution.

4　Effects of Social Change on Individual Development: The Role of Social and Personal Factors and the Timing of Events

Gisela Trommsdorff

Social change can be a gradual unfolding of different ways of life or can imply a sudden, fundamental transformation of economic, social, and political institutions, as was the case in Eastern Europe after the end of the Cold War. Individuals perceive, experience, and handle effects of social change on the basis of certain sociopsychological processes. This chapter focuses on how individuals deal with social change – how social change is perceived, experienced, and acted upon by the person and how these reactions affect human development.

Until recently, social change and individual development were studied separately in different disciplines. Attempting to relate these two complex topics of research may increase the risk of failing to deal successfully with either one. However, I believe that the study of individual development in a changing socioeconomic context will allow us to further our understanding of human development. This belief is based on the assumption that individual development is an active process taking place over the life course in multiple contexts. The *active* role of the individual is seen in the psychological processes of negotiating the self in relation to the environment, including goal setting, decision making, and behavior. The *contextual* view enlarges the individual-centered approach by specifying ecological conditions that affect individual development and by illuminating multidirectional processes in changing person–environment relations.

When dealing with the possible effects of social change on individual development, several issues have to be clarified:

1. Which aspects of social change have an impact on the individual person?
2. How is the individual person affected by such factors?
3. Why do some people gain from social change and others experience losses?
4. How does the outcome of social change affect further individual development?

From a theoretical perspective, the questions are, Can the view of development as an active, life-long process-in-context further our understanding of individual

Parts of this research were supported by the *Deutsche Forschungsgemeinschaft* (AZ Tr 169/5-1; 5-2).

development in periods of social change, and, Can this approach bridge two very different phenomena: social change and individual development? To begin to address these questions, contextual factors and dimensions of subjective experience will be discussed. Each is discussed in relation to the other according to a goodness-of-fit model.

Social change can induce significant modifications in the person's environment. However, these changes are only relevant for the person's further development if demands for certain behavior in the (new) environmental setting do not fit the person's psychological and social resources. Depending on the person and his or her environment, certain social changes may imply either stressors and risk factors or new options and opportunities for development. The person can experience environmental changes in such a way that previously successful goal attainment is blocked, or previously unattainable goals can now be reached. Internal processes of evaluating such experienced environmental change may induce cognitive and socioemotional reorientation: Previous goals are modified or abandoned, and this is followed by a restructuring of one's goals, active planning, and decision making. In this way social change stimulates individual development.

Socioeconomic changes such as economic hardship thus do not necessarily mean a stressful life event but could mean a challenge stimulating the person to engage in coping strategies that later lead to developmental gains in options and resources. This can be seen from Elder's (1974) famous study *Children of the Great Depression*. Girls and boys and children of different developmental ages experienced this social change in very different ways, some gaining and some losing from economic hardship. The differing outcomes were due to the ways in which contextual factors and previously established social and personal resources matched the changing contexts and related options and constraints.

This example suggests that the impact of social change on the individual depends on the context and the person as well as on the way both correspond and interact with each other. However, more detailed studies are needed concerning how external and internal factors affect human development and induce resilience or proneness to risk in times of social change. In the following section, contextual factors and person factors are examined in more detail with respect to their roles in the process by which social change affects individual development.

Contextual Factors: Mediators and Moderators

Context as Multifaceted Variable

Social change may be studied at the level of social context (e.g., changes in the labor market), at the level of individual behavior changes, or in terms of the relation between the two. Changes at the macrolevel of society (e.g., structural changes such as an increase in unemployment) may affect the person directly or indirectly. For example, information gained through the media or through interaction with other persons directly affects the individual. Indirect effects can also occur when a family member or the person himself or herself loses a job.

Contextual changes can be seen as both mediators and moderators of social change effects. To give an example, the family context may be a *mediator* of social change (e.g., when labor market changes lead to unemployment and economic hardship in the family, which in turn affect parent–child relations); the family context may also be a *moderator* of social change effects (e.g., when the family climate provides a buffer between external changes, such as dislocation, and the adolescent) in such a way that an otherwise negative impact of contextual changes is modified.

Here, we take the view that social change usually affects the individual indirectly; that is, filtered by multifaceted social contexts. Social contexts are understood here both as distal historical and cultural conditions and as proximal conditions (such as availability of social support in the family). The more distal social context and the more proximal social context may transmit social change. For the present purposes, however, we focus on the more proximal contexts affected by social change and their effects on human development.

Dynamic Approach. When looking for ways in which contextual factors transmit social change to the individual, one has to be aware of the ecological complexity of contextual variables and their different meaning in different cultural contexts. Also, one has to take into account that different components of social contexts may have different relevance for social and cognitive development at different periods of development (e.g., achievement demands in school, availability of attachment figures, etc.). By neglecting the process of individual development over time, a purely contextual approach clouds which factors have developmental implications. Instead, a *dynamic* model is needed that takes into account the social and psychological functions of contextual changes for individual development.

In line with this reasoning, the chapters by Elder and Russell and Brooks-Gunn, Schley, and Hardy in this volume demonstrate that one has to go beyond structural categories and static descriptions of context by differentiating between the following:

1. More distal contexts such as historical processes that allow us to place persons within their intergenerational histories (e.g., occupational career or life history of families and family members across generations).
2. More proximal contexts such as actual family processes.

These dimensions mediate and moderate effects of socioeconomic change on the development of children and adolescents. According to Elder and Russell (this volume), life course theory allows researchers to study individual development by locating a person in historical context and life stage, thereby focusing on the impact of historical, structural pathways and social strata and age-graded social trajectories (such as work or family). The focus on persons and their families takes into account history (through birth cohort) and the individual life course (through age). By interrelating these dimensions, the impact of biological and social factors (including the sociopsychological impact of birth cohorts and age strata) on individual development becomes another focus of attention. Reciprocal influences between social and developmental trajectories and mutual influences between people's life trajectories and their developmental processes (including choices and careers) are assumed.

Elder's position is that, to understand the developmental consequences of certain social changes, one should identify historical factors that account for changes in the life course. Both the proximal implications of social change (e.g., effects on family structure) and more distal consequences (e.g., labor market changes) for individual development are relevant. Therefore, Elder and Russell (this volume) differentiate between *framing statements* (proximal implications) and *nested points of entry*. This model allows us to measure the processes of change as an interplay between individual lives and a changing society. The advantage of this model is to "nest developmental analyses within a social change framework." Elder's studies make full use of birth cohorts in relating history to the life course and thus in *relating historical and individual time*. Therefore, Elder not only uses cohort-sequential designs but also studies *variations within specific cohorts*. Variations in family patterns (household economy, family relations, and strains) are viewed as linkages affecting children's developmental outcomes. This allows one to grasp the nested points of entry.

According to Elder's data, extreme hardship (e.g., economic depression) can strengthen certain psychological dispositions brought to the event such as emotional instability. Irritable men become more explosive and punitive in parenting, thus affecting the development of their children negatively. This can be a risk factor for children's development. This example also shows that changing societies do not necessarily affect the individual's development directly; rather, changes on the macrolevel are mediated and moderated by proximal conditions such as microlevel contextual factors and individual transitions.

Social Resources. During the life course, different aspects of the environment are important for the socioemotional and cognitive development of the person. In early childhood, attachment figures will be influential owing to their capacity to fulfill the child's basic needs for security and emotional bonding (Bowlby, 1969). Therefore, a critical question for effects of social change on early child development is whether and how the emotional availability of attachment figures (like the parents) is affected. During later development, multiple social agents will be important, such as siblings, peers, and adults. Accordingly, more has to be known about the psychological relevance of changes in the social environment over the course of development, especially with regard to close relationships and social resources.

Family. Social support in the family modifies risk factors and provides a protective influence on children's development. In their study of Iowa youth, Conger, Conger, Elder, Lorenz, Simons, and Whitbeck (1992, 1993) demonstrated a close association between objective family hardship and increased risk of parental depression, conflicts in marriage, and nonnurturing parental behavior (both parents). These outcomes, in turn, were associated with lower self-confidence, lower peer acceptance, and lower school performance in early adolescent boys. Elder and Russell (this volume) find the same pattern of relationships for displaced families (who lost their farmland). However, in the case of strong marriage bonds and effective problem solving by fathers, children of displaced families developed a positive self-image and suffered fewer developmental risks. Parents in emotionally strong marriages can counter stress and depressed moods more effectively, support a sense of self-efficacy, and serve as a model and a protective force for their children (Elder & Shanahan, 1996). Similarly, a strong emotionally based family and child orientation seemed to increase the resilience of East German children and adolescents during the dramatic transformation in the economic, political, and social system following unification (Trommsdorff & Chakkarath, 1996).

The wider *sociocultural and political context* in which families are living should also play an important role in their responses to social change. For example, after unification, families in West Germany were more stressed by the economic depression and suffered more in the quality of family interaction compared with families in the East (Hofer, Kracke, Noack, Klein-Allermann, Kessel, Jahn, & Ettrich, 1995). Although the families from different German regions presumably met objectively similar economic deprivations, they experienced these deprivations in different socioeconomic contexts and on the basis of quite dissimilar life histories. Thus, the same historical change had differential consequences.

Peers. The *wider social network*, especially peer relations, should also provide important mediating variables influencing the experience of change for children and adolescents. However, inter- and intracultural differences with respect to the relevance of peers for adolescents' development are also to be taken into account. In the former German Democratic Republic, peers had an important function in the socialization of children and adolescents (Schmidt, 1996), for nearly every child and adolescent joined well-organized peer groups (*Junge Pioniere*). Presumably, the breakdown of these youth groups negatively affected the sense of social integration, support, and control among East German adolescents, and some data suggest that this may have resulted in developmental risks (e.g., Zinnecker & Silbereisen, 1996). For example, East as compared with West German adolescents tend to prefer more aggressive behavior in cases of frustration; and East German females hold more pessimistic expectations for the future (Trommsdorff & Kornadt, 1995).

However, contextual factors alone cannot predict individual development in changing contexts. Rather, it is necessary to specify what the individual's resources are in order to analyze how well environmental changes and individual resources match each other.

The Subjective Experience of Social Change

Besides social resources in the family and in the peer group, specific individual resources such as cognitive, social, and emotional dispositions are the basis of a person's competencies, values, and goals and influence his or her way of negotiating social change. On the basis of prior socialization and developmental experiences, a person has built up certain options in the life course and certain competencies that serve as psychological resources. These mediate the way in which "objective" changes are experienced (e.g., as gains or losses, as threats or promises) and the way these changes activate and possibly modify individual values, beliefs, and goals, which, in turn, affect further development (See Figure 1). Thus, diversity in development when experiencing social change is not only related to contextual factors but also to the developmental status of the individual, including competencies and patterns of beliefs that are used to interpret environmental changes and that affect the person's abilities for coping. Moreover, interaction effects between contextual and personal factors are to be expected.

Empirical studies have shown that children growing up with a sense of self-worth and a belief in self-efficacy are better able to cope with economic deprivation. Elder, King, and Conger (1996) showed that children from Iowa farm families grew up with close emotional ties to the family and felt that their parents viewed them as significant persons who were important for the family enterprise. Farm as compared with nonfarm children were more aware of their family responsibility, spent more time with family and less with peers, and were more involved in communal activities; also, they showed lower vulnerability to materialistic and hedonistic values. The authors explain these differences as an effect of farm children's personal resources, which are seen as a result of their socialization experiences, including more intergenerational continuity, more feelings of interdependence, and less individualization. This study supports our hypothesis that sociopolitical and economic changes are experienced differently and have differential consequences that depend on one's personal and social resources.

Subjective Beliefs and Goals

Over the course of development, a person has built up certain individual resources such as a specific "internal working model" and related belief systems (including beliefs in self and control). These resources filter the subjective perceptions and evaluations of events, including changes in the environment. The "inner working

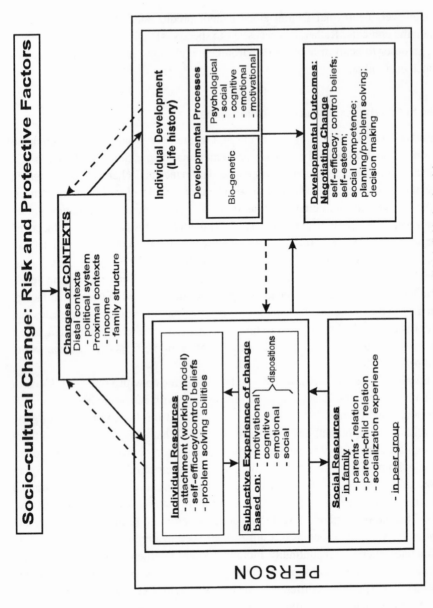

Figure 1. Effects of Social change on individual development as mediated by individual and social resources.

model" (Bowlby, 1969) is assumed to provide a basis for the person's belief system that serves to interpret oneself and the environment and the relation between them in a more positive or negative way. The same kinds of events could be subjectively experienced in very different ways, depending on the person's underlying belief system and internal working model. One's subjective experience of, and reactions to, changing events may serve either as a buffering factor or a risk factor in further development, implying either chances or an accumulation of risks in response to negative events such as an economic depression (See Figure 1).

Individuals act on their own development by setting goals (and disengaging from goals), by planning for achievement of these goals, and by carrying out the respective decisions. Certain changes may imply serious problems when previously established goals and related planning are disrupted. Some goals seem more difficult to achieve, whereas other goals (e.g., to pursue a certain career) seem to be completely blocked by ongoing changes (e.g., changes in the labor market). However, it may also be that certain wishes are transformed into goals and come to be viewed as realistic future outcomes.

The setting of goals and the evaluation of previous goals (in the light of the effects of social change on one's distal and proximal environment) are closely related to a person's identity and self-esteem and, more specifically, to his or her control beliefs (self-efficacy) and future orientation (Bandura, 1995; Scheier & Carver, 1985). These are part of the personal resources that affect the subjective experience of change (e.g., the degree of stress due to the perceived difficulty of achieving one's previously set goals) and also the way of actually dealing with such experience. Effective coping consists of reorganizing one's goals, values, attribution preferences, control beliefs, and planning behavior.

Scheduling of Changing Contexts and the Person's Developmental Transitions

So far, we have dealt with the role of context and person and the interaction between them in individuals' development in times of social change. Additionally, the roles of timing of effects of social change and timing of biographical events have to be taken into account. Here, two aspects are relevant: First, individual variations in timing (e.g., adolescents' leaving home to take a job) can be a consequence of social change; second, individual variations in timing of biographical events can imply potential risk factors for further development under certain conditions of social change. Here, we will focus on possible implications of personal variations in timing of events for individual development in times of social change.

Some events in a person's biography, such as giving birth to a child as a teenage mother, can happen at a period in the person's development when the individual is not yet "developmentally" prepared. Normally, a match between new roles and personality development is secured by providing the necessary contextual conditions and by stimulating anticipatory socialization, training, or other planning activities related to the new developmental tasks. However, the scheduling of events in times of social change can have problematic effects, especially in the case of multiple transitions (e.g., starting a job, having a child). Multiple transitions need a certain synchrony that may be disturbed by unexpected events. By disrupting this synchrony and contributing to off-time transitions, social change can contribute to developmental risk.

The "off-time" scheduling of events and new roles can induce stress and risk. This can lead to self-perpetuating disadvantages in further development and may even affect the next generation. In their longitudinal studies on early childbearing, Brooks-Gunn and Furstenberg (1987), and Holmbeck, Paikoff, and Brooks-Gunn (1995) demonstrated that children of teenage mothers perpetuate teenage parenthood and long-time welfare dependency from one generation to the next. Children of Black teenage mothers experience cumulative effects of *multiple* risks: They grow up in poverty, in a single-parent family, and they have less educated and less securely employed parents. One third of these teenage mothers' daughters also become teenage mothers (Brooks-Gunn et al., this volume).

When social change events occur in one's life course, the timing of such events may be a risk factor for some persons and an opportunity for others. As noted earlier, Elder and his coworkers demonstrated that for preschool children who grew up during the Great Depression, family economic hardship negatively affected their emotional development. In contrast, adolescents could profit from the Depression; they had already developed capacities to take over social responsibility in their families and had developed more self-confidence. Studies on effects of unification in East Germany also demonstrate that for some age groups the transformation was a risk factor, whereas for others it was an advantage. For example, East German males born around 1940 had a lower belief in internal control directly after unification than any other male group in East or West Germany (Trommsdorff, in press). Obviously, for a certain cohort (males around 50 year of age) the turmoil after the reunification turned out to be a risk mainly because of decreased chances for employment at this age and the related off-time disengagement from social roles and activities.

The developmental timing of events also affects social motivation in children (unpublished data). Immediately following reunification and 3 years later, preschool children and adolescents in the East showed more anger and aggression and fewer prosocial goals compared with those in the West; this pattern was not found for children of intermediate age, however. A longitudinal study demonstrated that this difference has now disappeared for the older children (Trommsdorff, Kornadt, & Hessel-Scherf, 1998) but has remained stable for adolescents. It seems that East German children who experienced social change at an intermediate developmental age could negotiate such changes more successfully than either younger children or older adolescents, both of whom were confronted with multiple transitions in and outside their family (e.g., the normative transition from preschool to school and from school to the job market).

Summary and Outlook

To summarize, individual development in times of social change can be conceived of as either a risk or a challenge, depending on the individual's personal and social resources. Such resources are part of one's past experiences and present (social) context, including the timing of transition. Social change does not affect a person's development negatively unless individual and social resources of the person do not match the new environmental demands. The context of the person, the timing of events, the person's developmental age, and related social and individual resources can each constitute risk or buffering factors. The main factors predicting how persons negotiate social change are the historical and sociocultural context, on the one hand, and the proximal context of family and social relationships, in combination with the individual resources and the scheduling and duration of events, on the other; these conditions allow us to predict how social change confers developmental gains or losses for the individual.

More precisely, a theoretical outline concerning development in changing contexts should specify which aspects of the social environment (social structure, economic conditions, family environment) relate in which way to individual resources in the dynamic process of transitions (see Figure 1). The timing of events and their fit with individual and social resources will affect a person's subjective experience of such events and contribute to the way the person acts on his or her development. Even in the case of mismatch between new environmental demands and the person's resources, problems of accommodation and assimilation can reestablish a person's control, reduce possible risks, and increase the person's potential for later coping with even more demanding changes in the environment. Therefore, further research should take into account *processes* of individual development in changing contexts.

In conclusion, future studies on social change and individual development should focus more explicitly on how the person perceives and experiences specific aspects of ongoing social change. Here, the view is taken that subjective experience of social change depends on the timing of events and on the accumulation and duration of transitions. Also, it depends on social relations (in the family and with peers) and on individual resources as transmitted by the person's life history and past socialization experiences (in a specific cohort, as male or female, and at a specific developmental age). Therefore, the timing of the person's encountering specific events of social change at a specific constellation of his or her personal development-in-context is a relevant starting point for empirical research. Because individuals are confronted with social change at different points in the process of change and at different times in terms of their social roles and developmental stage, social change can turn out to be a risk factor or a growth-fostering challenge for further development.

References

Bandura, A. (Ed.). (1995). *Self-efficacy in changing societies*. Cambridge, England: Cambridge University Press.

Bowlby, J. (1969). *Attachment and loss: Vol. 1. Attachment*. New York: Basic Books.

Brooks-Gunn, J., & Furstenberg, F. F. (1987). Continuity and change in the context of poverty: Adolescent mothers and their children. In J. J. Callagher & C. T. Ramey (Eds.), *The malleability of children* (pp. 171–188). Baltimore: Brooks.

Conger, R. D., Conger, K. J., Elder, G. H., Lorenz, F. O., Simons, R. L., & Whitbeck, L. B. (1992). A family process model of economic hardship and adjustment of early adolescent boys. *Child Development, 63,* 526–541.

Conger, R. D., Conger, K. J., Elder, G. H., Lorenz, F. O., Simons, R. L., & Whitbeck, L. B. (1993). Family economic stress and adjustment of early adolescent girls. *Developmental Psychology, 29,* 206–219.

Elder, G. H. (1974). *Children of the Great Depression: Social change and life experience*. Chicago: University of Chicago Press.

Elder, G. H., King, V., & Conger, R. D. (1996). Intergenerational continuity and change in rural lives: Historical and developmental insights. *International Journal of Behavioral Development, 19,* 433–455.

Elder, G. H., & Shanahan, M. J. (1996). *Social change, youth and agency: A perspective on the life course*. Unpublished manuscript, University of North Carolina.

Hofer, M., Kracke, B., Noack, P., Klein-Allermann, E., Kessel, W., Jahn, U., & Ettrich, U. (1995). Der soziale Wandel aus Sicht ost- und westdeutscher Familien, psychisches Wohlbefinden und autoritäre Vorstellungen [Social change from the point of view of East- and West German families, psychological well-being and authoritarian beliefs]. In B. Nauck, N. Schneider, & A. Tölke (Eds.), *Familie und Lebenslauf im gesellschaftlichen Umbruch* (pp. 154–171). Stuttgart, Germany: Enke.

Holmbeck, G. M., Paikoff, R. L., & Brooks-Gunn, J. (1995). Parenting adolescents. In M. H. Bornstein (Ed.), *Handbook of parenting: Vol. 1. Children and parenting* (pp. 336–374). Mahwah, NJ: Erlbaum.

Scheier, M., & Carver, C. (1985). Optimism, coping, and health: Assessment and implications of generalized outcome expectancies. *Health Psychology, 4,* 219–247.

Schmidt, H.-D. (1996). Erziehungsbedingungen in der DDR: Offizielle Programme, individuelle Praxis und die Rolle der Pädagogischen Psychologie und Entwicklungspsychologie [Conditions of education in the DDR: Official programs, individual practice and the role of educational and developmental psychology]. In G. Trommsdorff (Ed.), *Sozialisation und Entwicklung von Kindern vor und nach der Vereinigung. Beiträge zum Bericht "Individuelle Entwicklung, Bildung und Berufsverläufe im Transformationsprozeß" der KSPW, Bd. 4.1* (pp. 15–171). Opladen: Leske & Budrich.

Trommsdorff, G. (in press). Subjective experience of social change and developmental effects. In R. Silbereisen & J. Bynner (Eds.), *Adversities and constraints in the life course*. Berlin: de Gruyter.

Trommsdorff, G., & Chakkarath, P. (1996). Kindheit im Transformationsprozeß [Childhood in the process of transformation]. In S. E. Hormuth, W. R. Heinz, H.-J. Kornadt, H. Sydow, & G. Trommsdorff (Eds.), *Individuelle Entwicklung, Bildung und Berufsverläufe. Berichte zum sozialen und politischen Wandel in Ostdeutschland, KSPW Bd. 4* (pp. 11–77). Opladen: Leske & Budrich.

Trommsdorff, G., & Kornadt, H.-J. (1995). Pro- and antisocial motivation of adolescents in Eastern and Western Germany. In J. Youniss (Ed.), *After the wall: Family adaptions in East and West Germany. New directions for child development, No. 70* (pp. 39–56). San Francisco: Jossey–Bass.

Trommsdorff, G., Kornadt, H.-J., & Hessel-Scherf, M. (1998). Soziale Motivation ost- und westdeutscher Kinder [Social motivation of East- and West German children]. *Zeitschrift für Sozialisationsforschung und Erziehungssoziologie. 18,* 121–136.

Zinnecker, J., & Silbereisen, R. K. (Eds.). (1996). *Kindheit in Deutschland: Aktueller Survey über Kinder und ihre Eltern* [Childhood in Germany: Current survey on children and their parents]. Weinheim, Germany: Juventa.

Part II

Social Change and Adolescent Transitions

5   The Global Spread of Adolescent Culture

Alice Schlegel

Look at your fellow passengers on any train in Europe. If there are adolescents among them, try to guess their nationality. It will be difficult, because young people all over Europe wear the same kinds of clothing and style their hair in similar ways. Teenagers in Indonesia buy the magazine *Topchords* to learn the guitar chords and lyrics of popular Indonesian and Western songs. Within 2 years of the loosening of restrictions in China, urban adolescents and youth were using available fabrics to copy, to the best of their ability, the dress of their Western counterparts. Quechuan teenagers, in the high Andes Mountains, listen to tapes of popular North American music. In the small cities of Morocco, young people imitate their glamorous cousins who return home for visits from France or Germany with their emigrant parents. Adolescent culture has spread throughout Europe and is moving far from its European and American homeland. What is adolescent culture? Is it a product of the industrial or postindustrial age? How does it affect the lives of its participants?

Locating Adolescent Culture

Culture is one of those terms whose very usefulness, which lies in its flexibility and applicability to a number of distinct phenomena, makes it ambiguous. Anthropologists usually employ it to cover the total way of life of a people, focusing on either the behavioral or the ideological according to their theoretical stance. I am taking one aspect–expressive culture (the aesthetic, ritual, and leisure-time pursuits of a category of people) – and overlapping it with material culture (the products of human thought, effort, and skill). In brief, I am dealing with products designed to be used for primarily expressive rather than utilitarian purposes and that convey information about the user concerning such personal features as his or her social status, political ideology, sexual interest, and, in this case, the adolescent stage in

I thank Ellen Basso, Edward Nell, the editors of this book, and an anonymous reviewer for their comments and suggestions. Ruby Takanashi, Ulf Hannerz, Daniel Nugent, and Reed Larson provided valuable material, for which I am grateful.

71

the life cycle. Although such products, especially clothing, can be brought into the school or workplace, they are mostly used by students or young workers during their leisure time. Adolescent expressive culture includes products of human activity other than tangible material ones, such as speech patterns and expressions and the songs, dances, and games that adolescents themselves create. These, however, are not the cultural elements that are spreading rapidly, for they are usually localized by place or speech community.

Cultural artifacts are saturated with the meanings that users attach to them, which may or may not be the same as those their producers intended. Different users may attach divergent meanings to the same cultural artifact, as anyone attempting to launch a new product in a country outside that of its origin must foresee to market it successfully. Products that engage the viewer's or listener's personal experience, such as song lyrics and some visual arts, make direct, value-laden statements about experience. They inspire fantasies, recall events and feelings, and help to create and shape beliefs about how things are or should be.

These cultural products and their use by adolescents are the subject of this chapter. What I have labeled "adolescent culture" is actually a "culture" of both adolescence and youth, for these material objects are used primarily by young people at these two stages of life. Many researchers use *adolescence* to refer to young people anywhere from 11 to 20 years of age or even older. I find it truer to the reality of life in our contemporary society, and in some nonindustrial ones as well, to consider an additional stage between adolescence and adulthood. I apply the term *adolescent* to people from around the age of puberty to about 18 or 19 years of age, and I use the term *youth* for older ones who are not yet socially recognized as adults. Adolescence is a social category that is only imperfectly constructed onto a biological one (like middle age), and thus the exact ages of entry into, and exit from, this category vary by culture and even by social class. For the majority of peoples in the world, adulthood is achieved at marriage or at some other socially marked status change. Contemporary young people may delay marriage and settling down into their mid-20s or older (as did, incidentally, the youth of Shakespeare's day). The behavior of people in their 20s, and the way they are regarded by others, is very different from the behaviors and expectations of 14-year-olds. (For a longer discussion of the youth stage and its difference from social adolescence, see Schlegel and Barry [1991]).[1] Because the particular focus of this essay is adolescents (young people in their teens) rather than older youth, adolescent culture is more precise than "youth culture."

In most aspects of their lives, adolescents are absorbed into institutions designed and managed by adults. These are primarily the family and kinship networks; in many places they include school, workplace, and marketplace. There is little time or social space for developing a culture in any encompassing sense. Living at home, as most do, adolescents cannot create a style of life. Their culture consists of how they present themselves as a distinctive social category marked by age and activities. They do this through dress, manner, speech, and how they spend their free time. Popular music and clothing style are two of the most prominent and distinctive elements of adolescent culture, probably because clothing, recordings, and videos are relatively cheap, widely available, and obvious as signaling devices to adults and other adolescents. Unlike teenage slang, which is restricted to the native language, these cultural elements can readily be exported.

We tend to associate a culture of adolescence with industrial nations since World War II and the associated growth in more specialized products for an increasingly affluent teenage market. In fact, however, adolescent culture has a long history in Europe, and it has been found to some degree in almost all preindustrial societies. Historians of youth life tell of youth organizations and youth customs in towns of early modern Europe. Adolescent boys and youths served as a local militia in some parts of Europe, and the young people of both sexes were often mobilized by the church to organize processions and other events (Gillis, 1974). In the Provençal towns of the 16th to 18th centuries, groups of adolescents and youths, divided by social class, organized balls at Mardi Gras with the blessing of the town fathers (Roubin, 1977). Although some activities, like church processions, were organized by adults, others like town balls were for the benefit of the young people themselves. These festivities were entertaining, but their importance to young people lay in the opportunities they provided for girls and boys to meet and flirt. They were an aid to courtship, an important step toward marriage and adulthood.

Mitterauer (1992) gives details about adolescent and youth groups, particularly in German-speaking areas. One activity that resonates in contemporary life is the adolescent gang battles of German cities in the 18th and 19th centuries, a "pastime" rarely indulged in by adults. Mitterauer draws the important distinction between the all-village peer groups of rural communities and the peer groups in the towns and cities, which were restricted by district and social class. It is likely that adolescent groups in villages and towns sang their distinctive songs and uttered their distinctive slang terms, but there seems to be little information on these creative aspects of early modern adolescent life.

A cross-cultural study of adolescence in tribal and traditional societies (Schlegel & Barry, 1991) provided many examples of the activities characteristic of people in the adolescent stage of life. Visual markers of adolescence, such as clothing, hair style, or body decoration occurred in over 80% of the more than 100 societies for which there was evidence (Schlegel & Barry, 1991, p. 37). This study showed that there were many activities specific to the adolescence stage in a wide range of societies from foragers to the traditional farmers and pastoralists of Africa, Eurasia, and the Americas. These were often pastimes such as games or dancing, but they included service to the community done by young people of this age. There is little evidence for products used only by adolescents; but it is likely that songs accompanying the dances were sung predominantly, if not exclusively, by the young, and there may well have been adolescent slang terms, although ethnographers have not recorded them.

Although it is almost universal for adolescents to have an expressive style that distinguishes them as a socially defined age set, there are important differences between the adolescent cultures of earlier times and simpler places and the adolescent culture of modern adolescents and youths. There is much more emphasis on the consumption of commercial products and much less on homemade ones, and reliance on commercial recreational facilities has replaced many of the pastimes organized by adolescents themselves. In this, adolescents are like adults, whose expressive culture also relies heavily on what the market provides. But for adolescents, this means that they increasingly rely on adults to produce the material elements of their culture for them, even though they may be selective in what they buy. The distinctiveness of modern adolescent culture is aided by the mass marketing of popular culture with special products aimed at the youth market. It is to the advantage of producers of cultural products to enhance the distinctiveness of the market niche to which they appeal and to stimulate the acquisition of new goods.

A feature that distinguishes modern adolescence from adolescence of earlier times is the degree to which it turns inward: Modern adolescents are largely oriented toward one another with relatively little orientation toward adults. Formerly, children were more in contact with large numbers of adults than most are today. They worked alongside adults for much of the day, and many of their recreational activities took place in full view of the community, or at least the household, where they were under adult surveillance. More important, adolescents knew that they were being judged and assessed as the fellow citizens they would be in a few years' time. In this way, adolescence was not the self-contained stage that it has become now that a great many adolescents have infrequent contacts with adults outside the household except for a few authority figures like teachers or trainers or the adult sponsors of formal youth associations. Although involvement with adult neighbors and kin varies, it pales in contemporary Euramerican societies when compared with more traditional cultures. Adolescents now are out of sight and out of mind much of the time.

Many adolescents today are not making serious preparations for marriage, although this varies by social class. Although it is not unusual for working-class young people in their late teens to marry the "high school sweetheart," for middle-class adolescents, as well as for those of their working-class peers who look forward to further training, a marriage in the near future is out of the question. Thus, young people are selecting romantic and sometimes sexual partners for attachments that they know will probably be temporary.

Contemporary adolescent culture is spreading widely through the same channels that spread other aspects of material and expressive culture: the international media, entertainers on tour, migrants, the import–export market, and the travels of adolescents themselves. In many places outside of Europe and North America, adolescents may have more of the trappings of Western culture than their parents do. Cassettes of rock music show up in villages in India, Africa, and the Andes. I shall speak more about the global spread of adolescent culture; first, I wish to consider the meaning adolescent culture has for the lives of its participants.

The Functions of Adolescent Culture

It is common knowledge that the particular style of dress or manner adopted by any group sets it apart from other social groups. Modern adolescents are not unique in using stylistic markers: exhibits of 19th-century village costumes, a prominent feature of European folk museums, show that the Sunday clothing of physically mature but unmarried boys and girls differed from the festive garb of children and adults. In those same villages today, adolescents display a wide variety of styles, identifying themselves not only as members of a physically mature but unmarried age set but also as adherents of one or another set of preferences and even values.

A distinctive adolescent culture develops and becomes elaborated when adolescents share a strong common identity that this culture expresses and reinforces. It appears when adolescents are separated from their families in schools or places of work or constitute a formal age set in an age-graded tribe. When Navajo Indian children lived in isolated homesteads and had few opportunities to form peer groups, there was little content to adolescent culture, even though Navajo language contains special terms for adolescent girls and boys. Today, when they, like other American adolescents, spend much of their day in school, they have invented a teenage slang in their native language. Hopi Indians, neighbors of the Navajo, have always lived in compact villages and have had active peer groups; their adolescents have used Hopi teenage slang, consisting of particular verb endings, for as long as living adults can remember. These are just two examples of a widespread form of linguistic innovation.

The distinctive style or styles of behavior and self-presentation of adolescents set them off as a clearly marked social set. They use elements of this culture in competition for position among their peers. Goods and knowledge are their "cultural stock."[2] Although there are certainly other weapons in the arsenal of status competition, such as excellence in sports or achievement in various kinds of endeavors, modern adolescents learn from their larger cultural milieu that one measure of success is material attainment. Thus, displaying new products and the latest fashions in dress and music are ways that teenagers can gain the admiration of their peers and the envy of their rivals. Money counts. Although the administrators of the apprenticeship programs I studied in Germany emphasized the occupational and social skills their young workers are learning, the apprentices themselves gave their earnings as the major reason for participating. Most of their earnings were spent for immediate consumption or saved for cars or vacation trips that they planned to purchase within the next 1 or 2 years.

The Significance of Modern Adolescent Culture to Its Participants

Cultural items are used as signals. To adults, the artifacts of adolescent culture signal the distinctiveness of the age set, and to adolescents themselves they signal a common identity in an age cohort with interests of its own. When adolescent culture is elaborated, as it is in modern industrial nations, the consumption preferences and behavioral styles of adolescents may also signal identification with a social class or an interest group. British sociologists of youth (e.g., Hebdige, 1979) provided good descriptions of such signaling in their discussions of the appearance and manner of the Punks and Mods and other stylistic communities of England since the 1960s. The clothing and mannerisms adopted by gang members to signify membership are only the most blatant examples of this visual marking.

However, cultural products are more than just instrumental devices to the adolescents who use them. There is an involvement with these products – the almost desperate need to attend a particular rock concert or purchase a specific kind of jacket – that indicates that they have great emotional significance to their users. This is often difficult for adults to understand, for the clothes are usually unflattering and the songs, videos, and literature marketed to adolescents are frequently banal and tasteless.

Social Bonding and Social Status

In part, involvement in an adolescent culture mirrors the involvement adolescents have with one another. Less embedded in their families than children, and not yet responsible for families of their own, adolescents everywhere are free to spend time with peers and to find social satisfaction in their company. The separation of modern adolescents from adults and their activities intensifies this peer orientation. Adolescents are often thrown together with others adolescents with whom they have little in common, and yet they look to them for acceptance and affirmation. Exchanging recordings or information about new products, coming together to listen to music or watch a video, experimenting with cosmetics (girls) or new computer games (mostly boys) are ways that teenagers can communicate even when they share few other interests. The very banality of many of the products of adolescent culture, which demand little in the way of intellectual activity or prior knowledge, facilitates their use among a wide range of consumers. Young people who otherwise would have little to say to each other find common ground in their preferences for certain products and dislike of others. In short, the products become a medium through which social relations are formed and maintained. This common involvement with material goods gives content and meaning to the bonds adolescents form.

Among older adolescents and youths, preferences in clothing, music, and recreation differentiate subgroups by social class, future orientation, and political and personal values, dividing these adolescents, like adults, into communities of taste. At the same time that these preferences signal membership in a like-minded value set, they signal differences from other sets. "Communities of values" have always been present in heterogeneous societies. Christians, Jews, nobles, guild members, members of religious orders – the list goes on and on – have for centuries used signaling devices of speech, personal adornment, or insignia to identify themselves to others, whom they may or may not know, as alike or different. As these categories lose some of their social salience, taste emerges as a social signal. (Taste, of course, is not socially neutral but is itself conditioned by social status, education, ethnicity, and, as in this case, age status.) Taste rather than kinship, neighborhood, or attendance at a particular school becomes the basis for starting a friendship or forming a peer group. It also defines the outsider.

Experiments in Self-Presentation

Adolescent culture has personal as well as social significance. The products that adolescents use often are the stage props for fantasies, and their salience may lie in the depths of desire that these fantasies reveal and the ease with which these products lend themselves to fantasy construction. What do adolescents fantasize about? The same things adults do: success in their endeavors, power, wealth, sexual attractiveness, and the admiration of their companions. If the forms their fantasies take seem naïve and unrealistic, it is because adolescents are uncertain about how to achieve their goals or even what these goals should be. Those individuals who have attained wealth and fame through activities appealing to young people (primarily singers, musicians, and sports stars) are the figures on which adolescents can easily pin their fantasies and turn into heroes, particularly when they appear to be leading lives of freedom and luxury. Songs that speak of sex or love or empowerment allow listeners to pretend that the words are their own; weird clothes can be the costumes for role play, for trying out different styles of self-presentation. Some adolescents take these fantasies and their props more seriously than others. The more judicious, mature adolescents use their fantasies as mature adults do: as a form of play and as a vacation rather than an escape from the sober everyday world.

It is likely that most young people are somewhat conscious of the play element in their self-presentation. (I have observed rather fearsome-looking young Germans in black leather, heavy boots, and green or purple hair who turned out, when I spoke to them, to be entirely harmless, even friendly.) Nevertheless, there is the danger that fantasies can be mistaken for reality, that young people can begin to take their fantasies seriously, especially when these fantasies are encouraged by peers or adults. The thin line between faking a presentation and believing it is something all professional actors know, and in fact method-acting is based on the principle of inducing the emotion that the actor is portraying. When the self-presentation is designed to be shocking and antisocial, as in the case of neo-Nazi items or gang emblems that some young people might wear to horrify their elders, what began as fantasy can end in dangerous reality.

One product that particularly lends itself to adolescent fantasy construction is popular music. The words of songs often speak to adolescents' wishes and attitudes dealing with love or freedom and other topics that engage their interests, and the music itself is soothing or highly stimulating and provides a backdrop to thoughts, feelings, and imagined scenarios. It is a major component of adolescent culture and one that crosses social, cultural, and national boundaries.

The Use of Music as a Cultural Product

Over the last 50 years or so popular music has become one of the most important cultural products in signifying an adolescent's identification with a community of taste. Of all cultural elements, it also seems to have the greatest personal signifi-cance to adolescents. Christenson and Roberts (1990) have surveyed the literature on young people's use of music, drawing on research done by psychologists and communications specialists. This research showed that of all the media, music heard over the radio or from recordings is the one in which adolescents are most involved, both in the time they spend with it and the importance they attach to it. There are a number of differences in the kinds of music adolescents listen to and how they interpret the lyrics of songs, depending on age, gender, ethnicity, and social class, as well as identification with ideologies and values. Social usefulness plays a role in music listening because music is a necessary accompaniment to dancing and other festivities. Musical preferences act as social markers and signals, and groups of adolescents can find a basis for companionship in listening to or playing music together. Here, however, I will discuss the personal meaning music has for modern adolescents.

Listening to music increases from childhood to early adolescence and peaks in later adolescence. Although music may be listened to in public places or by small groups, as much as two thirds of music is heard in solitude. It is useful to examine the relation, then, between music listening and solitude in adolescence.

According to research reported in Larson (1990), solitude increases throughout the life span, from about 17% of time in the childhood years of 9 and 12 to about 29% in adulthood. Mood is lower for adolescents and adults when solitary than when in company, and there are more self-reports of loneliness and lower self-ratings of happiness and cheerfulness. However, mood when alone is not so low for adults as for adolescents. In spite of causing negative feelings, a good deal of adolescent solitude is voluntary: it takes place in the home and represents a conscious withdrawal from social activities, particularly with family members.

Larson (1990) posited two reasons for adolescent solitude. The first is the need for adolescents to take breaks from the new and difficult task of impression man-agement, which is a developmental task that emerges in adolescence. Adolescents, much more than younger children, are conscious of the effect they have on those around them. Adolescents report feeling much less self-conscious and much more like their true selves when they are alone. The second reason, drawing on Erikson (1968), is the desire for solitude to question and develop personal identity. This implies that there is a need for private reflection. That implication, however, is called into question because most music is listened to in solitude. By self-report, adolescents use music to pass the time and to relieve boredom, tension, and loneliness (Christenson & Roberts, 1990) or as a stimulus to imagination. Adolescents absorbed in listening to music or attending to lyrics do not seem to be reflective; they are more likely to be weaving webs of fantasy with themselves as hero or heroine.

I suggest that solitude, although somewhat painful for adolescents, is sought because, as Larson proposes, it is a temporary reprieve from the self-consciousness that is a feature of adolescence everywhere (for India, see Saraswathi & Dutta, 1998). Growing self-awareness no doubt occurs in the process of cognitive growth, but it is also a result of the development of one's social persona in anticipation of the demands of adult life. This developmental task is not limited to modern adolescence. One of the questions asked in Schlegel and Barry (1991) was whether adolescence is a time during which the person establishes a social persona that will determine what occupational or social roles, or what potential spouses, will be available in adulthood. We had information on more than 80% of cases in the sample of 186 societies. The answer was affirmative in 82% of these societies for boys, and 79% of them for girls (Barry & Schlegel, 1990). It is clear that impression management is a serious issue for adolescents in many, probably most, societies in the world and is related to resources adolescents need at present and in the future. However, this task may be more complex for modern adolescents, who receive less help from adults because of being somewhat isolated from them, than for young people in many of the more traditional societies.

At the same time that adolescents are seeking solitude, they are suffering from it by feeling bored or lonely. It is an ambivalent state. Listening to music is an attempt to relieve these negative feelings and thus reduce conflict over solitude. Music, then, is a form of self-medication. It is not surprising that involvement in music declines in adulthood (Christenson & Roberts, 1990), when there is not so much conflict over solitude because adults have a better sense of where they fit in their social world.

The Global Spread of Adolescent Culture

At the beginning of this essay I spoke of the worldwide spread of the elements of modern adolescent culture. Why do teenagers in Africa, Asia, South America – wherever Western commercial products have penetrated, which is almost everywhere – purchase, use, and imitate these products so eagerly? Is adolescent culture replacing local adolescent cultures? How do adolescents use these imported products and ideas? Is there any broader significance to this culture spread?

I shall address these issues through two case studies of modern adolescents in rather different political and cultural circumstances. Polish youth inhabit a European nation, but until recently they have been discouraged from using or copying those elements of Western adolescent culture that the Communist ruling elite saw as degenerate and socially harmful. Moroccan adolescents are not discouraged from this, but their access to the artifacts of adolescent culture is limited, and the ideology implicit in these artifacts does not fit very well with the cultural traditions of their families and communities.

I have now introduced a new concept into the discussion: the ideology implicit in the artifacts. One of the values inherent in the transformation of cultural products into commodities is innovation, the search for the new. It could hardly be otherwise in nations in which so many aspects of life have been commercialized, where the maintenance and expansion of the market are dependent on providing new products and tempting consumers to purchase them. The new way of playing music or staging a video or dressing directed at the adolescent niche of the market may seem absurd and trivial to adults, but it is a simple reflection of the search for the new that is inherent in capitalism.

Another value conveyed by these artifacts is the freedom of individuals to choose their clothing, their friends and lovers, their futures. This message is inherent in the wide range of products from which the individual can freely select, and it is made explicit in the words of songs and the actions portrayed in videos. Adolescents in Western Europe and North America are in the awkward position of preparing for independence at the same time that they remain subordinate in the family and school. They know that within a few years they will be leaving home and will be expected to make choices of a career and a spouse even though they may lack the knowledge and experience to make informed choices. At present, however, they are still children within their parents' home.[3] It is a common experience for these adolescents to feel constrained by parental authority. Conflict over autonomy may not be so marked in societies with other forms of family structure; that is, where adolescents will continue to live with older adults after they marry and therefore are not anticipating such a break from parental authority (see Schlegel & Barry, 1991). Nevertheless, even under such conditions the interests of parents may diverge from those of adolescents themselves, who may feel resentment even if they do not express it in open conflict. The message of individualism – freedom of choice and freedom from constraints – is a strong antidote to adolescent feelings of powerlessness.

If innovation and individualism are messages that are meaningful to Western adolescents, how are they perceived in cultures that place a higher value on tradition and familial solidarity? The case studies will illustrate this question.

Poland: Rejoining the West[4]

Within the last few years, St. Valentine's Day has sprung up as a day of celebration, a "sweetheart's day," spreading rapidly through the college-preparatory schools of cities and towns all over Poland. This addition to the ceremonial calendar of the school year has been instituted by the students themselves. Although St. Valentine was known in Poland, his day was never recognized or celebrated. Even today, these celebrations are restricted to these schools and are not found in primary schools, vocational schools, or among the general public. Decorations, cards, and gifts are all made by the students themselves, although within the last year a few printed cards have appeared on the market. Unlike Americans, who associate Valentine's Day with both romance and friendship, in Poland it is only for sweethearts, and those of a special kind – the fellow student toward whom one has romantic feelings.

Students celebrate Valentine's Day in various activities and by sending cards to the one they like very much through a "post office" set up in the school. To forestall embarrassment if the overture is rejected, the sender will sometimes claim it was only a joke. If a couple are already established as sweethearts, the boy may take the girl out for ice cream, or they may go for a romantic walk together. It is primarily girls who organize the school activities, but boys are willing participants. (In Poland, women and girls are responsible for domestic celebrations, and girls are experienced in organizing them.)

One reason for the celebration's popularity is that it imitates the West. Signs and posters are often in English. This is a land in which Western European, and especially American, words and objects mark one as sophisticated and in the know. A second reason is the greater tolerance toward mingling of the sexes in recent years. Although adolescents are expected to remain chaste, there is now a general acceptance of their romantic feelings and expressions.

That this celebration appears only in those schools with a predominantly middle-class student body, most of whom expect to go on to a university, bespeaks its class locus. Vocational school students tend to marry shortly after leaving school, and thus their flirtations and dating have serious meaning as forms of courtship. Academic high school students, however, know that marriage is far off in the future and that it is unlikely that they will marry their current romantic interest. In spite of strong feelings they may have, they are playing at romance. A cultural element, the Valentine rituals and their associated artifacts, has been borrowed from the West, but it has been transformed to express the attitudes and values of local adolescents.

Morocco: The Superficiality of Imported Adolescent Culture[5]

Moroccan adolescents and youths in the town of Zawiya have wide exposure to Western culture. Emigrants and their children bring items of clothing, recordings, and videos (including pornographic videos) with them on their visits home. American, French, and Egyptian programs are broadcast over local television, presenting ways of life that have little concordance with the daily lives of Moroccans. Teenagers go to mixed-sex schools and learn about Western traditions, but in the home and the community they are expected to behave like traditional Moroccan youth, obeying and respecting their parents and subordinating their private wishes to the well-being of the family, as decided by their elders. They do not contest their parents' right to make their marital arrangements.

There seems to be little intergenerational conflict, for these young people adhere to what is expected of them. However, a harmonious family setting may hide deep anxieties and emotional conflicts over one's present life. The area that seems to be the most uncertain, and causes the greatest frustration and dissatisfaction, is the relation between the sexes. The new opportunities for girls and boys to mingle at school and the knowledge that there is romantic freedom in the West give rise to dreams of possibilities that cannot be met in reality. Davis (1995, p. 70) asked, "What does an 18-year-old Moroccan male make of a reggae lyric 'No woman no cry' that he has written onto a poster in his bedroom?" Probably no more than his adolescent sister does of the American television series *Beverly Hills 90210* and its teenage characters. These adolescents can draw the line between fantasy and reality, and they know that Western ways are fantasies even though they may long for them.

Moroccan youths, like their Polish counterparts, look to the West as the place of glamor and freedom. However, they do not expect such freedom for themselves; they seem to be aware that their fantasies are just that and have little relevance to the realities of their present or future lives. For them, the artifacts of adolescent culture have a somewhat different meaning than they do in Poland.

Causes of Adolescent Culture and Its Spread

Adolescent cultures are not a recent innovation. As I have indicated, an adolescent social stage appears to be universal, and this stage is marked by its own activities, accoutrements, and stylistic elements. These all add up to local "cultures" of adolescence, rudimentary though they may be in some instances.

A full-blown culture of adolescence, such as we in the West experience, builds on the adolescent-culture elements of earlier times. It is the culture of a socially recognized and self-aware category of persons. Identifiable cultures of social categories appear when members of the category recognize themselves as unique and cultivate their specialness by drawing on and elaborating existing elements and inventing new ones. We see this in the self-conscious new ethnic cultures that have evolved or transformed themselves in the United States, Britain, France, and elsewhere in the modern world.

Changes in economic and social conditions that have set off adolescence as a distinct phase of life have given rise to this self-awareness and uniqueness. The major change is the isolation of so many adolescents from adults, which promotes an age-class consciousness and forces adolescents to turn primarily to one another (outside of the family) for social contacts and involvement. This is a result of widespread schooling. Even where adolescents work, in most of the industrial nations they do not work alongside adults but hold jobs defined as suitable for teenagers. (An exception is German-speaking countries, where the majority of older adolescents work with adults as apprentices.) Furthermore, adolescents remain in school until they are 15 or older (16 or 17 in most Western nations), by which time they have established a sense of themselves as an age-class apart. As I have indicated, the artifacts of adolescent culture play an important part in the social interchange of adolescents and in stimulating the fantasies of adolescents and aiding in their self-presentations.

The contemporary culture of adolescence is market driven, as is the leisure culture of adults and, increasingly, of children. Cash in their pockets, whether put there by their own efforts or by generous parents, allows adolescents to purchase the products assiduously offered to them. The purchase of items for entertainment or self-presentation, and as aids to fantasy, would not be possible without massive increases in the flow of money in Western and other nations. Without rises in income, adolescents would have to curb their consumer impulses, and those who worked would have to contribute to the family money supply.

Culture migrates. Sometimes it is carried by living persons; sometimes it is passed along through artifacts. Adolescent culture has been aggressively marketed in the West by Western producers, and outside the West by these producers and their local imitators, for the adolescent market. Adolescents have the motive and the means to acquire it; producers and marketers provide the method.

Conclusion

A danger that some foresee in the spread of Western culture is the homogenization of cultural forms. These observers fear that the global villages of the future will look pretty much the same, whether they are New York, Frankfurt, Karachi, or Timbuktu. Anthropologists used to dealing directly with people affected by the spread of Western culture have pointed out that neither is cultural transmission an automatic process nor do the recipients of new ideas simply accept them unchanged (see Hannerz, 1992). Human history is a chronicle of the diffusion of ideas and objects produced in one area and transported to another, where they are received in a variety of ways. At one extreme there might be local incorporation and adaptation of introduced beliefs and style. An example of this is Buddhism and its accompanying art, which moved from India to China. At the other extreme, foreign cultural products may be viewed as exotica that have entertainment value but little else, like the Andean music currently played by Bolivian and Peruvian musicians in the pedestrian shopping streets of Europe. What has changed in recent years is not the process but the speed by which goods and ideas are moving.

Adolescents may be using cultural artifacts produced elsewhere, but their lived reality is local, and "local" culture includes the reworking of imported themes. Adolescents take the ideas and artifacts of adolescent culture and use them for their own purposes. They transform them to meet local needs, as with St. Valentine's Day in Poland, or simply accept them as fantasy, as in Morocco. One need only scratch the surface to discover that the teenagers of different societies who dress alike and are avid purchasers of the same or similar cultural artifacts are really very different; and there is little likelihood that consumption patterns alone will bring about convergence of values, attitudes, and beliefs.

In earlier times, new influences on the local cultures of adolescents would have been filtered through adults. That is, adolescents had relatively little opportunity to acquire foreign cultural products, mostly because they lacked the money to do so. Today, however, young people have direct access to foreign goods and ideas through the media and through purchases of cheap mass-produced items. In fact, it may be adolescents who introduce foreign cultural products into the home. These products have become commodities, and one explanation for the spread of adolescent culture lies in the aggressive marketing techniques of culture producers – both Western producers and those local variants that imitate them. However, marketing strategies would not find fertile ground if conditions did not make these products meaningful. It is the increasingly common experiences of adolescents worldwide, I believe, that make adolescent culture appealing. As young people everywhere spend more time in school and have fewer relations with adults outside of the immediate family, the social setting of adolescents is coming more and more to replicate that of the West. The same factors that make Western adolescent culture appealing to Western teenagers make it appealing to adolescents in other places, and there is the added attraction of coming from the economic and political center of the modern world system.

Adolescent culture has sometimes been interpreted as an indication of resistance to adult tastes and values. This tack was taken by the Birmingham "school" of social theorists (Hebdige, 1979; Willis, 1981), who focused on the powerlessness of adolescents and their resistance to the authority of adults. In fact, however, most adolescent cultural products express mainstream values, as do the majority of song lyrics that adolescents listen to (Christenson & Roberts, 1990, p. 42). The adolescents who eagerly seek out the new to purchase are literally buying into the consumption pattern of capitalism.

It is a mistake to assume that adolescents, or any other powerless individuals, necessarily contest the imposition of authority. The adolescent children of elite families in prewar Japan were remarkably docile and complacent about subordination (Lebra, 1995). As another example, Hollos and Leis (1989) described adolescents in two Ijaw villages of Nigeria. In one, the more traditional village, these young people were breaking away from the control of their elders. In the other, the more modern village, adolescents cheerfully obeyed their elders and actively sought their approval through good behavior. The explanation for this is, I believe, that adolescents in the more modern village needed the help of older relatives, whereas in the more traditional village, elders had little to offer the next generation (Schlegel, 1995). Powerless people of any age are unlikely to contest the authority of the powerful if they require their goodwill in the present and the future.

Worldwide, the separation of adolescents from adults in the community is obviously more characteristic of upper- and middle-class urban adolescents than their counterparts in working-class families, where teenagers spend less time in school activities, and in the small towns and rural areas where life is more traditional. The teenage boys of Aswan or the popular quarters of Cairo spend many of their leisure hours hanging around the coffeehouses where men gather, whereas their elite peers in Cairo are following more age-segregated pursuits. Similar cases of class-differentiated patterns occur widely in places outside the West.

This raises an interesting question. The allocation of time, and the degree of association with adults, may differ considerably between middle- and working-class, or rural and urban, adolescents, and yet all of these young people may be trading cassettes, watching music videos, and wearing pieces of Western-style clothing. Are they responding to the same cultural products in the same way? We cannot assume that they are. As the examples of Poland and Morocco illustrate, adolescents of different cultural settings respond to Western influences in very different ways, and it is likely that adolescents of different backgrounds and social settings within a single nation do so as well, as in Poland. Urban middle-class adolescents may be using adolescent cultural products as their Western counterparts do. Rural or working-class youths, especially the poorer, less educated teenagers outside of America and Western Europe, may appear to be using the artifacts of adolescent culture of the West more as prestige items – for prestige emanates from the centers of world power – and as markers of catholic taste, much as Western intellectuals display African tribal masks or Peruvian textiles to attest to their sophistication and global vision.

As the artifacts of adolescent culture provide channels of communication for an age group, so do they provide a common store of experience when adolescents have become adults. It is possible that as adolescent culture becomes widespread, people in different parts of the world will draw from a common pool of memories, blurring the edges of cultural differences. I would not put too much weight on this, however, for we know that as adolescents become adults, the differences in the adult world that draw the boundaries between social groups and can lead to antipathy or hostility (e.g., nation, class, religion, and ethnicity) increase in importance. These differences already make themselves felt in adolescence, but communication through the artifacts of adolescent culture can mitigate or temporarily override these differences. However, adolescent and youth tastes fade into insignificance as people move further on in life. Youth may speak to youth across the barriers of class, language, and nationality, but it takes more to build bonds of understanding and cooperation than the ephemeral enthusiasms of the young for similar cultural products.

We have seen the impetus to moving adolescent cultural products out of their European and American homelands on the part of the producers who sell them and the receivers who desire them for a variety of purposes. The question remains of why these products are so transportable that they can be easily adapted by their receivers. If it were true that popular culture is a localized response to local conditions, then it could only be exported as a novelty, like the Andean music that entertains European pedestrians.

Adolescent culture has two features that contribute to its transportability. First, it is often banal; that is, it makes few demands on the listener, viewer, wearer, or participant. It can be intellectual and emotional "fast-food." Second, it is usually grounded in universal issues rather than local ones. These are love, sex, power, and achievement issues that concern adolescents everywhere because they are just moving into the realm where these are played out, the adult world.

I spoke earlier about the possibility that new cultural forms will drive out the old and that the everyday creation of songs, poetry, tales, and theatrical performances will fall into disuse. In many places this seems not to be the case, for the new forms stimulate adaptations of the old traditional ones and make them more up-to-date, whereas the old forms are often consciously preserved as part of the cultural heritage (e.g., Robertson, 1996). However, it is undeniable that when adolescents turn to commercial products, they tend to give up the homemade ones. A case in point is Malaysia, where teenagers no longer produce the wood and paper sculptures that used to decorate the towns in celebration of the end of Ramadan. Cultural production, whether of old or new forms, becomes more of an occupational specialization by adults and the minority of adolescents who develop their creative or performative abilities.

Is there any danger in bringing up a generation of young people who are more the consumers, and rather passive ones, than the creators of their expressive culture? Are productions and performances of expressive culture more important than just entertainment and recreation?

Competence and mastery of one's environment increase as young people learn that they can do or make something useful or enjoyable. For young people who take their schooling seriously, competence can come through working with ideas and learning how to solve intellectual problems. Those who are employed in craft production, which requires knowledge of materials and the fitting of task to time, and those with hobbies that require the management of objects or ideas, are also expanding their skills. There is no doubt that many adolescents use commercial products in creative ways: The costumes and room decors that some assemble could rank as "found art," and snippets of recorded music may be combined to create new tapes that can even rise above their origins. But many young people, the school-idlers or those in routine and unchallenging jobs, are locked into – or have locked themselves into – drifting through their days without any sense of accomplishment. They are not alone; many adults do the same. Fatigue, or lack of initiative, may keep them from using their leisure time any more constructively than sitting in front of the television set or the game on the computer screen.

In earlier times, before entertainment was a packaged commodity, leisure time activities provided a sphere of creative and social production available to those in even the most menial or routine occupations. Work songs, games that do not require purchased equipment, local festivities produced and managed locally – all these were, and for some still are, creative productions. But for many young people, as for their elders, homemade leisure pursuits are a thing of the past. If they are not extending their minds and skills at school or at work, are they still doing so at all? For such young people, their cognitive ability may fail to realize its potential, not because it is deadened by television but because it has not been sharpened by the problem solving and planning of cultural production.

References

Barry, H., III, & Schlegel, A. (1990). *Adolescence. HRAF Series in Quantitative Cross-Cultural Data: Vol. 4*. New Haven, CT: HRAF, Inc.

Christenson, P. G., & Roberts, D. F. (1990). *Popular music in early adolescence*. Working Paper, Carnegie Council on Adolescent Development. New York: Carnegie Corporation.

Dankowska, J. (1996, March). *St. Valentine in Poland*. Talk based on her dissertation (in Polish) *Youth attitudes toward selected family and annual customs (including informal youth customs)*. Institute of Ethnology and Anthropology, University of Poznan, Poland. Unpublished manuscript in the author's possession.

Davis, D. (1995). Modernizing the sexes: Changing gender relations in a Moroccan town. *Ethos, 23,* 69–78.

Davis, D., & Davis, S. S. (1989). *Adolescence in a Moroccan town*. New Brunswick, NJ: Rutgers University Press.

Erikson, E. (1968). *Identity: Youth and crisis*. New York: Norton.

Gillis, J. R. (1974). *Youth and history*. New York: Academic Press.

Hannerz, U. (1992). The global ecumene. In U. Hannerz (Ed.), *Cultural complexity* (pp. 217–268). New York: Columbia University Press.

Hebdige, D. (1979). *Subculture: The meaning of style*. London: Methuen.

Hollos, M., & Leis, P. E. (1989). *Becoming Nigerian in Ijo society*. New Brunswick, NJ: Rutgers University Press.

Larson, R. (1990). The solitary side of life: An examination of the time people spend alone from childhood to old age. *Developmental Review, 10,* 155–183.

Lebra, T. (1995). Skipped and postponed adolescence of aristocratic women in Japan: Resurrecting the culture/nature issue. *Ethos, 23,* 79–102.

Mitterauer, M. (1992). *A history of youth: Family, sexuality and social relations in past times*. Cambridge, England: Blackwell.

Robertson, R. (1996, February). *Comparison and communication: The intercultural communication movement and its consequences for comparative research*. Address to the Society for Cross-Cultural Research, Pittsburgh, PA.

Roubin, L. (1977). Male space and female space within the Provençal community. In R. Forster & O. Ranum (Eds.), *Rural society in France: Selections from the Annales* (pp. 152–180). Baltimore: Johns Hopkins University Press.

Saraswathi, T. S., & Dutta, R. (1988). *Invisible boundaries: Grooming for adult roles*. New Delhi: Northern Book Centre.

Schlegel, A. (1995, June). *Strangers or friends? The importance of adults in the lives of adolescents*. Frobenius Lecture, Frobenius Institute, University of Frankfurt, Frankfurt am Main, Germany.

Schlegel, A., & Barry, H. III. (1991). *Adolescence: An anthropological inquiry*. New York: Free Press.

Willis, P. (1981). *Learning to labour: How working class kids get working class jobs*. New York: Columbia University Press.

6   Social Change and the Sequencing of Developmental Transitions

John Bynner

Transitions in adolescence are part of developmental sequences reflecting those changes of state through which individuals pass on the route from childhood to adulthood. They contain biological, developmental, and the socially constructed components that determine the shape of the human life course in each society (Robins & Rutter, 1990; Chisholm, Kruger, & du Bois, 1995).

The physical maturational changes associated with puberty signal the beginning of adolescence, the acquisition of certain rights and responsibilities, and entry into adulthood. The process of developmental change includes the *developmental tasks* to be accomplished and the differentiation and commitment that accompany them in the construction of adult identity such as in the crystallization of gender identity (Erikson, 1968; Marcia, 1966). These are associated with the shifting *focal concerns* of adolescence: sexual relations, peer relations, and relations with parents (Coleman, 1974; Hendry, 1983), successful resolution of which is critical to adjustment to adult life. The change in focal concerns is paralleled in leisure life by the moves from family to single-sex peer group, to mixed group, to partner, parenting, and marriage (Hendry, 1983). Finally we come to the transitions that are most obviously socially defined. These include the transition from school to work, involving the changes in status from school student to trainee to adult worker with the accompanying shift in autonomy from dependent child to independent adult. Family formation may be formalized through the institution of marriage. Political participation will come through the right to vote. Contracts may be entered into and criminal responsibility shouldered. Such status changes are usually age based, as enshrined in legislation, and will vary between countries. They cut across the statuses associated with biologically based maturity, which may be only loosely related to chronological age. Taken together, these adult statuses define, in modern terms, the citizen; that is, the status bringing with it the rights and obligations that define full membership of a modern society (Bulmer & Rees, 1996; Jones & Wallace, 1992; Marshall, 1973).

Although the sequencing of the transitions within each of the different developmental areas may not be fundamentally altered by social change, the timings of the transitions and the length of the phases between them are and can themselves have substantial effects on sequencing *across* the different areas (Silbereisen, 1993, 1994). Extension of schooling in response to the increased demand for qualifications in the labor market is likely to prolong dependency on the family, which itself increases the pressure to postpone entry into permanent partnerships and marriage. But this is, of course, not always the case. The more biologically driven developmental pressures within one area of life may overturn the more socially driven pressures in another: The transition to parenthood, for example, may precede the transition of leaving home. It is ironic that "youth (leisure) culture" is spreading to ever younger preadolescent age groups while many of the defining features of adult citizenship, such as financial independence and autonomy, are continually postponed. Such phenomena lie behind the extension of the transition to adulthood to embrace the period of "postadolescence" (Hurrelmann, 1989) and "deferred" or "quasicitizenship" (Jones & Wallace, 1992; Coles,1995). These transitional statuses reflect the further detachment of the socially constructed life course from the roles and responsibilities that were in the past identified with biological maturity and financial independence.

The aim of this chapter is to set social change against the other major factors that influence the sequencing of developmental transitions. First, the sociocultural influences that previous research suggests are important factors in shaping youth transitions (e.g., country, cohort, gender, and education) are considered in isolation. Then, an analysis of variance comparing data on youth transitions in England and Germany is used to assess the effects of such factors separately and in combination. The data for this latter part of the paper come from a comparative study of youth transitions in England and Germany (Bynner & Roberts, 1991; Evans & Heinz, 1994).[1]

Sociocultural Factors in Youth Transitions

Changes in transition patterns often signify long-term trends related to the way a society, through its institutions, is evolving (in response to new technology, for example). Overlaid upon such trends can be the dramatic ruptures brought about by social, political, or economic transformation of the kind that occurred in the countries of Eastern and Central Europe at the end of the 1980s. National context is therefore central to understanding the impact social change is likely to have on transition patterns (Bynner & Chisholm, 1998). Table 1 presents statistics from the 12 countries of the European Economic Community on age at first marriage, economic activity rate (ages 14–24), participation in education and training, births outside marriage, and higher-education entry.

The figures show a degree of consistency related to the length of transition to adulthood in the different countries at the time the data were collected. Thus, high levels of post-16 participation in education and high economic activity rates in the 16–24 age group tend to be accompanied by later ages for marriage. But there

Table 1. *European Union transition and social change indicators.*

EEC countries	Age at marriage (years)[a]		Economic activity rate (% 14–24 year olds)[b]		Participation in education and training (% age group)[c]			Births outside marriage (% live births)[d]	Higher-education entry (% population)[e]	
	M	F	M	F	16	17	18		M	F
United Kingdom	26.4	24.2	71.7	69.1	77	60	34	30	16	14
Greece	27.7	23.2	69.6	60.3	75	58	44	4	–	–
Portugal	25.9	23.8	63.8	50.6	47	39	28	16	–	–
Germany	27.7	25.2	58.0	53.3	99	97	81	15	23	16
Denmark	29.4	26.8	57.4	55.0	82	75	68	47	30	25
Netherlands	27.2	25.0	54.1	50.6	98	88	71	12	14	11
Belgium	26.1	23.8	52.3	45.5	92	82	59	11	22	18
Luxembourg	26.6	24.6	48.9	40.0	70	63	50	12	–	–
Italy	27.9	24.9	48.2	39.6	81	75	70	7	28	28
Spain	26.7	24.5	47.7	35.7	60	55	44	10	15	16
Ireland	27.0	25.5	40.2	30.0	91	71	58	17	–	–
France	27.0	24.9	39.2	36.9	92	82	59	29	–	–

[a] Source: Eurostat (1990).
[b] Source: Eurostat (1990).
[c] Source: Labour Force Survey; Employment in Europe (1990).
[d] Source: Eurostat (1994).
[e] Source: Utting (1995).

are exceptions to this rule, and when we turn to the other societal characteristics (percentage of births outside marriage and percentage of entry into higher education) there is much more evidence of each country's distinctiveness. Britain turns out to have the highest economic activity rate for those aged 16–24 of all countries and, similarly, nearly the lowest percentage of young people participating in education and training at age 18. Yet, the incidence of higher education entry in Britain is slightly higher than in the Netherlands, which has twice the proportion in education and training at age 18 and five sevenths of the level of Britain's economic activity among those aged 14–24. On age at first marriage, however, Britain, as we might expect, is at the bottom end of the age range for men and near the bottom for women; along with Denmark, Britain also has one of the highest rates for births outside marriage. Finally, to take two extremes: the average age of marriage is 27.7 years for men and 25.2 for women in Germany compared with 26.4 years for men and 24.2 for women in Britain. At the same time, the percentage of births outside marriage in Britain is twice that of Germany: 30% compared with 15%.

These data point to the importance of the sociocultural factors bound up with the nation-state as factors in the shaping of transition patterns: Accelerated transitions tend to be the norm in Britain and the countries of southern Europe, whereas protracted transitions tend to be the norm elsewhere. But this rather oversimplified picture needs qualifying. First, the effect of social change has been to produce a degree of convergence between transition patterns in all domains of life (Lagree,

1996). Postponed labor market entry, delayed marriage, and parenting outside marriage are becoming more common in all countries across time. However, there is likely to be a cross-cohort lag between the occurrence of the change and the transformation of the transition patterns that follow it. Young people and their parents cling to past expectations and behaviors well after they have lost their relevance to the new socioeconomic situation they are in.

Thus, for example, when traditional manufacturing collapsed and the youth labor market virtually disappeared in the early 1980s, Britain experienced major social and economic upheavals. But the full effects of this were not felt until a series of policy interventions, including the government's youth training scheme (YTS), gradually worked their way into people's consciousness and, ultimately, their behavior. The most striking evidence of this effect was the rise in "staying on rates" in education, which first lagged behind the economic changes, but suddenly accelerated some 10 years after the major economic changes and then rose steadily year by year until leveling off in the mid-1990s. Thus, a post-16-rate of staying in school of 48% in 1983 was still at 50% in 1989, but by 1993 it had risen to 73%, where it has remained ever since (Department for Education and Science [DFE], 1994).

The second feature of the impact of social change on transition patterns is that the effects differ among various sections of the population as defined by such social structural factors as social class, gender, ethnicity, and locality (Chisholm, 1992; Coleman, 1993). Hence, variation in the distribution of such characteristics between countries is going to affect the transition patterns as well. Human and cultural capital, as manifested through qualifications and occupational achievement, are not only acquired through the system but are brought into it from family background. Thus, in Britain through the 1980s, in high-unemployment areas, middle-class young people pursuing further education en route to higher education and the professions were protected against the adverse labor market effects: Their transitions were relatively unaffected. In sharp contrast, those, typically from working-class backgrounds, who had traditionally left school at the minimum age to seek work, found themselves unemployed or in dead-end training schemes without jobs at the end (Bynner, 1991; Banks et al., 1992).

There was little evidence of gender differentiation in relation to such labor market transition patterns. With respect to marriage and family formation, however, the response of young men and young women tends to be different. Under conditions of rising unemployment young men are likely to resist partnership and long-term commitments as long as possible, preferring to hold on to a state of "perpetual adolescence" with dependence on their parents. Motivated in the opposite direction, unemployed young women frequently try to escape the domestic routines expected of them in the family home by seeking partnership and motherhood instead (Wallace, 1987).

Such interactions underline the point that under conditions of social change the relationships between biologically determined development, personal agency, societal institutions, and social structure become increasingly complex (e.g.,

Hurrelmann, 1988). The advent of new technology, for example, has transformed the labor market and employment practice (Brown, 1995) and consequently the routes to adult status. Technological change also lies behind the structural unemployment experienced in all industrialized countries. Moreover, it is no longer even clear that the first transition from education to employment is as important in determining employment destinations in adulthood as it was in the past. People are likely to change not only their employers but even their occupations through their lives as the skills associated with one field of work or occupation become redundant and are replaced by others (Jallade, 1989). There is now more frequently a revolving door scenario in which labor market "test runs" and cyclical trajectories between education, training, and employment replace the old transition route of education (training) to employment (Gershuny & Pahl, 1994). Early unemployment may stunt the whole process with the consequence that the young person leaving education may never completely achieve the transition to adult work. In turn, the other transitions, such as to marriage and parenting, are likely to take over; hence, the whole developmental sequence and the transitions within it are transformed.

Casualties are likely to increase in such an ever more demanding employment system. Those who fail to acquire the necessary skills and competencies of interest to employers face difficulties both in gaining work and holding on to it (Bynner, 1996). Ulrich Beck's term "Risk Society" (Beck, 1992) aptly sums up the increasing uncertainty of modern transition patterns and the need for protection against the risks of social and occupational exclusion. Thus, past certainties associated with the direction the occupational career was likely to take and rooted in social structural factors such as class, gender, ethnicity, and location give way to more "individualized" patterns whereby young people have to "navigate their way" to secure and continuing occupations (Evans & Furlong, 1997). Their success in doing this is still likely to depend strongly on the human and cultural "capital" they have acquired, as certified by qualifications. Consequently, education or quasieducation in the form of vocational training (Bynner, 1991) is increasingly the occupational status that young people are going to hold well into their 20s.

Transition to Adulthood in Germany and England

The previous section helps to set the parameters for an examination of the effects of social change on transition patterns on the basis of data from our Anglo-German study. Youth transitions are dominated in Germany by an extended period of training through the *dual system*: the combination of employer-based training and vocational education that prepares the young person for adult work. Before they reach adolescence, young people are faced with the choice of either moving along the academic route via the *Gymnasium* and the *Abitur* qualification to higher education and professional occupations or opting, via attendance at a *Realschule* (intermediate occupations) or *Hauptschule* (skilled manual occupations), for the apprenticeship (dual system) route. There has been a steady trend for more young people and their parents to opt for the *Gymnasium* or *Realschule* routes at the expense of the *Hauptschule*; the numbers attending the latter were down from two thirds in the 1960s to one fifth in the 1990s (Evans & Heinz, 1994). Those who fail to get apprenticeships may stay on at school or enter remedial schemes to help them get an apprenticeship. There is a generally accepted assumption among employers, young people, and their parents that apprenticeship is an essential prerequisite for adult employment.

Although the main routes to skilled employment in Germany conform to the classic dual system pattern, there are a myriad of other possibilities relating to the need to accommodate young people who fail to get apprenticeships, drop out from them, or, in the case of those on the *Gymnasium* route, opt to serve an apprenticeship before higher education as a kind of vocational insurance against unemployment. There is a statutory requirement that all stay in touch with the education system at least on a part-time basis up to the age of 18. An added complicating factor is military or community service for males, which not only extends the transition but may lead to further changes of direction. Under the upheavals of first, economic transformation, and, more recently, political and economic transformation through unification, the whole system has been under increasing strain. This has led to the gradual erosion of the number of occupations to which apprenticeship can lead and the steady extension of the period of vocational preparation to accommodate the increasingly complex choices involved. This phenomenon accounts for an average age of entry into apprenticeship of 19 and an average age of graduation from the university of 29 for males and 28 for females (Bundesminister Für Bildung und Wissenschaft, 1994).

In England, young people's transitions are characterized by speed of entry into adult work. There is not so much a system for preparing young people for employment as a diversity of routes to adult work, some of which involve little formal training at all. Entry to the professions is comparable to the German system and requires the "A level" qualification obtained through the academic "sixth form" at school, or through a further education college, to gain entry to higher education. With respect to entry into skilled work, the German and the English routes diverge. The majority of English young people who wish to enter skilled occupations will either go on to a further education college to obtain a vocational qualification or leave education for youth training (YT), preferably with a potential employer. The best of these will be accepted for the most prestigious form of YT, the "modern apprenticeship," which was targeted originally at 8% of the total 16 year-old school-leave cohort and is the closest to the German norm. A similar small proportion will enter a job directly after leaving school. The main difference from Germany is that there is no automatic assumption that a prior period of training is essential before adult work is entered. The dominant motive for a substantial proportion of young school leavers and their parents is to get *any* kind of job. A small proportion fail to achieve this and enter a period of unemployment interspersed with training schemes, none of which lead to a proper job. But because welfare benefits are no longer paid to this latter group, very few who do not have substantial parental support are able to opt to stay out of work.

The major changes in what the Organization for Economic Cooperation and Development describes as Britain's *mixed system* (Evans, 1990) were brought about by the upheavals of the early 1980s and resulted in more young people staying on in education beyond the minimum age of 16, but the transition to employment for the great majority was still over well before the German one. There is a kind of cultural imperative in Britain (endorsed by employers, young people, and their parents) towards gaining adult status at the earliest opportunity through full-time employment. Consequently, the youth training programs have never been more than a pale shadow of their German counterparts. German aspirations are much more deeply rooted in a "training culture" that accepts an extended period of vocational preparation as an essential preliminary to employment.

Sample Design

Although young people's transition routes differ between countries, the employment structures they will find at the end of their transitions are likely to be quite similar. There are likely to be professional occupations at the top of the occupational hierarchy, skilled jobs in the middle, and partly skilled or casual unskilled jobs at the bottom. In our Anglo-German project this common structure led to stratifying the samples into four groups: academic and professional, skilled, partly skilled, and unskilled. Although all German youth are expected to be trained for a *Beruf* identified with a particular set of vocational skills, large areas of occupational training within the apprenticeship system lead to what in Britain would be described as partly skilled or unskilled work, for which little prior training is considered necessary.

To balance up the two sets of routes, we selected representative samples of 40 young people in each career route in two cohorts aged 16–17 and 18–19 (equal numbers of boys and girls) in each of two economically contrasting German cities, Bremen (contracting) and Paderborn (expanding), and in each of two English cities, Swindon (expanding) and Liverpool (contracting). In the case of the British samples, the young people were selected on the basis of an initial questionnaire survey conducted as part of a British program of research funded by the Economic and Social Research Council, the 16–19 Initiative (full details are given in Banks et al., 1992). The German samples were selected directly from lists supplied by *Gymnasia* and training providers in the different sectors of the dual system. A further control on the selection involved the attempt to match young people heading for comparable occupational destinations as closely as possible between countries: A fitter in Paderborn was matched with a fitter in Swindon; a hairdresser in Bremen with a hairdresser in Liverpool, and so on. (For full details of the matching procedure, see Bynner and Heinz, 1991). This approach enabled us to identify much more precisely than is usually the case how the transition experience in comparable occupations differed between countries in similar labor markets.

The young people completed questionnaires about their vocational preparation and work experiences and also answered several other questions about their vocational preparation experiences and attitudes to them (see Bynner & Roberts, 1991). Selected sample members were also interviewed. For the purposes of the analysis reported here, the questionnaire data were used to assess several transition outcomes employing the same indicators in the two countries. The indicators used included scales measuring work-related skills, occupational confidence, age expecting to leave home, age expecting to marry, and interest in politics. Interest in politics was chosen as signifying the beginning of political participation, the hallmark of adult citizenship. In addition, the sample design included a measure of social change as embodied in the distinction between expanding and contracting labor markets: Swindon and Paderborn (expanding) versus Bremen and Liverpool (contracting). This factor can be set against other matching factors in the two samples: cohort (16–17 and 18–19), gender (males and females), and career route, which was previously defined as embodying education and type of occupational destination. Measurement details of all the variables used in the analysis are shown below.

Variables used in the Anglo-German analysis.[a]

Transition outcome variables

Work experience: score obtained by aggregating scores for 12 work-related skills and experiences, each scored on a 4-point scale: *never* (1), *rarely* (2), *sometimes* (3), *quite often* (4), *very often* (5). The following skills were assessed: "discussed in a group the best way to perform a task," "worked as a member of a team," "been asked for advice from others on how to tackle a problem," "felt a sense of achievement," "had a chance to use your initiative," "felt all your abilities were being used," "been able to make decisions for yourself," "been given responsibility," "felt stretched and challenged," "developed new skills and abilities," "set your own goals and targets," "had your skills tested."

Occupational confidence: score obtained by aggregating scores on five occupational confidence indicators, each scored on a five-point scale: *extremely doubtful* (1), *very doubtful* (2), *fairly doubtful* (3), *reasonably confident* (4), *very confident* (5). The following indicators were assessed: "In 10 years' time I will have the kind of job that I really want," "I will be able to impress an employer in a job interview," "I will be able to get on with the people I work with," "I will avoid unemployment," "I will not be dismissed from a job for unsatisfactory work."

Age expecting to leave home: age in years

Age expecting to marry: age in years

Interest in politics: measured on a four-point scale, in response to the question: "How interested are you in politics?" Scored on a scale of *very interested* (4), *quite interested* (3), *not very interested* (2), *not at all interested* (1).

Factors affecting transition outcome

Country: Germany (1), England (2)

Cohort: Younger (1); Older (2)

(younger = 16–17, older = 18–19)

Sex: Female (1), Male (2)

Career route: Academic or professional (1), skilled occupations (2), semiskilled occupations (3), Unskilled (4).

Labor market: Expanding (1), Contracting (2).

---

[a] Numbers in brackets denote the score for each category of each variable

Table 2 shows the mean scores for each of the transition outcome indicators for each category of the five factors for Germany and England separately. The notable features of these bivariate comparisons are the much higher levels of work experience and occupational confidence claimed by English young people compared with German young people and a higher desired age of marriage in Germany compared with England (though not higher age of leaving home). All the differences are in line with the more prolonged transition to adulthood in Germany. On the other hand, in Germany, there were higher levels of interest in politics than in England, suggesting a more developed sense of citizenship there despite the longer transition. The mean values also varied between cohorts, genders, career trajectories, and labor markets. Work experience was, as we might expect, higher in the older groups and, perhaps more surprisingly, higher in the professional and skilled categories than in the semiskilled and uncertain categories. Males and females barely differed in these respects. Surprisingly, there was also relatively little difference between the expanding and the contracting labor markets except more evidence of work experience in the former than in the latter and much higher occupational confidence, especially in the English expanding labor market. Age of leaving home and age of marriage related most strongly to cohort and gender (males opting for higher ages), and higher ages for leaving home and getting married were also preferred more often in the professional groups than in the unskilled groups in both countries. Interest in politics was very strongly connected with career route, and the professional groups showed the most interest by far, especially in England.

To determine which of the factors was related to each of the transition indicators, with the effect of other factors held constant, and to assess their interactions, analysis of variance of the transition indicators was carried out (see Table 3).

The results show that in relation to the transition indicators concerned with employment (work experience and occupational confidence), as indicated by the sums of squares, country emerged as by far the strongest factor. Career route and labor market factors came second in terms of importance. With respect to age of leaving home, only one factor (cohort) was significantly involved: the younger cohort tended to want to leave earliest. For age of marriage, however, gender, career route, country, and cohort were all involved, and career route followed by gender exhibited the strongest relationships. The Germans, the professional groups, men rather than women, and the older cohort rather than the younger cohort, all wanted to marry later. Finally, with respect to interest in politics, career route again showed the strongest relationship, and those on the professional route exhibited the most interest. This was followed by country and gender. Notably, the social change factor, labor market, had a significant relationship with all the transition indicators, except interest in politics.

As Table 3 also shows, there were many two-way, three-way and even four-way interactions between the factors, especially for occupational confidence. Finally,

Table 2. *Transition outcomes (mean scores) by cohort, labor market, sex, career route, and country.*

	Germany					England				
Factor	Work experience	Employment confidence	Age of leaving home	Age of marriage	Interest in politics	Work experience	Employment confidence	Age of leaving home	Age of marriage	Interest in politics
Cohort										
Older	3.1	4.1	21.2	26.8	2.7	3.8	4.9	21.9	24.8	2.5
Younger	3.1	4.2	19.6	25.0	2.5	3.6	4.9	20.5	24.9	2.3
Gender										
Male	3.1	4.2	21.1	26.8	2.8	3.6	4.9	20.9	25.3	2.5
Female	3.1	4.1	20.5	25.0	2.5	3.8	4.9	20.5	24.4	2.2
Career route										
Professional	3.3	4.4	20.7	27.4	3.2	3.9	4.9	20.0	25.9	3.0
Skilled	3.3	4.3	21.6	25.4	2.6	3.8	4.9	21.1	24.9	2.3
Semiskilled	3.0	4.1	20.6	26.1	2.6	3.8	4.9	21.5	24.3	2.1
Uncertain	2.8	4.0	20.3	24.4	2.1	3.3	4.8	20.3	24.0	2.1
Labor market										
Expanding	3.2	4.6	21.4	25.8	2.8	3.7	4.9	20.5	24.3	2.3
Contracting	3.0	3.7	20.4	26.0	2.5	3.7	4.9	20.9	25.3	2.5

for interest in politics, career route overrode every other factor, though country was also involved.

Conclusion

The Anglo-German and British examples point to the importance of the national context via each country's institutions in shaping transition patterns and demonstrate the complex interactions between personal attributes, structural factors, cultural factors, and social change in the sequencing of youth transitions. Thus, young people in declining labor markets tend to have less work experience and lower levels of occupational confidence. But there were interactions with many of the other factors. Of these, country and career route were the most important.

The representativeness of the sample was limited by the need to match individuals as closely as possible in terms of likely career and occupational outcomes. But the consistency of the differences revealed between countries, between educational levels, and between labor markets suggests that the direction of effects is likely to stand up to replication with other more representative and rigorous survey designs. Moreover, the qualitative insights gained from the biographical interviews conducted with selected young people point to underlying processes that conform with and help particularly to enhance our understanding of the different institutional arrangements surrounding transition in England and Germany (Bynner & Roberts, 1991; Evans & Heinz, 1994).

Thus, over and above the effects of social change on developmental sequences and between the cultural and institutional contexts in which they occur, we need to recognize their differential impact across different sections of young people, especially between the sexes and between those groups differing by educational level. Those in Britain with the lowest levels of human and cultural capital, as signified by poor educational qualifications, leave school at the earliest possible age and tend to experience training schemes rather than getting jobs. Yet in German terms, the training schemes they enter should be precisely the kind of vocational preparation they need. More typically, however, youth training in England is followed by periods of unemployment interspersed with unskilled, often part-time, casual work. The extent to which such employment is available varies from one part of the country to another. In those areas with contracting labor markets, prospects of employment are very limited, and a process of marginalization is set in motion: 36% of the 16–19 Initiative young people who were on the YTS–Unemployment route at age 18 were unemployed at 20 (Bynner, 1992). Boys with poor skills in this situation tended to report unemployment. For girls a different response was evident, as manifested by large numbers of them leaving the labor market to "look after their homes." This move of young women into their alternative career of parenting and motherhood is shown by the much higher tendency among them to have children early. The return of these young women to the labor market is, more

Table 3. *Analysis of variance of transition outcomes by country, cohort, sex, labor market, and trajectory: sums of squares and P values.*

	Work experience			Occupational confidence			Age wants to leave home			Age wants to marry			Interest in politics		
	SS	df	P's	SS	df	P's	SS	df	P's	SS	df	P's	SS	df	P's
Main effects	82.28	7		117.86	7		167.17	7		634.89	7	***	103.49	7	
Country (a)	55.22	1	***	83.63	1	***	0.03	1	NS	101.94	1	**	11.89	1	***
Cohort (b)	1.43	1	NS	0.07	1	NS	55.98	1	***	63.35	1	*	5.13	1	**
Sex (c)	0.13	1	NS	1.41	1	**	5.93	1	NS	116.05	1	***	9.81	1	***
Career route (d)	22.48	3	***	4.87	3	***	46.62	3	**	282.77	3	***	76.63	3	***
Labor market (e)	3.62	1	**	28.30	1	***	8.83	1	NS	58.95	1	*	0.17	1	NS
2-way interactions	11.97	18	NS	37.06	18	—	113.16	18	*	312.26	18	*	17.39	18	*
a × b	0.34	1	NS	0.32	1	NS	16.64	1	*	58.41	1	*	0.28	1	NS
a × c	0.54	1	NS	0.68	1	*	2.97	1	NS	39.12	1	*	0.00	1	NS
a × d	2.91	3	NS	1.65	3	*	6.00	3	NS	19.36	3	NS	4.30	3	NS
a × e	1.16	1	NS	30.92	1	***	28.42	1	**	40.85	1	*	7.50	1	***
b × c	0.54	1	NS	0.11	1	NS	4.81	1	NS	0.10	1	NS	0.67	1	NS
b × d	1.03	3	NS	1.07	3	NS	8.83	3	NS	22.53	3	NS	1.15	3	NS
b × e	0.29	1	NS	0.19	1	NS	0.03	1	NS	12.65	1	NS	0.02	1	NS
c × d	1.75	3	NS	1.36	3	*	22.91	3	NS	30.47	3	NS	0.92	3	NS
c × e	1.61	1	*	0.29	1	NS	0.14	1	NS	10.51	1	NS	0.17	1	NS
d × e	1.95	3	NS	0.79	3	NS	16.12	3	NS	60.25	3	NS	2.97	3	NS

	SS	df	P	SS	df	P	SS	df	P	SS	df	P	SS	df	P
3-way interactions	12.51	22		10.79	22	–	120.90	22	*	202.45	22		16.13	22	NS
a × b × c	0.50	1	NS	0.01	1	NS	0.47	1	NS	1.90	1	NS	0.33	1	NS
a × b × e	0.30	1	NS	0.18	1	NS	0.23	1	NS	1.84	1	NS	1.17	1	NS
a × d × e	0.67	3	NS	2.03	3	**	38.25	3	*	27.16	3	NS	1.90	3	NS
b × c × d	4.79	3	**	2.44	3	***	8.39	3	NS	2.52	3	NS	4.78	3	*
b × c × e	0.42	1	NS	0.02	1	NS	0.21	1	NS	2.64	1	NS	0.11	1	NS
a × b × d	1.01	3	NS	1.15	3	*	11.02	3	NS	21.37	3	NS	0.76	3	NS
a × c × d	1.56	3	NS	0.88	3	NS	2.46	3	NS	30.30	3	NS	2.01	3	NS
a × c × e	0.77	1	NS	0.37	1	NS	7.05	1	NS	0.97	1	NS	0.47	1	NS
b × d × e	1.69	3	NS	1.66	3	*	16.03	3	NS	78.32	3	NS	2.38	3	NS
c × d × e	0.90	3	NS	1.97	3	**	25.01	3	NS	25.50	3	NS	2.25	3	NS
4-way interactions	4.65	13	NS	4.45	13	–	28.62	13	NS	152.10	13	–	6.35	13	NS
a × b × c × e	1.24	1	NS	0.01	1	NS	0.23	1	NS	0.53	1	NS	0.02	1	NS
a × b × c × d	0.63	3	NS	1.40	3	*	15.99	3	NS	54.79	3	NS	0.96	3	NS
a × b × d × e	2.22	3	NS	1.32	3	*	6.21	3	NS	12.07	3	NS	2.87	3	NS
a × c × d × e	0.22	3	NS	1.25	3	*	7.54	3	NS	61.44	3	NS	0.37	3	NS
b × c × e × d	0.37	3	NS	0.47	3	NS	4.06	3	NS	19.86	3	NS	2.12	3	NS
5-way interactions	0.05	3	NS	0.82	3	–	–	–	–	77.96	3	–	0.93	3	NS
a × b × c × e × d	0.05	3	NS	0.82	3	NS	–	–	–	77.96	3	NS	0.93	3	NS
n	640			640			640			640			640		

* = $P < .05$; ** = $P < .01$; *** = $P < .001$; NS = not statistically significant; SS = sum of squares; df = degrees of freedom; P = probability

frequently, in lower-level kinds of occupations, often unskilled part-time, that they use to earn money to support their children (Joshi & Hinde, 1993).

The main conclusion to draw from these results is that social change does influence the sequencing of transitions. But the effects it has need to be viewed against the long-term trends taking place that are characterized by the distinctive arrangements for handling transitions in each country. In addition, these effects will vary depending on gender and the human capital, as reflected in qualifications, that young people have to bring with them to the opportunities available. Those with least to offer have the most difficulty in achieving positive transitions, not only in occupational life, but in the domain of private life, where the accelerated transitions carry increased risk of early family breakdown. The most compelling effect of social change on transition sequences is the increasing pressure toward marginalization of these groups. They have the most difficulty in making adjustments to new circumstances, for the transitions they experienced in the past no longer provide satisfactory routes to adulthood.

References

Banks, M., Breakwell, G., Bynner, J., Emler, N., Jamieson, L., & Roberts, K. (1992). *Careers and identities*. Buckingham, England: Open University Press.

Beck, U. (1992) *Risk society*. London: Sage.

Brown, P. (1995). Cultural capital and social exclusion: Some observations on recent trends in education, employment and the labour market. *Work, Employment and Society, 9*, 29–51.

Bulmer, M., & Rees, A. M., (Eds.). (1996). *Citizenship today*. London: University College Press.

Bundesminister für Bildung und Wissenschaft (1992). *Grund-und Struktur daten 1993/1994*. Bonn, Germany: Author.

Bynner, J. (1991). Transition to work: Results of a longitudinal study of young people in four British labour markets. In D. Ashton & G. Lowe (Eds.), *Making their way*. Milton Keynes, England: Open University Press.

Bynner, J. (1992). Transition to employment and citizenship: Findings on early careers and identities from a UK longitudinal study. In W. Meeus, M. de Goede, W. Kox, & K. Hurrelmann (Eds.), *Adolescence, careers and cultures*. Berlin: Walter de Gruyter.

Bynner, J. (1996). Resisting youth unemployment: The role of education and training. In M. P. M. de Goede, P. M. Klaver, J. A. C. Van Ophem, C. H. A. Verhaar, & A. de Vries, (Eds.), *Youth: Unemployment, identity and policy*. Aldershot, England: Avebury.

Bynner, J., & Chisholm, L. (1988). Comparative youth transition research: Methods, meanings and research relations, *European Sociological Review, 14*(2), 131–150.

Bynner, J., & Heinz, W. R. (1991). Matching samples and analysing their differences in a cross-national study of labour market entry in England and West Germany. *International Journal of Comparative Sociology, 32*, 137–153.

Bynner, J., & Roberts, K. (1991). *Youth and work*. London: Anglo German Foundation.

Chisholm, L. (1992, September). *Young people in the European community: Staking the terrain for European youth research*. Paper presented to the British Sociological Association Conference, A New Europe, Kent, England.

Chisholm, L., Kruger, H.-H., & du Bois, R. M. (1995). *Growing up in Europe*. Berlin: Walter de Gruyter.

Coleman, J. (1974). *The nature of adolescence*. London: Methuen.

Coleman, J. (1993). Adolescence in a changing world. In S. Jackson, & H. Rodriguez-Tomé, (Eds.), *Adolescence and its social worlds*. Hillsdale, NJ: Lawrence Erlbaum.

Coles, R. (1995). *Youth and social policy*. London: UCL Press.

Department for Education and Science. (1994). Statistical Bulletin, 10/94. London: Author.

Erikson, E. H. (1968). *Identity: Youth and crisis.* New York: Norton.

Evans, K. (1990). Post 16 education, training and employment: Provisions and outcomes in two contrasting areas. *British Journal of Education and Work, 3,* 41–59.

Evans, K., & Furlong, A. (1997). Metaphors of youth transitions: Niches, pathways, trajectories and navigations. In J. Bynner, L. Chisholm, & A. Furlong (Eds.), *Youth, citizenship and social change.* Aldershot, England: Ashgate.

Evans, K., & Heinz, W. R. (1994). *Becoming adults in the 1990s.* London: Anglo German Foundation.

Gershuny, J., & Pahl, R. (1994, October). *Lifetime employment in a new context.* Paper presented at the conference on Challenges of Unemployment in a Regional Europe, Ljonwert, Fryske Academy.

Hendry, L. B. (1983). *Growing up and going out: Adolescents and leisure.* Aberdeen, Scotland: Aberdeen University Press.

Hurrelmann, K. (1988). *Social structure and personality development.* Cambridge, England: Cambridge University Press.

Hurrelmann, K. (1989). The social world of adolescents: A sociological perspective. In K. Hurrelmann & U. Engel. (Eds.), The social world of adolescents. Berlin: Walter de Gruyter.

Jallade, J.-P. (1989). Recent trends in vocational education and training. *European Journal of Education, 24,* 103–125.

Jones, G., & Wallace, C. (1992). *Youth, family and citizenship.* Buckingham, England: Open University Press.

Joshi, H., & Hinde, A. (1993). Employment after childbearing: Cohort study evidence on contrasts within and across generations. *European Sociological Review, 9,* 203–227.

Lagree, J.-C. (1996). Youth in Europe. In H. Helve & J. Bynner (Eds.), *Youth and life management* (pp. 152–170). Helsinki: University of Helsinki Press.

Marcia, J. E. (1966). Development and validation of ego-identity status. *Journal of Personality and Social Psychology, 3,* 551–558.

Marshall, G. (1973). *Class, citizenship and social development.* Westport, CT: Greenwood.

Robins, L., & Rutter, M. (1990). *Straight and devious pathways from childhood to adulthood.* Cambridge, England: Cambridge University Press.

Silbereisen, R. (1993, August). *Psychosocial adversities and adolescent timetables: East versus West Germany.* Paper presented at the 101st Annual Convention of the American Psychological Association, Toronto.

Silbereisen, R. (1994). *Differential timing of vocational choice.* Paper presented to the 13th biennial meeting of the Society for the Study of Behavioural Development, Amsterdam.

Utting, D. (1995). *Family and parenthood.* York, England: Joseph Rowntree Foundation.

Wallace, C. (1987). *For richer and poorer: Growing up in and out of work.* London: Tavistock.

7   German Unification and Adolescents' Developmental Timetables: Continuities and Discontinuities

Rainer K. Silbereisen

The unification of Germany in 1989 represents a particular case of rapid rather than gradual social change. According to the dominant view of this event and its aftermath, the unification process, at least in the beginning, was primarily characterized as a replacement of East German social institutions by their West German equivalents (Zapf, 1996). An example is the dissolution of the Eastern system of comprehensive schools in favor of the three-track Western system, which distinguishes tracks leading to professional careers as opposed to academic careers from early on. In this sense, practically all social institutions dealing with education, labor, internal security, and many more concerns underwent rapid and encompassing changes (Kornadt, 1996).

Many of the postunification problems, such as the profound difference in what performances people in the two regions of the country expect from state authorities with regard to public welfare, seem to be rooted in the failure of the change of peoples' minds and attitudes to progress at the same pace as the institutional changes (Zapf, 1996). Put in other words, the situation, even several years after unification, still reflects what Elder described as inherent to social change in peoples' lives: Individuals experience a more or less pronounced mismatch between new challenges and established resources from the past. This mismatch is likely to be perceived as a partial loosening of personal control. Whether this focuses attention, with the result of more forceful attempts at regaining control, or whether it results in desperation, depends on many factors, including basic features of individuals' personality structures (Elder, Caspi, & Burton, 1988).

The studies reported in this chapter have been supported by grants received from the German Research Council (Si 296/14-1 bis 14-5; principal investigator: Rainer K. Silbereisen). Special thanks go to the colleagues of our research consortium at the University of Siegen (principal investigator: Jürgen Zinnecker) and the University of Bamberg (principal investigator: Laszlo Vaskovics). I owe much to the parents and their adolescent children who participated in the survey. Special thanks go also to Fred W. Vondracek, who helped to optimize earlier drafts of this chapter and whose research has inspired some of the analyses reported.

104

With regard to adolescence and human development in general, social change can be seen as affecting, through such mismatches, the basic organization of the life course, as sociologists would call it. If one utilizes the concept of developmental tasks more familiar to psychologists, what social change, as experienced in Germany after unification, produces is a more or less subtle or profound change in the fabric of biological growth, psychological aspirations, and social expectations that make up developmental tasks (Havighurst, 1972).

These changes of social expectations can affect the content of developmental tasks, their timing, or both. Certainly not all aspects of the life course will be affected alike (finding acceptance among one's peers may be as crucial now as it was before unification), and it is also not probable that all cohorts undergo similar experiences. Those who have resolved a particular developmental task under circumstances of the past (now gone forever) are in a different position than those who still face that task and can profit from new opportunities without being constrained by past experiences. One manifestation of such processes is that social change makes even adjacent cohorts different (Elder, 1998).

Individuals play an active role in resolving developmental tasks. Because these tasks do not represent any clear directive as to what exactly is expected to be accomplished when and by whom, adolescents need to select goals and choose settings with the aim of promoting their development (Lerner & Busch-Rossnagel, 1981; Silbereisen, Noack, & von Eye, 1992). New opportunity structures that result from social change will not directly translate into reformulated individual goals for development. Rather, this linkage between social change and individual development represents a "loose coupling" (Elder & O'Rand, 1995) because many factors, the family in particular, contribute to the linkage, and all have some impact and thereby produce interindividual differences.

This general framework on the relationship between social change and individual development, on the one hand, and the rapid changes of social institutions produced by the unification of Germany, on the other, formed the background for the research reported here. Our particular interest was to trace the timing (age) at which psychosocial transitions during adolescence and early adulthood take place. An example is the age at which individuals begin dating, an important initial way station in the development of romantic involvement. More specifically, transitions representing three behavioral patterns were investigated: behavioral autonomy, romantic involvement, and socioinstitutional achievements.

The timing of such steps in development belongs to the broader topic of life transitions, which is an important theme in sociology and psychology. According to George (1993), two conceptual precursors of modern perspectives on life transitions are important. Within role theory, the transitions of interest are entry and exit of role allocations, such as beginning and accomplishment of the college student role with its associated social expectations with regard to habits and behaviors. As such, role allocations are seen as governed by social norms, which individuals are socialized to follow. From this perspective, the only timing aspect of interest is whether the transition occurs off-time (i.e., unexpectedly), and consequently results in disturbances. Note, however, that many timed aspects of adolescents' negotiations of autonomy do not seem to be governed by social norms (as, in contrast, is true regarding the age for receiving a driver's license).

The other precursor of current approaches to life transitions noted by George (1993) is social stress research. Many of the hazards studied in this paradigm qualify in actuality as transitions (such as divorce), and, in contrast to role theory, interindividual differences in the consequences of such events are acknowledged. The normative underpinnings provided by social structure, however prominent in role theory and thus important in the predictability of transitions, are not central in social stress research. Interestingly enough, adversities such as divorce or serious illnesses are likely to have an impact on other, more age-correlated transitions such as the earlier assumption of household responsibilties by the young following a divorce.

Transitions represent a key concept in the modern sociological life course approach (Elder, 1985). The life course itself is conceived of as the intersection of social and historical factors with personal biography. Because context and person vary across time, space, and population, so do life course patterns; that is, sequences of socially recognized transitions. Transitions, such as the one from student to worker, do not occur in isolation. Rather, many transitions are elements of particular trajectories that give them meaning. For instance, the transition to worker may occur before the formation of one's own family, thus representing the traditional trajectory. Most of the studies conducted within the life course approach, however, focus on transitions in isolation rather than on trajectories, and the present investigation is no exception to this rule.

Past research on transitions was carried out in two modes. Concerning the population-based mode, trends were investigated across and within cohorts. The median timing of marriage, for instance, showed a decline during the first part of the century but increased again during the last decades (Watkins, Menken, & Bongaarts, 1987). Intracohort variability in the timing of such transitions is substantial across social, cultural, and national contexts. In conformity with this tradition in research, the first aim of the present study was to address differences and commonalities in median transition ages between the Eastern and Western parts of Germany and across periods. If equivalent samples soon after unification (1991) and a considerable period of time into unification (1996) are compared, some insight can be gained into the consequences of unification for developmental timetables.

Individual-based studies, the other mode described by George (1993), aim to obtain a better understanding of the mechanisms that connect the timing of transitions with antecedents and consequences. Research on the relationship between early family experiences and the timing of leaving home represents an instance of research on such antecedents. Children in step families are known to leave home earlier than age-mates raised in intact families, and according to Acquilino (1991) this phenomenon is mediated by the greater intergenerational conflict and stressful daily living in these families. On the basis of this line of thinking, the second aim of the present study was to investigate the relationship between adversities experienced during childhood and the timing of psychosocial transitions during adolescence. The remainder of this chapter is organized according to these two aims.

Median Transition Times

Studies on the timing of everyday manifestations of age-related achievements in autonomy and the other developmental tasks addressed in this section represent an established tradition in research on acculturation among immigrants. Feldman and Rosenthal (1994), for instance, found that young immigrants from a collectivist value background gradually changed some of their rather late developmental timetables. This was seen as rooted in the emphasis on individualistic orientations provided by behavioral models in the host country. The more new social institutions or the changed pragmatics of everyday life were involved in the timing of transitions, the faster this acculturation took place. Against this backdrop of the impressive plasticity of timetables, the following expectations were formulated.

First, given the common cultural heritage, which is unlikely to be wiped out by a few decades of separate political development, basically the same developmental timetables were expected for psychosocial transitions that are not influenced by societal institutions, which clearly differed between the two former Germanys. Concerning romantic involvement, the first aspect of developmental timetables addressed, the conditions were alike in both regions. The timing of way stations such as dating or first sexual relationships is influenced by physical development and by societal expectations (Dornbusch et al., 1981). Changes of the body are rooted in biological processes that certainly do not differ, given the common gene pool and more than satisfying nutrition, and societal expectations are influenced by cultural value orientations that are also not known to differ between the former German states.

The expectation of no mean timing differences between the two parts of the country should hold for 1991 and for 1996 as well. In challenging this, one could refer to the lower marriage age and lower age at the birth of the first child common in former East Germany (23.2 and 22.9 versus 25.7 and 26.7 years, respectively; Adler, 1997). Although such a difference might point to differences in the timing of first romantic involvement, this is actually unlikely. The reasons for earlier marriage and childbirth were related to government provisions (very generous family leave policies, for instance) and the eligibility of only young families and single parents for subsidized housing (Adler, 1997).

Concerning the timing of behavioral autonomy from parental supervision, the second aspect of developmental timetables, the same considerations apply. The general pattern should not differ between 1991 and 1996. The reason is that the aspects studied do not seem to be controlled by normative expectations that made the two former countries different. With closer scrutiny, however, an important particularity of life in the East comes to mind. Out of economic necessity, but also owing to politically induced equalizing mechanisms, the percentage of working mothers was twice as high in the former German Democratic Republic (GDR) as compared with the West (60% to 30%; Bundesministerium für Frauen und Jugend, 1992). Although the state deemed child care and other means that helped to combine full-time employment and family roles as public duty, there was still the problem of a double burden for women. Thus, one could imagine that adolescent children, particularly males, took over responsibilities in the household earlier than was the case in the West. This qualification of our expectation would also be supported by the fact that almost all children attended day care and were accustomed to spending the better part of the day in either kindergarden or school (Trommsdorff & Chakkarath, 1996). Such experiences may foster early autonomy.

The third aspect of timetables we addressed concerns the development of maturity with regard to socioinstitutional aspects of identity, or more specifically, the age at which adolescents formed their first occupational preferences and took part actively in political debates. We predicted differences in 1991 in favor of earlier timetables in the East, albeit for topic-specific reasons. Concerning political participation, the young in former East Germany had been raised from early on in a climate that virtually demanded the expression of (party line) political opinions. Although this was unlikely to represent independent action and judgment, there nevertheless were opportunity and necessity to care about political issues, at least in public. Moreover, it is possible that the radical societal changes around the time of unification led to an even higher sensitivity to, and interest in, political issues. As far as 1996 was concerned, it was difficult to predict, but our idea was that existing differences should have begun to fade away.

With respect to the age of first occupational preferences, we predicted an earlier timing in the East compared with the West in 1991. Issues of vocational education and job opportunities are a clear case of differences based on institutional under-pinnings. The former GDR had a system by which students' occupational interests were guided from early on in directions defined by the priorities of the state-run industries.

It was not clear whether this would hold in 1996. The school curriculum changed in 1992, and the West German system of several levels of schooling was introduced. Furthermore, the East German system of guidance and channeling of students into preselected professions was no longer in place. However, because initial occupa-tional preferences and their antecedents are likely to be formed quite early in life and social change is known to need time before it becomes effective on the individual level, we did not expect to find the differences predicted for 1991 to have disap-peared by 1996. In summary, our first expectation was to find no mean differences in those developmental timetables that reveal no clear institutional underpinnings, that is, way stations of romantic involvement and autonomy from parental super-vision (except the earlier assumption of household responsibilities). This should apply soon after unification and several years into the process. Where institutional underpinnings were relevant and differed, as in the case of the socioinstitutional transitions, differences were expected in 1991. More specifically, the timing of first occupational preferences was expected to be earlier in the East. The differences were expected to become smaller in 1996 owing to the ongoing social changes.

Methods

To investigate these hypotheses, we relied on several sets of data. The Shell Youth Study (1991) encompassed about 4,000 young people, aged between 13 and 29 years, from the former East and West Germany. Because of logistical problems at the time of unification, it was not possible to draw a random sample. Instead, quota samples were gathered, stratified by gender, education, and community size (Jugendwerk der Deutschen Shell, 1992). Younger age groups and participants from the East were oversampled to compensate for their smaller share in the population (East Germany had about 18 million citizens as compared with about 60 million in West Germany). (For details of sampling procedures, see Fischer, 1992). The same procedure concerning stratification criteria was used for the 1996 replication, which followed an equivalent sampling plan. This time about 3,000 young people in the same age range as in 1991 participated (Silbereisen, Vaskovics, & Zinnecker, 1996).

Results from those two studies are the focus of this chapter. On occasion the evidence is complemented by findings from a third data set, derived from about 700 adolescents, aged between 10 and 13 years. Gathered in 1993, the study was planned to expand the age range toward younger, prepubertal groups (Zinnecker & Silbereisen, 1996). Although the 1991 data in part, and the 1993 data more extensively, entail longitudinal assessments, the analyses in this chapter are confined to the assessments at the first wave of measurements in each study.

Owing to space and time constraints set by the established research protocol of the Shell Youth Studies, it was impossible to cover a full list of developmental tasks by a large number of representative manifestations. Only recently, a stan-dardized questionnaire has become available that addresses such everyday way stations to adulthood (Dekovic, Noom, & Meeus, 1997). The authors distinguish between personal tasks, such as autonomy with regard to decisions; relational tasks, such as forming romantic friendships; and socioinstitutional tasks, like choosing a profession. The way stations we formulated were based on the work of Feldman and Quatman (1988) and concern the three domains mentioned above, although at varying breadth and depth. The specific items used in the analyses reported in this chapter are shown in Table 1. The first four belong to the personal tasks, the next four concern romantic relationships, and the last two refer to socioinstitutional tasks; namely, occupational preferences and participation in political discussion.

Table 1. *Percentage of 13- to 19-year-olds who accomplished transitions.*

Transition	Percentage
1. To come and go as you please	47
2. Choose own looks even if parents disapprove	90
3. Warming up dinner when alone at home	86
4. Take care of household chores	88
5. First romantic relationship	54
6. First sexual experiences	51
7. Fall in love for the first time	76
8. Go out to discotheques	78
9. Talk about political issues	51
10. Initial occupational preference	69

Are there any obvious omissions? According to Dekovic et al. (1997), a few come to mind. For example, with regard to relational tasks, establishing friendships with peers was not included. Also, in relation to socioinstitutional tasks and personal tasks, the timing of several more transitions could have been gathered.

Because substantial interindividual variation in developmental timetables was to be expected, not all participants were likely to have already passed a particular transition. Leaving them out in the calculation of the timing would have led to biased results. Consequently, various models of event history analysis were used to provide optimal estimates of the age at which transtions were accomplished (Willett & Singer, 1991).

Results

The results of survival analyses of the 1996 data are presented first. We restricted ourselves to the group of the 13- to 19-year-olds. In Figure 1 the median ages are given at which the respective transitions were estimated to have taken place. For details of these analyses readers are referred to Wiesner and Silbereisen (1996). In comparing East and West, the similarity of the rank order is amazing. Relatively late achievements concern autonomy, intimate heterosexual relationships, active participation in political debates, and finally, freedom of decision regarding when to come and go, the latest accomplishment. In contrast, really early accomplishments refer to self-care, such as preparing food for oneself at home.

For each transition, statistical comparisons were made across the four groups formed by political region and gender. The following summary of the main trends in median survival ages relies on Bonferroni-corrected significance levels (nominal $p < .05$). First, concerning the issues of behavioral autonomy tapped in the questionnaire, as expected we found significantly earlier achievements in the East when

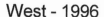

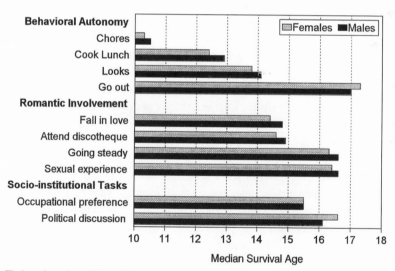

Figure 1. Timing of psychosocial transitions among adolescents in the West and East in 1996.

it came to taking care of oneself or taking over household responsibilities. Even more interesting, however, was that the usually earlier autonomy among females applied to the sample from the West only. In other words, taking over such responsibilities not only occurred earlier among adolescents who grew up in former East Germany, but there was also no gender-stereotypic differentiation, as was found in the West. Interestingly enough, the same pattern of gender differences in the West but not in the East also applied to the age at which adolescents decided about their style of appearance for the first time on their own.

With regard to the tasks related to romantic involvement, no differences between the political regions were expected, and none were found, except one. Going to a discotheque was an event that took place earlier in the East (and earlier among females within this sample) than in the West. It should be noted, however, that going to a discotheque in the East traditionally meant an informal gathering, not a commercialized entertainment as known in the West (even years after unification this holds true, in part because disposable incomes are not high enough to attend commercial facilities). With the exception of the timing of the first "real" sexual experience, the other way stations of romantic involvement did reveal, not too surprisingly, a faster pace among female adolescents.

Finally, there were clear differences between the samples from East and West Germany with regard to first political discussions and initial occupational preferences. As is revealed in Figure 1, next to the earlier assumption of household responsibilities in the East, the age at which first ideas about one's future vocation were formed represents an instance of earlier timing of a transition in the East. Whereas there were no gender differences in this domain, with respect to political discussions the earlier timing in the East was accompanied by a faster pace among males in both regions.

Note that the results on the differences, specifically in the timing of first occupational preferences, speak for one of the predictions put forward; namely, that some differences in the timing of psychosocial transitions were maintained even years after unification. This leads back to the question of differences between East and West 5 years earlier, in 1991. The answer, provided in a previous chapter by Silbereisen, Schwarz, and Rinker (1996), is very simple. The results basically resemble those just reported for 1996. It would be premature, however, to conclude that the societal changes did not have an impact. The median timing of early household responsibilities, for instance, refers to an age at which even the youngest adolescents studied in 1996 lived under the preunification conditions of development and socialization. With respect to occupational preferences, at least the oldest of the 1996 group had experienced the past East German system of school and vocational guidance up to early adolescence.

Seen against this background, the results of additional analyses on the 10-to 13-year-olds gathered in 1993 are revealing. Owing to the change of the school system in 1991, all attended the differentiated secondary level following the West German model. Concerning the relevant results reported by Rinker and Schwarz (1996), one has to note that the number and content of psychosocial transitions tapped in 1993 were not entirely identical with those of the other studies. The significant differences observed between East and West referred to taking part in political debates and the age at which youngsters did the shopping for the family for the first time.

Further, the early adolescents from the East decided later about their appearance. Although, as expected, there was no difference in the timing of first romantic contacts, at closer scrutiny females of the Eastern sample showed an earlier timing of going steady for the first time.

Most importantly, however, there was no regional difference in the timing of first occupational preferences. If one overlooks that these adolescents were much younger than the 13- to 19-year-olds of the other samples, the lack of a difference supports the notion of a gradual adaptation of timetables to the new circumstances. Note that most of the adolescents, seen in 1993, had been enrolled in the new system of secondary schools (established in 1991) from the time of leaving primary school. Nevertheless, at this time one cannot rule out that the results are characteristic of the young age and do not reveal a process of gradual adaptation of timetables.

When the main results concerning commonalties and differences in timetables are summarized, one fact stands out. In line with expectations, as far as the timing is concerned, differences between the political regions were confined to those psychosocial transitions that have more or less obvious institutional underpinnings, which clearly differed between the two regions. Thus, the faster pace with regard to first occupational preferences in the East is likely to reflect the higher efforts by schools and employers to guide adolescents into particular professions, and the earlier timing of self-care and responsibilities in household duties probably mirrors factors such as the higher share of working mothers in the East. The greater gender equality in the East, at least as far as labor opportunities were concerned, also manifested itself in the Eastern females' not taking over such duties earlier than males, whereas their age-mates in the West followed the gender-stereotyped pace.

Previous research has shown that adolescent girls who did more household work also ranked higher in their feelings of competence regarding work and motivation to perform work. They also reported more authoritative parenting. Because this pattern did not apply to boys, the conclusion was that girls' household work is more integrated within their psychological development than is the case for boys' household work (Russell, Brewer, & Hogben, 1997). It is an open question whether this description also applies to the Eastern situation in which boys and girls started performing household activities at about the same age (and earlier than in the West). That this pattern did not disappear in the 1996 data may indicate that boys' household work is similarly integrated psychologically. This, in turn, would lead to the expectation that such differences would persist for quite some time in spite of the changes in the employment situation of women after unification.

Basically, all of these differences and commonalties still applied in 1991 and in 1996, 5 years after unification. It is an issue for discussion whether this stability across different cohorts, in spite of quite remarkable social and political transformations, can be interpreted as revealing a loose coupling between macrolevel change and individual development or a relative insulation of individual development from such changes.

The Role of Cumulated Adversities

The second aim of the research reported here was to investigate the relationship between childhood adversities and the timing of psychosocial transitions. Beyond differences in central tendencies, contexts such as East and West Germany can reveal what in cross-cultural research is called patterning effects; that is, the differing correlates of timetables. Consequently, the question was whether the role of adversities would be the same across political regions and periods of time studied. Note that studying adversities such as divorce belongs to the broader program of research on transitions (George, 1993).

The point of departure is that it is not so much the particular event or experience but the accumulation of adverse happenings, each of which may have a minute effect but which in combination put individuals at risk to grow up more hastily than desirable. With this in mind, Rutter (Rutter & Smith, 1995) and others (Kolvin et al., 1990) have suggested the construction of measures of cumulated adversity consisting of items such as whether a parent had passed away, or suffered from serious illness, whether the family had to face economic strains, or whether a divorce had occurred. The relationship of such cumulated adversities to the pace of reaching developmental milestones is basically seen in two proximal processes. Earlier timing is presumed to be rooted in diminished parental surveillance due to the parents' being overtaxed by these adversities, to the fact that the young have to take over responsibilities that their less adversity-affected agemates are not yet required to face, or both (Conger et al., 1993).

A rather comprehensive array of studies and explanatory concepts exists on the effects of adversities on the timing of puberty (Steinberg & Belsky, 1996). Although pubertal timing is not a variable studied here, this research allows for making an important qualification concerning the linkage between adversity and developmental timing. As is the case with puberty, very serious adversities would probably result in a delay of development, including the psychosocial transitions of interest, rather than an acceleration. If one bears in mind that samples from the normal population are analyzed in this chapter, the adversities addressed do not represent a total lack of opportunities to grow, and thus a more or less pronounced acceleration of transition ages is expected. It is also important to note that adults seem to appreciate relatively early accomplishments in many developmental tasks (Grob, Flammer, & Rhyn, 1995) and hence may act to reinforce behaviors that point toward their achievement.

The general expectation was that adolescents who experienced a high load of adversities (following a convenient threshold this was identified as the upper 10% of the sample) would pass the psychosocial way stations at an earlier age. As far as differences among the topical domains are concerned, the effect should be stronger the more parental social capital is involved in achieving the respective accomplishment. Seen in this vein, the timing of first occupational preferences is a candidate for an earlier than usual orientation toward the future. This is so because the extensive exploration of options would be in conflict with the early responsibilities that foster premature commitments. This circumstance is likely to be aggravated by an increase in the freedom from parental supervision, which is also characteristic of adolescents who had faced adversities.

The timing of way stations concerning behavioral autonomy and romantic involvement is presumably less influenced by parental social capital, and thus it was expected that the difference between adolescents free of adversities and those burdened with many is likely to be less pronounced than in the case of occupational preferences.

Concerning the comparison of the samples from former East and West Germany, two opposing views can be taken. One would predict weaker effects of adversities in the East when thinking of the generally easily available and affordable public support systems for children and adolescents (Nauck, 1993). Thus, as far as relief from adversity-induced strains is concerned, child care and supervised after-school activities may have played a positive role.

The other view would stress these very activities and emphasize their potential risks; namely, the bringing together of peers. At least those already at risk can thus find the opportunities and forms of affiliations that are known to foster a more hasty assumption of adult-like behaviors (Patterson, DeBaryshe, & Ramsey, 1989).

Results

Table 2 shows the various adversities considered in the research reported here. In line with previous research, only adversities were included that happened at least once before the age of 9. The high-adversity group consisted of the upper 10%, which is equivalent to having experienced two or more individual adversities.

Silbereisen, Schwarz, and Rinker (1995) reported the estimated median ages at which the respective transitions in 1991 took place. They are in Figures 2–3. As can be seen, differences were all in favor of earlier transitions among the high-adversity group. This was particularly strong for the timing of autonomy concerning one's appearance, falling in love for the first time, and initial occupational preferences. This pattern applies basically to both genders and both regions.

When comparing East and West, the above-mentioned effects seem to be more pronounced in the East and, with respect to romantic involvement, more advanced way stations also appear to be affected. Finally, females of the high-adversity group from the East stand out compared with all others. Particularly in all manifestations of romantic involvement, and especially concerning initial occupational preferences, they are much faster in their developmental pace. Whereas the differences between

Table 2. *Percentage of adversities
experienced during childhood.*

	Percentages	
Adversity[a]	1991	1996
1. Relocation	20	15
2. Loss of a parent (death or divorce)	12	11
3. Own illness or illness of close relatives	9	8
4. Father (or, if missing, mother) without formal educational training	5	4
5. Repeated a grade at school	1	1
6. Unemployment of a parent	1	1

[a] Adversities until the age of 9 only.

the adversity groups vary in most cases between a few months and a bit more than a year, in the case of initial occupational preferences the difference in the estimated median transition ages amounts to about 2 years. As this point it is important to note that, according to additional analyses, the effects of cumulated adversities were not simply due to differences in the educational tracks attended. The tendency for stronger effects of the adversities among the female adolescents from the East was curious. Although there is no obvious interpretation, one should bear in mind that life prospects in the East were generally more predictable with regard to achievable aims. It could well be that the data mirror a tighter relationship between one's personal circumstances and knowledge about opportunities. Because the same pattern did not turn up in the 1996 data, however, a more parsimonious explanation in terms of fluctuation across samples may be appropriate.

Wiesner and Silbereisen (1996) replicated the analyses with the 1996 data set. Again, a faster pace of those who had faced cumulated adversities was observed as exemplified by an earlier timing of decisions about one's appearance or with regard to romantic involvement. In contrast to the 1991 results, however, differences in the timing of initial occupational preferences did not emerge. Further, when analyzing the 1993 sample of 10- to 13-year-olds, Rinker and Schwarz (1996) also did not find differences between the adversity groups in the timing of initial occupational preferences.

Taken together, the results with regard to occupational preferences are intriguing. The situation in 1996 was characterized by a heightened insecurity with regard to the future development of the job market. It was a common topic of public debate that the structural reorganization of the traditional industries would result in a scarcity of full-time jobs and, at the same time, a shift in the emphasis from manufacturing to jobs in the service sector (Kommission für Zukunftsfragen der Freistaaten Bayern und Sachsen, 1996). This characterization applies to East and West alike, and the results may thus point to a heightened awareness that early commitments might be

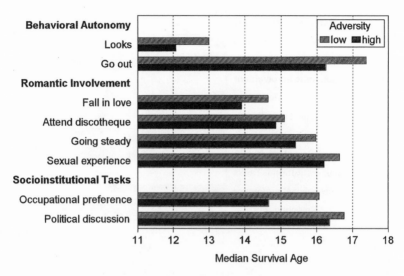

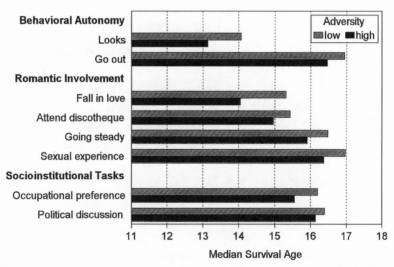

Figure 2. Timing of psychosocial transitions among female and male adolescents in the West in 1991: High vs. low adversity.

unwise. In other words, the lack of a difference between adolescents high and low in adversities, specifically with regard to occupational preferences, may indicate an adaptive response to the changes in the opportunity structures.

Some further results of the 1993 study again speak in favor of differences between East and West as far as the timing correlates of early family adversities are

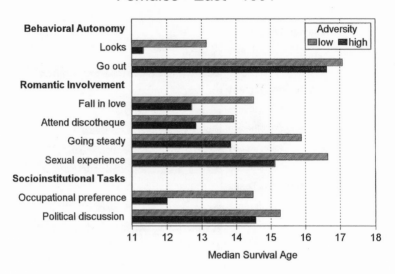

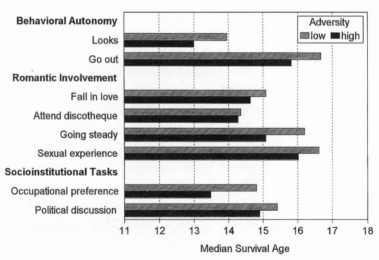

Figure 3. Timing of psychosocial transitions among female and male adolescents in the East in 1991: High vs. low adversity.

concerned. There seems to be a contrasting pattern induced by adversities charac-terized by earlier responsibilities for the family and oneself in the East and earlier falling in love and leeway for activities outside the home in the West. If one as-sumes that the adversities as such result in similar behavioral possibilities (greater responsibilities for others, more autonomy for oneself), then these differences in the actual behaviors reported can be seen as reflecting more general differences in socialization. Adolescents in the East may have experienced higher pressures to support the family household from early on. In this regard one could think of the much higher share of working mothers, the lower availability of services, and consequently the higher reliance on an intensive household economy (Adler, 1997). Because unsupervised peer activities were less prevalent in the East, consistent across the various samples studied (Reitzle & Riemenschneider, 1996), there were also fewer cliques and other peer groups to affiliate with.

Beyond such conditions that can result in the East–West differences just described, other more general issues may play a role. The research protocol of the 1991 and 1996 samples contained extended sets of statements that reflected the types of collectivist and individualistic values identified by Schwartz and Bilsky (1990). Although the rank orders showed a high degree of similarity, thus lending support to previous observations that Eastern teens had turned to Western-like values even before unification (Friedrich & Foerster, 1994), the adolescents raised in former East Germany endorsed values representing a collectivist orientation more than was common in the West (security, tradition, authority). According to Reitzle and Silbereisen (1996), the results for 1996 revealed similar differences, although they were less pronounced, particularly among the younger cohorts. Seen against this backdrop, similar adversities seem to put adolescents on differential tracks in East and West reflecting opportunities and more basic differences in the fabric of values.

Conclusion

The timing of developmental way stations to adulthood is an important aspect of adolescent development. From our research on acculturation among immigrants it was known that timetables in the domains of behavioral autonomy, intimate social relations, and socioinstitutional achievements, such as choosing a profession, differ between societies and cultural groups as a function of value orientations (among other things). Moreover, depending on the degree to which social institutions and the pragmatics of life dictate a different pace of development, adjustment to the standards of the host country takes place (Silbereisen & Schmitt-Rodermund, 1995).

Based in part on these observations, the postunification situation in Germany was conceived of as resembling various aspects of acculturation. In this case, however, it was not the population that moved, but the institutions. By taking over the West German system of secondary schools, occupational training, and justice, to name but a few instances of "institutional transfer," some developmental timetables obviously were affected (e.g., occupational preferences), whereas others were less likely to show any relationship at all (e.g., romantic involvement).

The first aim was to trace such differences and commonalties between the two former Germanys across a significant period of time into unification. The circumstances did not allow for a longitudinal study, and thus samples were gathered in 1991 and 1996 (additional data were gathered from a complementary sample in 1993). Every possible measure was taken to ensure equivalence between the 1991 and 1996 samples. Further, because the present research had to be conducted within the constraints of an existing research protocol, several weaknesses had to be accepted. The data are all self-report, in part retrospective, and the level to which individuals were actually affected by the various social changes was not assessed comprehensively (the few relevant data could not be used for the analyses reported in this chapter).

Nevertheless, some insights on how unification played a role in adolescents' developmental timetables were gained. As expected, it was the case that the timing of first occupational preferences differed in favor of an earlier age in the East compared with the West. Way stations that were less affected by institutional pacemakers, in contrast, did not differ. Moreover, the differences concerning occupational preferences were, for the most part, retained in 1996, thus suggesting a delayed response given that the institutional underpinnings had already changed quite dramatically. It is certainly tempting to interpret this result as an instance of the "loose coupling" that Elder (Elder & O'Rand, 1995) claimed to be a prominent characteristic of the linkage between macrosocial change and individual development. Obviously, further research is needed to make sure that it is indeed the presumed processes within the family that result in the delay, but at least the empirical fact (of the delay) is quite clearly demonstrated.

The second aim was to examine whether East and West would also differ in the antecedents of individual differences in adolescent timetables. The shared role of early adversities, which corresponds generally to earlier psychosocial transitions, was found, as expected. With regard to a better understanding of the role of social change, another result was revealing. Adolescents from East and West differed in the particular domain that seemed to be most affected by early adversities. In the East the trend was more towards earlier assumption of responsibilities for others, whereas in the West it was more towards claiming earlier autonomy for oneself. Although at present not more than a plausible speculation, it looks as if similar pressures (adversities) result in outcomes that reflect the more general opportunities and orientations of those affected.

Concerning social change (i.e., when comparing 1991 with 1996), the difference between those high and low in adversities in the timing of first occupational preferences no longer existed. Again, perhaps stretching the data too far, this can be seen as reflecting a situation now common in East and West: All feel more or less insecure regarding prospects in the job market, and thus virtually nobody, not even those pressed by adversities in the past, feels compelled to speed up the formation of occupational preferences.

In sum, social change in Germany, as studied here, seems to have some profound effects on the pace of youthful psychosocial transitions. Further research on particular aspects of the ongoing changes and on particular antecedents of interindividual differences is needed.

References

Adler, M. A. (1997). Social change and declines in marriage and fertility in Eastern Germany. *Journal of Marriage and the Family, 59,* 31–49.

Aquilino, W. S. (1991). Family structure and home leaving: A further specification of the relationship. *Journal of Marriage and the Family, 53,* 999–1010.

B. F. J. (Ed.). Bundesministerium für Frauen und Jugend (1992). *Frauen in der Bundesrepublik Deutschland* [Women in the Federal Republic of Germany]. Bonn Germany: Boehm Stendal.

Conger, R. D., Conger, K. J., Elder, G. H., Lorenz, F. O., Simons, R. L., & Whitbeck, L. B. (1993). Family economic stress and adjustment of early adolescent girls. *Developmental Psychology, 29,* 206–219.

Dekovic, M., Noom, M. J., & Meeus, W. (1997). Expectations regarding development during adolescence: Parental and adolescent perceptions. *Journal of Youth and Adolescence, 26,* 253–272.

Dornbusch, S., Carlsmith, J., Gross, R., Martin, J., Jennings, D., Rosenberg, A., & Duke, P. (1981). Sexual development, age, and dating: A comparison of biological and social influences upon one set of behaviors. *Child Development, 52,* 179–185.

Elder, G. H. (1985). Perspectives on the life course. In G. H. Elder, Jr. (Ed.), *Life course dynamics* (pp. 23–49). Ithaca, NY: Cornell University Press.

Elder, G. H. (1998). The life course as developmental theory. *Child Development, 69,* 1–12.

Elder, G. H., Caspi, A., & Burton, L. M. (1988). Adolescent transitions in developmental perspective: Sociological and historical insights. In M. Gunnar (Ed.), *Minnesota Symposia on Child Psychology,* (Vol. 21, pp. 151–180). Hillsdale, NJ: Erlbaum.

Elder, G. H., & O'Rand, A. M. (1995). Adult lives in a changing society. In K. S. Cook, G. A. Fine, & J. S. House (Eds.), *Sociological perspectives on social psychology.* Needham Heights, MA: Allyn & Bacon.

Feldman, S. S., & Rosenthal, D. A. (1994). Culture makes a difference or does it? A comparison of adolescents in Hong Kong, Australia, and the United States. In R. K. Silbereisen & E. Todt (Eds.), *Adolescence in context* (pp. 99–120). New York: Springer-Verlag.

Feldman, S. S., Quatman, T. (1988). Factors influencing age expectations for adolescent autonomy: A study of early adolescents and parents. *Journal of Early Adolescence, 8,* 325–343.

Fischer, A. (1992). Zur Stichprobe. In Jugendwerk der Deutschen Shell (Ed.), *Jugend '92, Vol. 4* (pp. 59–63). Opladen, Germany: Leske & Budrich.

Friedrich, W., & Foerster, P. (1994). Jugendliche in den neuen Bundeslaendern [Adolescents in the new federal states]. In H.-J. Veen (Ed.), *Eine Jugend in Deutschland? Orientierungen und Verhaltensweisen der Jugend in Ost und West* (pp. 119–152). Opladen, Germany: Leske & Budrich.

George, L. K. (1993). Sociological perspectives on life transitions. *Annual Revue of Sociology, 19,* 353–373.

Grob, A., Flammer, A., & Rhyn, H. (1995). Entwicklungsaufgaben als soziale Normsetzung: Reaktionen Erwachsener auf Loesungsmodi von Entwicklungsaufgaben Jugendlicher [Developmental tasks as social norms: Adults' reactions to adolescents' solving of developmental tasks]. *Zeitschrift für Sozialisationsforschung und Erziehungssoziologie, 15,* 45–62.

Havighurst, R. J. (1972). *Developmental tasks and education.* London: Longman Inc.

Jugendwerk der Deutschen Shell (Ed.) (1992). Jugend '92. Opladen, Germany: Leske & Budrich.

Kolvin, I., Miller, F. J. W., Scott, D. M., Gatzanis, S. R. M., & Fleeting, M. (1990). *Continuities of deprivation? The Newcastle 1000 family study.* Alershot: Avebury.

Kommission für Zukunftsfragen der Freistaaten Bayern und Sachsen. (1996). *Erwerbstätigkeit und Arbeitslosigkeit in Deutschland.* Bonn: Author.

Kornadt, H.-J. (1996). Erziehung und Bildung im Transformationsprozeß. [Education and training in the transformation process]. In S. E. Hormuth, W. R. Heinz, H.-J. Kornadt, H. Sydow, & G. Trommsdorff (Eds.), *Individuelle Entwicklung, Bildung und Berufsverläufe* (pp. 11–78). Opladen, Germany: Leske & Budrich.

Lerner, R. M., & Busch-Rossnagel, N. A. (Eds.). (1981). *Individuals as producers of their development: A life-span perspective.* New York: Academic Press.

Nauck, B. (1993). Sozialstrukturelle Differenzierung der Lebensbedingungen von Kindern in West- und Ostdeutschland [Socio-structural differentiation of developmental ecologies in West and East

Germany]. In M. Markefta & B. Nauck (Eds.), *Handbuch der Kindheitsforschung* (S. 143–163). Neuwied, Germany: Luchterhand.

Patterson, G. R., DeBaryshe, B. D., & Ramsey, E. A. (1989). Developmental perspective on antisocial behavior. *American Psychologist, 44,* 329–335.

Reitzle, M., & Silbereisen, R. K. (1996). Werte in den alten und neuen Bundesländern [Values in the old and new states]. In R. K. Silbereisen, L. A. Vaskovics, & J. Zinnecker (Eds.), *Jungsein in Deutschland* (pp. 41–569). Opladen, Germany: Leske & Budrich.

Reitzle, M., & Riemenschneider, U. (1996). Gleichaltrige und Erwachsene als Bezugsperson. In R. K. Silbereisen, L. A. Vaskovics & J. Zinnecker (Eds.), Jungsein in Deutschland [Peers and adults as significant other]. Opladen: Leske und Budrich.

Rinker, B., & Schwarz, B. (1996). Familäre Belastungen in der Kindheit und das Entwicklungstempo von Kindern [Family adversities and the rate of development in children]. In J. Zinnecker & R. K. Silbereisen (Eds.), *Kindheit in Deutschland* (pp. 359–370). Weinheim, Germany: Juventa.

Russell, A., Brewer, N., & Hogben, N. (1997). Psychological variables associated with the household work of girls and boys in early adolescence. *Journal of Early Adolescence, 17,* 197–215.

Rutter, M., & Smith, D. J. (Eds.) (1995). *Psychosocial disorders in young people: Time trends and their origins.* Chichester, England: Wiley.

Schwartz, S. H., & Bilsky, W. (1990). Toward a theory of the universal content and structure of values: Extentions and cross-cultural replications. *Journal of Personality and Social Psychology, 58,* 878–891.

Silbereisen, R. K., Noack, P., & von Eye, A. (1992). Adolescents' development of romantic friendship and change in favorite leisure contexts. *Journal of Adolescent Research, 7,* 80–93.

Silbereisen, R. K., & Schmitt-Rodermund, E. (1995). German immigrants in Germany: Adaptation of adolescents' timetables for autonomy. In M. Hofer, P. Noack, & J. Youniss (Eds.), *Psychological responses to social change: Human development in changing environments* (pp. 105–125). Berlin: Walter de Gruyter.

Silbereisen, R. K., Schwarz, B., & Rinker, B. (1996). The timing of psychosocial transitions in adolescence: Commonalities and differences in unified Germany. In J. Youniss (Ed.), *After the wall: Family adaptation in East and West Germany* (pp. 23–38). San Francisco: Jossey-Bass.

Silbereisen, R. K., Vaskovics, L. A., & Zinnecker, J. (Eds.). (1996). *Jungsein in Deutschland* [Being adolescent in Germany]. Opladen, Germany: Leske & Budrich.

Steinberg, L., & Belsky, J. (1996). An evolutionary perspective on psychopathology in adolescence. In D. Cicchetti & S. Toth (Eds.), *Adolescence: Opportunities and challenges* (pp. 93–124). Rochester, NY: University of Rochester Press.

Trommsdorff, G., & Chakkarath, P. (1996). Kindheit im Transformationsprozeß [Childhood in the process of transformation]. In S. E. Hormuth, W. R. Heinz, H.-J. Kornadt, H. Sydow, & G. Trommsdorff (Eds.), *Individuelle Entwicklung, Bildung und Berufsverläufe* (pp. 11–78). Opladen, Germany: Leske & Budrich.

Watkins, S. C., Menken, J. A., & Bongaarts, J. (1987). Demographic foundations of family change. *American Sociology Revue, 52,* 46–58.

Wiesner, M., & Silbereisen, R. K. (1996). Freizeitverhalten bei Jugendlichen in Ost und West als Funktion des Identitätsstatus [Leisure time conduct of young people in the East and West as a function of identity status]. *Unterrichtswissenschaft, 24,* 128–141.

Willet, J. B., & Singer, J. D. (1991). How long did it take? Using survival analysis in educational and psychological research. In L. M. Collins & J. L. Horn (Eds.), *Best methods for the analysis of change: Recent advances, unanswered questions, future directions* (pp. 310–327). Washington, DC: American Psychological Association.

Zapf, W. (1996). Zwei Geschwindigkeiten in Ost- und Westdeutschland [Two speeds in East and West Germany]. In M. Diewald & K. U. Mayer (Eds.), *Zwischenbilanz der Wiedervereinigung, Strukturwandel und Mobilität im Transformationsprozeß* (pp. 317–328). Opladen, Germany: Leske & Budrich.

Zinnecker, J., & Silbereisen, R. K. (Eds.). (1996). *Kindheit in Deutschland. Aktueller Survey über Kinder und ihre Eltern* [Childhood in Germany: Current survey on children and their parents]. Weinheim, Germany: Juventa.

8   Adolescents in Changing Social Structures: Bounded Agency in Life Course Perspective

Michael J. Shanahan and Kathryn E. Hood

The intersection of social change and human lives represents a paradigmatic theme of sociology and the life course (Elder & O'Rand, 1994). The profound social changes of the 18th and 19th centuries, encompassing the rise of the metropolis and the spread of factories, inspired scientific inquiries into human communities and their many groupings (Lepenies, 1988; Mazlish, 1989). Especially in France, Germany, and England, scholars began to examine the implications of urban life and the industrial mode of production for personal identity. However, the role of the individual in most early theories of social change was notably minimal. As Giddens (1979) observed, these treatments viewed the individual as a "cultural dope," the fully determined product of social forces that evolved independently of people. Thus, the city dweller invariably suffered from malaise, and the laborer of capitalism was necessarily alienated. Agency – in its broadest sense of something that causes something else – was located in the society's structural characteristics and normative dictates (Sztompka, 1993).

Such an orientation gradually came to include people as agents capable of constructing their lives. This theme became prominent with the widespread acceptance of dynamic models of individual development, as one finds, for example, in Piaget or Vygotsky (Bidell, 1988). Individuals proactively and reactively engage with challenges and resources, and these engagements often lead to the emergence and consolidation of new, adaptive capacities. In a life course framework, agency at the level of the person can be defined as *the individual's capacity to formulate and pursue life plans*. A central assumption of this definition is that agency extends across the phases of life, connecting earlier and later experiences with goals.

Yet life course agency can be complicated by social change: People make long-term plans about the direction and pace of their lives, but changing circumstances may interfere with these plans. That is, personal agency and social change are not always harmonious. Social change often brings with it pervasive modifications in a society's institutions, organizations, small groups, and interpersonal relationships.

The authors thank John Howell White for his original illustrations (Figures 1a and 1b).

In turn, these organizational and relational modifications can undermine an individual's ability to unify the life phases with goal-directed behaviors. This problem can be particularly acute for adolescents and young adults, who often formulate and begin to follow through with life course plans involving school, work, and family.

How can we conceptualize agency in adolescence as a life course phenomenon that interplays with social change? We examine conceptions of agency and its range of meanings in life course theory, from individual psychological mechanisms that effect and support life-long goals to models of relationships in the family that promote a sense of efficacy. We then turn to perspectives on macrosocial structures and historical change. What we find lacking in discussions to date is a theoretical integration of individual factors and societal change as co-constitutive elements. To address this lack, we adapt a probabilistic developmental model from biology, C. H. Waddington's "epigenetic landscape," to portray the interrelationships between personal agency and the constraints of changing social structures. The central theme of our chapter is that agency reflects the interplay among individual efforts, group-based strategies, and macrosocial structures – an interplay we term "bounded agency."

Adolescence and Agency in Life Course Perspective

Agency is the capacity to articulate life plans and carry through with them in a meaningful way that extends across the entire lifetime, including future orientations for education, work, and family. The psychological processes that support the formulation and pursuit of life goals include control beliefs (e.g., Bandura, 1995; Skinner & Chapman, 1987), goal-directed behaviors (e.g., Freese & Sabini, 1985; Heckhausen & Schulz, 1995) and reflexive monitoring, intelligence, and motivation (for an inclusive model, see Lerner, 1982). Agency also reflects the social structural conditions for individual development, which may promote or interfere with a young person's pursuit of life plans. However, models of agency in life course perspective typically have emphasized either the individual's capacity to shape the biography or the society's structures of opportunity with less attention to the relationship between these factors.

Agency as a Developmental, Psychological Characteristic

Charlotte Bühler made an early and influential contribution to the developmental study of agency with her conceptual model of "the goal-directed life" (Bühler & Massarik, 1968). According to this model, the life course must be analyzed in terms of "integrated strivings" to fulfill personal goals and aspirations viewed in relation to a self-consciously chosen life project. Drawing on an extensive sample of life-histories, Bühler concluded that between ages 8 and 12, children develop an achievement style that reflects their fundamental orientation to goals, including their work style, values, and beliefs. Particularly important is an "integrating tendency" that identifies the goals that best suit an individual's abilities and organizes these goals to arrive at a sense of meaningfulness in life. Life goals then remain vague and tentative until the adult years (extending from 25 to 45), which bring with them a definite and meaningful goal structure. Bühler's model is primarily focused on the dynamic self, the integrating tendencies of personality, creativity, intelligence, achievement motivation style, values, and beliefs that direct behavior and instill coherence and meaningfulness in life. She established several basic themes for the study of agency in the life course, including an emphasis on the life plan, its motivational nature, and the analysis of behaviors as strivings toward the fulfillment of goals (for related models, see Cantor & Fleeson, 1991; Little, 1983).

John Clausen's (1991a, 1993) model of planful competence in the life course also views agency as a fundamentally developmental characteristic of the individual. Planful competence is a personality characteristic related to the individual's self-confidence, intellectual investment, and dependability, all of which have broad relevance for life course mechanisms and outcomes (Clausen, 1991b). Critical to his model is developmental timing in the acquisition of planful competence. Clausen argues that most adults possess a functional degree of planfulness, whereas children possess very little; however, individuals who have a solid sense of planful competence by the end of the high school years will "better prepare themselves for adult roles and will select, and be selected for, opportunities that give them a head start" (Clausen, 1993, p. 21). Thus, those who are more planfully competent at midadolescence will experience life course transitions with greater ease and enact adult roles with greater success.

Clausen's (1991a) studies of children from the Berkeley and Oakland samples partially support this model. Planful competence in senior high school (age 15 to 18 years) significantly predicts personality resemblance between ages 18 and 60, marital stability, and educational attainment for males and females as well as occupational attainment and career stability for males. Although the data do not allow for an examination of his central hypothesis – that the timing of the acquisition of planful competence determines its significance in the life course – his studies nevertheless demonstrate that planfulness in later adolescence has pervasive implications for the life course, perhaps extending into old age.

Bühler and Clausen locate the significant beginnings of agency in the early life course. For Bühler, these processes begin in late childhood, although they are not fully articulated until much later in life. For Clausen, the level of planful competence that is achieved between the ages of 15 and 18 is critical. However, neither of these models addresses social context or historical change.

Agency in Social Settings

Contextual issues have been addressed by social structural orientations that emphasize (1) groups and interpersonal relationships as sources of agency and (2) the constraining and enabling nature of macrosocial structures. The foundations for the first perspective were established by W. I. Thomas, an influential sociologist of the Chicago School, and later elaborated to a considerable degree in the studies of Glen H. Elder, Jr. The second perspective is illustrated in instructive ways in the chapters by Bynner, Schlegel, and Silbereisen in the present volume.

Group-Based Agency. Thomas's model identifies how agency functions within the family and other groups (Thomas & Thomas, 1932; see also Volkart, 1951). Central to the model is the "crisis," any situation in which habitual behaviors are no longer effective. The crisis is an abstract category that is highly inclusive: As Thomas (1909) notes, the interruption of habit may follow from "an incident, a stimulation, [or] a suggestion" (p. 18). The crisis elicits attention followed by efforts to reestablish control. Thomas viewed this basic cycle of crisis-attention-control as integral to the life course: "The incidents of birth, death, adolescence, and marriage, while not unanticipated, are always foci of attention and occasions for control" (1909, pp. 13–26). Thus, agency is found in the context-specific adjustive behaviors enacted to regain control and habit through life.

The analysis of agency as a group-based process has been carried forward by Glen Elder's Social Change Project, which has focused in part on how young people surmounted three contexts of disadvantage: the Great Depression, an economically distressed rural area, and the inner city. Like Thomas, Elder begins with a detailed inquiry into context, including its history, resources, and points of risk for youth. One recurring observation made in the course of these studies is the prominent role of parents as socially based sources of agency for their children and their families.

For example, Elder's (1974) studies of the Great Depression showed that families often responded as a unit to economic decline, and that greater work responsibilities were assumed by young children. Boys from the Oakland sample (ages 7 and 8 at the time of the Stock Market crash in 1929) who acquired paid jobs were viewed as more socially independent and responsible in financial matters in later life. By making genuine contributions to the household economy as part of a larger effort, the Oakland boys were able to surmount the crisis and enhance their sense of maturity and efficacy (for similar findings in the distressed rural sample, see Shanahan, Elder, Burchinal, & Conger, 1996). In contrast, the children of the Berkeley sample (newborns in 1929) were too young to participate in these household strategies. Indeed, at age 30 the Oakland men exhibited more stable careers and assigned a greater priority to dependable behavior than the Berkeley men. Studies of children in the inner city suggest that proactive and nurturant parenting is another family-based source of agency for young people in inner-city neighborhoods (Elder, Eccles, Ardelt, & Lord, 1995). Similarly, other research points to the potentially important role of school teachers in young people's lives (Eccles et al., 1993; Silverberg & Gondoli, 1996).

These findings clearly move the focus of analysis away from the agency of the child to the efficacy of his or her parents and the school. A sense of efficacy among parents and teachers may translate into the ability of the family, including its younger members, to surmount hard times, which is a relationship mediated by parenting practices (see also Schneewind, 1995, on families; Oettingen, 1995, on schools).

Changing Social Structures. Social change can expand or limit the range of choices that exist for an adolescent. When social change creates conditions with few viable choices, individual and family-based agency may become less consequential for later life outcomes. Rainer Silbereisen's chapter (this volume) documents the implications of German reunification for the timing of the transition to adulthood. When compared with the role of the state in individual lives in the former West, the more extensive regulatory structures of the former East largely determined the timing of transitions to adulthood. These structures restricted the available options, channeling young people into adult roles in school and the workplace. However, the ongoing process of reunification of the former East and West Germany should act as an enabling source of change, relaxing the restrictions on life options for young people in the former East by disassembling some of the state's role in regulating the life course. This possibility in turn suggests that the influence of individual and family-based agency on the timing of the transition to adulthood will increase for young people in the former East when compared with their predecessors. Yet the disadvantage, as Blossfeld (1994) noted, is that less bounded social systems bring with them a greater potential for unpredictability in one's life history with more possibilities for career floundering and identity diffusion among unprepared youth.

This theme – that macrosocial structures can influence the importance of personal agency in pursuing life plans – is also illustrated by a study of adolescent planful competence and life-time educational achievement in cohorts of men who grew up during the Great Depression (Shanahan, Elder, & Miech, 1997). The study involved men born between 1900 and 1920 from the Terman Sample of Gifted Children. The research distinguished between the older cohort, those born between 1900 and 1910 who were in college and would normally have begun careers during the Great Depression, and the younger cohort, those born between 1910 and 1920 whose college years postdated the Depression; this latter group would have begun their careers in the post–World War II economic boom. For the older cohort, it was hypothesized that adolescent planful competence would not predict adult educational attainment. Rather, very high levels of unemployment during the Depression would support prolonged schooling for this cohort, regardless of their planfulness (see Bynner, this volume; Duncan, 1965; Walters & O'Connell, 1988). In contrast, planful competence in adolescence was expected to predict adult educational attainment in the younger cohort, which was presented with viable choices involving employment opportunities and continuation in school.

As expected, planfulness at age 14 positively predicted educational attainment, but only for the men born between 1910 and 1920 who finished school during the postwar economic boom. Planful competence did not predict educational attainment for men from the older cohort who remained in school regardless of their planful competence, presumably to avoid the poor economy (Shanahan et al., 1997). Thus, for the older cohort, the lack of economic opportunity precluded entry into the workplace, and, under these circumstances, personal agency did not predict level of schooling. In short, the Terman men's lives reflect bounded agency as found in the intersection of economic opportunities and their planful competence.

Bynner's chapter (this volume) shows further that in times of social change individuals lacking socioeconomic resources and human capital are likely to become even more highly marginalized. The implications of social change and the range of options that are effectively available to an individual not only reflect society's broader structures but also the individual's status in the society. For example, expansions in the American economy have been more likely to pull students of lower- or middle-class backgrounds from school than students from upper socioeconomic strata (Shanahan, Miech, & Elder, 1998). The important role of socioeconomic status is also evident in Schlegel's (this volume) observation that, in contemporary Poland, St. Valentine's Day is celebrated only by an upper stratum of students who plan to go to college. This group typically defers the transition to marriage, relying on a prolonged period of dating for intimacy. Students adopted St. Valentine's Day, but this adoption was conditioned by the anticipated life course of the college bound.

In short, social change can serve as a source of enablement, increasing the range of pathways into adulthood. At the same time, experiences of the former East Germany and of the older cohort in the Great Depression illustrate that the state, economic change, and institutions can become overwhelming forces, restricting the range of pathways and allocating individuals into pathways. Options reflecting social structures, agency, and the individual's status in a stratified society together shape adolescent transitions into adulthood.

The Episocial Landscape and "Bounded Agency"

How can theory encompass the combinations of macrostructural pressures and individual propensities that are interactively embedded in social history? We adapt a descriptive model of biological development, C. H. Waddington's (1971) "epigenetic landscape," to represent the life course dynamics of bounded agency. Waddington's landscape consists of an inclined plane with an undulating surface through which balls move by the force of gravity. The elevations and depressions of the surface represent developmental pathways to predictable outcomes (as in Figures 1a and 1b). Waddington proposed that predictability occurs through corrective tendencies that "canalize" organisms into particular patterns or "chreods" (Waddington, 1975; see also Gottlieb, 1992). The model has considerable intuitive appeal, as demonstrated by its wide use in developmental science, including biology, psychobiology, behavioral genetics, and psychology (e.g., McCall, 1981).

a 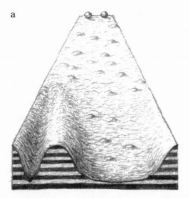   b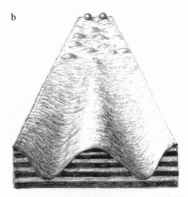

Figure 1. Changing Social Structures and Life Histories Portrayed as Episocial Landscapes. Individual agency (low and high agency represented by the two starting points in each figure) will be less predictive of pathways of education during historical periods with fewer available choices (Figure 1a) when compared with periods with viable options (Figure 1b).

The visual metaphor can also represent the interactions between agency and social structures in the life course. The landscape is seen as a probability surface that corresponds to the social structure of opportunity. Historical time can be represented by changing patterns of hills and valleys: The downward movement of balls through the landscape indicates possible life histories. Thus, the chreods represent temporally specific pathways to adulthood.

According to this perspective, the landscape is a developmental topology that differentiates life histories. It begins with little surface variation, as in the figures; this represents the relative similarity of young children with respect to social opportunities when compared with older age groups (Dannefer, 1984). However, by late adolescence, the individual is situated in a chreod, a pathway to adulthood, with less likelihood for a major shift into a different chreod. The steeper sides of the deepening valleys prevent an individual from changing into a neighboring chreod. This steepness reflects the merging of social roles with personal identity, expectations from others, specific forms of certification, and rites of passage into specific jobs, interpersonal relationships, and memberships in organizations–all of which serve to promote stability in the life course. The greater distance between chreods at the end of the life course represents the greater variability in attained status observed among adults.

Adolescence is a transitional life period in this model. Chreods first begin to form in adolescence, although there is still an appreciable probability that an individual headed toward one pathway could switch to a different pathway. This corresponds to Clausen's argument that planfulness in adolescence is especially determinative of pathways into adulthood. However, the steep valleys of later life indicate a decreasing probability that an individual could switch to a different chreod or pathway.

Unlike other landscape diagrams, which have smooth surfaces, our representation (Figures 1a and 1b) adds randomly situated bumps that perturb the course of development. These reflect chance encounters and accidental events of life that may have a high degree of influence on the pathways taken by an individual. Bandura (1982) noted that separate chains of events may intersect fortuitously, producing novel branching in a life plan for good or for ill. Bandura's early discussions presage themes of the dynamical systems (or "chaos") approach to development, which emphasizes that very small changes early in development may produce large effects later in life (see Hood, 1995; Smith & Thelen, 1993; Thelen & Smith, 1994.) These events may be evidenced in oral life histories by such rhetorical formulations as "the defining moment," "the turning point," "the big break," or "where things started to go wrong" (see also Crockett, 1995).

This episocial landscape model can be illustrated with results from Shanahan, Elder, and Miech's (1997) study, as shown in Figures 1a and 1b. Two groups of individuals possess different amounts of planful competence: The group to the left in each diagram possesses relatively little planful competence, whereas the group to the right in each diagram has relatively high planful competence. Because the older cohort graduated from college during a period of high unemployment, most chose to continue for a master's degree regardless of their earlier level of planful competence. As shown in Figure 1a, at that historical time, it is probable that from both starting points (low or high planfulness), individuals would be canalized into the chreod to the right, which indicates a higher level of education. By contrast, the younger cohort faced a viable choice between continuing school and taking a job in the postwar economic boom; only those with high planfulness continued their educational careers, as shown by Figure 1b.

The model suggests that across societies and through historical time, the role of agency in the transition to adulthood can be studied in terms of the number of pathways (or chreods) an adolescent has access to based on initial status in the society, the role of the state in allocating individuals to pathways, how early in the life course these pathways form (as hills and valleys begin to differentiate), and how quickly the pathways entrench individuals (or deepen), making change into other pathways less likely. These parameters interact to determine the relative importance of individuals, group-based agency, and macrosocial structures.

Bidirectional Processes in Chreod Formation

The metaphor of the episocial landscape raises two relatively neglected issues in studies of adolescence: how cohorts of adolescents change their own opportunity structures and why models of adolescent behavior often have low explanatory power. The metaphor suggests that as cohorts of adolescents first meet the resistance of chreods (i.e., life histories encounter distinctly structured pathways into adulthood, such as tracking in high schools), a process of erosion may occur that changes the shape of the chreods themselves. Indeed, historical studies show that cohorts of adolescents have redefined their life phase and the transition to adulthood through spending patterns and cultural innovations, sexual mores and behaviors, and religious and political activism (Kett, 1977; Moran, 1991). An example is the youth peace movement in the United States during the war in Vietnam: in resistance to the military draft, older adolescents helped to bring the war to an end, and the draft was abolished.

Unpredictable outcomes are inherent in this model deriving from properties of development itself. It is well known that flow patterns can give rise to unpredictable turbulence. Applied to the episocial landscape, the concept of *epigenetic turbulence* suggests that, as developmental flow meets the chreod walls, behavioral patterns at that point in the life course will exhibit more variability within and between individuals. Young people respond to increased social constraints with accommodation but also with attempts to redefine the self, change social structures, and select new pathways. As chreods deepen sharply (i.e., structured pathways entrench individual life histories more quickly), epigenetic turbulence is likely. Patterned and continuous turbulence can in turn lead to new pathways for development as established chreods give way to new structures. From this perspective, behavior in adolescence will be characterized by a relatively high degree of unpredictability, and this indeterminacy will occur as a reaction to newly encountered structured pathways to adulthood.

Summary and Implications for Empirical Research

Our theoretical analysis suggests that a fully specified model of agency must include the conceptualization and measurement of adolescents (1) across multiple dimensions that reflect their capacity to formulate and pursue goals, (2) their close relationships and proximal settings that mold goals and facilitate or hinder their pursuit, and (3) the macrostructural context as it defines the structured pathways of education, work, and family. It is the confluence of these elements that produces "bounded agency," the dynamic interplay between individual efforts, group-based strategies, and social structures. Furthermore, the capacity of structured pathways to sort adolescents into adult roles and positions within society reflects several factors, including a young person's initial status in a stratified society, the number of pathways available, the role of the state in allocating individuals to pathways, how early in the life course various pathways form, and how quickly these pathways entrench individuals to the exclusion of alternative routes through life. Thus, agency cannot be understood without measurement, sampling, and design strategies that are longitudinal and include features of context from the household to the more broadly defined society. Indeed, cross-national studies that focus on variability in the social organization of the life course have shed much light on the role of macrostructures in the transition to adulthood (e.g., Bynner & Heinz, 1991).

Comparative strategies must extend to inequalities among children within societies. Issues of race, social class, and gender have been powerful canalizing factors because they provide and limit access to developmental pathways into adulthood. For example, in the Terman Sample of Gifted Children (discussed earlier), almost all of the girls, even those girls with childhood IQ scores above 170, became office workers or housewives who were supported by their husbands' careers. Among these women, there was no evidence of the relationship between ability and attainment so frequently observed among the Terman men. Measurement, sampling and research design strategies must attend both to macrostructural variations through time and across societies and to the powerful social forces of inequality operating within societies.

Finally, our discussion of the life course as an episocial landscape suggests that the standard approach to analyzing data, involving variants of the general linear model, is but one of several methodological orientations that should be used. When young people encounter structured pathways into adulthood, unpredictable behavior is likely. Qualitative methodologies are ideal in such cases, especially because the unpredictable behaviors of youth may lead to the restructuring of the pathways. Theoretical models and empirical realities require the careful juxtaposition of quantitative and qualitative strategies.

In short, the chapters in this volume illustrate the progress that has been achieved in thinking about the central role of agency in the transition to adulthood and the new challenges that must be faced for further progress. These challenges include drawing upon diverse measures of agency's multiple aspects, using research designs that allow for comparisons across different social structures (including the same society through time and multiple societies), and viewing lives as they are shaped by socially based inequalities. Addressing these challenges will in turn lead to a better understanding of young people, their many social worlds, and their many futures in times of risk and uncertainty.

References

Bandura, A. (1982). Self-efficacy mechanism in human agency. *American Psychologist, 37,* 122–147.

Bandura, A. (1995). Exercise of personal and collective efficacy in changing societies. In A. Bandura (Ed.), *Self-efficacy in changing societies* (pp. 1–45). New York: Cambridge University Press.

Bidell, T. (1988). Vygotsky, Piaget, and the dialectic of development. *Human Development, 31,* 329–348.

Blossfeld, H.-P. (1994). *Different systems of vocational training and transition from school to career: The German dual system in cross-national comparison.* Paper presented at The Determinants of Transitions in Youth conference, Barcelona, Spain.

Bühler, C., & Massarik, F. (Eds.). (1968). *The course of human life: A study of goals in the humanistic perspective.* New York: Springer-Verlag.

Bynner, J., & Heinz, W. (1991). Matching samples and analyzing their differences in a cross-national study of labour market entry in England and West Germany. *International Journal of Comparative Sociology, 1–2,* 137–153.

Cantor, N., & Fleeson, W. (1991). Life tasks and self-regulatory tasks. In M. L. Maehr & P. R. Pintrich (Eds.), *Advances in achievement motivation, vol. 7* (pp. 327–369). Greenwich, CT: JAI.

Clausen, J. (1991a). Adolescent competence and the shaping of the life course. *American Journal of Sociology, 96,* 805–842.

Clausen, J. (1991b). Adolescent competence and the life course, or why one social psychologist needed a concept of personality. *Social Psychology Quarterly, 54,* 4–14.

Clausen, J. (1993). *American lives: Looking back at the children of the Great Depression.* Berkeley: University of California Press.

Crockett, L. J. (1995). Developmental paths in adolescence: Commentary. In L. J. Crockett & A. C. Crouter (Eds.), *Pathways through adolescence* (pp. 75–84). Mahwah, NJ: Erlbaum.

Dannefer, D. (1984). Adult development and social theory: A paradigmatic reappraisal. *American Sociological Review, 49,* 100–116.

Duncan, B. (1965). Drop-outs and the unemployed. *Journal of Political Economy, 73,* 121–34.

Eccles, J,. Midgeley, C., Wigfield, A., Buchanan, C., Reuman, D., Flanagan, C., & MacIver, D. (1993). Development during adolescence: The impact of stage-environment fit on young adolescents' experiences in schools and families. *American Psychologist, 48,* 90–101.

Elder, G. H., Jr. (1974). *Children of the Great Depression.* Chicago: University of Chicago Press.

Elder, G. H., Jr., Eccles, J. S., Ardelt, M., & Lord, S. (1995). Inner-city parents under economic pressure: Perspectives on the strategies of parenting. *Journal of Marriage and the Family, 57,* 771–784.

Elder, G. H., Jr., & O'Rand, A. M. (1994). Adult lives in a changing society. In K. Cook, J., House, & G. Fine (Eds.), *Handbook of social psychology: Sociological perspectives* (pp. 452–475). New York: Basic Books.

Freese, M., & Sabini, J. (Eds.) (1985). *Goal-directed behavior: The concept of action in psychology.* Hillsdale, NJ: Erlbaum.

Giddens, A. (1979). *Central problems in social theory: Action, structure, and contradiction in social analysis.* London: MacMillan.

Gottlieb, G. (1992). *Individual development and evolution: The genesis of novel behavior.* New York: Oxford.

Heckhausen, J., & Schulz, R. (1995). A life-span theory of control. *Psychological Review, 102,* 284–304.

Hood, K. E. (1995). Dialectical and dynamical systems of approach and withdrawal: Is fighting a fractal form? In K. Hood, G. Greenberg, & E. Tobach (Eds.), *Behavioral development: Concepts of approach-withdrawal and integrative levels: The T. C. Schneirla Conference Series, Vol. 5.* New York: Garland.

Kett, J. (1977). *Rites of passage: Adolescence in America 1790 to the present.* New York: Basic Books.

Lepenies, W. (1988). *Between literature and science: The rise of sociology.* Cambridge, England: Cambridge University Press.

Lerner, R. M. (1982). Children and adolescents as producers of their own development. *Developmental Review, 2,* 342–370.

Little, B. R. (1983). Personal projects: A rationale and method for investigation. *Environment and Behavior, 15,* 273–309.

Mazlish, B. (1991). *A new science: The breakdown of connections and the birth of sociology.* University Park, PA: Pennsylvania State University Press.

Moran, G. F. (1991). Adolescence in Colonial America. In R. M. Lerner, A. C. Petersen, & J. Brooks-Gunn (Eds.), *Encyclopedia of adolescence* (pp. 157–171). New York: Garland.

McCall, R. B. (1981). Nature-nurture and the two realms of development: A proposed integration with respect to mental development. *Child Development 52,* 1–12.

Oettingen, G. (1995). Cross-cultural perspectives on self-efficacy. In A. Bandura (Ed.), *Self-efficacy in changing societies* (pp. 149–176). New York: Cambridge University Press.

Schneewind, K. A. (1995). Impact of family processes on control beliefs. In A. Bandura (Ed.), *Self-efficacy in changing societies* (pp. 114–148). New York: Cambridge University Press.

Shanahan, M. J., Elder, G. H., Jr., Burchinal, M., & Conger, R. D. (1996). Adolescent paid labor and relationships with parents: Early work-family linkages. *Child Development, 67,* 2183–2200.

Shanahan, M. J., Elder, G. H., & Miech, R. A. (1997). History and agency in men's lives: Pathways to achievement in cohort perspective. *Sociology of Education 70,* 54–67.

Shanahan, M. J., Miech, R. A., & Elder, G. H., Jr. (1998). Changing pathways to adult attainment: historical patterns of school, work, and family. *Social Forces, 77,* 231–256.

Silverberg, S. B., & Gondoli, D. M. (1996). Autonomy in adolescence: A contextualized perspective. In

G. R. Adams, R. Montemayor, & T. P. Gulotta (Eds.), *Psychosocial development during adolescence: Progress in developmental contextualism*. London: Sage Publications Ltd.

Skinner, E. A., & Chapman, M. (1987). Resolution of a developmental paradox: How can perceived internality increase, decrease, and remain the same across middle childhood? *Developmental Psychology, 23*, 44–48.

Smith, L. B., & Thelen, E. (Eds.). (1993). *A dynamic systems approach to development: Applications*. Cambridge, MA: MIT Press.

Sztompka, P. (1993). *The sociology of social change*. Oxford: Blackwell.

Thelen, E., & Smith, L. B. (Eds.). (1994). *A dynamic systems approach to the development of cognition and action*. Cambridge, MA: MIT Press.

Thomas, W. I. (1909). *Source book for social origins*. Boston, Richard G. Badger.

Thomas, W. I., & Thomas, D. S. (1932). *The child in America*. New York, Knopf.

Vallacher, R. R. (Ed.). (1994). *Dynamical systems in social psychology*. San Diego, CA: Academic Press.

Volkart, E. H. (1951). Introduction: Social behavior and the defined situation. In E. H. Volkhart (Ed.), *Social behavior and personality: Contributions of W. I. Thomas to theory and social research* (pp. 1–32). New York: Social Science Research Council.

Waddington, C. H. (1971). Concepts of development. In E. Tobach, L. R. Aronson, & E. Shaw (Eds.), *The biopsychology of development*. New York: Academic Press.

Waddington, C. H. (1975). *The evolution of an evolutionist*. Ithaca, NY: Cornell University Press.

Walters, P. B., & O'Connell, P. J. (1988). The family, economy, work, and educational participation in the United States, 1890 to 1940. *American Journal of Sociology, 93*, 1116–1152.

Part III

Social Change and Adolescents' Social Contexts

9   Adolescent Peer Relations in Times of Social Change

Peter Noack

Adolescent Peer Relations in Times of Social Change

Peer relations are an issue of major interest in adolescent research. The role peers play in adolescents' lives and their influence on psychosocial development during the transition to adulthood are well documented. The strength and quality of family–peer linkages, teenagers' susceptibility to peer influence, and the developmental outcomes of parent–peer cross-pressure are but a few well-studied examples. So far, most attention has focused on the qualitative and quantitative nature of peer relations, their consequences, and their proximal antecedents, such as experiences in the family or school. Effects of more distal contextual conditions have mostly been neglected (Furman, 1993; Hartup, 1993). The present study sets out to examine possible variations of peer bonds among adolescents who grew up under considerably different societal conditions, namely in East and West Germany, and to explore influences of social change on relationships with age-mates in both parts of the country, which are differentially affected by societal transformations resulting from German unification.

In the following, studies investigating consequences of social change on the relationship and individual level are reported first. Then, peculiarities of the situation of the two Germanys before the unification of the country as well as changes resulting from the process of unification are addressed. This second section focuses particularly on adolescent peer relations. The third section draws together empirical findings to arrive at some tentative hypotheses for the empirical study of peer relations after German unification reported upon in the remaining part of this chapter.

The study is based on an investigation of individuation and social change conducted in collaboration with Manfred Hofer, Elke Wild, and Bärbel Kracke at the University of Mannheim and Klaus Udo Ettrich and Rolf Krause at the University of Leipzig. It is supported by the German Research Council as part of the program Childhood and Adolescence in Germany Before and After Unification. This chapter was previously published in Noack (1999), which appeared in R. K. Silbereisen & A. von Eye (Eds.), *Growing up in times of social change*, published by Walter de Gruyter. Reprinted with permission of Walter de Gruyter, publishers.

137

Influences of Social Change on Individual and
Relationship Development

Influences of macrosocial conditions on adolescent development have mostly been addressed by way of cross-cultural comparison (Kagitcibasi & Berry, 1989; Thomas, 1993). The virtual lack of studies directly examining the impact of social change is surprising, for probably more adolescents are growing up in societies undergoing considerable changes than in a stable macrocontext (cf. Youniss, Noack, & Hofer, 1995). Moreover, in the popular discourse – at least in Europe – rapid transformations of the societal context are pointed out as an important factor jeopardizing the functioning of family and institutional socialization, which may, in turn, drive adolescents into deviant peer goups. Still, the empirical basis for these considerations is far from satisfactory.

A notable exception is a line of work starting with Glen Elder's (1974) seminal study *Children of the Great Depression*. Focusing on economic changes, in particular, as reflected by financial losses on the family level or unemployment of family members, Elder provided evidence for a destabilization of family bonds as a consequence as well as for effects on children's and adolescents' adjustment that were partly mediated by changes of the family system. The central findings could essentially be replicated by studies addressing various background situations such as an economic recession in Germany during the early 1980s (Walper, 1988), the recent farm crisis in the American Midwest (Conger & Elder, 1994), or the transformations taking place in Albania after the collapse of the Eastern bloc (Kloep, 1994). Extending Elder's approach in our own work, we included experiences of social change beyond variations in the family budget in assessments with families in the former East and West Germany. An instrument was developed capturing family members' perceptions of, for instance, growing uncertainty and anomie in society (Noack, Hofer, Kracke, Wild, & Boehnke, 1999). Our analyses showed that relative financial losses as well as other experiences of change, such as a perceived increase of anomie, impact family relationships (Noack, Oepke, & Sassenberg, 1998), different aspects of adolescents' psychosocial adaptation, and political orientations (Hofer, Kracke, Noack, & Klein-Allermann, 1995; Noack, Hofer, Kracke, & Klein-Allermann, 1995).

Despite several successful replications under varying historical and cultural conditions showing the harmful role of losses in the family budget, Elder himself (e.g., Elder & Caspi, 1991; cf. Silbereisen, 1991) points out the complexity of the processes of macrocontextual influence. Its outcomes, for instance, depend on the age of the children in the family. Moreover, initial personality and family characteristics affect the workings of contextual influences. The process of accentuation is a case in point. Changes in the family household economy often seem just to intensify the given situation. Thus, it should be possible to find improvements as well as declines in family relations in response to adverse experiences. Garbarino (1991) makes the general point that the answer to the question of whether given conditions turn out to be developmental opportunities or risks also depends on peculiarities of the societal context. This is convincingly illustrated by Elder's (1974) findings of differential effects of macrosocial conditions at different historical points in time. Likewise, Franz and Herlyn (1995) call for caution when deriving predictions from historical "precedents" in discussing the consequences of German unification among families in the eastern part of the country.

Given the scarcity of earlier research, even less is known concerning adolescents' peer relations in the context of macrosocial conditions and their changes. Consequently, this study of peer relations among young people in postunification Germany is exploratory. A short review of the situation in Germany and the peculiarities of German unification may facilitate the formation of some general hypotheses.

Adolescence in Germany Before and After Unification

In terms of immediate changes, German unification meant a dramatic transformation of the living conditions of East Germans in particular. Almost from one day to the other, new laws, new institutions, and a new economic system governed their lives. The institutional provisions for the young such as day-care and school in the former German Democratic Republic (GDR) differed markedly from those in West Germany, offering an organized exposure to peers for almost every child starting at a very early age (Oswald & Krappmann, 1995). Concerning adolescents, the institutional influence was not confined to the school. Extracurricular activities provided by party youth organizations, state-controlled youth clubs, and vacation camps are but a few examples that sharply contrast with the mainly private and commercialized nature of adolescent leisure time in the western part of the country (Schmidt, 1996).

There is no doubt that organized leisure for adolescents in the GDR was established as a means of directly enforcing educational goals serving societal needs, which were defined by the ruling Socialist party, and to secure collective control over the young. Still, two considerations are necessary at this point. First, adolescents *were* offered various inexpensive leisure pursuits, many of which met the interests of at least younger age groups. After unification, very little of this was still available. Consequently, young former East Germans mentioned the shortage of leisure activities offered, the lack of adequate leisure places, and the costs of interesting activities as problems more often than young former West Germans (Institut für empirische Psychologie, 1995). Secondly, the nature of the explicit and implicit goals guiding the institutional care for young people tells only half of the story of adolesent leisure in the GDR. During the 1980s, young people showed quite some reservation concerning the GDR, for their interest in the country and their loyalty were systematically decreasing (Schmidt, 1996). Thus, many seem to have taken advantage of what was offered only to the extent that it matched their individual interests. This was particularly true for older adolescents who preferred informal gatherings with peers and self-organized activities just as their age-mates in the West. In other words, differences between East and West German adolescents were probably smaller in reality than often assumed. "Hanging out" with friends, watching television, and listening to music, for instance, ranked highly on the leisure time agendas of young people in both parts of the country. Consequently, similarities in leisure time pursuits of adolescents in the former East and West Germany noted in recent survey studies (Institut für empirische Psychologie, 1995; Jugendwerk der Deutschen Shell, 1997; Strzoda & Zinnecker, 1996) have only partly resulted from a trend towards convergence during the years after unification. A major difference can be observed, however, when it comes to membership in clubs, which is systematically more widespread in former West Germany. It is open to speculation whether this divergence is due to a stronger reservation of young former East Germans concerning organized activities or just to the problems of establishing an infrastructure of private sports and leisure time organizations in the East after the closing of state-run institutions.

Likewise, the early exposure to peers in the GDR, collectivist education, and stricter adult surveillance of peer activities seem to have affected young people's peer relations only to a small extent (Jugendwerk der Deutschen Shell, 1997; Oswald, 1992; Oswald & Krappmann, 1995; Zinnecker & Strzoda, 1996). Even though somewhat more young West Germans reported having close friends, being members of cliques, and spending their leisure time together with friends, these differences were small in absolute terms. At the same time, young people from East Germany seemed to be part of slightly larger friendship groups, with members who were more often schoolmates, than in the West. Less is known concerning the quality of peer relations. A thorough investigation into the subjective shades of meaning making up young people's friendship concepts (Oswald & Krappmann, 1995), again points to negligible variations comparing East and West German subsamples. Young Easterners, however, reported higher levels of rejection by normative peers. There is little reason to assume that unification has caused comprehensive changes in these respects.

Unification brought about more dramatic changes concerning the family that could indirectly affect opportunities for, and the nature of, adolescent peer relations. In the GDR, the vast majority of women, including mothers of children and adolescents, participated in the work force, whereas parallel figures for West German women are among the lowest in Europe. Full-time employment of East German women was facilitated by the extensive system of day-care mentioned before. Earlier biographical transitions than in West Germany such as marriage and first childbearing can partly be attributed to these circumstances (Buba, Fruechtel, & Pickel, 1995; Nauck & Joos, 1997). With unification, employment (particularly female full-time employment), birth rates, and the number of marriages swiftly decreased in the East whereas age at first marriage, for instance, went up. Related to these changes, the acceptance of a family model, including no maternal employment or only part-time work of mothers, which is quite widespread in West Germany, also increased among East Germans. It has to be noted that, again, some of these changes had already started before the collapse of East Germany and were then accentuated by the process of unification (Nauck & Joos, 1997). Moreover, what may look like strong differences resulting from markedly disparate political systems can be partly explained in terms of regional variations dating back to the time before the political system of the GDR and its institutions were established. Differences in birth rates and the distribution of nonnormative family forms are cases in point.

In any case, higher rates of maternal full-time employment could be expected to result in lower levels of surveillance of leisure time and friendship activities among adolescents. Indeed, times without adult control in the afternoon were far higher in the GDR than in West Germany despite the system of organized activities provided in the East (Institut für praxisorientierte Sozialforschung, 1993). Curiously, this does not mean that bonds between East German parents and their offspring were weaker than in West German families. In cases where findings of empirical studies revealed any systematic differences, they suggested the opposite (Noack et al., 1995; cf. Oswald & Krappmann, 1995). Young East Germans, for instance, placed a higher premium on parental advice than did their West German age-mates. This situation could have been changed by German unification. On the basis of Elder's findings, economic uncertainty and rising unemployment rates could have set family relations at risk. At the same time, however, family bonds in East Germany may also have improved in response to contextual strain due to the often-discussed role of GDR families as niches providing retreat and support for people whose public lives were governed by an authoritarian rule (e.g., Kabat vel Job, 1991). Both considerations suggest systematic, albeit different, indirect effects on the quality of adolescent peer relations.

Peer Relations of East and West German Adolescents in the Wake of Unification

In the present study, adolescent peer relations are examined drawing on data from a longitudinal study that began in 1992 (Hofer & Noack, 1992); that is, shortly after German unification. The first objective is to compare the quality of different types of peer relations among East and West German adolescents. The second research question addresses possible changes in the quality of peer relations in response to experiences of societal changes in both parts of the country. Hypotheses concerning the first question might refer to the East–West dichotomy as a rough indicator of social change. In fact, the pace of societal transformation clearly differed in both parts of the country. As mentioned, a considerable continuity characterized the situation in the West, at least concerning the economic and political system as well as most public institutions, whereas hardly any aspect of everyday life has remained the same for the citizens of the former GDR. This line of thought, however, draws on an interpretation of German unification as a "natural experiment," which Nauck and Joos (1997) strongly criticized by referring to preexisting differences and similarities as a consequence of the previously disparate political systems as well as of more deeply rooted regional variations. Put more generally, this approach could easily be misleading, as is often the case with aggregate-level approaches, because a host of variables beyond variations in the societal transformation is confounded with living in the East or West (cf. Silbereisen, Robins, & Rutter, 1995). As far as empirical evidence is available, only minor differences between adolescent peer relations in East and West Germany can be expected, namely, a slightly lower quality of relations with age-mates among young East Germans. One must bear in mind that the predicted difference does not have to result from the differential pace of change in East and West Germany.

Given the problems of an aggregate-level approach, the second research question is addressed employing a more molecular approach to the effects of social change on peer relations. Different aspects of change are captured in terms of experiences on the family level. This approach capitalizes on variations in the experiences of social change within both parts of the country (Noack et al., 1999). As mentioned, more objective reflections of change, such as a relative decrease of purchasing power, are considered as well as subjective perceptions of, for example, growing uncertainty in society. We examined to what extent variations in experienced change influence different aspects of adolescent peer relations. In addition, the quality of family bonds is also included in these analyses as a possible source of influence on relationships between adolescent age-mates. This makes it possible to address the old question of linkages between the family and peer contexts and to explore possible differences when comparing the East and West German subsamples. More important, it is thus possible to examine to what extent family bonds may operate as a link mediating associations between experiences of social change and adolescent peer relations.

The body of available evidence from earlier research does not yield straightforward hypotheses concerning effects of social change on how adolescents get along with age-mates. Given the broader empirical bases, possible indirect effects are discussed first. The majority of findings addressing the long-lasting debate of continuity between adolescent family and peer contexts as opposed to antagonistic roles played by the two microsystems seem to favor the continuity hypothesis (Cooper & Cooper, 1992; Noack, 1992; Rubin & Coplan, 1992; Savin-Williams & Berndt, 1990). Only in a situation in which family relationships are highly conflictual and the bonds between parents and their offspring have become weak does the peer system tend to assume a compensatory function (e.g., Henderson, Kahn, & Youniss, 1990). Even though the directions of effects linking family and peers have often not

been spelled out in empirical analyses, experiences in the family are clearly considered to affect the quality of relationships with age-mates. Parental influences on
children's and adolescents' social development and similarity of partners in peer
relationships due to selection and mutual socialization (cf. Kandel, 1986) are suggested as processes responsible for continuity (cf. Savin-Williams & Berndt, 1990).
If, as suggested before, social change sets family relations at risk, peer bonds should
also be jeopardized as a consequence. Only when the parent–child relationship is
extremely strained in response to macrocontextual pressures could a compensatory
pattern be expected.

One must bear in mind, however, that in the course of adolescence at the latest, the
peer system becomes somewhat more independent from the family. Although this
does not contradict the observation of positive (contemporaneous) linkages between
family and peers, this continuity may originate in earlier phases of development.
In this case, an acute disturbance of the relationship between parents and their
adolescent sons and daughters may be of limited importance for interactions with
age-mates.

Possible effects of social change not mediated by the family system could thus
be of equal or higher relevance. Referring to these effects as direct influences does
not deny the operation of intervening variables. The likely processes of mediation,
however, would be of an intrapersonal nature and are not addressed empirically in
the following analyses. Parallel to parents', responding to, for instance, a situation
of financial shortage by depressive symptoms (Conger et al., 1992), adolescent
adjustment can be assumed to be impaired by experiences of social change for the
worse. Internalizing or externalizing problems of adolescents may, in turn, affect
their interaction with friends and other peers. Along the same lines, experiences of
social change could also affect adolescents' perspective on social relationships and
result in behavior detrimental to peer bonds or a withdrawal from age-mates. The
perception of an increasingly cold and competitive social world would be a likely
candidate of subjective experiences of changes in the society that could influence
the individual's integration into the world of peers. Still, the hypothesis is less
certain in regard to former East German adolescents. First, the traditional meaning
of close personal relations in the GDR as a niche in a hostile world may also
result in a strengthening of peer bonds when the society is perceived to change for
the worse. Secondly, young former East Germans have more extreme experiences
of social change in absolute terms than former West German adolescents. Even
though this may lead them to withdraw from normative peer groups, it could result
in new bonds with nonconforming age-mates (cf. Elliott, Huizinga, & Ageton,
1985; Kaplan, 1980). Thus, the analysis concerning effects on peer relations among
former East German adolescents is mainly exploratory. Finally, a positive quality
of parent–adolescent relationships is expected to predict sound peer relations. We
will examine to what extent social change effects are mediated by the quality of
family relationships.

Empirical Study

Method

The study is part of a more comprehensive longitudinal investigation of adolescent development in the wake of German unification (Hofer & Noack, 1992). The analyses of peer relations draw on the data sets from the first two assessments conducted during the winters of 1992–93 and 1993–94.

Sample. The two-wave sample is comprised of about 300 male and female adolescents who attended 9th grade at first measurement. About half of these 15-year-olds lived in Mannheim; the other half was from Leipzig. The partly pragmatic decision for the two cities as sites of the study also aimed at an acceptable comparability of subsamples as a basis for the interpretation of the results. Leipzig and the twin city of Mannheim–Ludwigshafen are densely populated urban areas with a population of about 500,000 inhabitants. The economy of both areas is based on a mixture of heavy industry as well as midsized and small companies involved in production and services. Even though the eastern part of Germany is subject to a far more dramatic economic transition, it is not only Leipzig that is suffering from rising unemployment rates. Still, both areas fare better than the average of eastern and western Germany. A geographic similarity is also worth mentioning. Both areas are located close to Germany's borders. From our point of view, this situation contributes to a more typical portrayal of eastern and western German cities than is the case with places in the vicinity of the former inner German border, where direct mutual influences and a peculiar basis for social comparison result in an unusual ecology.

Subjects attended the major tracks of the state school systems in Mannheim (*Hauptschule, Realschule, Gymnasium*) and Leipzig (*Mittelschule, Gymnasium*). As in the institutionalized tracking system of German schools, the attended track is roughly indicative of socioeconomic status, and the sample represents a wide range of social strata. Still, it has to be acknowledged that this longitudinal sample cannot be considered representative. The urban context as well as regional peculiarities have already been mentioned. Moreover, analyses of attrition revealed a systematic middle-class bias, particularly among former West German subjects. Interestingly, however, a systematic bias concerning major psychological variables included in the analyses is virtually absent. Owing to a participation rate of about 50% of adolescent subjects' parents, the second set of analyses, which also considered parental data, is based on roughly 140 subjects.

Variables. Three measures addressing different aspects of adolescent peer relations that vary in the extent of closeness were included in the analyses. Our measure of friendship quality addresses adolescents' relationships with their best friends; that is, the relationship characterized by the highest level of connectedness and intimacy besides family bonds. Three items (e.g., "I can rely on my best friends") elicited global evaluations of the friendship relationship. Sum scales of adolescents' self-ratings on four-point scales ($1 = does\ not\ apply$; $4 = fully\ applies$) were included in the following analyses.

The second scale, peer rejection, focuses on more distant peer relations that are less close but still based on face-to-face interactions. Furman (1993) has under-scored the importance of distinguishing friendship and other peer relations. They are not only different in character but also seem to have a differential impact on ado-lescents' psychosocial adaptation. Likewise, there is reason to assume that close friendships and more distant relations with other adolescents vary differentially in response to contextual challenges. The distant relations may deteriorate more rapidly under conditions of strain that could, however, also strengthen these peer bonds in the sense of solidarity if young people notice that they are in an essentially similar situation. Following Kaplan (1980), particular interest is paid to normative peers such as classmates in school. Lack of acceptance within this context has been shown to drive adolescents towards peer groups that challenge societal norms and encourage deviant behavior. The scale employed in this study draws on Kaplan's (e.g., Kaplan, Martin, & Robbins, 1984) earlier empirical work, thus capturing rejection by peers as opposed to closeness or supportive relations. It comprises three items (e.g., "I don't feel well with my classmates in school") that adolescents judged using the same response format as described before.

Finally, peer orientation was measured as a general tendency of adolescents to value their own generation highly and see age-mates as those to turn to for ad-vice and support. The construct was developed in youth research (Georg, 1992) to contrast those for whom peers are the major reference group with other young people oriented rather towards their parents and the generation of adults. It has to be noted that empirically parent and peer orientation scales show strong nega-tive correlations but do not turn out as a bipolar measure. Even though the word-ing of individual items is concrete, the composition of items aims at captur-ing a more general orientation as opposed to actual relationships. In this study, six items (e.g., "About important school-related things I talk with my friends") capture the variable. Again, four-point rating scales served to elicit adolescents' responses.

Despite the brevity of the first two measures, all scales showed good internal consistencies at both assessments (Cronbach's alpha = .65–.82). At the same time, the longitudinal data set also provides the opportunity to examine the stability of the peer relation measures. Longitudinal correlations point to a considerable stability of all three aspects across 1 year ($r_{tt} = .52$–.60). In comparisons of groups from different societal or cultural backgrounds, there is often doubt concerning the validity of measures; that is, concerning the meaning of scales in the different groups. Oswald and Krappmann's (1995) convincing findings providing evidence for the similarity of friendship concepts of young East and West Germans clearly speak against the expectation of systematic differences in the understanding of the three peer relations scales employed in this study. Moreover, the parallel pattern of intercorrelations of the measures in the East and West German subsamples gives reason to assume a valid measurement. The slightly smaller (negative) correlations involving the peer rejection scale among young East Germans may be due to school-related changes after unification, resulting in a higher likelihood of newly composed classrooms in Leipzig schools.

To capture experiences in the family reflecting changes of the societal context, three scales included in the first assessment were considered in the analyses. Following the line of research intiated by Elder (1974), a major focus was on more objective manifestations of change; namely, variations in the family household economy. Purchasing power (e.g., Noack et al., 1995) addresses the extent to which it has become easier or more difficult for the family to cover the costs for various regular expenditures or whether the financial situation has remained the same. Fathers and mothers were asked to indicate change or stability concerning three types of expenditures (rent, child care, cultural and leisure time pursuits) in the course of the preceeding 5 years on five-point rating scales (1 = *far easier*, 3 = *remained the same*, 5 = *far more difficult*). The time interval spanned the period when German unification took place and was chosen to cover the time of most dramatic changes – at least for the families in Leipzig. Maternal and paternal responses were summed, resulting in a highly reliable scale (Cronbach's alpha = .75–.84).

The other two measures addressed subjective experiences of social change. As part of a more extensive instrument (Noack et al., 1999), family members were asked to report their perceptions of changes concerning uncertainty (anomie, lack of predictability of the future; five items, e.g., "Everything is so uncertain that anything could happen"), and competition (decline of prosocial behavior in public; three items; e.g., "Life is a rat race") on the societal level. Responses on five-point scales (1 = *much less*, 3 = *the same*, 5 = *much more*) again referred to a 5-year time interval before the first assessment. Items were coded in a way that high scores indicate a deterioration of the situation. In the present analyses, responses from adolescents and both parents were combined to arrive at a single family score for each variable. The internal consistency of the scales (Cronbach's alpha) varied between .61 and .79.

Retrospective accounts of change are subject to different sources of bias such as memory effects. Obviously, family members' reports cannot be seen as an accurate portrayal of the societal transformation. Given the interest in psychological consequences guiding this study, a look at subjective change rather than at the objective course of the transformations taking place in Germany seems to be more instructive. Still, it should be mentioned that findings of two investigations of subjective perceptions of macrosocial conditions (Haeder & Nowossadeck, 1993; Noack et al., 1999) suggest a considerable consistency of perceptions of change referring to a defined time interval, on the one hand, and changes in contemporaneous accounts of the societal situation during the same time interval, on the other hand. Even though both measures are subjective reports, their convergence supports the assumption that they are systematically influenced by aspects of actual social change. Moreover, there is some evidence pointing to a considerable accuracy of retrospective reports covering time intervals even more extensive than the 5-year period used in this study (Kracke, Nowak, Thiele, & Silbereisen, 1992).

The quality of *family relations* was assessed by a measure of *connectedness*. This aspect of the parent-adolescent relationship is a global and at the same time central characteristic of family bonds during the adolescent years (Youniss & Smollar, 1985). The sum scale consisted of five items (e.g., "I care about getting along with my parents") that the adolescent subjects judged on four-point scales (1 = *does not apply*; 4 = *fully applies*; Cronbach's alpha = .72).

Analyses. In a first step, differences between peer relations of East and West German adolescents were tested by way of multivariate analysis of variance with the three peer relations measures as dependent variables, gender and place (East vs. West) as between-subject factors, and measurement point (t_1, t_2) and type of measure (friendship quality, peer rejection, peer orientation) as within-subject factors.

In the second step, multiple regression analyses were conducted separately for the three aspects of peer relations that directly addressed effects of social change experiences. In contemporaneous analyses based on t_1 data, place was entered as the first predictor followed by uncertainty, competition, and purchasing power, which were included *en bloc*. Then, family connectedness was entered in the regression equation. Finally, we tested whether the same associations held for the East and West German subsamples. To this aim, we examined whether entering the different multiplicative terms of place and the respective other predictors resulted in a significant increase of explained variance. Multiple regression analyses drawing on two-wave data were employed to specify the assumed directions of effects. The procedure was essentially the same as before. This time, however, the t_2 assessment of a given peer relations measure was considered as criterion, and the corresponding t_1 measure was entered first to partial out the stability of the measure.

Results

Adolescent peer relations in East and West Germany. The multivariate analysis of variance yielded main effects of gender ($F[1/271] = 23.25$, $p < .001$) and type of measure ($F[2/542] = 540.36$, $p < .001$). The overall gender difference resulted from females' more positive reports on their peer relations. The systematic variation between the types of dependent measures is more trivial. The general tendency of adolescents to describe their peer relations in positive terms is reflected by comparably higher scores with regard to friendship quality and peer orientation as opposed to a relative denial of peer rejection. Given several significant multivariate interaction effects, including the type-of-measure factor (Measure × Gender, Measure × Place, Measure × Measurement Point, Measure × Place × Measurement Point; all $ps < .05$), univariate analyses conducted separately for the three measures served to examine the findings further.

Following the main hypothesis, place effects are considered first. Univariate analyses yielded significant differences between reports of East and West German adolescents concerning friendship quality ($F[1/295] = 8.70$, $p < .01$), and peer rejection ($F[1/299] = 5.83$, $p < .05$). As expected, young East Germans portrayed their peer relations less favorably. Although they indicated lower levels of friendship quality, they also more often felt rejected by their peers. A marginal Place × Measurement Point interaction effect on peer rejection [$F[1/299] = 3.34$, $p < .10$) points to a slight increase of the observed difference. Whereas the scores of East German adolescents remained about the same across the 1-year interval in focus, peer rejection felt by their West German age-mates declined from age 15 to 16. No place-dependent differences were identified for peer orientation. Variations of friendship quality and peer rejection as a function of place and measurement point are shown in Figure 1.

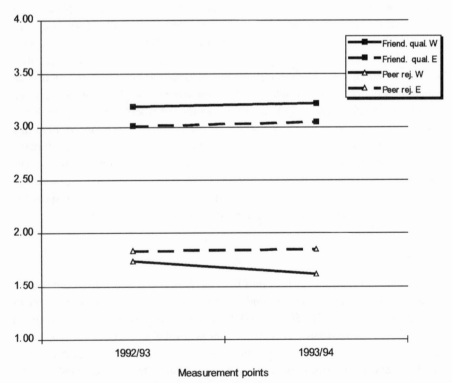

Figure 1. Changes of friendship quality and peer rejection among East and West German adolescents across a one-year time interval.

Table 1. *Multiple regression of aspects of adolescents' peer relationships by place, experiences of social change, and family connectedness: correlations, betas, and R^2.*

	Friendship quality		Peer rejection		Peer orientation	
Predictor	r	β	r	β	r	β
Place	−.23***	−.20**	.00	−.02	−.11+	−.08
Uncertainty	−.05	−.01	−.02	−.03	.08	.09
Competition	−.07	−.07	.06	.07	−.13*	−.16*
Purchasing power	−.04	−.04	−.02	.00	.12+	.09
Connectedness	.24***	.23**	−.13*	−.12+	.11+	.09
R^2		.11**		.02		.05+

Notes: $N = 185$.
*** $p < .001$, ** $p < .01$, * $p < .05$, + $p < .10$

Moreover, univariate analyses suggest that gender differences in friendship quality ($F[1/295] = 8.45$, $p < .01$) and peer orientation ($F[1/291] = 29.00$, $p < .001$) are mainly responsible for the multivariate gender effect. In both instances, female adolescents provided more positive reports. Finally, adolescents' peer orientation varied across assessments ($F[1/291] = 5.93$, $p < .05$). Peer orientation increased with age.

Experiences of social change and adolescent peer relations. The analyses of contemporaneous associations between experiences of social change, the quality of parent–adolescent relationships, and place, on the one hand, and the peer relations measures, on the other hand, yielded no significant interaction effects involving place. Consequently, findings are presented for the total sample. Beta coefficients and R^2s of the last step of the multiple regression analyses as well as zero-order correlations are shown in Table 1.

The findings can be presented concisely. Whereas all three aspects of peer relations varied depending on family connectedness, experiences of social change have hardly any effect. As hypothesized, connectedness predicted higher levels of friendship quality and lower levels of peer rejection. Even though the positive beta concerning peer orientation is not significant, at least the zero-order correlation with connectedness indicates a mariginal association of the expected sign. Entering connectedness into the regression equation contributed between 1 to 5% of explained variance above and beyond place and social change. Experiences of social change significantly contributed to the explanation of peer orientations only ($R^2_{\text{change}} = .03$, $p < .10$). The negative effect of competition ($\beta = −.16$, $p < .05$) reflects the corresponding zero-order correlation. Interestingly, the correlation of purchasing power and peer orientation is positive ($r = .12$, $p < .10$), but the beta coefficient remained insignificant.

Table 2. *Multiple regression of adolescents'
friendship quality at t_2 by friendship quality at t_1,
experiences of social change, and family
connectedness separately for place: partial
correlations,[a] betas, and R^2.*

Predictor	West		East	
	r_{part}	β	r_{part}	β
Friendship quality (t_1)	—	.58***	—	.44***
Uncertainty	−.09	.02	−.28**	−.23+
Competition	−.15+	−.12	−.03	.03
Purchasing power	−.05	−.01	−.14	−.08
Connectedness	.03	.03	.17+	.10
R^2		.37***		.35***

Note: $N = 132$.
*** $p < .001$, ** $p < .01$, * $p < .05$, + $p < .10$
[a] Partial correlations of each predictor (t_1) and friendship quality
(t_2) controlled for friendship quality (t_1).

The analyses of two-wave longitudinal data yielded significant interactions of place and social change variables concerning friendship quality and peer rejection as criteria. Consequently, regression analyses were conducted separately for the East and West German subsamples, whereas the analysis concerning peer orientation was based on the complete sample. Partial correlations of the t_1 predictors and friendship quality at t_2 (controlled for friendship quality at t_1), and betas and R^2s of the last step of the regression analysis are shown in Table 2.

Above and beyond the considerable stability of friendship quality, which alone explained 36% the of variance in the West German subsample and 28% of the variance in the East, influences of social change resulted in changes of friendship quality among young East Germans only. A decrease of friendship quality depending on experiences of uncertainty is mainly responsible for the observed 7% increase of explained variance. In the West German subsample, a marginal partial correlation suggests slight decreases of friendship quality when competition in the society has been perceived as growing. The nonsignificant beta coefficient can be attributed to the intercorrelation of the three social change variables entered in one step. Finally, a marginal partial correlation of connectedness and friendship quality of East German adolescents points to a longitudinal influence of the family context. Still, the effect does not hold beyond the influence of social change.

Findings for peer rejection partly correspond to those reported before. The respective coefficients are listed in Table 3.

The pattern of findings concerning peer rejection mostly parallel those reported before. Besides the high stabilities, there is a decrease of peer rejection as a function

Table 3. *Multiple regression of adolescents' peer rejection at t_2 by peer rejection at t_1, experiences of social change, and family connectedness separately for place: partial correlations[a], betas, and R^2.*

	West		East	
Predictor	r_{part}	β	r_{part}	β
Peer rejection (t_1)	–	.57***	–	.40***
Uncertainty	.13	.04	−.19+	−.16
Competition	.24*	.18+	−.06	.02
Purchasing power	.14	.08	−.21*	−.17
Connectedness	.04	.03	−.22*	−.24*
R^2		.37***		.36***

Notes. $N = 135$.
*** $p < .001$, ** $p < .01$, * $p < .05$, + $p < .10$
[a]Partial correlations of each predictor (t_1) and peer rejection (t_2) controlled for peer rejection (t_1).

of family connectedness in the East German subsample. Moreover, West German adolescents' feelings of being rejected were intensified if they experienced increases of competition. This time, however, both betas are significant. Curiously, however, analyses of peer rejection among young East Germans revealed negative influences of social change; that is, perceived changes for the worse resulted in a decrease of peer rejection. Despite an increase of explained variance ($R^2_{change} = .07$, $p < .10$) when the three change scales are entered into the regression equation, the betas of the interrelated predictors are not significant. The partial correlations for uncertainty ($r_{part} = -.19$, $p < .10$) and purchasing power ($r_{part} = -.21$, $p < .05$), however, corroborate the counterintuitive finding.

The last longitudinal analysis focused on peer orientation as criterion. The findings show no substantial effects above and beyond the stability of the measure. Partial correlations, betas, and explained variance are shown in Table 4.

Conclusions

The major objective of this study was to examine to what extent adolescents' peer relations are affected by the dynamics of social change. Given the scarcity of previous research as well as the early stage of the reported work, the findings that could be presented so far raise questions rather than provide straightforward insights. Nevertheless, the results seem clearly to confirm the expectation that swift changes of macrocontextual conditions do not systematically drive young people into the peer world but rather lead to a deterioration of relations with age-mates. The pattern of findings parallels observations suggesting that social change can be

Table 4. *Multiple regression of adolescents' peer orientation at t_2 by peer orientation at t_1, place, experiences of social change, and family connectedness: partial correlations,[a] betas, and R^2.*

Predictor	r_{part}	β
Peer rejection (t_1)	—	.61***
Place	−.07	−.05
Uncertainty	−.12+	−.02
Competition	−.14+	−.08
Purchasing power	−.16*	−.10
Connectedness	.00	−.01
R^2		.40***

Notes: $N = 135$.
*** $p < .001$, ** $p < .01$, * $p < .05$, + $p < .10$
[a]Partial correlations of each predictor (t_1) and peer orientation (t_2) controlled for peer orientation (t_1).

a risk factor for family relationships (Noack, Oepke, & Sassenberg, 1998). In this regard, it is not necessary to rely on the assumption that differences related to the social addresses (cf. Bronfenbrenner & Crouter, 1983) "East vs. west Germany" are mainly due to a differential pace of societal transformation that explains closer peer relations of young people in the West. Findings yielded by a more molecular approach focusing on different aspects of social change as experienced by family members point in the same direction. One must keep in mind, however, that relations with nonnormative or deviant peers were not considered in the analyses. In our longitudinal study, data on age-mates' challenging adult rules and norms are only available starting from the third wave of assessment. Future analyses might show that rapid changes of the society do bear the risk of deviant affiliations.

One finding, however, is not in accordance with the general pattern. Social change for the worse seemed to result in a decrease of peer rejection as felt by East German adolescents. In the introduction, I pondered whether the peculiar meaning of close relationships in the former GDR might lead to intensified peer relations as a response to the strains of societal transformation. Negative effects of social change on friendships and peer orientation of young former East Germans, however, cast doubt on this interpretation. Alternatively, a decline of peer rejection could be seen as an indirect indication of withdrawal from more distant relationships such as in the classroom. In other words, experiences that lead to feelings of being rejected could be reduced by a move away from age-mates. Still, the latter interpretation is quite speculative and also raises the question as to why responses of young people in former East and West Germany would be different.

One could further speculate that peer relations among young former East Germans are generally less stable in a context undergoing dramatic transitions. The pattern of stability coefficients is consonant with this assumption. Systematic transformations of the East German school system, such as the change from comprehensive schooling to institutionalized tracks that include newly composed groups of classmates, provide a plausible explanation. Unfortunately, the data presented here do not allow examination of the identity – or changing identity – of the friends and other peers adolescents referred to in their responses. It would be worthwhile, however, to address this question in future research.

In line with most earlier findings, the analysis of contemporaneous associations provided evidence for continuity between adolescents' family and peer contexts. Connectedness in adolescents' families was related to positive relations with age-mates. It would be premature to conclude that experiences at home have an influence on peer bonds. Only cross-lagged effects on friendship quality and peer rejection reported by former East German adolescents favor this interpretation. The cross-sectional associations could mainly result from influences of the opposite direction; namely, adolescent–parent relationships being affected by experiences in the world of peers. Even though this view cannot be discarded by the present analyses, it seems more plausible to assume that existing continuity has been transported by the stability of peer relations. If peer relations among East German adolescents were, indeed, less stable in times of change as suggested before, it would be more easy to understand why there were longitudinal effects of family connectedness in the Eastern subsample.

Finally, the limits of the present study have to be addressed. The size and composition of the sample certainly calls for a replication of the findings. Moreover, the 1-year time interval between data collections in the course of the longitudinal assessments has mainly been chosen for pragmatic reasons. It cannot be ruled out that the processes in focus follow a different temporal pattern. In this case, the findings could underestimate the actual associations. Finally, it should be underscored that the size of effects reported here is mostly small. Still, the findings are encouraging and point out the importance of considering macrosocial conditions (especially their variation across time) to arrive at an adequate understanding of adolescents' integration in the world of age-mates.

It should also be pointed out that only specific aspects of the societal transformation have been considered. In each instance, the social change variables that were analyzed captured a deterioration of the situation. For young people, in particular, times of swift societal development may also provide fresh opportunities. It is far from obvious, however, if improving aspects of the living conditions, such as new opportunities for travel, education, or self-direction, in general foster peer relations or set them at risk. Another limitation results from the particular cohort studied in this investigation. For the young people in this study, German unification roughly coincided with their regular change from elementary school to high school. Older adolescents or young adults who more consciously experienced school education and the leisure landscape of the preunification years may respond quite differently to the societal transformation. Although there is no empirical evidence bearing on the meaning of this constellation for effects on peer relations, research on stability and change of value orientations among young East and West Germans (Reitzle & Silbereisen, 1997) calls for caution when findings in one cohort are extrapolated to other groups. Finally, there is some indication that the time shortly after unification when the data analyzed here were collected may have been a peculiar one insofar as changes in several variables addressing, for instance, patterns of relationships and individual psychosocial adaptation reached a culmination and turning point (e.g., Friedrich & Foerster, 1997; Nauck & Joos, 1997). It is questionable if these individual findings represent a general pattern. In any case, more dramatic macroeconomic consequences have become salient at the site of this study in former West Germany only in the years after the first two assessments. Although our database will eventually allow testing of the effects of this region-specific timelag with regard to our sample, the examination of variations in reponses to accelerated change depending on cohorts and age groups (cf. Elder, 1974) will be an objective of future research.

References

Bronfenbrenner, U., & Crouter, A. (1983). The environmental models in developmental research. In P. H. Mussen (Ed.), *Handbook of child psychology, Vol. 1* (pp. 357–414). New York: Wiley.

Buba, H. P., Fruechtel, F., & Pickel, G. (1995). Haushalts- und Familienformen junger Erwachsener und ihre Bedeutung im Ablösungsprozess von der Herkunftsfamilie – Ein Vergleich in den alten und neuen Bundesländern. [Household and family forms among young adults and their meaning concerning the individuation from the families of origin]. In B. Nauck, N. F. Schneider & A. Toelke (Eds.), *Familie und Lebensverlauf im gesellschaftlichen Umbruch* (pp. 119–136). Stuttgart, Germany: Enke.

Conger, R. D., Conger, K. J., Elder, G. H., Lorenz, F. O., Simons, R. L., & Whitbeck, L. B. (1992). A family process model of economic hardship and adjustment of early adolescent boys. *Child Development, 63*, 526–541.

Conger, R. D., & Elder, G. H. (1994). *Families in troubled times. Adapting to change in rural America.* New York: Aldine de Gruyter.

Cooper, C. R., & Cooper, R. G. (1992). Links between adolescents' relationships with their parents and peers: Models, evidence, and mechanisms. In R. D. Parke & G. W. Ladd (Eds.), *Parent-peer linkages.* Hillsdale, NJ: Erlbaum.

Elder, G. H. (1974). *Children of the Great Depression.* Chicago: University of Chicago Press.

Elder, G. H., & Caspi, A. (1991). Lebensverläufe im Wandel der Gesellschaft: soziologische und psychologische Perspektiven [Life course in the face of social change: Sociological and psychological perspectives]. In A. Engfer, B. Minsel, & S. Walper (Eds.), *Zeit für Kinder* (pp. 32–60). Weinheim, Germany: Beltz.

Elliott, D. S., Huizinga, D., & Ageton, S. (1985). *Explaining delinqency and drug use.* Beverly Hills, CA: Sage.

Franz, P., & Herlyn, U. (1995). Familie als Bollwerk oder als Hindernis? Zur Rolle von Familienbeziehungen bei der Bewältigung der Vereinigungsfolgen [Family as support or problem? On the role of family relations in coping with consequences of unification]. In B. Nauck, N. F. Schneider, & A. Toelke (Eds.), *Familie und Lebensverlauf im gesellschaftlichen Umbruch* (pp. 90–102). Stuttgart, Germany: Enke.

Friedrich, W., & Foerster, P. (1997). Politische Orientierungen ostdeutscher Jugendlicher und junger Erwachsener im Transformationsprozeß [Political orientations of East German adolescents and young adults during the process of transformation]. In H. Sydow (Ed.), *Entwicklung und*

Sozialisation von Jugendlichen vor und nach der Vereinigung Deutschlands (pp. 17–73). Opladen, Germany: Leske & Budrich.

Furman, W. (1993). Theory is not a four-letter word: Needed directions in the study of adolescent friendships. In B. Laursen (Ed.), *Close friendships in adolescence* (pp. 89–103). San Francisco: Jossey-Bass.

Garbarino, J. (1991). Kinder in Familie und Gesellschaft: Eine ökologische Perspektive [Children in the family and in society: An ecological perspective]. In A. Engfer, B. Minsel, & S. Walper (Eds.), *Zeit für Kinder* (pp. 72–89). Weinheim, Germany: Beltz.

Georg, W. (1992). Die Skala Jugendzentrismus im Zeitreihen- und Kulturvergleich [The Youth Centrism scale under a longitudinal and cross-cultural perspective]. In Jugendwerk der Deutschen Shell (Ed.), *Jugend '92* (pp. 15–26). Opladen, Germany: Leske & Budrich.

Haeder, M., & Nowossadeck, S. (1993). Anstieg der Lebenszufriedenheit in Ostdeutschland – Ergebnisse aus der Untersuchungsreihe 'Leben DDR/Ostdeutschland' [Increases in life satisfaction in East Germany – Findings from the 'Life GDR/East Germany studies']. *ZUMA-Nachrichten, 17,* 25–44.

Hartup, W. W. (1993). Adolescents and their friends. In B. Laursen (Ed.), *Close friendships in adolescence* (pp. 3–22). San Francisco: Jossey-Bass.

Henderson, S. H., Kahn, C., & Youniss, J. (1990, March). *Adolescents' friendships in intact and divorced families.* Poster session presented at the third biennial meetings of the Society for Research on Adolescence, Atlanta, GA.

Hofer, M., & Noack, P. (1992). *Individuation und sozialer Wandel. Antrag an die Deutsche Forschungsgemeinschaft* [Individuation and social change. Grant proposal submitted to the German Research Council]. University of Mannheim, Germany.

Hofer, M., Kracke, B., Noack, P., & Klein-Allermann, E. (1995). Der soziale Wandel aus Sicht ost- und westdeutscher Familien, psychisches Wohlbefinden und autoritäre Vorstellungen [Social change as perceived by East and West German families, psychological well-being, and authortarian orientations]. In B. Nauck, A. Tölke, & N. Schneider (Eds.), *Familie und Lebensverlauf im gesellschaftlichen Umbruch* (pp. 154–171). Stuttgart, Germany: Enke.

Institut für empirische Psychologie (1995). *"Wir sind o.k.!"* ["We are o.k.!"] Cologne, Germany: Bund Verlag.

Institut für praxisorientierte Sozialforschung (1993). *Jugendliche und junge Erwachsene in Deutschland* [Adolescents and young adults in Germany]. Mannheim, Germany: IPOS.

Jugendwerk der Deutschen Shell (1997). *Jugend '97.* Opladen, Germany: Leske & Budrich.

Kabat vel Job, O. (1991). Zum Wandel familialer Lebensformen in Ostdeutschland [On the change of family life styles in East Germany]. In P. Buechner & H.-H. Krueger (Eds.), *Aufwachsen hüben und drüben.* Opladen, Germany: Leske & Budrich.

Kagitcibasi, C., & Berry, J. W. (1989). Cross-cultural psychology: Current research and trends. *Annual Review of Psychology, 40,* 493–531.

Kandel, D. B. (1986). Processes of peer influence in adolescence. In R. K. Silbereisen, K. Eyferth, & G. Rudinger (Eds.), *Development as action in context* (pp. 203–227). Berlin: Springer Verlag.

Kaplan, H. B. (1980). *Deviant behavior in defense of self.* New York: Academic Press.

Kaplan, H. B., Martin, S. S., & Robbins, C. (1984). Pathways to adolescent drug use: Self-derogation, peer influence, weakening of social controls, and early substance use. *Journal of Health and Social Behavior, 25,* 270–289.

Kloep, M. (1994, May). *Concurrent and predictive correlates of girls' depression and antisocial behavior under conditions of economic crisis and changing values: The case of Albania.* Paper presented at the fourth biennial conference of the European Association for Research on Adolescence, Stockholm, Sweden.

Kracke, B., Nowak, M., Thiele, G., & Silbereisen, R. K. (1992). Gedächtniseffekte und Antworttendenzen in der Shell-Jugendstudie [Memory effects and response biases in the Shell Youth Study]. In Jugendwerk der Deutschen Shell (Ed.), *Jugend '92* (pp. 55–58). Opladen, Germany: Leske & Budrich.

Nauck, B., & Joos, M. (1997). Wandel der familiären Lebensverhältnisse von Kindern in Ostdeutschland [Changing conditions of life of families with children in East Germany]. In G. Trommsdorff (Ed.),

Sozialisation und Entwicklung von Kindern vor und nach der Vereinigung (pp. 243–298). Opladen, Germany: Leske & Budrich.

Noack, P. (1992). Freunde, Bekannte, Peers: Die Familie und Beziehungen zu Gleichen [Friends, acquaintances, peers: The family and relationships with "equals"]. In M. Hofer, E. Klein-Allermann, & P. Noack (Eds.), *Familienbeziehungen.* (pp. 82–104). Göttingen, Germany: Hogrefe.

Noack, P., Hofer, M., Kracke, B., & Klein-Allermann, E. (1995). Adolescents and their parents facing social change: Families in East and West Germany after unification. In P. Noack, M. Hofer & J. Youniss (Eds.), *Psychological responses to social change* (pp. 129–148). Berlin: de Gruyter.

Noack, P., Hofer, M., Kracke, B., Wild, E., & Boehnke, K. (1999). Assessments of family experiences of social change in East and West Germany. Unpublished manuscript.

Noack. P., Oepke, M., & Sassenberg, K. (1998). Sozialer Wandel und familiale Individuation [Social change and family individuation]. *Zeitschrift für Sozialisationsforschung und Erziehungssoziologie 2*, 199–214.

Oswald, H. (1992). Beziehungen zu Gleichaltrigen [Peer relations]. In Jugendwerk der Deutschen Shell (Ed.), *Jugend '92*, Vol. 2 (pp. 319–332). Opladen, Germany: Leske & Budrich.

Oswald, H., & Krappmann, L. (1995). Social life of children in a former bipartite city. In P. Noack, M. Hofer, & J. Youniss (Eds.), *Psychological responses to social change* (pp. 163–185). Berlin: Walter de Gruyter.

Reitzle, M., & Silbereisen, R. K. (1997, April). *Adolescents' values in Eastern and Western Germany: What has changed since unification?* Paper presented at the Biennial Meeting of the Society for Research in Child Development, Washington, DC.

Rubin, K. H., & Coplan, R. J. (1992). Peer relationships in childhood. In M. H. Bornstein & M. E. Lamb (Eds.), *Developmental psychology* (pp. 519–578). Hillsdale, N.J.: Erlbaum.

Savin-Williams, R. C., & Berndt, T. J. (1990). Friendship and peer relations. In S. S. Feldman & G. R. Elliott (Eds.), *At the threshold* (pp. 277–307). Cambridge, MA: Harvard University Press.

Schmidt, H.-D. (1996). Erziehungsbedingungen in der DDR: Offizielle Programme, individuelle Praxis und die Rolle der Pädagogischen Psychologie und Entwicklungspsychologie [Conditions of education in the GDR: Official programs, individual reality, and the role of eductional and developmental psychology]. In G. Trommsdorff (Ed.), *Sozialisation und Entwicklung von Kindern vor und nach der Vereinigung* (pp. 15–171). Opladen, Germany: Leske & Budrich.

Silbereisen, R. K. (1991). Elders Untersuchungen zu den Auswirkungen sozialen Wandels: fachliche Hintergründe und aktuelle Bezüge [Elder's research on consequences of social change: Scientific background and present relevance]. In A. Engfer, B. Minsel, & S. Walper (Eds.), *Zeit für Kinder* (pp. 61–70). Weinheim, Germany: Beltz.

Silbereisen, R. K., Robins, L., & Rutter, M. (1995). Secular trends in substance use: Concepts and data on the impact of societal change on alcohol and drug use. In M. Rutter & D. J. Smith (Eds.), *Psychological disorders in young people* (pp. 490–543). Chichester, England: Wiley.

Strzoda, C., & Zinnecker, J. (1996). Interessen, Hobbies und deren institutioneller Kontext [Interests, hobbies, and their institutional context]. In J. Zinnecker & R. K. Silbereisen (Eds.), *Kindheit in Deutschland* (pp. 41–79). Weinheim, Germany: Juventa.

Thomas, A. (1993).(Ed.). *Kulturvergleichende Psychologie* [Cross-cultural psychology]. Göttingen, Germany: Hogrefe.

Walper, S. (1988). *Familiäre Konsequenzen ökonomischer Deprivation* [Consequences of economic deprivation on the family level]. Munich: PVU.

Youniss, J., Noack, P., & Hofer, M. (1995). Human development under conditions of social change. In P. Noack, M. Hofer, & J. Youniss (Eds.), *Psychological responses to social change* (pp. 1–6). Berlin: de Gruyter.

Youniss, J., & Smollar, J. (1985). *Adolescent relations with mothers, fathers, and friends.* Chicago: The University of Chicago Press.

Zinnecker, J., & Strzoda, C. (1996). Freundschaft und Clique. Das informelle Netzwerk der Gleichaltrigen [Friendship and clique. The informal network of age-mates]. In J. Zinnecker & R. K. Silbereisen (Eds.), *Kindheit in Deutschland* (pp. 81–97). Weinheim, Germany: Juventa.

10 Life Course Dynamics and the Development of New Relations Between Generations

Hans Bertram

For them, modernity is basically a break with the ligatures of former times. Gone is the idyllic past with its holy shudders. The exit of man from his dependence, brought on by himself, is at the same time his exit from the nest warmth of stable human relations in fixed corporative structures. All fixed deep-rutted relationships are dissolved. And what are they replaced by? Not much... At the end of this world without ligatures, the false gods are not far off. They have led astray many and some followed them even to Jonestown. (Dahrendorf, 1994, p. 424).[1]

The Change in Forms and Course of Life

According to Dahrendorf (1994), Giddens (1988), and Beck (1986), the options of choice and opportunities have increased clearly for the individual in modern times to find a satisfying way of life, to fulfill oneself, and to live the way one wants regardless of tradition and family background. This is true especially for the modern welfare state, which secures the individual against life risks to a high degree. That these freedoms have to be paid for with a high price in the area of private life with the loss of security and stability of private relationships is the initial thesis of many authors (Etzioni, 1993; Berger & Luckmann, 1995).

These recently won freedoms are also to be found in the new scripts of life and biographies (Buchmann, 1991), which have become less closed and unitary and open more different courses. Several names have been found for this new open status of the life course such as destandardization of the life course or individualization (Giddens, 1991). Modern men and women have become free of traditional ligatures and are no longer oriented towards the values of the past transferred by the Church, the school, and parents but instead towards life visions that are actual and supposed as "modern." Their lives, their interactions, and their biographies more and more resemble a patchwork without a clear structure. Authors such as Beck (1986, 1993), Giddens (1991, 1995), and Lasch (1995) worked out the opportunities as well as the risks of this process of individualization. Others like Etzioni (1988, 1993), Coleman (1997), and Berger and Luckmann (1995) pointed out the negative consequences for the family and the child's socialization. Bondlessness, a focus on

157

one's own needs, and little readiness to take responsibility for others are not good premises for the child's development. Coleman (1995) showed that the increasing external orientation of mothers minimizes the chance to build social capital in families.

This development, which some authors (Beck, 1997; Giddens, 1997) call the "second modernism," can be documented in many ways. A glance at the official statistics seems to confirm this interpretation of the rising risk of failure in private relations. In the Federal Republic of Germany and the United States, the divorce rates have been rising steadily over the past 15 to 20 years. The number of single mothers has reached a high level. Newspapers report more and more about elderly people who have to suffer infirmity and death undiscovered, lonely, and without stable support from their own families.

Some authors (Münch, 1993, pp. 206ff) have even claimed that the insecurity of private relations, the disruption of traditional relations with the group of origin, and the attendant liberation of the individual from the rule of the group of origin are the indispensable conditions for individualized societies. This is the only way that the necessary mobility of individuals can be established and the requirements of the postindustrial societies met.

In this chapter, these concepts will be seen as evident interpretations of the second modernism. All evident interpretations need empirical proof to be regarded as valid. To document the changes in and development of familial life forms with the thesis of the breaking of traditional bonds empirically, one must include a sufficiently long historical period, for life courses, familial life forms, and social interactions can be investigated only in terms of comparisons between the generations or the age-cohorts of this century. Only a comparison between 80-year-olds and 20-year-olds of today as age-cohorts will confirm statements on the processes of change described earlier. For example, the increasing proportion of singles in the last 5 or 10 years does not yet say anything about the structural change of life forms. Only a comparison between the proportion of 40-, 50-, and 60-year-old singles at the beginning or in the middle of this century and today will substantiate statements about the process of individualization.

In other words, processes of change in the forms and the courses of life can only be investigated through a historically far-reaching empirical analysis that includes at least several generations. Investigating change in the forms of life for three generations requires one to scrutinize a period of some 80 years. Furthermore, just how far the private life style has really changed can only be verified by defining the forms of life exactly.

We talk lightly of family without reflecting that we actually mean the neolocal conjugal family with young children. This family form, described by Parsons (Parsons & Bales, 1955) as the dominant family of the 1950s, is characterized by the conjugal subsystem and by children to be socialized in a common household. Has only this conjugal system changed, perhaps through more frequent divorce with a continued rearing of the children in the parental household because divorces only take place once the children have undergone early childhood socialization, or are children especially affected by divorce in the early childhood phase?

Moreover, the change in the forms of life that distinguish the modern age does not take place in the same way through all the regions of a modern society. Munich, Hamburg, Berlin, and Düsseldorf, for example, have developed different life styles and forms of life than Passau, Neuss, or Oldenburg. Lower Bavaria, the Ruhr area, and Mecklenburg–Vorpommern do not necessarily follow the regional developments of Berlin and Hamburg (Bertram, Bauereiss & Bayer, 1993).

In the final analysis, the change and the differentiation of life courses and life designs in the modern age cannot be read from the existing sources of data alone. Most data collected this century, and this is true for the official statistics as well as for social research, are cross-sectional data in which activities of people are registered irrespective of the time sequence on which these activities are based. Without an investigation of the time sequence of life events, statements on the change in life courses are barely possible. Life courses are constituted by a bundling of events from specific constellations of events or sequences of life events. A patchwork biography may be distinguished empirically from clearly structured life courses simply by comparing their sequential structures.

The interpretation of current insecure forms of life, modern biographies patched together and patchwork families, is part of a characterization of the present that may only be validated empirically if several generations are compared with regard to their life courses in a time perspective spanning at least our century. The different aspects of the life forms have to be distinguished from one another, the differing regional developments have to be reflected upon, and the socially determined structure of the time sequence of life events has to be investigated.

Design and Methods of the Investigation

Since 1888, official statistics have been collected in Germany containing data on family, children, births, marriages and divorces that allow comparison of age-cohorts with respect to these topics at different times in this century. By working up the data of the Deutsches Reich and the Federal Republic of Germany, one can analyze those processes of change relevant to discussions of family forms and life courses. It never, however, was the task of the official statistics compilers of the Deutsches Reich or the Federal Republic of Germany to describe parent–child relationships or interactions between relatives through the life course but rather to compile data on families defined as the persons living together in a household. Thus the information derived from these sources is always at the macrolevel with respect to common characteristics in the units of the districts. Because the thesis of individualization always stresses the increasing bondlessness of modernity, one must complete the official data sets by individual information and combine these data pools. I therefore conducted a series of investigations[2] (Bertram, 1991, 1992, 1995) involving about 16,000 persons between 18 and 80 years of age. The focus was the perceived and reported social relations constructed as an ego-centric network. In this approach, each person was first asked to tell all the first names (up to 20) of other persons with whom he or she shared a relationship. In the second step, the person received a list of family-centered activities such as common meals, personal communication, common leisure time, personal bonding, and also aspects like financial support that might involve each named person. Then the person was asked to indicate the professions or jobs of the respective named persons and, last but not least, to indicate his or her social relation to each of the named persons (e.g., the first child, the partner, a friend, a colleague, a neighbor, etc.). Here, up to 18 possibilities of relations could be chosen. In this way, a three-dimensional matrix as an ego-centric net of each person's perceived relations with their named persons together with a list of activities by which each person is linked with a named one was derived. The influences of social desirability or social normativeness on the answers are largely excluded by this procedure because the type of relationship is asked in the last step. Such matrices are handled by means of relational data banks (e.g., Bender, 1993) and then analyzed through the usual statistical methods (Bertram, 1995).[3]

The Change in Forms of Life: Single Middle-Aged Men and Widows

The trend away from traditional life forms is often seen as the origin of the large increase in the singles population in modern societies (Beck, 1986; Beck & Beck-Gernsheim, 1993; Giddens, 1991; but also Etzioni, 1993, Berger & Luckmann, 1995). To comprehend this increase in the number of singles historically by taking comparable age groups and at the same time considering the historical events in Germany throughout the century, 1991 must be taken as the latest year of investigation because these statistics refer to West Germany. The developments in East Germany are not to be described by the individualization thesis. The oldest comparable West German statistic dates from 1950 (in 1949, the Federal Republic of Germany was founded). With respect to the 1920s, one must take a year far enough away from the end of World War I in 1918 as well as from the Great Depression of 1929 because such historical events influence the behavior of people in a profound way. Furthermore, to take a longitudinal perspective by comparing age groups at two time points, (i.e., to look at the men and women born in 1898 in the years 1925 and 1950), one must take into account that the age groups of the different cohorts may differ about ±5 years. This is due to the extraordinary history of Germany within this century. In spite of such restrictions, it is evident that historical events are obviously more important than general trends.

Single women between 77 and 87 years old today, born in the period of 1908 to 1918, have developed greatly differing links and relations throughout the course of their lives, and this is due to historical events with which they have been confronted in their lives. One portion of them, that is to say some 10%, have been widows since between the ages of 30 to 40. As a result of World War II, 8% of the women who were 30 then and 10% of those who were 40 years of age were already widows in 1950 (see Figure 1). Other groups have remained single throughout their lives

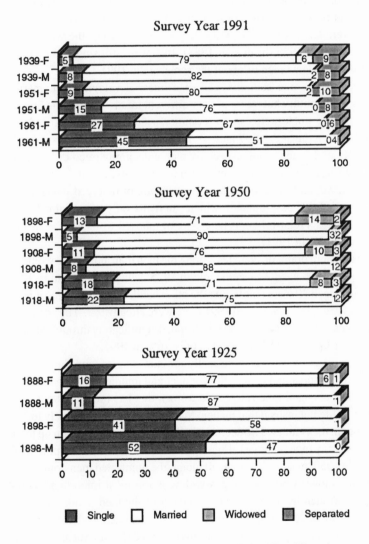

Figure 1. Family status and age, 1991–1925. (Data first published in Bertram (1995). Reprinted with permission of Leske and Budrich, publishers.)

or have become widows after they turned 60 owing to the more frequent deaths of men in that age group. The probability that they were divorced, however, is relatively low. When one compares the women of age 30 today (1991, year of study) with women aged 30 in 1925 or 1950, significant changes among the singles are evident. In 1991, some 27% of the women aged 30 were single and 6% were divorced. In 1950, only 18% of the women aged 32 were single and 3% were divorced. Forty-one percent of the women born in 1898, who were 27 years old in 1925, were single then and 58% were married. Even of the women who were 37 years of age in 1925 (birth year 1888), 16% were still single as compared with some 9% of single women of about the same age in 1991.

In other words, one cannot speak of a linear development of marital status throughout the century but rather of very different trends. During the first quarter of this century, the single status was as common a status as being married among the women between the ages of 37 and 40. In 1950, there was a high share of widows (10 to 14%) in this age group especially with a declining trend of being single. In 1991 there was more or less the same level of single status, but the share of widows had gone down, and there was a larger proportion of divorced women (6%). The consequence of this development, which can really only be explained historically, is that there was a relatively constant share of married women (77% in 1925, 71% in 1950, and 79% in 1991).

There are more dramatic changes among the men than among the women. Eleven percent of the men aged 37 were single in 1925, which is less than in 1991, when 15% of men aged 40 were single. On the other hand, there were almost no divorced men aged 40 in 1925, whereas in 1991 there were already 9%. The share of married men between the ages of 37 and 40 has dropped significantly throughout the century from 87% in 1925 and 88% in 1950 to only 76% in 1991.

These statistics show that there really are new singles, and they are the single and divorced or separated men of the younger and middle-aged groups. It is not the much quoted change in the role of the women that has brought about a change in the forms of life but instead that men up to the age of 40 are less likely to be married than earlier in the century. The decrease in the group of married men up to the age of 40 surpasses any other changes. Figure 2, which shows the development of marital status since 1950, makes clear that, all along, the unmarried men dominated among those living alone, whereas being a widow is the most important marital status among the women living alone. Sixty percent of the men living on their own are single, only about 25% of them are divorced or separated, and 15% are widowers. Of those women living alone, 30% are single, about 15% are separated or divorced, and 55% are widows.

Owing to an increase of single men among those living alone, the share of single people in this group has surpassed all other forms of marital status since the middle to the end of the 1980s.

Figure 2. Development of the family status of singles by sex, 1950–1992 (percentages). (Data first published in Bertram (1995). Reprinted with permission of Leske and Budrich, publishers.)

This analysis shows clearly that gender is more important for being classified as a single than other factors; secondly, the status as a single among men underlies more shifts than among women. The proportion of singles does not reflect a general trend toward individualization but among men reflects the increasing divorce rate and among women widowhood. This consideration of the marital status does not yet take into account the actually lived relations of the persons. Living alone does not necessarily mean living without intense social relations. Just considering aspects of psychohygienics, one must ask whether the change in marital status may be seen as a sufficient indicator for the so-called change of relationships.

The prevalence of "living apart together," a form of life that has made a career in literature as the new ideal of the modern society of singles, was established in our study with a maximum 9.5% of the 18- to 80-year-olds in the Federal Republic of Germany. In East Germany, some 5% of the interviewees chose this form of life; that is to say about half the rate in West Germany. The analysis of "living apart together" shows that this form of life cannot be regarded as a continuous form of life, which would allow the assumption of a certain life design (Schlemmer, 1995). This life status changes its characteristics in tandem with age and thus does not constitute an alternative to marriage.

"Living apart together" is rather a transitional period to another form of life for those of our study born between 1953 and 1970. The interviewees of this age group and form of life are single and childless, and most of them still live in the households of their parents. Usually, they have the university entrance qualification, and the majority undergo a long period of training. As job starters, they belong to the lower income brackets. "Living apart together" is continued far beyond the average age of marriage and is thus characterized by an independent nature also among the younger interviewees. The partial link to the family of origin obviously secures career-oriented training and job planning for women, and for men, the mother substitutes for a wife, enabling the men to follow independent career planning.

The middle-aged group (born 1933–52) are divorced, and most of them have children. Because the children live with their mothers in most cases, the majority of the women in this age group are one-parent families. It is especially among them that this form of life seems to take on a more permanent nature. Men of this age group, living this form of life usually live alone after a divorce. Because men of the middle-aged group are to be found with a not more than coincidental frequency, one may assume that the new single only chooses this form of life as one trend but otherwise has no permanent relationship.

It becomes clear already at this point that the manifold trends of change in the private forms of life and life styles in modern societies are not only to be characterized through the empirical description of structural changes. Should these processes be made the subject of a consistent approach, then we believe that it would be better to do so via a historical and sociological investigation of relations between the generations and the conditions of the generations and thus to reformulate existing approaches to generation.

The Stability of Child Relations

This process of individualizing forms of life in certain regions and social groups of our society has had few consequences for children growing up. If one-person households occur mostly in the metropolitan areas, the probability of families with many children is not very large there. Thus, it comes as no surprise that the historical comparison up to the year 1991 (year of study) discloses that the majority of the children grew up with their real parents (see Figure 3).

The chances of the children to grow up with their real parents has been influenced throughout this century far more strongly by historical events than by trends of change over the past 15 to 20 years. The highest share of children who grew up with a one-parent family is to be found in the generations of 1933 to 1938. Even foster parent families are rarer today than in those years. Thus, it is difficult to comprehend that researchers now lament the crisis in the parent–child relationship of today and the threat to the children's growing up in stable conditions. The percentages of children who grow up with both their parents are higher at present or at least are just as high as the average of this century. Taking into consideration, at the same time, that the share of children who live in homes or other institutions away from their

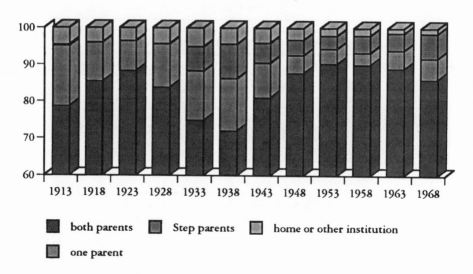

Figure 3. Growing up until the 15th or 18th year of life. (Data first published in Bertram (1995). Reprinted with permission of Leske and Budrich, publishers.)

parents has dropped considerably (to 1.5% in the group interviewed in this study), one can even speak of a stronger trend towards the family in the children growing up in our society. Some 86% of those born after 1968 grew up with both their parents, according to their own statements, 6% with the mother only, and some 7% with foster parents. Why the stable social relations with the parents or foster parents have allegedly become more insecure than among the age groups of those born in 1913, 1933, or 1938 remains the secret of those who adopt the individualization of modern societies as their subject without an extended time perspective.

From the Neolocal Conjugal Family to the Multilocal Family of Several Generations

Whereas the development of children has been little influenced by such trends of individualization, family relations have changed thoroughly as the result of changes in the age structure of society. In 1950, there were about 6.7 million people in Germany who were older than 65 years of age and more than 15 million children up to the age of 14 (see Figure 4). After a peak of some 17 million in the year 1970, the number of children dropped to a little over 12 million in 1991. The number of elderly people had risen to just under 11 million already by 1975 and reached about 12 million in 1991. Whereas the ratio of old to young people was about 1:2 in the 1950s, it is 1:1 today.

Figure 4 summarizes these developments once more and makes clear that this trend did not only start over the past 15 to 20 years. The increase in elderly

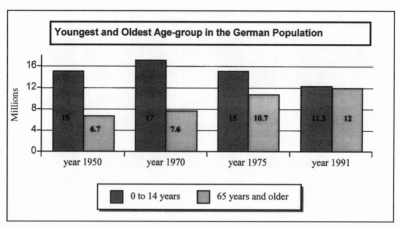

Figure 4. Youngest and oldest age group in the German population. (Data first published in Bertram (1995). Reprinted with permission of Leske and Budrich, publishers.)

had been evident since 1950, without this finding receiving much attention; the increase among the children occurred since the mid 1970s. Today this trend is judged primarily from an economic point of view without attention to the accompanying change in family relations that results from the decrease in the number of children on the one hand and the increase in the security of life on the other. This demographic revolution can only be interpreted in relation to gender from the perspective of the theory of family and relations. Widowers or single men are rarely found in the higher age groups: If men grow older than 60, the majority of them are married. The share of married men among the 60-year-olds is about 87%, and among the 70- to 75-year-olds there are still about 75% married men; even among the 80-year-olds this share is still about 55%. In contrast, only 66% of the 60-year-old women are married versus 36% of the 70-year-olds, and the proportion drops to about 10% among those women aged 80 and over. Owing to the dramatic changes in life expectancy and the different development among men and women, there is not only a group of young men and women living on their own and men of the middle-aged group living alone but also a rising number of widows growing much older. This group cannot really be called singles, but they are just as significant in the change of household structures, especially the one-person households, as the younger age groups.

Thus, the question arises as to whether individual social relations follow similar patterns; that is, if the trends toward individualization in our society are an expression of a stronger differentiation among age groups resulting from a rising life expectancy, different developments in the regions of the Federal Republic of Germany, and a change in the opportunities for men in the marriage market. An egocentric, network-theoretical approach permits us to investigate this issue for all age groups. To establish a clear relation to the process of change, as described in the official statistics, marital status (single, married, divorced, widowed) is used to counter the claim that the results put forward in this chapter can be put down more or less to a new definition of the term "single." On the contrary, the following analyses of interactions between individuals and their families are related explicitly to the debate about individualization, which uses the rising number of divorces, the change in the share of singles, and the decreasing willingness to marry as indicators of a growing insecurity in private relations. This return to the definition of marital status, changes in which are now being used as indicators of trends reflecting crisis in the private structure of relations, enables us to verify that these definitions and their changes serve little to explain the stability or crisis of private relations in a family context.

Extending the Function of the Family as a Consequence of a Secure Lifetime

The structures of social contacts and relations in families may be depicted relatively easily with the help of network-theoretical approaches. At the same time, the model of the neolocal nuclear family can be verified empirically with regard to its validity through lived social relations. In contrast to unmarried single people, married couples with children have to develop a pattern of relations that concentrates essentially on the partner and the children during the childhood phase of socialization and is reduced to relations between the partners once the children leave their family home. This double break in the course of people's lives – first when they find their own marriage and second when the children leave the family context – represents a stark contrast to the multigeneration (extended) family in which patterns of relations also have to change throughout the course of life but where this process of change follows the life rhythm of the parents, the partners, and the children. Relations with one's parents do not become weaker abruptly but rather gradually during the course of one's life as other persons enter, such as the partner and the children; they disappear finally through the death of the parents. Similarly, the children's leaving the family does not lead to an immediate severing of all relations but rather to a continuous breaking away and a possible new start of relations, for instance, between grandparents and grandchildren.

Such a life course theoretical pattern of lived relations between members of a family should actually be verified empirically through a longitudinal study, for the dynamics of lived relations may only be reconstructed through a longitudinal design. But to conduct such a longitudinal study is extremely difficult because the life of one researcher usually does not suffice. The data introduced and analyzed in the following paragraphs are cross-sectional data with which a comparison of age groups is conducted to establish whether there are specific patterns within the framework of age group comparisons.

The age group comparisons, however, relate to the age groups of 18 to 80 years of age, and thus the normal life span of a person in this century can be taken into consideration. If one analyzes the pattern of relations of 18- to 80-year-olds on the basis of a network-theoretical approach, this approach lends itself especially to the investigation of relations that traditionally concern the family. Apart from the elements already known since Weber (1985), for instance, shared meals and leisure time, there are also those items that Parsons and Bales (1955) mentioned: the intimate elements of relations such as how personal matters are discussed and how a close emotional relationship with somebody is developed. Intimacy, familiarity, and close feelings are defined in theory as constitutive elements of the reproductive and educational functions in the private sphere of the family. Apart from these elements of relations, there are of course the joint activities outside the job, especially in the area of leisure time, as well as the joint meals that are regarded as typical elements of patterns of family relations. Within the framework of a network-theoretical approach, it was possible to ask all the interviewees, 16,124 persons (Bertram, 1995, pp. 442ff), to mention the person with whom they have meals, spend their leisure time, share personal and close feelings, and discuss personal matters. Checking all patterns of relations with the help of these four indicators according to the possible family relations of the person, one learns that the relations of people in the age group comparison are determined by two elements regardless of sex, marital status, or social origin of the interviewee. On the one hand age is the decisive variable in explaining to a sufficient degree the differentiation between the age groups, and on the other hand, it is the existence of children. Younger interviewees, those born between 1970 and 1978, who did not have any children at the time of the study, are determined decisively through friends and their own parents in their pattern of relations. Partners do not play a very great role yet, and the brothers and sisters drop behind the significance of the parents. Others, be they acquaintances, relatives, children-in-law, partner parents, or grandparents, may be more or less neglected. As soon as there are enough children among the older interviewees (roughly as of 1953), the children are the dominant group in the pattern of relations among the interviewees. The partners, too, gain in importance then, but the children remain the most important reference group in the person's networks for all interviewees up to the age of 80 insofar as children are around. In comparison, the partners, even if they are of greater significance during the middle-age phase, rarely play such a great role as the children, who usually appear as more than 30% of the persons mentioned in all age groups. A drop in this proportion when the children leave their family home, as would be expected on the basis of Parsons' theory, cannot be identified, for children still have as dominating a role among the oldest interviewees, those born in 1913, as among those born in 1953 (that is to say among the 40- to 43-year-old interviewees).

In differentiating the analysis in Figure 5 according to individual activities and distinguishing single and married interviewees to test the suspected transition to the multilocal family of several generations, one comes to the conclusion, when comparing the emotional ties (compare Figure 6), that, in this case, too, there is no

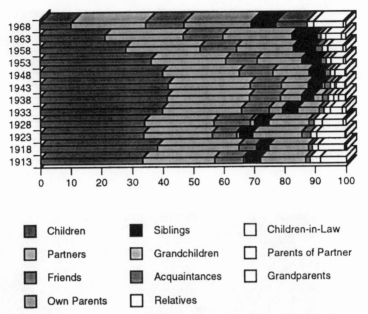

Figure 5. Social relations of married people by age groups. (Data first published in Bertram (1995). Reprinted with permission of Leske and Budrich, publishers.)

break between the family of origin and the new family and that age and marital status are the determining variables. Because single people usually have no children, they cannot develop any close feelings towards them. These close feelings among single people remain with their own parents to a dominating extent.

The decrease in the close feelings towards the parents with age corresponds to the growing incidence of death among the parents, and thus the parents do not leave the emotional world of the singles by the latter's leaving their parental home but only through the death of the parents. Apart from the parents, partners and friends are of some significance. In the higher age bracket, after the death of the parents, brothers and sisters or other relatives take the place beside friends. Thus, a withdrawal from the family context by the single interviewees neither takes place during youth nor during very old age; rather, the singles remain in the family relation patterns throughout their lives. The decisive difference between singles and married interviewees seems to be that singles remain within the relational pattern of their original family, whereas the married interviewees with children and partners build up a new context of relations with regard to their own feelings that is not oriented toward their family of origin any longer but more and more towards their own neolocal family. Among married people, the pattern of relations in the area of feelings is dominated by their children and partners. Parents, siblings, friends, and other relatives play a subordinate role.

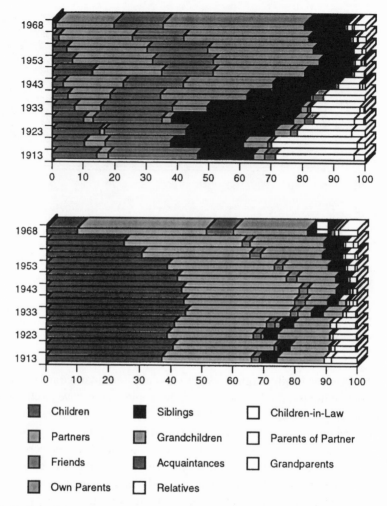

Figure 6. Feelings of closeness among single (top) and married (bottom) persons. (Data first published in Bertram (1995). Reprinted with permission of Leske and Budrich, publishers.)

This pattern, which is evident in close feelings, is also true for the single and the married interviewees for personal discussions and leisure time activities and meals. Married people behave in conformity with Parsons' theory in many points, insofar as this can be verified with the network-theoretical approach, for they really build up a new pattern of relations with the founding of their own family based primarily on children and the partner. Singles remain more or less within the relational pattern of their family of origin. One can also state that for the married interviewees the establishment of new relations does not necessarily mean that the pattern of relations breaks down when their children leave the parental home and that from then on the partners have to rely on one another. The pattern of relations between parents and children remains in place in many points even once the children have founded a family of their own. This is true especially for personal close feelings and personal discussions. It is not true, however, for leisure time activities and joint meals. The impact of children's moving away from the parental home is also documented with these two indicators insofar as joint activities with children decrease significantly and are mainly replaced by joint activities with partners, if they are still around. At higher ages, activities with children are also replaced by joint activities with grandchildren.

The Multilocal Family: Solidarity Among Generations
as a New Function of the Family

The preceding analyses of relations already show relatively systematically that one cannot talk of breaks in the patterns of relations throughout the course of people's lives, as is assumed in the theory of the modern small family. However, the analysis of frequency of contact between members of the nuclear family (parents, children, partners, and siblings, as well as grandparents as nonmembers of the nuclear family) shows that a differentiation between the nuclear family and the extended family has to be regarded as obsolete for the Federal Republic of Germany. Looking at contact frequency and the nuclear family in Figure 7, which is depicted in its regional differentiation, one will find that it follows certain patterns.

By comparing the patterns of contact among family members (Figure 8), one sees that the level of daily contact with grandparents in comparison with siblings makes clear that brothers and sisters are of much less significance in the contact structure of German families than are the grandparents. For instance, there was no region in which brothers and sisters were mentioned more frequently than the grandparents. In whatever way this result may be assessed in detail, one can state that the classic differentiation of nuclear family and extended family (that the relations vary depending on the children and the age of the parents and other relatives) is not reflected. In the regional comparison, the grandparents have a greater significance with regard to the contact frequency than do brothers and sisters, and thus a differentiation between the nuclear family and the extended family cannot be maintained any longer.

The fifth Family Report (Bundesministerium für Familie und Senioren, 1994) disclosed a transition from horizontal structures of relatives (i.e., structures of relatives that relate mainly to the same generation) to vertical structures of relatives due to increasing security of life time. This thesis of the fifth Family Report is confirmed impressively, to my mind, by the data discussed here. Increasing security of lifetime for a greater percentage of the population is thus also leading to an extension of the traditional functions of the family. More or less all theories of family development regard the family dynamics as finished with the move of the children from the parental home (the empty-nest phase). The data introduced here

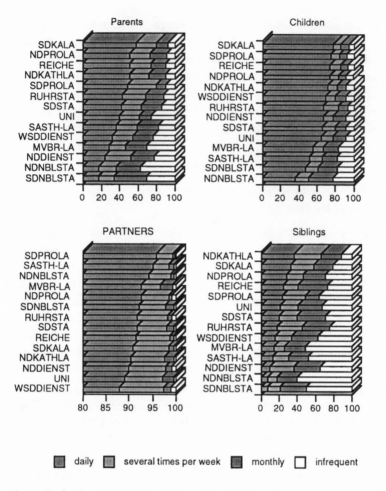

daily ▨ several times per week ▦ monthly ☐ infrequent

Legend of abbreviation in the Figures 7 und 8:

SDKALA	South German Catholic region
NDPROLA	North German Protestant region
Reiche	Wealthy Suburbs
NDKATHLA	North German Catholic region
SDPROLA	South German Protestant region
RUHRSTA	Ruhr area
SDSTA	South German cities
UNI	University towns
SASTH-LA	Saxon, Saxon-Anhalt, Thuringia-region
WSDDIENST	West/South German service centers
MVBR-LA	Brandenburg/Mecklenburg-Vorpommern region
NDDIENST	North German service centers
NDNBLSTA	Brandenburg/Mecklenburg-Vorpommern cities
SDNBLSTA	Saxonian, Thuringian cities

Figure 7. Frequency of contact between members within the nuclear family. (Data first published in Bertram (1995). Reprinted with permission of Leske and Budrich, publishers.)

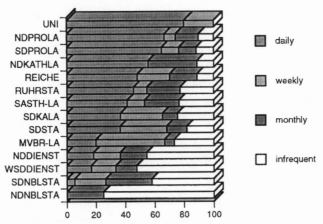

Figure 8. Contact with grandparents. (Data first published in Bertram (1995). Reprinted with permission of Leske and Budrich, publishers.)

show, however, that the empty-nest phase does indeed mark the move of the children from the parental home, but this does not mark the end of family development. Because relations between increasingly older parents and their increasingly older children do not end with the establishment of new households but remain in place until the death of the parents, both parents and children are required to develop new strategies to integrate these relations into the course of their lives.

Thus one can conclude that the increasingly secure lifetime and the decreasing percentage of children in our population have not led to the family being rendered obsolete as a model of relations and life. Rather, the emphasis in family relations has moved from socialization during early and later childhood to the relations between older children and very old parents. Maybe it makes sense to place another function beside that of socialization. One could call this function generation solidarity, which has perhaps turned into another category, a third key element, of family relations apart from those of socialization and regeneration. Unfortunately, family research, apart from a few exceptions, has not attached the necessary attention to this element of solidarity among the generations as a new function of the family. It would, however, be desirable if future family research and family theory would no longer regard the empty-nest phase as the end of family development and would empirically scrutinize the solidarity among generations more closely than has been the case so far.[4]

The results may be summarized by saying that the sequence of generations is decisive for the security and stability of private relations, for only with children and grandchildren may the private relations remain stable throughout the course of life. Parents with children (and grandparents with grandchildren) live in patterns of relations with the subsequent generation, whereas people without children only have relations to their family of origin, relations that naturally end with the death of their parents and cannot really be supported by surviving brothers and sisters and other relatives. Living together, too, is not as important for the security of private relations as the existence of grandchildren and children. The findings of this section show that Parsons' model of the household family is now really only a transitory phase in the course of people's lives. In contrast, the multilocal family of several generations has become reality in the Federal Republic of Germany as a trend, and thus the relations between the generations, the conditions of these generations, and the generational issue move to the center of family sociological studies in a completely new way.[5]

The Individual and the Family: Generation Relations and Generation Conditions

Reflecting about marriage and family from the perspective of life course theory and basing the analysis of families and family development during the course of life on the changed composition of the age groups of the German population, one inevitably arrives at the following five findings:

1. The increase in the number of older parents and grandparents and the decrease in the number of younger children in our society have not led to a decline in the significance of the functions of marriage and family, but, on the contrary, as so often in the history of family, have resulted in a clear transfer of functions and even to their extension. In the 1950s and 1960s, the socialization and reproduction function of the family dominated in the discussion, whereas today generation solidarity has become a decisive part of family relations and thus of the family along with the socialization and reproduction functions.

2. Family relations do not follow the ideas developed by Parsons in the 1950s in all points. It is correct that the formation of a family leads to the fresh establishment of lifelong relations with the partner and the children; however, it is not correct that these new relations represent a complete break with the family of origin. Children's moving out of their parent's home does not at all mean that parents necessarily give up their relations with the children. On the contrary, relations with the children are of greater significance throughout the course of life, with regard to frequency, than are relations with partners. Contrary to traditional theories of socialization, it is not the crisislike breakaway from the parental home that is the central problem in the development of adult personality but rather the development of lifelong relations with parents and grandparents accompanied by independence from early youth onwards. Such lifelong relations necessarily change the view of the parents with regard to the children's development just as adolescence, the link between the childhood lack of independence and the growing support of the adult children, takes on a different significance for their own parents. Longer support of the children through their parents ("Hotel Mom") gains a high degree of functionality in the life courses of the parents. The parental solidarity in the young adult life provides the children with a different background of experience for the solidarity they will render themselves during the old age of their parents.

3. This change in the pattern of family relations, reflected clearly in the data submitted here, has been largely overlooked until now. Because the definition of the family was restricted to persons of a family living together in one household, Parsons' concept was taken over implicitly without verifying within the framework of empirical

analysis whether the household concept is still adequate for the family relations lived today. This, one may conclude, leads to an image of marriage and family that concentrates very much on the family with young children, which only covers a part of the adult's life course and neglects a priori that part of family following in old age. Consideration of a broader definition of family as extending beyond the household has led to a reassessment of the relations between old parents and old children. Thus it will be important for future research to supplement the family development models, which stop at the empty-nest phase nowadays, to formulate a life course theoretical concept of family. Furthermore, it will be significant to make the extension of the functions of family and family relations, which was only hinted at here, the subject of more detailed studies.[6]

4. Thus there cannot be any doubt that the processes of individualization in modern societies, which have led to a differentiation of life and household forms, have also thoroughly changed the relations of the individual with his or her family. This change can neither be interpreted as individualization, singularization, or disintegration of family relations but rather as a transition from the neolocal conjugal family with young children to a multilocal family of several generations with lifelong relations between the generations without these generations having to live under one roof. These lifelong relations of generations with one another will also have to lead to a new theoretical understanding of generations and a respective empirical concept. The simultaneous presence of parents and grandparents for a long period of life will contribute to a change in the self-perception between the generations. Grandparent–grandchild relations gain their own standing side by side with the parent–child relations.

5. For decades socialization has been regarded as the development and nurturance of little children by parents and school. In the 1960s and 1970s, Bronfenbrenner (1986) and Kohn (1977) could demonstrate that, besides parents and school, the occupational experience of parents and the extended ecological conditions of children influence the socialization process. The work of Elder (1974) made clear that history and economic development are of substantial relevance for the socialization of children. These theoretical and empirical approaches had great influence on socialization research. The development of juveniles and young adults was for a long time not the focus of sociological and psychological socialization research because youth in Freud's tradition were seen as breaking with the parents and orienting themselves toward the peer group. The results described here, however, show that the developmental tasks of youth are not limited to loosening bonds and gaining independence; in addition, youth must develop a consciousness of generations as a lifelong partnership between young adults and elder generations on the basis of equal rights.

References

Beck, U. (1986). *Risikogesellschaft. Auf dem Weg in eine andere Moderne* [Risk society. On the way in a different modernity]. Frankfurt am Main: Suhrkamp.

Beck, U. (1997). *Kinder der Freiheit* [Children of freedom]. Frankfurt am Main: Suhrkamp.

Beck, U., & Beck-Gernsheim, E. (1993). Nicht Autonomie, sondern Bastelbiographie. Anmerkungen zur Individualisierungsdiskussion am Beispiel des Aufsatzes von Günter Burkhart [Not autonomy, rather a patchwork biography. Remarks about the individualization discussion from the example of Günter Burkhart's essays]. *Zeitschrift für Soziologie, 22*, 178–187.

Bender, D. (1993). *Von Meta-Daten zur Wissensbank. Ein theoretischer Beitrag mit einer Anwendung relationaler Datenbanktechniken zur Vorbereitung wissensbasierter Speicherung von empirischen Informationen der Sozialwissenschaften. Dissertation. Humboldt-Universität zu Berlin.* [From meta-data to knowledge banks. A theoretical contribution with an appliance of relational data bank techniques for the preparation of knowledge-based memory of empirical information from the social sciences. Ph.D. Thesis].

Berger, P., & Luckmann, T. (1995). *Modernität, Pluralismus und Sinnkrise* [Modernity, pluralism, and the crisis of meaning]. Gütersloh, Germany: Bertelsmann.

Bertram, H. (1991). *Die Familie in Westdeutschland* [The family in West Germany]. Opladen, Germany: Leske & Budrich.

Bertram, H. (1992) *Die Familie in den neuen Bundesländern* [The family in the new Bundesländer]. Opladen, Germany: Leske & Budrich.

Bertram, H. (1995) *Das Individuum und seine Familie. Lebensformen, Familienbeziehungen und Lebensereignisse im Erwachsenenalter* [The individual and his family: Life styles, family relations, and life events in adulthood]. Opladen, Germany: Leske & Budrich.

Bertram, H., Bayer, H., & Bauereiß, R. (1993). *Familienatlas* [Family atlas]. Opladen, Germany: Leske & Budrich.

Bronfenbrenner, U. (1986). Ecology of the family as a context of human development. *Developmental Psychology, 22,* 723–742.

Buchmann, M. (1989). *Script of life.* Chicago: University of Chicago.

Bundesministerium für Familie und Senioren (Ed.). (1994). *Familien und Familienpolitik im geeinten Deutschland. Zukunft des Humanvermögens. Fünfter Familienbericht* [Families and family politics in a united Germany. The future of human capital. The fifth family report]. Bonn.

Clausen, J. (1993). *Kontinuität und Wandel in familialen Generationsbeziehungen* [Continuity and change in family generational relationships]. Constance, Germany: Universitätsverlag Constance.

Coleman, J. S. (1995). *Grundlagen der Sozialtheorie: Körperschaften und die moderne Gesellschaft* [Bases of social theory: Corporations and modern society]. Munich: Oldenberg.

Conger, R. D., & Elder, G. H. (1995). *Families in troubled times.* New York: Aldine de Gruyter.

Dahrendorf, R. (1994). Optionen und Ligature n. D. Die Utopie der Weltbürgergesellschaft [Options and ligatures. The utopia of cosmopolitan society]. In U. Beck, & E. Beck-Gernsheim. (Eds.), *Riskante Freiheiten* [Precarious freedoms]. Frankfurt am Main: Suhrkamp.

Elder, G. H., Jr. (1974). *Children of the Great Depression.* Chicago: University of Chicago.

Etzioni, A. (1988). *The moral dimension.* New York: Crown.

Etzioni, A. (1993). *The spirit of community.* New York: Crown.

Giddens, A. (1988). *Die Konstitution der Gesellschaft. Grundzüge einer Theorie der Strukturierung* [The constitution of society: characteristics of a structural theory]. Frankfurt am Main: Campus.

Giddens, A. (1991). *Modernity and self-identity.* Stanford, CA: Stanford University.

Giddens, A. (1997). *Jenseits von Links und Rechts* [Beyond left and right]. Frankfurt am Main: Suhrkamp.

Kohn, M. L. (1977). *Class and conformity* (2nd ed.). Homewood, IL: Dorsey.

Lasch, C. (1995). *Die blinde Elite* [The blind elite]. Hamburg: Hoffmann & Campe.

Lüscher, K., & Schultheiß, F. (Eds.). (1993). *Generationenbeziehungen in "postmodernen" Gesellschaften* [Generational relationships in "postmodern" societies]. Constance, Germany: Universitätsverlag Constance.

Mannheim, K. (1964). Das Problem der Generationen [The problem of generations]. In K. H. Wolff (Ed.), *Wissenssoziologie.* [Knowledge sociology]. Berlin: Luchterhand.

Matthes, J. (1985). Karl Mannheims *"Das Problem der Generationen," neu gelesen. Generationen–"Gruppen" oder "gesellschaftliche Regelungen von Zeitlichkeit?"* [The problem of generations newly read. Generational "groups" or "social structure of time?"] Zeitschrift für Soziologie, 14(5), 363–372.

Münch, R. (1993). *Das Projekt Europa. Zwischen Nationalstaat, regionaler Autonomie und Weltgesellschaft* [Project Europe. Between nation-state, regional autonomy and world society]. Frankfurt am Main: Suhrkamp.

Parsons, T., & Bales, R. F. (1955). *Family, socialization and interaction process.* New York, NY: Free Press.

Rossi, A. S., & Rossi, P. H. (1990). *On human bonding: Parent-child relations across the life course*. New York: Aldine de Gruyter.

SAS (1996). JMP Statistics and graphics guide version 3.2. Cary, NC: SAS Institute Inc.

Schlemmer, E. (1995). "Living apart together," eine partnerschaftliche Lebensform von Singles? ["Living apart together," A partnership life style of singles?]. In H. Bertram (Ed.), *Das Individuum und seine Familie*. Opladen, Germany: Leske & Budrich.

Vaillant, G. E., (1995). Adaptation to life. Cambridge, MA: Harvard University.

Weber, M. (1985). *Wirtschaft und Gesellschaft* [The economy and society]. Tübingen, Germany: Mohr & Siebeck.

11 A Neighborhood-Level Perspective on Social Change and the Social Control of Adolescent Delinquency

Robert J. Sampson

This chapter explicates the central ideas animating a neighborhood-level approach to what is often treated as a purely "familial" or within-household phenomenon: informal social control. I first outline a theory of neighborhood social control with a focus on the role of social change reflected in concentrated structural disadvantage and patterns of residential instability. Specifically, I examine how unexpected changes in concentrated disadvantage and residential instability relate to variations in informal social control at the neighborhood level. In turn, I provide a preliminary assessment of the mediating role that informal social control plays in the explanation of rates of adolescent delinquency. The data are taken from a recent multilevel study of 80 neighborhoods in Chicago.

Social Disorganization and Social Control

My conceptual framework begins with the classic "Chicago School" tradition of urban sociology pioneered by Robert Park and Ernest Burgess (1921) and later extended by Clifford Shaw and Henry McKay. In *Juvenile Delinquency and Urban Areas*, Shaw and McKay (1942) argued that three structural factors – low economic status, ethnic heterogeneity, and residential mobility – fostered the disruption of community social organization, which in turn accounted for variations in crime and delinquency rates. *Social disorganization* is conceptualized as the inability of a community structure to realize the common values of its residents, and hence, to maintain effective social controls (Kornhauser, 1978; Bursik, 1988). As Janowitz (1975) has argued, social control refers to the capacity of a social unit to regulate itself according to desired principles – to realize *collective*, as opposed to forced, goals. According to this view, social control should not be equated with repression

This chapter was supported by the Project on Human Development in Chicago Neighborhoods and completed while the author was a Fellow at the Center for Advanced Study in the Behavioral Sciences, Stanford, CA. I am grateful for financial support provided by the Carnegie Corporation of New York (Grant B-6346), the John D. and Catherine T. MacArthur Foundation, and the National Institute of Justice. Portions of this chapter appeared in Sampson (1997a,b).

or forced conformity. One of the most central of shared goals is the desire of community residents to live in safe environments free of predatory crime (Bursik, 1988).

The social disorganization approach is grounded in what Kasarda and Janowitz (1974) labeled the "systemic" model in which the local community is viewed as a complex system of friendship and kinship networks, formal and informal associational ties rooted in family life, ongoing socialization processes, and local institutions. Structural components of the systemic model of community social organization include the prevalence and interdependence of social networks in a community (e.g., the density of acquaintanceship; intergenerational ties), institutional strength and mobilization capacity, and the span of collective attention that the community directs toward local problems. Social organization and social disorganization are thus conceived as different ends of a continuum; the systemic structure of a community facilitates or inhibits social control.

Community-level social control emerges from informal role relationships established for other purposes and more formal, purposive efforts to achieve social regulation through institutional means (e.g., arrest, juvenile court sanctions). In this chapter, I highlight the role of *informal* mechanisms by which residents themselves achieve the social control of adolescents. Examples of informal social control with respect to public order include the monitoring of spontaneous play groups among children, the willingness to intervene in preventing acts such as truancy and street-corner "hanging" by teenage peer groups, and confronting young persons who are exploiting or disturbing public space. As discovered originally by Thrasher (1963, p. 25), the origin of much delinquency can be traced to unsupervised, spontaneous play groups among children. Even nongang delinquency tends to be a group phenomenon, suggesting that the capacity of a community to control the group-level dynamics of children and adolescents is a key theoretical mechanism accounting for variations in delinquency rates. Not only is much crime committed by and against young people, but even among adults it regularly arises in public disputes in the context of illegal markets (e.g., prostitution, drugs) and in the company of peers. The capacity of residents to control group-level processes and visible signs of social disorder is thus a key mechanism influencing opportunities for interpersonal crime.

It is important to note that social control does not require homogeneity, whether cultural or sociodemographic. Culturally diverse populations can and do agree on common goals such as safe streets. And social conflicts can and do rend communities along the lines of economic resources, race, political empowerment, and the role of criminal justice agents in defining and controlling social deviance (e.g., drug use, gangs, panhandling, police misconduct). It is around the distribution of resources and power that conflict usually emerges, not the content of core values (Kornhauser, 1978). As Selznick has argued, the goal of community is the reconciliation of partial with general perspectives on the common good (Selznick, 1992, p.369). This sociological conception of social control addresses the long-standing criticism (Whyte, 1943) that theories of community social organization downplay social conflict.

Neighborhood Context and Social Change

Macrolevel social change manifests itself in important ways at the more proximate level of neighborhoods. Two neighborhood-level structural factors are especially relevant for understanding informal social control: residential instability and the increasing concentration of poverty.

Instability

The systemic model of community highlights the system of social ties embedded within ecological, institutional, and normative community structures. The basic hypothesis derived from this conceptualization is that residential change is an exogenous factor influencing local social organization. As Kasarda and Janowitz (1974, p. 330) have argued, "Since the assimilation of newcomers into the social fabric of local communities is necessarily a temporal process, residential mobility operates as a barrier to the development of extensive friendship and kinship bonds and widespread local associational ties."

I recently tested a version of the basic systemic model by examining length of residence at the individual and community levels (Sampson, 1988). Using data from a 1982 national survey of England and Wales that permitted construction of community-level variables for 238 areas, I showed through my empirical analysis that local friendship ties varied widely across communities and that these variations were positively related to residential stability. In particular, neighborhood stability was strongly associated with local friendship ties in both urban and rural areas and had independent effects on collective attachment to community and rates of participation in social and leisure activities. However, I did not examine the direct link between residential change and the informal social control of adolescents. Addressing this need, I draw on the systemic model of community to test the hypothesis that neighborhoods undergoing unexpected residential change are at risk for disrupted patterns of local social control (see also Sampson, 1997a,b).

Changes in Concentrated Disadvantage

A second dimension of social change concerns inequality and structural disadvantage, especially in urban neighborhoods of American cities. Consider first the large base-rate differentials in poverty by neighborhood and race. Although the majority of poor non-Hispanic Whites live in nonpoverty areas in the largest U.S. central cities, less than 20% of poor Blacks do (Wilson, 1987; Massey, 1996). Moreover, whereas less than 10% of poor Whites live in extreme poverty or ghetto areas, almost 2 in 5 poor Blacks live in such areas. The majority of poor Blacks also live in communities characterized by high rates of family disruption (Sampson, 1987).

These patterns underscore what Wilson (1987) has labeled "concentration effects" – living in a neighborhood that is overwhelmingly impoverished.

Perhaps most important for the theme of social change, the transformation of U.S. cities in recent decades has resulted in an increased concentration of the most disadvantaged *and* advantaged segments of the urban population. Among poor, female-headed families with children, the proportion residing in ghetto or extreme poverty areas increased in the period 1970–1990. But as Massey (1996) has recently noted, there have been concomitant increases in the concentration of affluence as well. The rich increasingly isolate themselves in enclaves of wealth and privilege. The result is a growing schism between advantaged and disadvantaged residents of American cities.

This process of social transformation has been fueled by macrostructural economic changes related to the deindustrialization of central cities where disadvantaged minorities are concentrated (e.g., a shift from goods-producing to service-producing industries, increasing polarization of the labor market into low-wage and high-wage sectors, and relocation of manufacturing out of the inner city). The exodus of middle- and upper-income Black families from the inner city has also removed an important social buffer that could potentially deflect the full impact of prolonged joblessness and industrial transformation. Wilson (1987, p. 56) argues that the basic institutions of a neighborhood (e.g., churches, schools, stores) are more likely to remain viable if the core of their support comes from more economically stable families.

Wilson's (1987) concept of social isolation in areas of concentrated poverty is consistent with findings by Land, McCall, and Cohen (1990) and also those of Taylor and Covington (1988), who found that increasing entrenchment of urban poverty was associated with increases in violence. The results of Land et al. (1990) also go beyond Wilson's by suggesting that the clustering of economic and social indicators appears not only in 1980 and in neighborhoods of large cities but for the two previous decennial periods and at the level of macrosocial units as a whole. Moreover, Land et al. present evidence in support of Wilson's argument that concentration effects grew more severe from 1970 to 1980 in large cities: "the numerical values of the component loadings of percent poverty, percent Black, and percent of children under 18 not living with both parents are larger in 1980 than 1970" (1990, p. 945). Therefore, various indicators of urban disadvantaged populations are not only highly related but are increasing in concentration (see also Massey & Eggers, 1990).

Inner-city neighborhoods have also suffered from population and housing loss of the sort identified earlier as disruptive of the social and institutional order. Skogan (1986, p. 206) has noted how urban renewal and forced migration contributed to the wholesale uprooting of many urban Black communities, especially the extent to which freeway networks driven through the hearts of many cities in the 1950s destroyed viable, low income areas. Nationwide, fully 20% of all central-city housing units occupied by Blacks were lost in the period 1960–1970 alone (for a more extensive review, see Sampson, 1997b).

In short, linking social disorganization theory with research on urban poverty suggests that both historic and contemporary changes in segregation, migration, housing discrimination, and the macro economy bear on changes in community-level factors – especially residential turnover and concentrated poverty – that impede the social control of adolescence. This viewpoint focuses attention on the proximate neighborhood characteristics and mediating processes of social control that help explain crime while recognizing the larger historical, social, and political changes that shape local communities (Sampson, 1997b; Massey & Denton, 1993). I thus hypothesize that neighborhood-level social control explains variations in adolescent delinquency, mediating, in part, the broader effects of social change as manifested in concentrated disadvantage and residential instability.

Research Design and Data

The present study builds on recent efforts to measure the collective dimensions of neighborhood social control empirically (Sampson & Groves, 1989; Elliott et al., 1996; Sampson, 1997a). The goal is to explain neighborhood-level variations in rates of informal social control and adolescent delinquency. The data stem from an ongoing study, the Project on Human Development in Chicago Neighborhoods (PHDCN).

I define neighborhoods on the basis of territoriality and leave the extent of solidarity problematic (see also Tilly 1973, p. 212). Formulated in this way, the dimensions of social control are variable and analytically separable not only from potential sources of variation (e.g., concentrated poverty, instability) but from the operational definition of the units of analysis. To operationalize neighborhood, Chicago's 847 populated census tracts were combined to create 343 "neighborhood clusters" (NCs). The overriding consideration in forming NCs was that they should be ecologically meaningful units composed of geographically contiguous census tracts and should be internally homogeneous for a variety of census indicators (for a fuller description of procedures, see Sampson, 1997a).

The sample design for the PHDCN is predicated on probabilistic sampling methods. Eighty sampled neighborhood clusters were selected for intensive study stratified across 21 cells defined by cross-classifying socioeconomic status (SES) and race and ethnicity. Census data were used to define the two stratification variables: racial–ethnic mix (three homogeneous strata and four heterogeneous strata) and an SES scale trichotomized into equal thirds (see Table 1).

Reflecting the unfortunate pattern of segregation by race and class that is predominant in American society, the number of NCs falling into the 21 strata created by the cross-classification of racial–ethnic mix and SES was uneven. Although the aim of the PHDCN was to obtain nearly equal numbers of NCs from each of the

Table 1. *Racial–ethnic composition by socioeconomic strata (SES):[a] Distribution of 80 sampled neighborhood clusters in the Project on Human Development in Chicago Neighborhoods (PHDCN)*

		SES	
Race–ethnicity	Low	Medium	High
75% Black or more	9	4	4
75% White or more	0	4	8
75% Hispanic or more	4	4	0
20% Hispanic or more 20% White or more	4	5	4
20% Hispanic or more 20% Black or more	4	4	0
20% Black or more 20% White or more	2	4	4
Neighborhood clusters not classified above	4	4	4
Total	27	29	24

[a] SES was defined by a six-item scale that summed standardized neighborhood-level measures of median income, percentage of college educated, percentage with household income over $50,000, percentage of families below the poverty line, percentage on public assistance, and percentage with household income less than $5,000. In forming the scale the last three items were reverse coded.

strata, in fact, 3 of the 21 strata were empty (e.g., low SES White), and an additional three cells had fewer than five NCs. Neighborhood clusters were thus selected with certainty in these three cells. In other strata, four NCs were selected systematically after sorting by SES and housing density. Because of the sparseness of several strata, a sample of 4 NCs per stratum could not produce the desired total sample of 80 NCs. The balance of NCs were sampled from the largest strata. The resulting sample of 80 NCs (Table 1) thus capitalizes on, to the maximum extent possible, the range of racial and ethnic diversity and SES stratification that currently exists in the city of Chicago.

The Community Survey (CS) of the PHDCN is a multidimensional assessment by residents of the structural and cultural organization of their neighborhoods. To gain a complete picture of the city's neighborhoods, 8,782 Chicago residents representing all 343 NCs were interviewed in their homes. However, the major effort was concentrated in the 80 stratified NCs, where 3,864 interviews were conducted for an average of 48 per NC. The remainder of this chapter focuses on the 80 NCs and the sample of 3,864, reflecting a final response rate of 78%.

Measuring Social Control

To tap the informal social control of neighborhood life, especially regarding children, the following five interview questions were examined:

1. If a group of neighborhood children were skipping school and hanging out on a street
   corner, how likely is it that your neighbors would do something about it?,
2. If some children were spraypainting graffiti on a local building, how likely is it that
   your neighbors would do something about it?,
3. If a child was showing disrespect to an adult, how likely is it that people in your
   neighborhood would scold that child?,
4. If there was a fight in front of your house and someone was being beaten or threatened,
   how likely is it that your neighbors would break it up?, and
5. Suppose that because of budget cuts the fire station closest to your home was going
   to be closed down by the city. How likely is it that neighborhood residents would
   organize to try to do something to keep the fire station open?

For each question, respondents were asked, Would you say it is *very likely, likely,
unlikely*, or *very unlikely*?[1] Note that this measure was designed to tap the likelihood
of *neighbors'* (not the respondent's) willingness to intervene. Consistent with the
neighborhood-level focus, each respondent thus was utilized as an informant and
asked to rate the collective properties of neighborhood social control.

Note also that the respondents were asked about collective expectations for action
rather than the frequency of actual social-control events. The latter is confounded
with the presence or absence of delinquency itself; some neighborhoods may exhibit
relatively few acts of social control simply because there is less need to do so.
Hence, the study opted for using vignettes that tap a latent capacity for taking
action.

The aggregate reliability for the measure of informal social control is .85 –
higher even than the individual-level Cronbach's alpha – indicating that the items
successfully tap mean levels of between-neighborhood variation (for details, see
Sampson, 1997a). Thirteen percent of the variance is between clusters, and hence
there were considerable differences in perceptions among individuals within the
same neighborhood on the level of social control. Still, the between-neighborhood
portion of variation is consistent with previous research using global ratings of
social contexts (Elliott et al., 1996). More important, the relatively high aggregate-
level reliability indicates that we were able to assess, with precision, meaningful
differences among neighborhoods in informal social control.

From the community survey, three questions were selected that tapped patterns
of conduct typical of adolescent delinquency: gang fights, graffiti, and instigating
trouble in groups. With respect to gangs, each respondent was asked how often in the
past 6 months there were gang fights in the neighborhood (*often, sometimes, rarely,
never*). Respondents were asked also how much of a problem in the neighborhood
"graffiti on buildings and walls" and "groups of teenagers or adults hanging out in
the neighborhood and causing trouble" (*a big problem, somewhat of a problem*, or

not a problem) presented. Not surprisingly, when aggregated to the neighborhood level these three items were correlated highly (at .74 or higher). They were thus combined to form a composite *delinquency rate* scale. The aggregate reliability of delinquency rate was .89 – even higher than the neighborhood-level reliability of informal social control. Moreover, almost 20% of the variance in delinquency was between clusters.

The measures of informal social control and delinquency were correlated at $-.64$ ($p < .01$), indicating that neighborhoods with high levels of collective social regulation of children also exhibit substantially lower rates of adolescent delinquency in the form of gang fights, graffiti, and peer-group disorder. This finding conforms to the predictions of the social disorganization theory articulated earlier and in Sampson and Groves (1989).

Social Change and Neighborhood Structure

Three predictors were examined based on a prior principal components analysis of 1990 census data in Chicago (Sampson, 1997a). The first factor, concentrated poverty, represents economic disadvantage in racially segregated urban neighborhoods and is dominated by high loadings ($> .8$) for poverty, public assistance, unemployment, and female-headed families with children, followed by, to a lesser extent, percentage of Blacks. Hence, the predominant interpretation revolves around the neighborhood concentration of economic disadvantage, to which African Americans and single-parent families with children are disproportionately exposed. The second factor captures areas of the city undergoing immigration. The variables that define this dimension are percentage of Latinos (approximately 70% of Latinos are Mexican American in Chicago), percentage of foreign born, percentage under age 18, and percentage with no college education. The third factor is dominated by just two variables with very high ($> .8$) loadings: percentage living in the same house as 5 years earlier, and percentage of owner-occupied homes. The clear emergence of a residential stability factor is consistent with much past research. Using factor loadings as weights, summary scales were created to reflect all three dimensions.[2]

Using parallel items from the PHDCN community survey aggregated to the neighborhood level, I also calculated factor scores for structural disadvantage, residential instability, and ethnicity and immigration for the year 1995. Then, to better capture notions of change with respect to the two key variables of disadvantage and instability, I created residual change scores from 1990 to 1995. Specifically, I regressed the 1995 survey-based disadvantage and instability factor scales on the analogous factor scales from the 1990 census and saved the residuals. These residual values represent changes in 1995 not accounted for by prior levels, taking into account ongoing city-wide dynamics.

Table 2. *Correlations of informal social control with neighborhood characteristics: 80 Chicago neighborhoods (PHDCN, 1995)*

	Informal social control
Structural disadvantage	−.39*
Ethnicity–immigration	−.40*
Residential instability	−.49*
▲ In disadvantage	−.19
▲ In instability	−.43*

Note: $*p < .05$

Table 3. *Weighted least-squares regression of informal social control on neighborhood characteristics: 80 Chicago neighborhoods (PHDCN, 1995)*

	Informal social control	
	β	t ratio
Structural disadvantage	−.29*	−3.35
Ethnicity–immigration	−.19	−1.77
Residential instability	−.57*	−6.79
▲ In disadvantage	−.23*	−2.08
▲ In instability	−.19*	−2.14
	$R^2 = .60$	

Note: $*p < .05$

Main Results

Table 2 presents the simple correlations of informal social control with the structural predictors – both static and change scores. One notes that informal social control is lower in disadvantaged, heterogeneous, and residentially unstable neighborhoods. The correlation with instability is of the greatest magnitude (−.49). Interestingly, informal social control is substantially lower in neighborhoods undergoing unexpected increases in instability ($r = −.43$) but is only modestly related to increases in disadvantage (−.19).

Table 3 turns to a multivariate weighted least-squares (WLS) regression of variations in social control predicted by concentrated poverty, ethnicity and immigration, residential instability, and the two change scores.[3] Consistent with social disorganization theory, the disadvantage and instability factors are the major predictors of variations in social control. By far the largest predictor is neighborhood instability: the higher the level of residential instability, the lower the reported

Table 4. *Weighted least-squares*
neighborhood-level regression of changes
in neighborhood social control and
adolescent delinquency, controlled for prior
crime: 80 Chicago neighborhoods
(PHDCN, 1995)

| | Adolescent delinquency | |
| | Model 1 | Model 2 |
	β	β
Lagged crime rate	.34*	.21*
▲ In disadvantage	.52*	.44*
▲ In instability	.23*	.11
Informal social control	–	−.43*
	$R^2 = .50^*$	$R^2 = .64^*$

Note: $^*p < .05$. Entries are standardized coefficients.

levels of collective neighborhood regulation (beta $= -.57$). Furthermore, informal social control is significantly lower in neighborhoods characterized by unexpected *increases* in structural disadvantage and residential instability. Social change at the neighborhood level apparently adds an important element to our understanding of patterns of social control. Indeed, both change scores add significantly to the prediction of informal social control on top of the lagged census-based factor scales.

Table 4 completes the analysis by presenting the predictors of between-neighborhood variations in delinquency rates. To provide the strictest test possible in assessing the predictive validity of informal social control, neighborhood-level variations in prior crime were introduced as a control variable. Skogan (1986) has provided an overview of some of the feedback processes of crime itself, including (a) physical and psychological withdrawal from community life, (b) erosion of the informal social control processes that inhibit crime, and (c) a decline in the organizational life and mobilization capacity of the neighborhood. He argues that residents in neighborhoods with high crime rates may be deterred from engaging in collective social control or other forms of mobilization out of fear of retaliation from neighborhood youth.

To account for this possibility, crime incident data from 1993 were aggregated to the cluster level for each of the 80 NCs and normalized by population size.[4] Informed by principal components analysis, a crime-rate scale was created that summed standardized rates of homicide, robbery, aggravated assault, weapon use, and drug violations. These crime rates were highly related, reflecting the nexus of predatory violence and drug dealing found in many neighborhoods. Controlling for a lagged measure of criminal violence should provide a strict test of the independent effect of collective social control on delinquency rates.

Prior crime also helps to account for unmeasured causes of current delinquency. Not surprisingly, prior crime is highly correlated with the lagged census factors – especially disadvantage ($r = .85$). To achieve empirical and theoretical parsimony I thus examine the lagged crime scale in conjunction with the two 1990–1995 change scores as explanatory predictors. Recall further that, by definition, the change scores are statistically independent of the lagged census factors measured in 1990. Hence, the lagged predictors are not included in the model because our primary interest is in the change estimates.

The results in Table 4 continue to validate the neighborhood social control measure. The standardized estimate of informal social control is not only still significant but double the magnitude for the violent crime. (The bivariate correlation between violent crime and later delinquency was .38, $p < .05$). Moreover, informal social control mediates about half of the effect of changes in residential instability. Note that the standardized coefficient drops from .23 to .11 once social control is introduced (compare Models 1 and 2). The direct association of increases in structural disadvantage with delinquency remains. Thus, delinquency is explained primarily by increases in concentrated disadvantage, prior levels of violent crime, and low informal social control, the latter of which mediates the role of changes in residential instability.

Conclusion

Overall, variations in neighborhood-level informal social control accorded reasonably well with theoretical predictions. There are limitations of the study to be sure, especially given that social controls were measured at only one point in time and were inferred from informant perceptions of latent neighborhood capacity. Nonetheless, prior levels and ecological changes in concentrated poverty and residential instability explained significant amounts of variation in social control and delinquency in the direction expected. Informal social control also mediated much of the effect of residential instability, consistent with one of the major themes in social disorganization theory. Even after adjustment for prior levels of crime in the neighborhood, informal social control emerged as a significant inhibitor of adolescent delinquency.

On the basis of these patterns, I would argue that changes at the neighborhood level – induced by wider structural changes in society at large – have important consequences at the local level for the understanding of social control and adolescent delinquency. One agenda for future research will be to extend the logic of the present study to consider other dimensions of social change relevant for adolescents. Changes in drug distribution networks, the availability and lethality of weapons, and changes in family relations may be such factors. Furstenberg (1993), for example, has argued that community-level context has an indirect influence on adolescence through family management practices. The monitoring of youth activities and time spent with peers, ties between parents and their children's friends and parents, and the effective and consistent discipline of children may be especially sensitive to secular changes and their manifestations at the neighborhood level. Research designed to uncover the influence of changes in family structure, family management practices, and community social control on adolescent delinquency is one of the major goals now being addressed in the PHDCN.

Another research need is to examine these issues in a cross-national, comparative framework. To the extent that generic patterns of informal social control, adolescent delinquency, and social change emerge in different international contexts, we will have increased confidence in general theories of community-level social change. Motivated by this concern, current research is now attempting to replicate the present findings in the neighborhoods of Stockholm, Sweden (Wikström & Sampson, 1997). Stockholm and Chicago are worlds apart in their crime rates, but from a comparative perspective, this is nearly ideal if our goal is to uncover general, structural characteristics that transcend cultural and national boundaries. Following the "most different" research design for comparative studies put forth by Przeworski and Teune (1970, pp. 34–46), our goal is to assess whether there are common relationships between changing structural characteristics, informal social control, and crime rates in these disparate cities.

References

Bursik, R. J., Jr. (1988). Social disorganization and theories of crime and delinquency: Problems and prospects. *Criminology, 26,* 519–52.

Elliott, D., Wilson, W., Huizinga, D., Sampson, R., Elliott, A., & Rankin, B. (1996). The effects of neighborhood disadvantage on adolescent development. *Journal of Research in Crime and Delinquency, 33,* 389–426.

Furstenberg, F. (1993). How families manage risk and opportunity in dangerous neighborhoods. In W. J. Wilson (Ed.), *Sociology and the public agenda* (pp. 231– 258). Newbury Park, CA: Sage.

Hanushek, E., & Jackson, J. (1977). *Statistical methods for social scientists.* New York: Academic.

Janowitz, M. (1975). Sociological theory and social control. *American Journal of Sociology, 81,* 82–108.

Kasarda, J., & Janowitz, M. (1974). Community attachment in mass society. *American Sociological Review, 39,* 328–339.

Kornhauser, R. (1978). *Social sources of delinquency.* Chicago: University of Chicago Press.

Land, K., McCall, P., & Cohen, L. (1990). Structural covariates of homicide rates: Are there any invariances across time and space? *American Journal of Sociology, 95,* 922–963.

Massey, D. (1996). The age of extremes: Concentrated affluence and poverty in the twenty-first century. *Demography, 33,* 395–412.

Massey, D., & Denton, N. (1993). *American apartheid: Segregation and the making of the underclass.* Cambridge, MA: Harvard University Press.

Massey, D., & Eggers., M. (1990). The ecology of inequality: Minorities and the concentration of poverty, 1970–1980. *American Journal of Sociology, 95,* 1153–1188.

Park, R., & Burgess, E. (1921). *Introduction to the science of sociology.* Chicago: University of Chicago Press.

Przeworski, A., & Teune, H. (1970). *The logic of comparative inquiry.* New York: Wiley.

Sampson, R. J. (1987). Urban Black violence: The effect of male joblessness and family disruption. *American Journal of Sociology, 93,* 348–382.

Sampson, R. J. (1988). Local friendship ties and community attachment in mass society: A multilevel systemic model. *American Sociological Review, 53,* 766–779.

Sampson, R. J. (1992). Family management and child development: Insights from social disorganization theory. In J. McCord (Ed.), *Facts, frameworks, and forecasts: Advances in criminological theory* (Vol. 3, pp. 63–93). New Brunswick, NJ: Transaction.

Sampson, R. J. (1997a). Collective regulation of adolescent misbehavior: Validation results from eighty Chicago neighborhoods. *Journal of Adolescent Research, 12,* 227–244.

Sampson, R. J. (1997b). The embeddedness of child and adolescent development: A community-level perspective on urban violence. In J. McCord (Ed.), *Childhood and violence in the inner city* (pp. 31–77). New York: Cambridge University Press.

Sampson, R.J., & Groves, W.B. (1989). Community structure and crime: Testing social-disorganization theory. *American Journal of Sociology, 94,* 774–802.

Selznick, P. (1992). *The moral commonwealth: Social theory and the promise of community.* Berkeley, CA: University of California Press.

Shaw, C., & McKay, H. (1942). *Juvenile delinquency and urban areas.* Chicago: University of Chicago Press.

Skogan, W. (1986). Fear of crime and neighborhood change. In A. J. Reiss, Jr., & M. Tonry (Eds.), *Communities and crime* (pp. 203–229). Chicago: University of Chicago Press.

Taylor, R., & Covington, J. (1988). Neighborhood changes in ecology and violence. *Criminology, 26,* 553–590.

Thrasher, F. (1963). *The gang: A study of 1,313 gangs in Chicago* (Rev. ed.). Chicago: University of Chicago Press.

Tilly, C. (1973). Do communities act? *Sociological Inquiry, 43,* 209–240.

Wikström, P., & Sampson., R. J. (1997, November). *On the comparative study of neighborhood context: Stockholm and Chicago.* Paper presented at the annual meeting of the American Society of Criminology, San Diego, CA.

Whyte, W. F. (1943). *Street corner society: The social structure of an Italian slum.* Chicago: University of Chicago Press.

Wilson, W. J. (1987). *The truly disadvantaged: The inner city, the underclass, and public policy.* Chicago: University of Chicago Press.

12   Social Change and the "Social Contract" in Adolescent Development

Constance A. Flanagan

In the 20 years since the publication of *The Ecology of Human Development* (Bronfenbrenner, 1979), social scientists have increasingly become cognizant of the ways that human development is contextualized. The chapters in this section of the volume are no exception. In Bronfenbrenner's framework, they focus on microsystems – families, peer groups, neighborhoods – and illustrate how conditions in, as well as the very definition of, these proximal settings are affected by macrolevel changes.

My commentary is organized in two parts. The first employs the metaphor of a social contract as a conceptual framework for understanding adolescent development in the context of social change. In the second part I take the liberty of rearranging the title of the volume from *Negotiating Adolescence in Times of Social Change* to *Adolescents Negotiating Social Change* to highlight the active role of youth as agents of change. As a complement to the three chapters in this section I draw from a program of work I have been directing on adolescents' interpretations of the "social contract." The first study in this research program compares youth from three stable democratic and capitalist nations (Australia, Sweden, and the United States) with their peers in Bulgaria, the Czech Republic, Hungary, and Russia. The latter nations are in the throes of change from command to market economies and from one-party to multiparty political systems. The second study concerns American adolescents' perceptions of race and ethnic relations in the broader context of their ideas about justice, opportunity, and membership in American society.

By the social contract I refer to the bargain or deal that inheres between persons and their society. It is a useful construct for understanding how macrolevel phenomena are linked with proximal settings under stable conditions but is even more advantageous for illustrating how changes at the macrolevel disrupt those links.

Adolescents' Interpretation of the "Social Contract" is a collaborative project directed by Connie Flanagan and supported in part by grants from the William T. Grant Foundation and the Johann Jacobs Foundation. The study Intergroup Understanding, Social Justice, and the "Social Contract" in Diverse Communities of Youth is funded by the Carnegie Corporation as part of their initiative on improving youth intergroup relations.

191

The metaphor implies that, in the course of growing up, children develop an under-standing of their social order and of the principles that make it "work." Their social theories incorporate core values of the dominant ethos in their society because its principles guide the practices of daily life and the very structures of developmental settings (Moscovici, 1988; Goodnow, Miller, & Kessel, 1995).

For example, in our comparative study we found that it was common across coun-tries to expect that children, by age 8, would be responsible for some household chores (Bowes, Chalmers, & Flanagan, 1997). However, the function and form of this practice differed in ways that were consonant with a society's economic con-tract. Whereas it was common practice in the three capitalist nations to pay children an allowance for doing chores, in those nations that were just beginning to adopt market principles, it was not. The link between wages and work was even more obvious in the United States, where a piecework principle (i.e., that children should be paid for *each* job they did) was endorsed by a sizable minority of participants.

Furthermore, the developmental function of household chores (i.e., in terms of the lessons children were expected to learn) varied on an individualist–collectivist dimension. American and Australian adolescents felt that doing chores was good training in self-discipline, an opportunity to learn responsibility for oneself and one's property. In contrast, youth from nations with a strong social welfare con-tract held that the primary value of having children help around the house was to teach them responsibility to the group. In summary, there were logical links be-tween practices in the proximal settings of development and the principles of the politicoeconomic order, and we concluded that it was through such routines in the proximal settings of development that the principles of the social contract were reproduced (Giddens, 1984).

However, in a context of social change, such connections are broken. When the bargain or deal changes, customary ways of behaving that were functional in the old system may be maladaptive in the new. The chapter by Noack is illustrative, especially for the youth from the former German Democratic Republic (GDR) who were raised under one set of rules but would make their transition into adulthood under another. Were adolescents' peer relations affected by these changes? Among youth in the East and in the West, negative perceptions of social change were associated with some distancing from peers. The peer relations of youth from the West were more vulnerable to their perceptions of increased competitiveness in society. The perception that life had become a rat race appeared to compromise their friendships (i.e., in the context of increased competition, friends became more rejecting and less reliable).

By comparison, the peer relations of youth in the East were susceptible to their feelings of anomie and uncertainty about the future. These perceptions of social change were associated with less confidence in peer networks. Whereas those net-works might have provided support for coping with the breakdown of the social order, instead youth who were anxious about the future seemed to retreat from their friends. The contrasting sensitivities and patterns in the two parts of the country resonate with the implications of reunification as well as with the ways that youth were differentially prepared to deal with stress. Reunification did exact an economic burden on the western part of Germany and increased competition for slots in higher education and apprenticeships. And, although there had been little autonomy in the East, security about one's future was a given in the old order. However, what had been functional ways of coping under earlier conditions left youth in the former GDR poorly prepared to engage friends as a support system in the new social order. Revealing private feelings to others outside of one's family or closest relations was done with great caution during the Soviet era (Scheye, 1991), especially if those feelings reflected discontent with the social order.

Whereas Noack's work draws attention to precipitous change in the conditions of a nation's contract, Sampson's reminds us that the costs of change may be borne disproportionately by certain groups. Borrowing from the metaphor, one observes that the terms of the social contract may vary significantly across communities with vastly different opportunity structures and safety nets for their residents. The social change at the heart of Sampson's study (i.e., the concentration of the most disadvantaged groups in large urban areas), is the result of the combined effects of economic restructuring, the redirection of social policies, and the migration of the middle class out of urban areas in the United States.

The stubborn association between poverty and delinquency has long been known. But Sampson demonstrates how this relationship is mediated by the lack of a neighborhood's collective resolve to intervene in the actions of its youth. Whereas the public's attribution for delinquency typically falls squarely on the shoulders of individual parents, Sampson draws attention to the larger ecology of the neighborhood and the collective will of its residents to do something on behalf of the community. Such social organization within a neighborhood ensures the rights of residents to safety. It also makes the neighborhood a good place to grow up. What are the messages implied in the collective resolve of a community to act? I suggest that there is a civic ethic communicated in this resolve. First, that members of the community have a right to free, open, and safe public spaces. Second, that members are prepared to work together to protect those rights. And third, although the teenagers may not process the message in so many words, their neighbors are insisting that the youth themselves have an obligation to the community. They will not be permitted to contribute to its disintegration.

However, social change in the forms of concentrated poverty and residential mobility erodes the social integuments that connect members of a neighborhood together in defense of their public spaces. Under such conditions, there is a disintegration of the sense of place, membership, and goals held in common. Youth are doubly jeopardized in communities of concentrated poverty. Not only is their safety and quality of life compromised, but these communities typically lack the social connections and cachet that might link residents to opportunities in mainstream society. Social isolation extends to the political process as well. Over and above the negative effects of family poverty on a community's political efficacy, high levels of poverty reduce the number of civic organizations, church groups, and indirect ties to public officials that enable residents to address their community's problems (Cohen & Dawson, 1993).

The concentration of poverty among urban minority residents in the United States did not just happen. Elective policy decisions, including cutbacks in social programs, disinvestment in the urban infrastructure, and regressive tax policies, exacerbated the problems of economic restructuring and increased what were already some of the largest income disparities in the industrialized world (Wilson, 1991). Income trends of the past two decades corroborated F. Scott Fitzgerald's pronouncement of the 1920's: The rich got richer and the poor poorer. The percentage of income received by the top 20% of the population was the highest ratio recorded since 1949, when the Census Bureau began keeping such records. During this same era the incomes of the poorest 10% of American households declined by 8.6% (Center for Budget and Policy Priorities, 1990). Since the era of the federal War on Poverty, there have been significant changes in the American social contract that have displaced large numbers of families to the margins of society and attenuated opportunities for minority youth in poor urban communities. As a result, in a nation built on the principle of a level playing field, adolescents' chances for a fair deal vary considerably, depending on the community in which they grow up. What do children growing up in communities with vastly different ecologies conclude about the principles of the social contract that bind people to their society?

We have tried to address this issue in a study of American high school students, teens whose neighborhoods span the spectrum of opportunity in America. Because the motivation behind this program of work was to understand the evolving political theories of young people, we have obtained samples in social studies and civics classes in the schools. This tends to bias the samples of inner-city youth towards those most committed to education and the promise of the work ethic and opportunity. Our samples include several hundred high school students evenly distributed across communities we have referred to as the inner city, urban ring, and wealthy suburb (Flanagan, Ingram, Gallay, & Gallay, 1996). Like many northern industrial areas, this region experienced high levels of unemployment during the past 15 years and, despite the economic recovery in the nation, the poor have been bypassed. The urban area in our study is one of the five cities in the United States accounting for the growth in persistently poor communities in recent years (Wilson, 1991).

To understand how the terms of the social contract as they are manifest in the opportunity structures and safety nets of different communities may relate to emergent political theories, we have posed two kinds of questions to youth. First, we look at their attributions for economic problems in the country by asking, If some foreigners were visiting our country and they asked you to explain some things to them, how would you explain unemployment to them? Poverty? Homelessness?

Wealth? Second, we ask youth about the values and world views they encounter in their families and schools.

We find that youth from communities that are advantaged by the economic system seem to expect that system to work. They were more likely than their disadvantaged peers to blame unemployment on plant closings or to hold the government accountable for homelessness. They noted that social connections or inheritance as well as hard work were ways that people became wealthy. In contrast, those adolescents living in neighborhoods of concentrated poverty (and who themselves were still in school) held individuals accountable for their success or failure. People were poor because they had not studied or applied themselves in school. The unemployed did not try hard enough to find work. Their answers to the second set of questions reinforced this view of the world. In school or at home the youth in more privileged communities were scaffolded by a dense network of support. Teachers were ready to help them, and parents would "be there" for them no matter what problems they might face. In contrast, the youth in the inner city painted a world in which they were on their own. Their teachers were less supportive, and fellow students were more alienated. At home, they heard strong messages of self-reliance (i.e., that it was incumbent on individuals to create their own opportunities and, if they failed, they would have only themselves to blame). We concluded that, although minority youth from poor neighborhoods may be aware of the system's failures, it may be necessary to disregard those failures to remain committed to education and the American dream. As Taylor and his colleagues found, to the extent that Black youth blamed "the system" for the job ceilings facing African Americans, they were more likely to have given up on their own education (Taylor, Casten, Flickinger, Roberts, & Fulmore, 1994).

Adolescents Negotiating Social Change

In the remainder of this chapter I want to focus attention on adolescents as agents of change, as creators of history. The title of the volume, *Negotiating Adolescence in Times of Social Change* implies two things. First, it frames social change as an exogenous variable, something "out there" that affects conditions in the proximal settings of development. In this framework, change impacts individuals, and they are in a reactive stance to it. Change challenges established patterns of behavior, causes individuals to question what they have taken for granted, and creates stress. This is the typical way that social scientists, including myself, have studied social change.

But social change is not only a force to which people react. It is also the result of the collective decisions and actions of people and the social policies of nations. Collective action played a role in the fall of the Soviet-backed regimes in Central and Eastern Europe. The Soviet empire was challenged in Budapest in 1956, in Prague in 1978, and in Gdansk in the 1980s. Furthermore, in contexts where political parties were banned, people managed to challenge the authority of the state and voice dissent about the quality of their lives publicly through voluntary associations and nongovernment organizations such as environmental groups (Fisher, 1993).

One can point to environmental actions before 1990 in each of the Central and Eastern European countries that ultimately led to the demise of the old regimes. In 1989 public demonstrations protesting the low quality of air and water engaged whole families in Czechoslovakia. In October 1988, 40,000 demonstrated in Budapest against plans to dam the Danube River. Pollution of the Danube from chemical plants in Romania was a focus of protest movements in Bulgaria. Such collective action ultimately led to the demise of the old regimes. According to Havel (1990) the roots of citizen movements such as KOR, Solidarity, *Neues Forum*, Charter 77, and Civic Forum can be traced to opportunities for people to create places where they could feel free to voice their opinion and to challenge the status quo. And, as in most historical movements, youth played a prominent role (Cipkowski, 1991; Feffer, 1992).

The second implication of the volume's title, negotiating adolescence, implies a stable developmental period, one that can be defined apart from its historical context. As Bertram tells us in his chapter on families, a developmental period cannot be defined in such a way. In fact, our very theories of adolescence are colored by the economic and political constraints of the era in which adolescents come of age. Whereas an 18 year old is perceived as an adult when a nation is at war, he or she is more likely to be seen as immature, emotionally unstable, and in need of additional training when a nation is in the throes of an economic depression (Enright, Levy, Harris, & Lapsley, 1987).

Again I turn to Bertram's chapter in which the historical grounding of "the family" can be seen as the sine qua non for understanding both its form and its function in the life course of individuals. By turning a long historical lens on this proximal context, Bertram cautions against a myopic, albeit popular, view that the modern single-parent family signals a crisis in family relations. He notes, for example, that it is not change in the professional and work roles of women that accounts for increases in the single-adult population in Germany. Rather, the new singles are never married, divorced, or separated men under the age of forty. The more myopic view misidentifies the social trend and the change in the proximal context of intimate, private relations. Bertram also cautions demographers that living alone does not imply being alone. In his studies, "living apart together" is identified as a new form of personal life, one that appears to be a transitional adult stage rather than an alternative to marriage.

But the most important lesson of Bertram's work for the social sciences is that dynamic models of social change and human development are indispensable to the enterprise. Without them, we may jump to erroneous conclusions about the impact of change in the proximal settings of development. We may also risk locking ourselves into unidirectional models and ignore ways that the collective actions of people and the decisions of adolescents charting their own and their society's future are a driving force behind social change. In concluding, I draw attention to what can easily be overlooked in Bertram's and Sampson's chapters (i.e., the choices that people make). In Sampson's case, it is the likelihood that neighbors will do something, will decide to intervene. In Bertram's, the change in family form and the stability of its function as a source of intimacy and security are the result of individuals' choices. The isolation that modernity has introduced into personal life has been redressed through the intergenerational bonds that adult family members forge, despite the geographical distance between them.

In closing, I want to comment on the voluntary sector (i.e., voluntary youth organizations, community service) as a proximal context worthy of more attention in the setting of global change. Globalization implies an end to work as we know it and to the salience of work in personal identity (Rifkin, 1995). Globalization can also erode our sense of place and obligation to community. In this context we need to pay more attention to the leisure time choices of adolescents and to the opportunities they have to connect with a broader community. In our cross-national study we have examined voluntary work as an opportunity which enables youth to feel like members who count in their communities, members with something to offer. Not only is some form of voluntary work common across these different types of polities, we believe it provides an opportunity for adolescents to identify with a common good. Using the "nation as context" approach, we have compared volunteers within each country with their compatriots who had not been volunteers and found that, across all seven countries, engagement in such work was consistently and significantly related to youth's civic commitments (i.e., their desire to help the less fortunate, improve their communities, and sustain the environment for future generations; Flanagan et al., 1998). Thus, volunteer work may serve as an outlet for youth who already have such civic commitments or as a means of fostering those commitments. Whatever the direction of effects, the voluntary sector is likely to play an important role in a global environment. Rifkin (1995) argues that, in the context of global change, voluntary organizations, non government organizations, and civic groups will form an essential third sector, the "social economy," which will compensate for the private and public sectors' failures, challenge their methods of resource allocation, and build the competencies of ordinary citizens working together in the process.

Adolescence is an ideal time to participate in this sector because it is a time when identity is focal. Opportunities to participate in the voluntary sector may enhance the likelihood that young people planning their future will also reflect on the direction of their society. Adolescents are not yet fully integrated into adult society and are therefore free to search and to define their relationship to the social order (Erikson, 1968; Mannheim, 1952). Thus, not only does this period afford an opportunity for individual growth, but social change itself is inevitable:

To be sure, those who have had a youth – who have seriously questioned their relationship to the community that exists, who have a self and a set of commitments independent of their social role – are never likely to be simple patriots, unquestioning conformists, or blind loyalists to the *status quo* (Keniston, 1968, p. 272).

References

Bowes, J. M., Chalmers, D., & Flanagan, C. (1997). Children's involvement in household work: Views of adolescents in six countries. *Family Matters: Australian Journal of Family Studies, 46,* 26–30.

Bronfenbrenner, U. (1979). *The ecology of human development: Experiments by nature and design.* Cambridge, MA: Harvard University Press.

Center for Budget and Policy Priorities. (1990). *Drifting apart: New findings in growing income disparities between the rich, the poor, and the middle-class.* Washington, DC: Congressional Budget Office.

Cipkowski, P. (1991). *Revolution in Eastern Europe.* New York: Wiley.

Cohen, C. J., & Dawson, M. C. (1993). Neighborhood poverty and African American Politics. *American Political Science Review, 87,* 286–302.

Enright, R., Levy, V., Harris, D., & Lapsley, D. (1987). Do economic conditions influence how theorists view adolescents? *Journal of Youth and Adolescence, 16,* 541–549.

Erikson, E. H. (1968). *Identity: Youth and crisis.* New York: W. W. Norton.

Feffer, J. (1992). *Shock waves: Eastern Europe after the revolutions.* Boston: South End Press.

Fisher, D. (1993). The emergence of the environmental movement in Eastern Europe and its role in the revolutions of 1989. In B. Jancar-Webster (Ed)., *Environmental action in Eastern Europe: Responses to crisis* (pp. 89–113). New York: M. E. Sharpe.

Flanagan, C., Ingram, P., Gallay, E. M., & Gallay, E. E. (1996). Why are people poor? Social conditions and adolescents' interpretation of the "social contract." In R. Taylor (Ed.), *Social and emotional adjustment and family relations in ethnic minority families* (pp. 169–185). Hillsdale, NJ: Erlbaum.

Flanagan, C., Jonsson, B., Botcheva, L., Csapo, B., Bowes, J., & Macek, P. (1998). Adolescents and the "Social Contract": Developmental roots of citizenship in seven countries. In M. Yates & J. Youniss (Eds.), *International perspectives on community service and civic engagement in youth.* (pp. 135–155). New York: Cambridge University Press.

Giddens, A. (1984). *The constitution of society.* Berkeley: University of California Press.

Goodnow, J. J., Miller, P. J., & Kessel, F. (1995). Cultural practices as contexts for development. *New Directions for Child Development, Number 67,* San Francisco: Jossey-Bass.

Havel, V. (1990). *Disturbing the peace: A conversation with Karel Hvizdala.* New York: Alfred Knopf.

Keniston, K. (1968). *Young radicals: Notes on committed youth.* New York: Harcourt, Brace, & World.

Mannheim, K. (1952). The problem of generations. In P. Kecshevich (Ed.), *Essays on the sociology of knowledge* (pp. 276–322). London: Routledge & Kegan Paul. (Original work published 1928)

Moscovici, S. (1988). Notes towards a description of social representations. *European Journal of Social Psychology, 18,* 211–250.

Rifkin, J. (1995). *The end of work: The decline of the global labor force and the dawn of the post-market era.* New York: G. P. Putnam's Sons.

Scheye, E. (1991). Psychological notes on Central Europe 1989 and beyond. *Political Psychology, 12*(2), 331–344.

Taylor, R. D., Casten, R., Flickinger, S. M., Roberts, D., & Fulmore, C. D. (1994). Explaining the school performance of African-American adolescents. *Journal of Research on Adolescence, 4,* 21–44.

Wilson, W. J. (1991). Studying inner-city social dislocations: The challenge of public agenda research. *American Sociological Review, 56,* 1–14.

Part IV

Implications of Social Change for Adolescent Health and Well-Being

13   The Role of Economic Pressure in the Lives of Parents and Their Adolescents: The Family Stress Model

Katherine J. Conger, Martha A. Rueter, and Rand D. Conger

Social change in the form of economic restructuring and recessions has occurred across the United States throughout the country's history. The Depression of the 1930s brought hardship to all regions of the country and produced a mass migration of farmers leaving the land. More recently, widespread unemployment resulting from worldwide competition in the Rust Belt's steel industry, stagnation of U.S. car manufacturing in the face of foreign competition, the oil boom and bust in Texas, and the decline of the aerospace industry in the Northwest are all examples of macroeconomic change influencing the lives of thousands of families. Studies of unemployed autoworkers and their families, for example, revealed the staggering effects of unemployment: marriages fell apart, emotional and physical health problems increased, incidents of spouse and child abuse increased, and the demand for social services escalated (e.g., Kessler, Turner, & House, 1988; Perrucci & Targ, 1988). A similar period of economic decline struck agriculture in the 1980s and continues to plague rural areas of the country today.

Riding the 1970s crest of unprecedented prosperity that included easy credit, escalating land values, and an increasing demand for grain, farmers of the Midwest mortgaged the family farm to modernize and expand, buying larger machinery and farming larger tracts of land. In many cases, plans were made to expand their operations to make room for their sons and daughters. These economic boom times also benefited the small towns that served farm families with increased retail sales, well-paying jobs related to agriculture, and an increased tax base that spurred local economic development such as new schools and community improvements. Viewed from the agricultural prosperity of the 1970s, almost no one would have predicted an economic collapse for families living in the rural Midwest just one decade later

During the past several years, support for this research has come from multiple sources, including the National Institute of Mental Health (MH00567, MH19734, MH43270, MH48165, MH51361), the National Institute on Drug Abuse (DA05347), the Bureau of Maternal and Child Health (MCJ-109572), the MacArthur Foundation Research Network on Successful Adolescent Development Among Youth in High-Risk Settings, and the Iowa Agriculture and Home Economics Experiment Station (Project No. 3320).

(Davidson, 1990; Lasley, 1994). Unfortunately, the boom times started to unravel in the late 1970s and early 1980s because of the confluence of several international economic events.

Just as U.S. crop production was reaching its peak, spurred on by agricultural policies designed to balance trade deficits in other areas of the U.S. economy, crop production rose worldwide, and countries such as Brazil became exporters rather than importers. Reduced demand, combined with the Russian grain embargo, forced commodity prices to decline (Lobao & Lasley, 1995). As grain prices fell, American farmers responded by producing more grain to keep up their profits and their payments to the bank. The resulting glut of grain on the market further depressed its price (Davidson, 1990). As commodity prices fell, so too did land values, which declined "almost 60% in some of the major farming states" (Leistritz & Murdock, 1988 in Lobao & Lasley, 1995, p. 5). These falling land values meant that the farmers' most precious resource, the land, now was often no longer worth as much as was owed. Meanwhile, in an effort to curb "runaway inflation," the Federal Reserve raised interest rates in late 1979 (Lasley, 1994), forcing many banks to call in loans and many farmers to lose their operations. Farms often were sold at auctions held by the same bankers who had encouraged the farmers to borrow against the land to expand (Davidson, 1990; Lasley, 1994; Rosenblatt, 1990). As the economic situation of farmers declined, so too did that of many small town businesses. Iowa, with an economy that was heavily dependent on agriculture, was particularly hard hit. "The ripple effects created by the 1980s crisis jeopardized the nonfarm economies and fiscal bases of rural communities located in these regions" (Lobao & Lasley, 1995, p. 4).

The declining economic conditions in Iowa and their negative influence on families and children led to the development of the research project that is the focus of the present chapter. This investigation involves research from a longitudinal study of Iowa families who were living in small towns and on farms during the farm crisis of the 1980s. In a broader sense, this research was designed to assess how the macrosocial change and economic upheaval that occurred across the United States during the 1980s influenced family functioning and the well-being of parents and their children.

Responding to Economic Change

Although the farm crisis no longer is front page news, the impact of this dramatic social and economic change still is being felt throughout the Midwest. Crosses on courthouse lawns, symbolizing lost farms and shattered lives, remain as vivid images from the mid-1980s as hundreds of farmers and small town businesses went bankrupt (Davidson, 1990; Friedberger, 1989; Lasley, Leistritz, Lobao, & Meyer, 1995). However, it is the mostly unseen lives of families in rural areas and small towns that tell the continuing story of this economic change.

For every family that lost a farm, a job, or business on main street, many others survived financially only because both parents worked one or more jobs to stave off economic ruin. There were children who gave up dreams of college, careers, or taking over the family business; couples who divorced, unable to withstand the stresses and strains of the crisis years; and adolescents whose development suffered because of the negative pressures within their families, schools, and communities.

Just as important are the families who came through this same crisis stronger in ways not yet fully appreciated, whose parenting was not significantly disrupted and whose children did well in school. In addition, many couples survived multiple transitions and economic upheavals without terminating their relationship. These resilient families provided valuable information regarding individual characteristics and social processes that promote well-being during stressful times. All in all, few lives in the rural Midwest were left untouched by the social and economic upheaval that occurred as a result of the agricultural crisis in the 1980s.

To address these issues, in 1989 we initiated the Iowa Youth and Families Project (IYFP). This panel study was conducted from 1989 to 1992 and included 451 families living in an area heavily dependent on agriculture in north-central Iowa. The project was designed to examine the effects of the farm crisis on Midwestern families in rural areas and to learn how changing economic conditions influence family functioning and individual adjustment. Four members of each family – the father, mother, a target seventh grader, and a near-age sibling – participated in the study.

Each family member reported on his or her family interactions, relationships with one another, personal characteristics, economic and demographic circumstances, and extrafamilial activities and relationships during two visits each year to the family home. In addition, four separate structured family interactions were videotaped as part of the second visit to the family. The videotapes were rated by trained observers using the Iowa Family Interaction Rating Scales (Melby et al., 1990). All measures were designed to develop a picture of how families of various economic backgrounds were influenced by, and adapted to, changes in the local economy and their family's specific economic situation. For a complete description of the study, see Conger and Elder (1994).

The first section of this chapter describes the empirical and theoretical foundations for the Family Stress Model, the conceptual framework that guided the study (Conger & Elder, 1994). The sections that follow summarize findings from both the IYFP and other studies relevant to the various processes and mechanisms proposed in the Family Stress Model. We also consider research on hypothesized protective mechanisms or dimensions of vulnerability that may moderate the causal linkages proposed in the theoretical model. After reviewing the possible applied significance of this work, we close the chapter with a discussion of conclusions that can be drawn from the research conducted thus far and the implications of these findings for future investigations of family economic stress.

The Family Stress Model of Economic Hardship

During the height of the farm crisis, Iowa endured economic conditions approximating those of the 1930s in rural America (Lasley, 1994; Rosenblatt, 1990). Rural families experienced increased risk of health and behavioral problems that are known to be associated with economic hardship (see Angell, 1965; Elder, 1974; Komarovsky, 1940; Voydanoff, 1990). Of particular interest was the investigation of family and individual responses to economic hardship as possible linking mechanisms to adolescent adjustment. Accordingly, the IYFP focused on families with at least one seventh-grade adolescent and on insight into the effects of various social and economic changes on adolescent development within the context of family relationships.

It is well documented that adolescence is a time of rapid and complex developmental changes involving biological, psychological, and social processes (e.g., Crockett & Crouter, 1995; Feldman & Elliot, 1990; Steinberg, 1996); thus, adolescence may represent a period of particular vulnerability to economic stress and its negative impact on family relationships. At a time when the family best promotes positive adjustment by providing a "zone of comfort" that helps the adolescent accommodate multiple life transitions (Simmons & Blyth, 1987), parents who are challenged by economic difficulties and related stresses may not have the emotional or physical energy required to maintain a safe and secure environment. Adolescents living in a family situation disrupted by economic concerns may be at increased risk for experiencing detrimental outcomes such as depressed or anxious mood, substance use, poor school performance, and other problem behaviors. The Family Stress Model seeks to identify the pathways through which such detrimental outcomes may occur, as well as biological, psychological, and social resources or vulnerabilities that may reduce or intensify the economic stress process.

Consistent with these ideas, research evidence continues to accumulate suggesting that economic hardship, such as that experienced in the rural Midwest, has an adverse influence on the psychological well-being of family members and on the quality of family relationships (e.g., Brody et al., 1994; Conger, McCarty, Yang, Lahey, & Kropp, 1984; Dodge, Pettit, & Bates, 1994). In accordance with this growing evidence, the Family Stress Model (see Figure 1) postulates that economic hardship (e.g., severe income loss, sharp increases in resource demands, chronic economic disadvantage) leads to economic pressure (difficulties in dealing with stressful economic conditions such as the inability to pay bills or to meet basic material needs for food, clothing, etc.). Economic pressure describes the daily problems that give psychological meaning to hardship experiences. It is these day-to-day frustrations associated with hardship that affect family life. Thus, the model indicates that parents experiencing these economic difficulties may subsequently become frustrated, angry, and otherwise emotionally distressed consonant with findings from a growing research literature (McLoyd, 1989; Voydanoff, 1990).

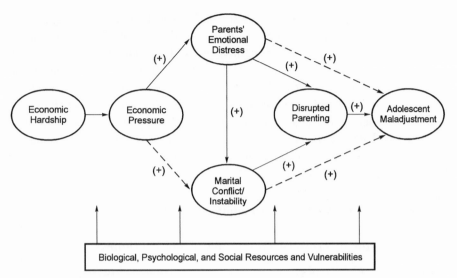

Figure 1. The family stress model.

This fundamental connection between economic pressure and emotional distress draws upon Berkowitz's (1989) reformulation of the frustration–aggression hypothesis. Berkowitz demonstrated that many stressful, frustrating, punishing, or painful events and conditions are lawfully related to increased emotional arousal that varies from despondency to anger in humans and other animal species. According to the Family Stress Model, economic pressure provides the stressful, frustrating impetus for the emotional and behavioral processes proposed by Berkowitz. Consistent with our interpretation of Berkowitz's reformulation of the frustration–aggression hypothesis, then, the Family Stress Model proposes a direct path from economic pressure to emotional distress (i.e., depressed mood, symptoms of anxiety, and angry and hostile feelings of adults and parents). Berkowitz also proposed that it is the emotional distress or negative affect that results from aversive life experiences that increases risk for withdrawal and irritability in social interactions, as suggested by the paths from emotional distress to marital conflict and disrupted parenting.

The final paths in the model propose that economic pressure is linked to adolescent adjustment through adults' emotional distress, their marital relationship, and their ability to parent. These proposed paths are consistent with Coyne and Downey's (1991) thesis that stressful life experiences, like economic hardship, have their most negative impact on individual well-being through disruptions in close personal relationships. The solid lines in the model indicate the pathways proposed to have the primary causal influences, whereas the dashed lines indicate secondary or mediated effects. For instance, the model suggests that the influence of economic pressure on marital conflict and instability is primarily indirect through its impact on adult emotional distress.

Finally, the Family Stress Model also considers biological, psychological, and social resources or vulnerabilities that may condition the influence of the various pathways included in the conceptual framework. This addition to the model recognizes that not all families or individual family members are likely to be equally influenced by economic stress. Werner and Smith (1992), for example, found that youth who were sociable, conscientious in their studies, and who had significant support from an adult or adults in their lives were relatively resilient, even to a background of severe disadvantage. With the general outlines of the model in mind, we now turn to empirical findings that help to evaluate the credibility of this perspective on family economic stress processes.

Empirical Studies Related to the Family Stress Model

Economic Hardship, Economic Pressure, and Emotional Distress

Studying the influence of economic conditions on families' lives required that we develop a set of measures that would adequately capture relevant dimensions of economic hardship. Four dimensions of economic hardship (see Figure 2) were chosen based on research traditions that focus on the economic experiences of families.

The first construct, per capita income, represents the current economic state of the family, a construct found in most contemporary research on poverty and families

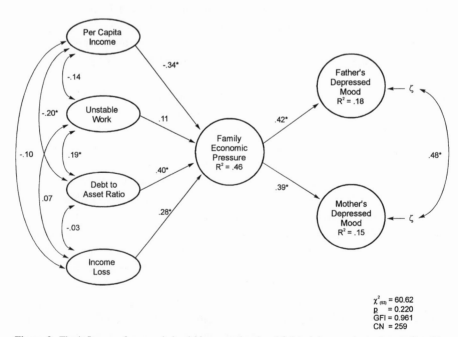

Figure 2. The influence of economic hardship on mothers' and fathers' depressed mood as mediated by economic pressure. (Adapted from Conger, Conger, Elder, Lorenz, Simons, & Whitbeck, 1993.)

(e.g., Duncan, 1984; Duncan & Brooks-Gunn, 1997). The second, unstable work, comes from the research tradition on unemployment and job disruptions (Atkinson, Liem, & Liem, 1987; Garraty, 1978; Komarovsky, 1940). The third construct, the ratio of family debts to assets, is used by rural social scientists such as Murdock and Leistritz (1988) as an important indicator of family hardship. From research on Depression-era families of the 1930s, changing economic circumstances of families are captured by the fourth construct, income loss (e.g., Elder, 1974). These four constructs are used in the conceptual model to represent conditions of family hardship hypothesized to predict economic pressure (e.g., Conger et al., 1992).

As noted earlier, the construct of economic pressure was developed to reflect difficulties associated with stressful economic conditions. Indicators for the construct include parents' reports of whether or not (1) they have enough money to pay their bills and to make ends meet each month; (2) they have sufficient resources for life's necessities such as food, clothing, medical care, and housing; and (3) they have had to make significant financial cutbacks or adjustments (e.g., give up health insurance, major purchases, etc.) in an attempt to adapt to declining revenues. Although economic pressure often is confused with financial strain, our conceptualization of economic pressure makes an important distinction. Economic or financial strain, a construct often used in research on economic stress, may be completely subjective and even assess future expectations (e.g., Vinokur, Price, & Caplan, 1996) rather than actual experiences. Economic pressure, on the other hand, attempts to portray as objectively as possible the actual experiences brought on by economic conditions that may be disruptive of family relations and individual well-being (see Conger et al., 1994). These indicators of economic pressure are expected to be key components in translating economic circumstances into daily experiences that could demoralize family members and disrupt family interaction processes. Tested in a series of incremental models (see Figure 2), the exogenous hardship conditions in the Family Stress Model explained a significant proportion of the variance in economic pressure (46%) in this representative set of analyses. Moreover, all of the influence of hardship conditions was indirect, through economic pressure (Conger et al., 1993). These findings are supportive of the initial links in the Family Stress Model.

Despite some conceptual and assessment differences, a number of research studies support these findings, which are consistent with the hypothesis that economic hardship exacerbates economic pressure or strain and, through this disruption in the daily lives of families, increases risk for adult or parent emotional distress. Kessler, Turner, & House (1988), for instance, demonstrated that job loss and related economic problems had an adverse influence on emotional distress primarily through a person's experience that bills could not be paid or necessities could not be purchased. Recent research in other countries also reports a link between economic difficulties and psychological distress. Gutkowski, Winter, and Njue (personal communication, 1998), for instance, found that economic pressure was the primary mechanism through which financial hardship affected adult emotional distress in

Polish households. Lorenz, Hraba, Conger, and Pechcova (1996) reported similar findings for families in the Czech Republic. To summarize, empirical findings are consistent with predictions by the Family Stress Model that (1) economic hardship produces daily financial stresses and strains in the family conceptualized as economic pressure, and (2) it is these daily financial disruptions that link economic conditions to emotional distress.

Economic Pressure, Emotional Distress, and Marital Relationships

According to the Family Stress Model, it is the combination of emotional distress and economic pressure that disrupts the marital relationship as the next stage in an unfolding cascade that ultimately threatens the well-being of adolescents. For example, a recurring theme in the videotaped interactions of husbands and wives in the IYFP was that financial problems often took the couple's attention away from their marital relationship. Time pressures, demoralization, and conflicts were common themes in the interviews with economically distressed Iowa couples. Ethnographic studies of disadvantaged rural families report similar findings (e.g., Rosenblatt, 1990). Support for this step in the stress process also is found in research concerned with the association between economic distress and family relationships (e.g., Brody et al., 1994; McLoyd, Jayaratne, Ceballo, & Borquez, 1994; Sampson & Laub, 1994; Voydanoff & Donnelley, 1988).

These contemporary findings are consistent with several decades of research demonstrating the potentially adverse impact of economic stress on family relations (Bakke, 1940; Conger et al., 1984; Dooley & Catalano, 1988; Elder, 1974; Heffernan & Heffernan, 1986; Lasley & Conger, 1986; Straus, Gelles, & Steinmetz, 1990; Voydanoff & Donnelly, 1988). For two-parent families with children, the marital relationship is a central link between financial difficulties and child and adolescent development. This focus on family relationships in relation to economic conditions is consistent with the more general perspective on psychosocial stress processes discussed earlier. Coyne and Downey (1991) argued that the impact of stresses and strains on individual adjustment can best be understood in the context of one's closest social relationships. Therefore, to understand the impact of financial concerns and worries on the lives of husbands and wives, we first consider the dynamics of the marital relationship.

In evaluating the Family Stress Model, we were particularly interested in the impact of economic uncertainty on the marital relationship because the findings from earlier research are somewhat inconsistent. Atkinson, Liem, and Liem (1986) found a significant inverse relationship between duration of unemployment and marital quality for white-collar but not blue-collar respondents. Perrucci and Targ (1988) found no significant correlations between economic strain and marital happiness. However, Liker and Elder (1983) reported that income loss during the early 1930s was positively associated with marital tension later in the decade. Marital tension also was associated with higher rates of marital instability (separation or divorce), which is consistent with other studies linking economic hardship to marital dissolution (Teachman, Polonko, & Scanzoni, 1987).

Conger et al. (1990) suggested that the lack of consistent findings may be due in part to a dearth of information about the quality of marital interactions in previous studies (e.g., Liker & Elder, 1983). They hypothesized that the quality of behaviors during spousal interactions is the mechanism that links economic difficulties to satisfaction or happiness in the marriage. The association between economic pressure and the quality of marital interactions was first studied in an independent sample of 76 Midwestern rural families (see Conger et al., 1990). The results of these analyses were consistent with the hypothesized relationships in the Family Stress Model. Economic conditions influenced wives' and husbands' hostile and warm marital interactions indirectly through economic pressure. The overall picture was one in which couples with serious financial difficulties experienced lower marital satisfaction and greater marital instability.

Consonant with increasing empirical evidence that demonstrates the link between economic stress and emotional distress such as anxiety and depression (Conger et al., 1992; Kessler et al., 1988; Voydanoff & Donnelly, 1988), depressed mood was added to the marital model in an attempt to explain the association between economic pressure and marital interactions. Conger, Ge, Elder, Lorenz, & Simons (1994) reported that economic pressure mediated the relationship between economic conditions and individual adjustment and subsequent marital quality. In addition, using self, spouse, and observer report, the study found that each parent's depressed mood mediated the relationship between economic pressure and his or her own hostility toward a spouse. Furthermore, each spouse's hostility had a significant negative effect on the marital quality of the other spouse. These results suggest that depressed mood, an emotional problem more commonly attributed to women (Downey & Coyne, 1990), links economic difficulties to men's as well as to women's hostile, irritable behaviors and clarifies wives' role in responses to economic stress. An important extension of these findings with rural Iowa couples was reported by Vinokur et al. (1996), who noted that economic strain increased depressed mood, which led to hostile interactions and reduced relationship quality for urban couples. Taken together, these findings provide significant support for our theoretical proposition that economic pressure, primarily through its impact on emotional distress, increases risk for hostility and conflict in marital relations (see Figure 1).

From Economic Pressure to Disrupted Parenting
and Adolescent Adjustment

Thus far the results are supportive of the first links in the Family Stress Model (Figure 1); emotional distress brought about by the demands of economic pressure leads to disruptions in the marital relationship. Emotional distress and marital conflict, in turn, are hypothesized to affect adolescent adjustment by diminishing or disrupting effective parenting behaviors. This is consistent with the suggestion by Patterson and his colleagues (e.g., Patterson, DeBaryshe, & Ramsey, 1989) that stressful family circumstances have their greatest impact on children and adolescents through disruptions in parent–child relations and effective parenting behaviors. Fauber, Forehand, Thomas, and Wierson (1990) reported that conflicts between spouses influenced early adolescent adjustment primarily through disruptions in parenting. Patterson (1991) reported similar findings for early adolescent boys living in intact families.

Support for the pathway linking economic pressure to adolescent adjustment through parenting was found in cross-sectional analyses of IYFP data for seventh-grade boys and girls (Conger et al., 1992, 1993). The expected associations were evaluated separately for boys and girls because of the considerable evidence that boys and girls respond differently to economic problems in their families (Elder, 1974; Elder & Caspi, 1988; Elder, Van Nguyen, & Caspi, 1985; McLoyd, 1989). For example, Rutter (1990) proposed that, during times of family stress, the more disruptive and oppositional behavior of boys, as compared with girls, may place them at greater risk for suffering the consequences of impaired childrearing practices. Girls, on the other hand, may be at greater risk for adjustment problems as a result of their heightened sensitivity to the emotional state of those around them (Belle, 1990; Conger, Lorenz, Elder, Simons, & Ge, 1993).

Figure 3 presents the combined results from the cross-sectional analyses for boys and for girls (Conger et al., 1992, 1993, respectively). The results are consistent with the primary hypothesized relationships in the Family Stress Model. That is, economic pressure influenced adolescent adjustment indirectly through other processes occurring within the family. Specifically, disruptions in adult functioning,

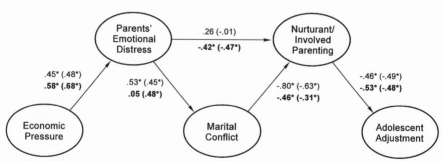

Figure 3. The influence of economic pressure on seventh-grade girls' and boys' competence mediated by fathers' and mothers' depressed mood, marital conflict, and nurturant and involved parenting. Results for girls are the top numbers (source: Conger et al., 1993); results for boys are the bottom numbers in bold (source: Conger et al., 1992). Structural coefficients for mothers are within parentheses; coefficients for fathers are outside parentheses.

conceptualized as emotional distress that leads to marital conflict, negatively affected adolescent adjustment through problematic childrearing practices. There
were some interesting gender differences related to the secondary hypotheses, as
represented by the dashed lines, in the Family Stress Model (see Figure 1). For example, consistent with the notion that girls may be more sensitive to the emotional
state of those close to them (e.g., Belle, 1990), both mothers' and fathers' depressed
mood had a significant negative influence on girls' competence, measured as self-
confidence, relations with friends, and academic competence (coefficients for girls
are the top numbers in Figure 3). These results are in contrast to the boys' results
(coefficients on bottom in bold), which show no direct effect of mothers' or fathers'
emotional distress on adolescent competence (see Conger et al., 1992).

In the analyses for boys, however, there was a direct path from parents' depressed mood to nurturant and involved parenting that was not observed for girls.
This conforms to Rutter's (1990) idea that boys may be a more irritating stimulus to emotionally distressed parents. Similarly, Bolger, Patterson, Thompson, and
Kupersmidt (1995), in a longitudinal study of White and African American elementary students and their families, reported that boys were more affected than girls by
family economic hardship. Ge, Conger, Lorenz, Shanahan, & Elder (1995) suggest
"that the emotional distress of either parent may negatively affect the psychological
functioning of either boys or girls when it contributes to incompetent parenting and
interpersonal negativity" (p. 417). Taken together, then, these analyses illustrate
the significance of parents' emotional distress as an important pathway linking
economic difficulties to adolescent adjustment through parenting behaviors.

In an attempt to further explicate how parental mood and marital conflict influence parenting behaviors, Conger, Ge, Elder, Lorenz, & Simons (1994) examined
parent–adolescent conflicts over money. They postulated that economic pressure
would increase parent–adolescent conflicts over the family's financial situation.
Similar to Patterson's (1982) theory of coercive family exchanges, this construct
brings into play contingent, aversive interactions that may occur when parents experiencing economic problems cannot provide the level of material support desired
or expected by their children. In other words, adolescents may resort to coercive
techniques to meet their desired material wishes at the same time that parents
are cutting back in an attempt to adjust to the family's diminished economic resources. Just as Liker and Elder (1983) found that spousal disagreements over
money contributed to marital tensions, this study found support for the idea that
economic pressure was associated with financial conflicts between parents and
their adolescent children. Economic pressure was also associated indirectly with
financial conflicts through parents' depressed mood and marital conflict. In the
final analysis, economic pressure was indirectly related to problems in adolescent development, in this case internalizing and externalizing symptoms, through
parental distress, marital conflict, parent–child conflicts over money, and generalized parental hostility toward the adolescent. Conger et al. (1994) suggested that

"Future analyses should examine how specific family stressors (e.g., time pressures in dual-earner households) lead to arguments and disagreements of particular types (e.g., concerning child and adolescent household responsibilities) and how these coercive family exchanges affect child and adolescent development" (p. 558). We suspect that additional research on this question will help to illuminate the processes through which economic and other potent family stressors influence parents and children.

Other IYFP Research Examining the Link Between Parents' Behaviors
and Adolescent Adjustment

It is well documented that marital conflict is associated with various child and adolescent adjustment problems (e.g., Cummings & Davies, 1994; Emery, 1988). High levels of marital conflict have been associated with externalizing behavior problems (Grych & Fincham, 1990; Reid & Crissafulli, 1990), interpersonal relationship difficulties (Emery & O'Leary, 1984; Long, Forehand, Fauber, & Brody, 1987), and problems at school (Long, Slater, Forehand, & Fauber, 1988). Consonant with these reports, the Family Stress Model hypothesizes that marital conflict affects adolescent adjustment primarily indirectly by diminishing or disrupting parents' childrearing skills. Parents distracted by frequent problems with each other likely have less time and energy for their roles as parents. Moreover, conflicts between parents may spill over into interactions with children (Conger et al., 1992, 1993). Another mechanism that may help explain the influence of marital conflict on adolescent well-being is adolescent awareness of conflicts in the marriage and the relation of this awareness to adolescents' perception of parents' hostility (Harold & Conger, 1997). That is, when parents behave in an angry fashion toward one another, adolescents may interpret their behavior as being more hostile in general. Harold and Conger (1997) found support for this hypothesis and showed that adolescent perceptions of parental hostility predicted increased risk for adolescent adjustment problems.

Other research with the IYFP families has added to the evidence regarding associations among family stress, parenting behaviors, and adolescent adjustment. Conger, Rueter, and Conger (1994) reported that a harsh, inconsistent parenting style was significantly and positively associated with early adolescent drinking as was older sibling alcohol use. Mothers' problems with alcohol were also related to adolescent drinking directly as well as indirectly through their influence on mothers' harsh, inconsistent parenting. Fathers' drinking was only indirectly related to adolescent alcohol use through their harsh and inconsistent parenting. An examination of the interaction between parenting behavior and older sibling drinking revealed that when parents were above the median on harsh, inconsistent parenting, or below on nurturant, involved parenting, sibling drinking was significantly and positively related to seventh-grader alcohol use. These results are consistent with the Family Stress Model's hypothesis that some adolescents will be more resilient, and some more vulnerable, to family stress processes. In the present illustration, nurturant and involved parenting promoted resilience and harsh and inconsistent parenting exacerbated vulnerability to an older sibling's deviant behaviors.

Similar results were observed for the association between parental behaviors and tobacco use by young adolescent males (Melby, Conger, Conger, & Lorenz, 1993). Parents' tobacco use was related only indirectly to boys' tobacco use via the boys' association with deviant peers. However, tobacco use by siblings was significantly, directly, and positively associated with boys' tobacco use and their interaction with tobacco-using peers. Harsh, inconsistent parenting had an indirect affect on adolescent tobacco use through the boys' association with deviant peers. Other research has also demonstrated that parents who are suffering the effects of economic pressure are more likely to be harsh and inconsistent, less nurturant, and less involved in closely monitoring and supervising their adolescents' activities with friends, thereby putting them at increased risk for problem behaviors (e.g., Conger et al., 1992; Simons, Conger, & Whitbeck, 1988; Whitbeck et al., 1991).

Academic performance is another indicator of adolescent adjustment that suffers from the negative consequences of family economic distress (Conger et al., 1992, 1993). More recent research focused on the impact of parenting behaviors (both hostile and supportive) on academic performance over a 4-year span during mid-adolescence. Melby and Conger (1996) reported that " displays of hostile affect by the parent toward the adolescent decreased the adolescents' subsequent school performance. Conversely, school performance was enhanced by an involved parental management style" (p. 130). Parents' level of education was associated with their own behavior and with adolescent academic performance, which is consistent with previous research (DeBaryshe, Patterson, & Capaldi, 1993; Steinberg, Lamborn, Dornbusch, & Darling, 1992).

Family Processes and Modifying the Stress Process

In addition to the mediational relationships explicitly represented in the Family Stress Model, the theoretical framework also includes biological, psychological, and social mechanisms predicted to moderate the various hypothesized linkages in the model (see Figure 1). Although research to date has been limited regarding these proposed moderating influences, several analyses have been completed that address this issue.

First, a report by Conger, Rueter, and Elder (1999) generated results, shown in Figure 4, that were consistent with the Family Stress Model as described thus far. This earlier research reported that economic difficulties due to job and income loss posed less of a threat to husbands and wives who were in strong, satisfying marriages (Liem & Liem, 1990; Liker & Elder, 1983). However, the global measures of

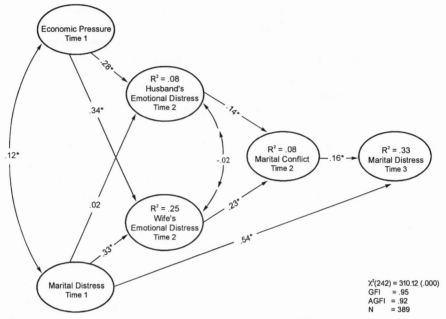

Figure 4. Predicting marital distress from economic pressure, emotional distress, and marital conflict with earlier marital distress controlled. (Adapted from Conger, Rueter, & Elder, 1999.)

marital satisfaction used by earlier researchers provided little information about the specific behaviors used by spouses to reduce the negative consequences of economic distress. Therefore, these investigators developed a longitudinal model that hypothesized couple-specific behaviors that might help explain the protective role of marital quality.

Two aspects of marital quality were chosen for study. First, on the basis of the theoretical ideas of Pearlin and McCall (1990) and Weiss (1990), interspousal support or empathy was chosen for study. Second, the work of Levinger and Huston (1990) on collaborative problem solving among married couples pointed to problem-solving skills as another possible protective resource. As expected, couples high in marital empathy (the ability to demonstrate concern, caring, sensitivity, and helpfulness towards one's spouse) were significantly less likely to suffer emotional distress as a result of economic difficulties.

However, empathy did little to protect the marriage from the deleterious effects of marital conflict. Rather, the findings indicated that couples who demonstrated the ability to negotiate, bargain, and reach agreement on realistic solutions regarding their conflicts were less likely to suffer instability in their marriages as a result of such conflicts. These results indicate that interaction patterns make a difference in response to stressors, and that couples who are more resilient in the face of economic difficulties are so, at least in part, because these types of positive behaviors occur in the relationship. These results also suggest that programs designed to enhance prosocial communication strategies and effective problem-solving skills may protect husbands and wives from some of the negative consequences of economic hardship.

Similarly, Simons, Lorenz, Conger, and Wu (1992) reported that level of support from a spouse facilitated supportive, involved parenting for mothers and fathers even in the face of economic pressure. Furthermore, spousal support moderated the impact of economic pressure on supportive parenting for mothers but not for fathers. That is, mothers with supportive husbands were resilient to economic pressure in terms of disruptions in parenting. This gender difference may be an indication of the different way that men and women approach marriage and parenthood. That is, the psychological well-being of women, as compared with men, appears to be more strongly affected by their marriage and other close personal relationships (e.g., Glenn & Weaver, 1981; Lee, 1978; Coleman, 1980; Wright & Keple, 1981). These results suggest that effective programs for preventing adverse consequences of economic pressure in families should teach parents and spouses the skills necessary to handle conflicts that arise reasonably as well as to promote a more satisfying relationship. A more satisfying marital relationship can lead, in turn, to the ability to carry out parental responsibilities in a more constructive fashion, thus reducing risks for adolescent adjustment problems during times of stress.

Extrafamilial Support

Just as support within the marriage can mitigate the negative impact of economic distress, so too can the support of family and friends outside the marriage. Lorenz, Conger, & Montague (1994) reported that husbands' and wives' level of depression was strongly predicted by economic pressure, but support from family and friends had significant, negative effects on depressive symptoms. The relationship between both types of support and depression was stronger for women than for men in the study. In an attempt to further our understanding of these support mechanisms, the sample was split into two groups according to high or low per capita family income. This analysis revealed significant differences between wives in the two groups, suggesting that wives from low-income families focus more of their efforts and resources on their family and that, if support is not forthcoming, these women are more likely to feel depressed. In contrast, wives from higher-income families are more likely to work outside the home and be involved in community activities that provide larger networks of friendships. The supportive quality of these extrafamilial friendships appears to be a relatively important factor in determining whether these women will feel depressed. This research extends earlier work on the role of supportive relationships within stress processes and begins to clarify the relative importance of family compared with friends (Reis, 1990; Wills, 1990) and the mechanisms through which support is garnered (Cutrona, Suhr, & MacFarlane, 1990; Hobfoll & Stokes, 1988).

Family Climate

Just as effective problem solving moderated the association between marital conflict and marital instability, the successful resolution of conflicts between parents and adolescents may alter the course of the stress process. Developmental researchers are beginning to include family context or climate as an influential factor in the course of parent–adolescent conflict (e.g., Cooper, 1988; Hill, 1993; Paikoff & Brooks-Gunn, 1991; Steinberg, 1990). According to this theoretical approach, emotional closeness and trust among family members are antecedents to the successful negotiation and resolution of disagreements. Family interactions that are typified by hostile, coercive exchanges, such as those described by Patterson (1982), interfere with effective problem-solving activities and may contribute to protracted disagreements. Furthermore, unresolved disputes can escalate in duration and intensity, weakening the parent–adolescent relationship and ultimately having a negative impact on adolescent development (Brook, Whiteman, & Finch, 1993; Forehand, Long, Brody, & Fauber, 1986; Montemayor, 1983; Rutter, 1980).

On the basis of this theoretical framework, Rueter and Conger (1995a) tested two models, one positive and one negative, to address the role of family context in predicting parent–adolescent conflict over time. The results were supportive of the proposed theory: a family's emotional climate sets the stage for future parent–adolescent conflicts. From early to midadolescence, families that demonstrated a pattern of supportive interactions tended to grow warmer and closer, worked on conflicts well together, and reported a decline in the number of disagreements with one another. On the other hand, difficulties in families characterized by hostile, coercive interactions appeared to worsen over the same period. In addition, a hostile interactional style directly predicted destructive problem-solving behaviors and indirectly predicted family problem-solving effectiveness (Rueter & Conger, 1995b). Additional support for these hypothesized relationships was found in longitudinal analyses of the reciprocal influences between parents' childrearing strategies and adolescents' problem-solving behaviors (Rueter & Conger, 1998). Similar results were found for reciprocal influences of parent–adolescent conflict and cohesion (Conger & Ge, 1999). Rueter and Conger (1995a) suggest "that interventions should initially focus on reducing hostility and increasing warmth among family members. Programs directed at improving problem-solving behavior should be paired with efforts to teach positive communication and supportiveness" (p. 446).

Conclusions

The stresses and strains associated with social change, such as the downturn in the agricultural economy that occurred in the 1980s, can have serious consequences for individuals and families. The Family Stress Model (Figure 1) is presented as a framework for studying and understanding how stressful economic conditions influence adolescent well-being through the disruptions they create in marital relations and in parent–child relations. The three pathways of influence (parents' emotional distress, marital conflict, and parenting behaviors) work singly and together to influence the developmental course of children. In other words, adolescents, too, suffer the effects of economic uncertainty and decline due to the spillover into their lives from all aspects of their most salient proximal environment – their family. Furthermore, as macrosocial change affects individuals and families across the social spectrum, disruptions in family life may be accompanied by related changes in the social networks of adolescents such as school, peers, and church, further heightening their risk for developing problems. As we stated in the beginning of this chapter, "few lives in the rural Midwest were left untouched . . . ."

The results from tests of specific hypotheses postulated by the Family Stress Model provide support for the idea that adolescents are at risk for developing problems such as depressed mood, antisocial and delinquent behaviors, poor school performance, and other problems when their parents experience disruptions in their lives associated with economic change and uncertainty. Although not tested in its entirety, support was found, concurrently and over time, for specific relationships postulated by the model. Taken together, these results help us understand the complex interrelationships of economic conditions, economic pressure, family functioning, and adolescent adjustment.

The recurring theme of emotional distress as a response to uncertain economic conditions provides a clear marker for people and organizations working with economically distressed families. Knowing that emotional distress is a common response will not in itself solve economic problems but may help individuals prepare for or avoid negative consequences to their marriage and their relations with their children.

Limitations. Although the findings reported here are consistent with a growing body of research in this area (e.g., Brody et al., 1994; McLoyd, Jayaratne, Ceballo, & Borquez, 1994; Voydanoff, 1990), several limitations of the IYFP should be noted. First, despite the examination of the hypothesized social processes over time, a longitudinal study of this type does not rival an experiment in terms of causal inference (Dwyer, 1983). However, the longitudinal panel design, with temporal ordering of constructs where possible, provides greater confidence in making causal inferences than does a cross-sectional design. Second, the generalizability of the mechanisms and processes in the proposed model should be tested in urban as well as rural settings, with different family structures, and with families of various racial and ethnic groups. Along those lines, results supportive of the model have been reported for urban couples (Vinokur et al., 1996). Moreover, similar findings are emerging in a parallel longitudinal study of single-mother families in Iowa with same-age adolescents (for details, see Simons & Associates, 1996). The Family Stress Model will also be tested with data from a just-initiated study of rural African-American families in Georgia and Iowa. Results supportive of the Family Stress Model are also emerging in other countries hard hit by macrosocioeconomic change such as Poland and the Czech Republic (e.g., Gutkowski et al., personal communication, 1998; Lorenz et al., 1996).

Summary. If the findings reported here prove robust upon further examination, they will provide a basis for understanding the social and psychological processes through which economic stress has adverse developmental consequences for adolescents and their families. Although we typically cannot prevent macrosocial changes from occurring, we can temper the impact of stressful social changes on the lives of adolescents by furthering our understanding of how stress processes influence family functioning and adolescent adjustment. Equipped with this better understanding, we can help families and communities anticipate the problems associated with economic distress and design strategies for preventing these problems from occurring or for intervening when they do occur. The prevention of stress-related emotional and relationship problems should reduce long-term difficulties for adolescents and their families. Hauser and Sweeney (1997) suggested "that the developmental pathways leading from childhood to achievement and aspiration in late adolescence ought to be the main targets of policy intervention" (p. 575). Furthermore, research demonstrating "the large influence of other social background characteristics suggests that policies affecting income alone are unlikely to compensate fully for social disadvantage" (p. 575). Through local, state, and national programs designed to assist economically distressed families, family members can obtain information that will reassure them that they are not the only ones experiencing the negative aspects of living in uncertain economic times.

References

Angell, R. C. (1965). *The family encounters the depression.* Gloucester, MA: Peter Smith.

Atkinson, T., Liem, R., & Liem, J. (1986). The social costs of unemployment: Implications for social support. *Journal of Health and Social Behavior, 27,* 317–331.

Bakke, E. W. (1940). *Citizens without work: A study of the effects of unemployment upon the worker's social relations and practices.* New Haven, CT: Yale University Press.

Belle, D. (1990). Poverty and women's mental health. *American Psychologist, 45,* 385–389.

Berkowitz, L. (1989). Frustration–aggression hypothesis: Examination and reformulation. *Psychological Bulletin, 106,* 59–73.

Bolger, K. E., Patterson, C. J., Thompson, W. W., & Kupersmidt, J. B. (1995). Psychosocial adjustment among children experiencing persistent and intermittent family economic hardship. *Child Development, 66,* 1107–1129.

Brody, G. H., Stoneman, Z., Flor, D., McCrary, C., Hastings, L., & Conyers, O. (1994). Financial resources, parent psychological functioning, parent co-caregiving, and early adolescent competence in rural two-parent African-American families. *Child Development, 65,* 590–605.

Brook, J. S., Whiteman, M., & Finch, S. (1993). Role of mutual attachment in drug use: A longitudinal study. *Journal of the American Academy of Child and Adolescent Psychiatry, 32,* 982–989.

Coleman, J. C. (1980). Friendship and the peer group in adolescence. In J. Adelson (Ed.), *Handbook of adolescent psychology*. New York: Wiley.

Conger, R. D., Conger, K. J., Elder, G. H., Jr., Lorenz, F. O., Simons, R. L., & Whitbeck, L. B. (1992). A family process model of economic hardship and adjustment of early adolescent boys. *Child Development, 63,* 526–541.

Conger, R. D., Conger, K. J., Elder, G. H., Jr., Lorenz, F. O., Simons, R. L., & Whitbeck, L. B. (1993). Family economic stress and adjustment of early adolescent girls. *Developmental Psychology, 29,* 206–219.

Conger, R. D., & Elder, G. H., Jr., (with Lorenz, F. O., Simons, R. L., & Whitbeck, L. B.) (1994). *Families in troubled times: Adapting to change in rural America*. Hillsdale, NJ: Aldine.

Conger, R. D., Elder, G. H., Jr., Lorenz, F. O., Conger, K. J., Simons, R. L., Whitbeck, L. B., Huck, S. M., & Melby, J. N. (1990). Linking economic hardship to marital quality and instability. *Journal of Marriage and the Family, 52,* 643–656.

Conger, R. D., & Ge, X. (1999). Conflict and cohesion in parent–adolescent relations: Changes in emotional expression from early to mid-adolescence. In M. Cox & J. Brooks-Gunn (Eds.), *Conflict and closeness: The formation, functioning, and stability of families* (pp. 185–206). Mahwah, NJ: Erlbaum.

Conger, R. D., Ge, X., Elder, G. H., Jr., Lorenz, F. O., & Simons, R. L. (1994). Economic stress, coercive family process and developmental problems of adolescents: Children and Poverty [Special issue]. *Child Development, 65,* 541–561.

Conger, R. D., Lorenz, F. O., Elder, G. H., Jr., Simons, R. L., & Ge, X. (1993). Husband and wife differences in response to undesirable life events. *Journal of Health and Social Behavior, 34,* 71–88.

Conger, R. D., McCarty, J., Yang, R., Lahey, B., & Kropp, J. (1984). Perception of child, child-rearing values, and emotional distress as mediating links between environmental stressors and observed maternal behavior. *Child Development, 55,* 2234–2247.

Conger, R. D., Rueter, M. A., & Conger, K. J. (1994). The family context of adolescent vulnerability and resilience to alcohol use and abuse. *Sociological Studies of Children, 6,* 55–86.

Conger, R. D., Rueter, M. R., & Elder, G. H., Jr. (1999). Couple resilience to economic pressure. *Journal of Personality and Social Psychology, 76,* 54–71.

Cooper, C. R. (1988). The role of conflict in adolescent-parent relationships. In M. R. Gunnar (Ed.)., *Minnesota symposia on child psychology* (Vol. 21, pp. 1181–1187). Hillsdale, NJ: Erlbaum.

Coyne, J. C., & Downey, G. (1991). Social factors and psychopathology: Stress, social support, and coping processes. *Annual Review of Psychology, 42,* 401–425.

Crockett, L. J., & Crouter, A. C. (1995). *Pathways through adolescence: Individual development in relation to social contexts*. Mahwah, NJ: Erlbaum.

Cummings, E. M., & Davies, P. (1994). *Children and marital conflict: The impact of family dispute and resolution*. New York: Guilford Press.

Cutrona, C. E., Suhr, J. A., & MacFarlane, R. (1990). Interpersonal transactions and the psychological sense of support. In S. Duck with R. D. Silver (Eds.), *Personal relationships and social support* (pp. 30–45). London: Sage.

Davidson, O. G. (1990). *Broken heartland: The rise of America's rural ghetto*. New York: Free Press.

DeBaryshe, B. D., Patterson, G. R., & Capaldi, D. M. (1993). A performance model for academic achievement in early adolescent boys. *Developmental Psychology, 29,* 795–804.

Dodge, K. A., Pettit, G. S., & Bates, J. E. (1994). Socialization mediators of the relation between socioeconomic status and child conduct problems. *Child Development, 65,* 649–665.

Dooley, D., & Catalano, R. (Eds.). (1988). Psychological effects of unemployment. *Journal of Social Issues, 44,* 1–12.

Downey, G., & Coyne, J. C. (1990). Children of depressed parents: An integrative review. *Psychological Bulletin, 108,* 50–76.

Duncan, G. J. (1984). *Years of poverty, years of plenty: The changing economic fortunes of American workers and families*. Ann Arbor: Survey Research Center, Institute of Social research, University of Michigan.

Duncan, G. J., & Brooks-Gunn, J. (1997). *Consequences of growing up poor*. New York: Russell Sage Foundation.

Dwyer, J. H. (1983). *Statistical models for social and behavioral sciences*. New York: Oxford University Press.

Elder, G. H., Jr. (1974). *Children of the Great Depression: Social change in life experience*. Chicago: University of Chicago Press.

Elder, G. H., Jr., & Caspi, A. (1988). Economic stress in lives: Developmental perspectives. *Journal of Social Issues, 44,* 25–45.

Elder, G. H., Jr., Van Nguyen, T., & Caspi, A. (1985). Linking family hardship to children's lives. *Child Development, 56,* 361–375.

Emery, R. E. (1988). *Marriage, adjustment, and children's adjustment*. Newbury Park, CA: Sage.

Emery, R. E., & O'Leary, R. D. (1984). Marital discord and child behavior problems in a nonclinical sample. *Journal of Abnormal Child Psychology, 12,* 411–420.

Fauber, R., Forehand, R., Thomas, A. M., & Wierson, M. (1990). A mediational model of the impact of marital conflict on adolescent adjustment in intact and divorced families: The role of disrupted parenting. *Child Development, 61,* 1112–1123.

Feldman, S. S., & Elliott, G. R. (Eds.). (1990). *At the threshold: The developing adolescent*. Cambridge, MA: Harvard University Press.

Forehand, R., Long, N., Brody, G. H., & Fauber, R. (1986). Home predictors of young adolescents' school behavior and academic performance. *Child Development, 57,* 1528–1533.

Friedberger, M. (1989). *Shake-out: Iowa farm Families in the 1980s*. Lexington: University Press of Kentucky.

Garraty, J. A. (1978). *Unemployment in history: Economic thought and public policy*. New York: Harper and Row.

Ge, X., Conger, R. D., Lorenz, F. O., Shanahan, M., & Elder, G. H., Jr. (1995). Mutual influences in parent and adolescent psycological distress. *Developmental Psychology, 31,* 406–419.

Glenn, N. D., & Weaver, C. N. (1981). The contribution of marital happiness to global happiness. *Social Forces, 43,* 161–168.

Grych, J. H., & Fincham, F. D. (1990). Marital conflict and children's adjustment: A cognitive-contextual framework. *Psychological Bulletin, 108,* 267–290.

Harold, G. T., & Conger, R. D. (1997). Marital conflict and adolescent distress: The role of adolescent awareness. *Child Development, 68,* 333–350.

Hauser, R. M., & Sweeney, M. M. (1997). Does poverty in adolescence affect the life chances of high school graduates? In G. J. Duncan & J. Brooks-Gunn (Eds.), *Consequences of growing up poor* (pp. 541–595). New York: Russell Sage Foundation.

Heffernan, W. D., & Heffernan, J. B. (1986). Impact of the farm crisis on rural families and communities. *Rural Sociologist, 6,* 160–170.

Hill, J. P. (1993). Recent advances in selected aspects of adolescent development. *Journal of Child Psychology and Psychiatry, 34,* 69–99.

Hobfoll, S. E., & Stokes, J. P. (1988). The process and mechanics of social support. In S. Duck, D. E. Hays, S. E. Hobfoll, W. A. Ickes, & B. M. Montgomery (Eds.), *Handbook of personal relationships* (pp. 497–517). New York: Wiley.

Kessler, R. D., Turner, J. B., & House, J. S. (1988). Effects of unemployment on health in a community survey: Main, modifying, and mediating effects. *Journal of Social Issues, 44,* 69–85.

Komarovsky, M. (1940). *The unemployed man and his family*. New York: Octagon Books.

Lasley, P. (1994). Rural, economic and social trends. In R. D. Conger & G. H. Elder Jr. (Eds.), *Families in troubled times: Adapting to change in rural America* (pp. 57–78). Hawthorne, NY: Aldine de Gruyter.

Lasley, P., & Conger. R. D. (Eds.). (1986). *Farm crisis response: Extension and research activities in the north central region*. Ames: North Central Regional Center for Rural Development, Iowa Sate University.

Lasley, P., Leistritz, F. L., Lobao, L. M., & Meyer, K. (1995). *Beyond the amber waves of grain: An examination of social and economic restructuring in the heartland*. Boulder, CO: Westview Press.

Lee, G. R. (1978). Marriage and morale in later life. *Journal of Marriage and the Family, 40,* 131–139.

Levinger, G., & Huston, T. L. (1990). The social psychology of marriage. In F. D. Fincham & T. N.

Bradbury (Eds.), *The psychology of marriage: Basic issues and applications* (pp. 19–58). New York: Guilford Press.

Liem, J. H., & Liem, G. R. (1990). Understanding the individual and family effects of unemployment. In J. Eckenrode & S. Gore (Eds.), *Stress between work and family* (pp. 175–204). New York: Plenum Press.

Liker, J. K., & Elder, G. H., Jr. (1983). Economic hardship and marital relations in the 1930s. *American Sociological Review, 48,* 343–359.

Lobao, L. M., & Lasley, P. (1995). Farm restructuring and crisis in the heartland: An introduction. In P. Lasley, F. L. Leistritz, L. M. Lobao, & K. Meyer, *Beyond the amber waves of grain: An examination of social and economic restructuring in the heartland* (pp. 1–28). Boulder, CO: Westview Press.

Long, N., Forehand, R., Fauber, R., & Brody, G. (1987). Self perceived and independently observed competence of young adolescent as a function of parental marital conflict and recent divorce. *Journal of Abnormal Child Psychology, 15,* 15–27.

Long, N., Slater, E., Forehand, R., & Fauber, R. (1988). Continued high or reduced interparental conflict following divorce: Relation to young adolescent adjustment. *Journal of Consulting and Clinical Psychology, 56,* 467–469.

Lorenz, F. O., Conger, R. D., & Montague, R. (1994). Doing worse and feeling worse: Psychological consequences of economic hardship. In R. D. Conger & G. H. Elder, Jr. (Eds.). *Families in troubled times: Adapting to change in rural America* (pp. 187–206). Hawthorne, NY: Aldine de Gruyter.

Lorenz, F. O., Hraba, J., Conger, R. D., & Pechacova, Z. (1996). Economic change and change in well-being in the Czech Republic, with comparisons to married women in the United States. *Czech Sociological Review, 4,* 43–62.

McLoyd, V. C. (1989). Socialization and development in a changing economy: The effects of paternal job and income loss on children. *American Psychologist, 44,* 293–302.

McLoyd, V. C., Jayaratne, T. E., Ceballo, R., & Borquez, J. (1994). Unemployment and work interruption among African American single mothers: Effects on parenting and adolescent socioemotional functioning. *Child Development, 65,* 562–589.

Melby, J. N., & Conger, R. D. (1996). Parental behaviors and adolescent academic performance: A longitudinal analysis. *Journal of Research on Adolescence, 6,* 113–137.

Melby, J. N., Conger, R. D., Book, R., Rueter, M., Lucy, L., Repinski, D., Ahrens, K., Black, D., Brown, D., Huck, S., Mutchler, L., Rogers, S., Ross, J., & Stavros, T. (1990). *The Iowa family interaction rating scales*: Unpublished manuscript, Center for Family Research in Rural Mental Health, Iowa State University, Ames.

Melby, J. N., Conger. R. D., Conger, K. J., & Lorenz, F. O. (1993). Effects of parental behavior on tobacco use by young male adolescents. *Journal of Marriage and the Family, 55,* 439–454.

Montemayor, R. (1983). Parents and adolescents in conflict: All families some of the time and some families most of the time. *Journal of Early Adolescence, 3,* 83–103.

Murdock, S. H., & Leistritz, F. L. (1988). *The farm financial crisis: Socioeconomic dimensions and implications for producers and rural areas.* Boulder, CO: Westview.

Paikoff, R. L., & Brooks-Gunn, J. (1991). Do parent–child relationships change during puberty? *Psychological Bulletin, 110,* 47–66.

Patterson, G. R. (1982). *Coercive family process.* Eugene, OR: Castalia.

Patterson, G. R. (1991, April). *Interaction of stress and family structure, and their relation to child adjustment: An example of across-site collaboration.* Paper presented at the biennial meeting of the Society for Research in Child Development, Seattle.

Patterson, G. R., DeBaryshe, B. D., & Ramsey, E. (1989). A developmental perspective on antisocial behavior. *American Psychologist, 44,* 329–335.

Pearlin, L. I., & McCall, M. E. (1990). Occupational stress and marital support: A description of microprocesses. In J. Eckenrode & S. Gore (Eds.), *Stress between work and family* (pp. 39–60). New York: Plenum.

Perrucci, C. C., & Targ, D. B. (1988). Effects of a plant closing on marriage and family life. In P.

Voydanoff & L. C. Majka (Eds.), *Redundancy, layoffs, and plant closures: Their character, causes, and consequences* (pp. 181– 207). London: Croom Helm.

Reid, W. J., & Crissafulli, A. (1990). Marital discord and child behavior problems: A meta-analysis. *Journal of Abnormal Child Psychology, 18,* 105–117.

Reis, H. T. (1990). The role of intimacy in interpersonal relations. *Journal of Social and Clinical Psychology, 9,* 15–30.

Rosenblatt, P. (1990). *Farming is in our blood: Farm families in economic crisis.* Ames: Iowa State University Press.

Rueter, M. A., & Conger, R. D. (1995a). Antecedents of parent-adolescent disagreements. *Journal of Marriage and the Family, 57,* 435–448.

Rueter, M. A., & Conger, R. D. (1995b). Interaction style, problem-solving behavior, and family problem-solving effectiveness. *Child Development, 66,* 98–115.

Rueter, M. A., & Conger, R. D. (1998). Reciprocal influences between parenting and adolescent problem-solving behavior. *Developmental Psychology, 34,* 1470–1482.

Rutter, M. (1980). *Changing youth in a changing society: Patterns of adolescent development and disorder.* Cambridge, MA: Harvard University Press.

Rutter, M. (1990). Psychosocial resilience and protective mechanisms. In J. Rolf, A. S. Masten, D. Cicchetti, K. H. Nuechterlein, & S. Weintraub (Eds.), *Risk and protective factors in the development of psychopathology* (pp. 181–214). New York: Cambridge University Press.

Sampson, R. J., & Laub, J. H. (1994). Urban poverty and the family context of delinquency: A new look at structure and process in a classic study. *Child Development, 65,* 523–540.

Simmons, R. G., & Blyth, D. A. (1987). *Moving into adolescence: The impact of pubertal changes and school context.* Hawthorne, NY: Aldine de Gruyter.

Simons, R. L., & Associates. (1996). Co-authors, Beaman, J., Chao, W., Conger, K. J., Conger, R. D., Elder, G. H., Jr., Goldberg, E., Johnson, C., Lorenz, F. O., Russell, S. T., & Whitbeck, L. B. *Understanding differences between divorced and intact families: Stress, interaction, and child outcome.* Thousand Oaks, CA: Sage.

Simons, R. L., Conger, R. D., & Whitbeck, L. B. (1988). A multistage social learning model of the influences of family and peers upon adolescent substance abuse. *Journal of Drug Issues, 18,* 293–315.

Simons, R. L., Lorenz, F. O., Conger, R. D., & Wu, C. (1992). Support from spouse as mediator and moderator of the disruptive influence of economic strain on parenting. *Child Development, 63,* 1282–1301.

Steinberg, L. (1990). Interdependency in the family: Autonomy, conflict, and harmony in the parent–adolescent relationships. In S. S. Feldman & G. R. Elliott (Eds.), *At the threshold: The developing adolescent* (pp. 255–276). Cambridge, MA: Harvard University Press.

Steinberg, L. (1996). *Adolescence* (4th ed.). New York: McGraw-Hill, Inc.

Steinberg, L., Lamborn, S. D., Dornbusch, S. M., & Darling, N. (1992). Impact of parenting practices on adolescent achievement: Authoritative parenting, school involvement, and encouragement to succeed. *Child Development, 63,* 1266–1281.

Straus, M. A., Gelles, R. J., & Steinmetz, S. K. (1990). *Behind closed doors: Violence in the American family.* Beverly Hills, CA: Sage.

Teachman, J. D., Polonko, K. A., & Scanzoni, J. (1987). Demography of the family. In M. B. Sussman & S. K. Steinmetz (Eds.), *Handbook of Marriage and the Family* (pp. 3–6). New York: Plenum Press.

Vinokur, A. D., Price, R. H., & Caplan, R. D. (1996). Hard times and hurtful partners: How financial strain affects depression and relationship satisfaction of unemployed persons and their spouses. *Journal of Personality and Social Psychology, 71,* 166–179.

Voydanoff, P. (1990). Economic distress and family relations: A review of the eighties. *Journal of Marriage and the Family, 52,* 1099–1115.

Voydanoff, P., & Donnelly, B. W. (1988). Economic distress, family coping, and quality of family life. In P. Voydanoff & L. C. Majka (Eds.), *Families and economic distress: Coping strategies and social policy* (pp. 97–117). Newbury Park, CA: Sage.

Weiss, R. S. (1990). Bringing work stress home. In J. Eckenrode & S. Gore (Eds.), *Stress between work and family* (pp. 17–37). New York: Plenum.

Werner, E. E., & Smith, R. S. (1992). *Overcoming the odds: High risk children from birth to adulthood.* Ithaca, NY: Cornell University Press.

Whitbeck, L. B., Simons, R. L., Conger, R. D., Lorenz, F. O., Huck, S., & Elder, G. H., Jr. (1991). Family economic hardship, parental support, and adolescent self-esteem. *Social Psychology Quarterly, 54,* 353–363.

Wills, T. A. (1990). Social support and the family. In E. A. Blechman (Ed.), *Emotions and the family: For better or for worse* (pp. 75–98). Hillsdale, NJ: Erlbaum.

Wright, P. H., & Keple, T. W. (1981). Friends and parents of a sample of high school juniors: An exploratory study of relationship intensity and interpersonal rewards. *Journal of Marriage and the Family, 43,* 559–570.

14 "Spread Your Wings and Fly": The Course of Well-Being and Substance Use During the Transition to Young Adulthood

John Schulenberg, Patrick M. O'Malley,
Jerald G. Bachman, and Lloyd D. Johnston

The period between adolescence and adulthood represents a critical developmental transition. Diversity in life paths becomes more clearly manifest during this transition (Sherrod, Haggerty, & Featherman, 1993), and interindividual variability in the timing and content of developmental milestones increases. This greater diversity is due to the realization of life path preferences established before the transition as well as to the creation of new paths as a function of experiences during the transition. The emergence of new roles and social contexts provides increased opportunities for successes and failures, which in turn may set the stage for potential discontinuity in functioning between adolescence and young adulthood (e.g., Aseltine & Gore, 1993; Petersen, 1993; Schulenberg, Wadsworth, O'Malley, Bachman, & Johnston, 1996).

At the broader societal level, there is relatively little institutional structure to facilitate the transition to young adulthood (Hamilton, 1990; Hurrlemann, 1990). For example, there is far less institutionally and culturally imposed structure on the roles, experiences, and expectations of young people when they make the transition out of adolescence compared with when they make the transition into adolescence. This relative lack of structure is undoubtedly developmentally beneficial for some older adolescents. For others, however, the lack of structure creates a developmental mismatch that adversely influences their health and well-being (see, for example, Eccles et al., 1997; Lerner, 1982; Schulenberg, Maggs, & Hurrlemann, 1997).

Moreover, as Clausen (1991), Elder (1986), Mortimer (1992), and Schuman and Scott (1989) have shown, decisions and experiences during this transition can have powerful reverberations throughout the course of one's adulthood. Certainly, much

This analysis is part of a larger study funded by a grant from the National Institute on Drug Abuse (DA01411). This chapter is based in part on an invited presentation by the first author to the International Conference on Negotiating Adolescence in Times of Social Change: Concepts and Research, Pennsylvania State University, March 1996, sponsored by the Pennsylvania State University and the Friedrich Schiller University of Jena, Germany. We thank Lisa Crockett, Rainer Silbereisen, and an anonymous reviewer for helpful feedback on previous drafts as well as Jonathon Brenner, Nicole Hitzemann, Jeanette Lim, and Katherine Wadsworth for assistance with data management and analysis.

of one's foundation is set, and many of the initial decisions regarding future plans are made before leaving high school. But the actual experiences of young adulthood – the joining of intentions and realities, the deflections of initial plans and making of new ones, the episodes of successes and failures with the various normative tasks – set the stage for the course of one's adult life.

Life Paths into Young Adulthood and Health and Well-Being

The present study was undertaken to examine the impact of these new social roles and contexts on health and well-being between the senior year of high school (age 18) and 4 years post–high school (age 22) using multicohort national panel data drawn from the Monitoring the Future (MtF) study (e.g., Johnston, Bachman, & O'Malley, 1995; Bachman, Wadsworth, O'Malley, Johnston, & Schulenberg, 1997). This launching period immediately following high school is an important one, for it is when initial plans combine with experiences to set into motion the paths that will take the young person through the transition and into adulthood (Gore, Aseltine, Colten, & Lin, 1997). We build upon previous research with the Monitoring the Future data that has shown the importance of such experiences as marriage and living arrangements on post–high school substance use (e.g., Bachman, O'Malley, & Johnston, 1984; Bachman et al., 1997) and take a pattern-centered approach to focus on individual life paths defined by the combination of individual's social roles and experiences during the transition. Specifically, individuals were placed into mutually exclusive life path groups on the basis of their experiences during this launching period.

This life paths strategy, which draws upon Elder's (1995, 1998) conceptualizations regarding social life course and Magnusson's (1995) pattern-centered holistic approach to studying change, rests on the assumption that decisions regarding the pursuits typical of the transition are not made independently; rather, certain pursuits (e.g., full-time education) typically make others (e.g., full-time employment) unlikely. In addition, it is assumed that certain pursuits take precedence over others in terms of impact on people's lives. For example, the power that marriage tends to have on increasing health and well-being makes getting married during the launching period a pivotal experience that likely overshadows the impact of educational and occupational pursuits. Furthermore, individuals' experiences during this transition are structured at least to some extent by whether they remain in their parents' home (e.g., Bachman et al., 1997; Flanagan, Schulenberg, & Fuligni, 1993; Graber & Dubas, 1996).

A Needed Focus on Inter- and Intracohort Differences and Similarities

Research conducted in the past two decades should give scientists interested in the study of adolescence some measure of satisfaction. The sheer amount of knowledge generated has been impressive; more important, the quality of the research has improved. Contextually sensitive and cross-cultural studies have become much more common, and cross-sectional studies have given way to longitudinal studies. Nevertheless, it is clear that our current scientific knowledge about adolescents is based largely upon conceptualizations and data that are culture-bound and time-bound. Only recently have we seen sustained efforts to compare adolescents from different countries and cultures. Similarly, with few exceptions (e.g., Elder, 1974; Modell, Furstenberg, & Hershberg, 1976; Nesselroade & Baltes, 1974), only during the past decade or so have there been systematic attempts to address directly basic questions about the effects of historical change on the experience of adolescence (e.g., Crockett, 1997; Elder, Modell, & Parke, 1993; Noack, Hofer, & Youniss, 1995).

A primary focus of the present study is on cohort differences in well-being and substance use with a particular emphasis on determining whether the course of well-being and substance use during the transition to young adulthood varies as a function of cohort. Although some studies suggest that the transition to young adulthood is accompanied by increased well-being (e.g., Aseltine & Gore, 1993; Bachman, O'Malley, & Johnston, 1978), few have included multiple cohorts. Likewise, an abundance of studies suggests that substance use increases during the transition, but other than the MtF study, few have tracked multiple cohorts (but see, for example, Elliot, Huizinga, & Menard, 1989). Thus, the extent to which changes in well-being and substance use during the transition reflect cohort-dependent experiences that vary with social change remains an open question.

In the past two decades in the United States, macrolevel social change is probably best conceptualized as emerging fairly continuously (e.g., increased availability of personal computers, increased maternal employment, increased college attendance and age of first marriage) rather than as a function of single defining historical events (e.g., the Great Depression). This, of course, makes it difficult to isolate social change and to capture its nature and impact. Still, in terms of "youth culture," the last two decades have witnessed some important macrolevel changes. For example, during the late 1970s (when Jimmy Carter was president), conservative and materialistic values were low and altruistic values were high; this pattern was reversed during the early and middle 1980s (when Ronald Reagan was president) and then reversed again during the early 1990s (when George Bush was president) (see, for example, Schulenberg, Bachman, Johnston, & O'Malley, 1995). During these same three historical periods, there were important changes in illicit drug use among young people: a decline in illicit drug use during the 1980s followed by an upturn in the early 1990s (Johnston, O'Malley, & Bachman, 1998). Another important historical trend was that by the end of the 1970s, the last birth cohorts of the baby boom generation had progressed through high school, whereas the post–baby boom cohorts (sometimes popularly referred to as "Generation X") experienced adolescence during the 1980s, when economic and demographic forces led many to believe that career prospects would be more limited (e.g., Holtz, 1995).

Given these macrolevel social changes and the opportunities and constraints in our data set, we focus the present study on three cohort groups: Cohort 1 consisted of those who were seniors in high school during the period 1976 through 1981; Cohort 2 consisted of the 1982–86 senior year cohorts; and Cohort 3 consisted of the 1987–92 senior year cohorts. It is important to recognize that this emphasis on cohort groups, although appropriate given our purposes here, nevertheless serves to confound period effects (i.e., secular trends) with cohort effects and to a lesser extent with age effects.

Intercohort comparisons are especially important when intracohort comparisons are also conducted (e.g., Ryder, 1965). Social change hardly ever strikes a cohort uniformly, and intracohort comparisons permit us to see how pervasive the effects of social change may be as well as to begin to understand the mechanisms that connect historical and individual change. In the present study, we focus on how cohort interacts with life paths and gender in influencing the course of well-being and substance use during the transition to young adulthood.

In summary, the present study was undertaken to examine the courses of well-being and substance use during the transition to young adulthood. We used multi-cohort U.S. national panel data spanning ages 18 to 22 to describe the courses of well-being and substance use and to determine whether the courses varied as a function of cohort, gender, life paths, and their interactions.

Method

Three waves of national panel data from 17 consecutive cohorts were obtained from the MtF project, which is an ongoing cohort-sequential longitudinal study designed to understand the epidemiology and etiology of substance use and, more broadly, psychosocial development during adolescence and young adulthood. The project has surveyed nationally representative samples of about 17,000 high school seniors each year in the United States since 1975 using questionnaires administered in classrooms. About 2,400 individuals are randomly selected from each senior year cohort for follow-up. Follow-up surveys are conducted on a biennial basis through mailed questionnaires. Additional details regarding the MtF project procedures and purposes are provided elsewhere (Bachman et al., 1997; Johnston et al., 1998; Johnston, O'Malley, Schulenberg, & Bachman, 1996).

Sample

The panel sample used in the present study consisted of 17 consecutive cohorts of respondents who were surveyed as high school seniors (Wave 1) from 1976 through 1992 and who participated in the first two biennial follow-up surveys

(Waves 2 and 3). The biennial follow-up surveys began 1 year post–high school for one random half of each cohort and 2 years post–high school for the other half. For these analyses, the two random halves were combined such that Wave 2 covered the first and second year out of high school (modal ages 19–20), and Wave 3 covered the third and fourth year (modal ages 21–22).

The life path analyses made it desirable to restrict the sample to respondents present at all three waves. Although retention rates for any one follow-up survey averaged 75–80%, this more demanding restriction resulted in a sample size of 21,134 weighted cases[1] (56.5% were women), representing a retention rate of approximately 68%. Previous attrition analyses with similar MtF panel samples have shown that, compared with those excluded, those retained in the panel sample were more likely to be female, white, higher in high school grade point average and parental education level and lower in high school truancy and senior year substance use (e.g., Schulenberg, Bachman, O'Malley, & Johnston, 1994; Schulenberg, Wadsworth, et al., 1996).

There were five separate questionnaire forms (six, beginning with the 1989 senior year cohort), and although the substance use measures were included on all forms, the well-being measures appeared on only one form. (The different questionnaire forms were distributed randomly within schools at the senior year.) In addition, the well-being measures were not included for the 1976 cohort and were not available at the time of analysis for the 1992 cohort. Thus, approximately one fifth of the panel sample from the 1977–91 senior year cohorts was available for the well-being analyses, including 3,586 weighted cases.

Subsample Groups

Cohort Groups. The senior year cohorts were arranged into three groups: Cohort 1 included the 1976–81 senior year cohorts (1977–81 for the well-being analyses), Cohort 2 included the 1982–86 senior year cohorts, and Cohort 3 included the 1987–92 senior year cohorts (1987–91 for the well-being analyses). This trichotomous grouping reflects an historically appropriate one, as discussed earlier.[2] Nevertheless, this strategy ignores within-cohort-group period differences, which is an important limitation in as much as Cohort 1 experienced the 4 years following high school between 1977 and 1985 (when substance use peaked and then declined among the youth population), Cohort 2 between 1983 and 1990 (when substance use declined among the youth population), and Cohort 3 between 1988 and 1996 (when substance use declined and then began to increase among the adolescent population) (Johnston et al., 1998). Furthermore, as discussed previously, an important limitation of this strategy is that period effects are confounded with cohort and age effects (i.e., between-cohort differences may reflect both cohort and period effects, and age-related changes may reflect both age and period effects). These limitations should be kept in mind when considering the findings.

Table 1. *Life paths into young adulthood: Group definitions and percentages.*

Group	Percentage of sample	Full time student (wave 2/3)	Full time employed (wave 2/3)	Live with parent(s) (wave 2/3)	Marital status (wave 2/3)	Children (wave 2/3)
1. College–away	16.3%	Y & Y	N & N	N & N	N & N	N & N
2. College–home	5.1	Y & Y	N & N	Y & Y	N & N	N & N
3. College–home and away	3.5	Y & Y	N & N	Y & N	N & N	N & N
4. Employed–away	3.6	– & –	Y & Y	N & N	N & N	N & N
5. Employed–home	7.7	– & –	Y & Y	Y & Y	N & N	N & N
6. Employed–home and away	3.4	– & –	Y & Y	Y & N	N & N	N & N
7. Married, no child	9.0	– & –	– & –	– & N[a]	– & Y	N & N
8. Married and parent	7.7	– & –	– & –	– & N[a]	– & Y	Y &/or Y
9. Single parent	4.5	– & –	– & –	– & –	N & N	Y &/or Y
10. Uncommitted	14.1	N &/or N[b]	N &/or N[b]	– & –	N & N	N & N
11. Other	25.1					

Note: Wave 2 = age 19–20; Wave 3 = age 21–22. Y = yes; N = no; – = either yes or no. weighted n = 21,134; cohorts = 1976–92.
[a] In addition to not living with own parent(s), respondent could not be living with spouse's parent(s).
[b] To be included in the Uncommitted group, it was necessary for respondent to be neither a full-time student nor employed full time at Wave 2 *and/or* at Wave 3.

Life-Path Groups. The life-path groups were constructed based on young adulthood demographic characteristics gathered at Waves 2 and 3: full-time college attendance during the past year, full-time employment during the past year, living arrangements (i.e., whether residing with parents) during the past year, current marital status, and current parental status (i.e., whether respondent had one or more children or stepchildren). An important premise in forming the groups was that certain pursuits and experiences take precedence over others during this launching period, and these defining pursuits and experiences serve to sort individuals into different paths. Furthermore, given finite time and financial resources, choosing one set of pursuits (e.g., full-time education) typically precludes other sets of pursuits (e.g., full-time employment). As shown in Table 1, 11 mutually exclusive life-path groups were formed.[3]

The first three life-path groups comprised about 25% of the total sample and consisted of those respondents who were full-time college students at *both* Wave 2 and Wave 3 and at the same time were not employed full-time, were not married, and had no children. These are the individuals whose primary "occupation" immediately following high school was to attend college and remain there for at least 3 to 4 years. The distinction among these three college groups was whether they lived away from home at both follow-ups, lived at home with parent(s) at both follow-ups, or moved from home at Wave 2 to away from home at Wave 3.

The next three groups comprised about 15% of the total sample and consisted of those who were employed full time at both Wave 2 and 3 and at the same time were not married and had no children. Although it was possible that individuals in these groups could also be part-time or even full-time college students, their primary occupation was full-time employment. The distinction among these three was whether they lived at home with parents.

The next three groups comprised about 21% of the total sample and consisted of those who were married, had children, or both, at Wave 2, Wave 3, or both. Individuals in these groups were on the "family fast track" (i.e., the average ages for first marriage and first pregnancy were in the mid-20s for the cohorts represented in the sample). In forming these three groups, given the relative infrequency of these family experiences during the launching period, no restrictions were placed on student or employment status. Furthermore, in forming the single parent group, no restrictions were made on living arrangements.

The uncommitted group consisted of those who were neither married nor had children at both Waves 2 and 3, and at least at one of these waves, were neither attending college nor employed full time. This group comprised about 14% of the total sample.

Finally, the other group consisted of the remainder of the sample that did not fit into any of the first 10 groups. This group comprised about 25% of the total sample, indicating that three fourths of the total sample fit into one of the 10 defined life-path groups.

With respect to gender differences, men were somewhat more likely than were women to be in the college-away group (17.9 vs. 15.9%), the employed groups (17.6 vs. 12.1%), and the uncommitted group (15.2 vs. 13.3%); men were much less likely to be in the marriage and children groups (14.4 vs. 25.9%). With respect to cohort group differences, the college-away group increased in prevalence across the three cohort groups (13.6 vs. 16.5 vs. 20.2%), and the two marriage groups decreased (20.9 vs. 16.2 vs. 12.7%).

Measures

Well-Being Measures. Well-being was considered in terms of overall satisfaction with life (one item) and three pairs of similar but opposing constructs: positive self-esteem (four items, average alpha of .77; based on Rosenberg, 1965; see also O'Malley & Bachman, 1979, 1983) and self-derogation (four items, average alpha of .78); self-efficacy (three items, average alpha of .50; based on Nowicki & Strickland's, 1973, internal locus of control subscale) and fatalism (two items, average alpha of .63); and social support (three items, average alpha of .66) and loneliness (three items, average alpha of .66). The same measures were used at all three waves. The magnitude of senior year correlations ranged from .19 between life satisfaction and self-efficacy to −.55 between positive self-esteem and self-derogation. Details of the measures are provided in Table 2.

Table 2. *Summary of measures.*

		Total sample means (standard deviations)		
Scale and item	Description and sample item	Wave 1	Wave 2	Wave 3
Well-Being				
Life satisfaction	How satisfied are you with your life as a whole these days?[a]	4.95 (1.21)	4.95 (1.21)	4.97 (1.22)
Self-esteem	I take a positive attitude toward myself.[b]	4.20 (.58)	4.26 (.57)	4.31 (.56)
Self-derogation	I feel my life is not very useful.[b]	2.03 (.75)	1.84 (.73)	1.72 (.70)
Self-efficacy	When I make plans, I am almost certain I can make them work.[b]	3.86 (.68)	3.92 (.69)	4.01 (.66)
Fatalism	Every time I try to get ahead, something or somebody stops me.[b]	2.08 (.73)	1.97 (.72)	1.91 (.71)
Social support	There is always someone I can turn to if I need help.[b]	4.28 (.70)	4.41 (.63)	4.41 (.62)
Loneliness	I often wish I had more good friends.[b]	2.94 (.88)	2.77 (.90)	2.66 (.87)
Substance use				
Cigarette use	How frequently have you smoked cigarettes during the past 30 days?[c]	1.66 (1.24)	1.78 (1.40)	1.84 (1.49)
Alcohol use	On how many occasions have you had alcoholic beverages to drink during the past 30 days?[d]	2.49 (1.51)	2.76 (1.57)	2.92 (1.58)
Binge drinking	Think back over the last 2 weeks. How many times have you had five or more drinks in a row?[e]	1.75 (1.22)	1.84 (1.26)	1.87 (1.26)
Marijuana use	On how many occasions (if any) have you used marijuana or hashish during the past 12 months?[d]	2.15 (1.93)	2.23 (1.99)	2.17 (1.97)

Note: Total sample includes senior year cohorts 1976–92 ($N = 21,134$ for substance use measures; $N = 3,586$ for the well-being measures); modal ages were 18, 19–20, and 21–22, for the three waves, respectively.

[a] Possible responses ranged from 1 (*completely dissatisfied*) to 7 (*completely satisfied*).

[b] Possible responses ranged from 1 (*disagree*) to 5 (*agree*).

[c] Possible responses ranged from 1 (*not at all*) to 7 (*two packs or more per day*).

[d] Possible responses ranged from 1 (*0 occasions*) to 7 (*40 or more*).

[e] Possible responses ranged from 1 (*none*) to 6 (*10 or more times*).

Substance Use Measures. Substance use measures included cigarette use (frequency in the past 30 days), alcohol use (occasions of use in past 30 days), binge drinking (frequency of having five or more drinks in a row during the past 2 weeks), and marijuana use (occasions of use in the past 12 months). These MtF substance use items have been shown to demonstrate adequate psychometric properties, and their reliability and validity have been reported and discussed extensively (e.g., Johnston & O'Malley, 1985; O'Malley, Bachman, & Johnston, 1983). The same measures were used at all three waves (see Table 2). Senior year correlations ranged from .33 between cigarette use and binge drinking to .74 between alcohol use and binge drinking.

Analysis Plan

To address the purposes of this study, we conducted 11 repeated-measures analyses of variance (ANOVAs) that were conducted as multivariate analyses of variance (MANOVAs), one for each well-being and substance use measure. These 11 measures at the three waves (ages 18, 19–20, and 21–22) were treated as the dependent variables in these analyses. The independent variables included cohort (3 levels), gender (2 levels), and life-path group (11 levels) as between-subject variables; and age (3 waves) as a within-subjects variable.[4] The MANOVAs were full-factorial (i.e., all two-, three- and four-way interactions were included).[5] Age effects (i.e., intraindividual change across the three waves) were partitioned into orthogonal polynomial contrasts to test for linear and quadratic age effects in well-being and substance use. (Additional details regarding the analyses and findings are provided in Schulenberg, O'Malley, Bachman, & Johnston, 1998.)

Results

The purpose of this study was to determine whether the individual-level course of well-being and substance use during the transition from adolescence to young adulthood varied as a function of cohort, gender, and life paths. There were four phases of the analyses: (1) total sample consideration of the course of well-being and substance use during the transition from adolescence to young adulthood, (2) cohort comparisons, (3) gender comparisons (including cohort by gender interactions), and (4) life-path comparisons (including cohort, gender, and life path interactions).

Phase 1. Course of Well-Being and Substance Use in Total Sample

An overview of the findings from the 11 repeated-measures MANOVAs is provided in Table 3. Of primary concern in this first phase of the analysis is the first set of rows for "age" in the "within-subjects effects" section.

Well-Being. As shown in Table 3, there were statistically significant main effects for age for all of the well-being measures except life satisfaction, and in each case the shape of the significant age-related change was entirely or primarily linear. The total sample means for each well-being measure are displayed in Figure 1 (and provided in Table 2). In considering Figure 1, note that all measures had the same 1-to-5 response format except life satisfaction (1-to-7 response format; see Table 2). As illustrated in the left panel, life satisfaction remained unchanged across the waves. Self-esteem, self-efficacy, and social support increased significantly during the transition, and the increase was linear for self-esteem and self-efficacy and linear and quadratic for social support (i.e., for social support, most of the increase occurred between Waves 1 and 2). Likewise, as is shown in the right panel, self-derogation, fatalism, and loneliness decreased significantly during the transition,

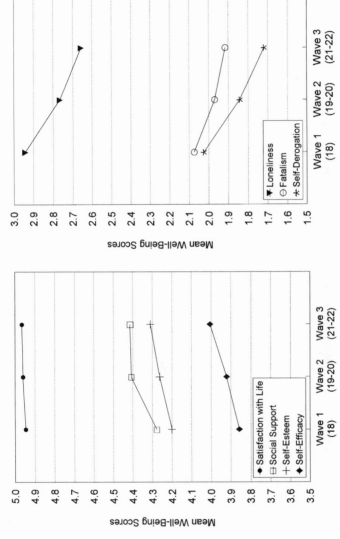

Figure 1. Age-related change in well-being during the transition to young adulthood: total sample. *Note:* Response formats range from 1 to 5 for all measures except life satisfaction, for which the range is 1–7 (see Table 2).

Table 3. *Overview of repeated-measures ANOVAs results for well-being and substance use.*

	Well-being							Substance use			
	Life satisfaction	Self-esteem	Self-derogation	Self-efficacy	Fatalism	Social support	Loneliness	30-day cigarette	30-day alcohol	Binge drinking	12-month marijuana
Between-subjects effects											
Cohort (C)								***	***	***	***
Gender (G)		***	***	**		***	**	*	***	***	***
Life path (P)	***	***	***	***	***		***	***	***	***	***
C*G											
C*P							*	**	**	*	***
G*P				*		*		**	***	*	*
C*G*P											
Within-subjects effects											
Age (A)											
linear		***	***	***	***	***	***	***	***	***	***
quadratic		**	***	***	***	***	***	***	***	*	*
C*A											
linear				*	*			**	*	**	***
quadratic				**	**	**		***	***	*	***
G*A											
linear				**		**		***	***	**	***
quadratic				**		**		***	***	***	***

P*A

linear

quadratic

C*G*A

linear

quadratic

C*P*A

linear

quadratic

G*P*A

linear

quadratic

C*G*P*A

linear

quadratic

Notes: See Schulenberg *et al.*, 1998, for a full summary of the analyses and findings.
*** = $p < .001$, ** = $p < .01$, * = $p < .05$.

and, in each case, the decrease was linear. Thus, at least in the total sample, the transition to young adulthood was accompanied by increased well-being, and the rate of increase was generally constant across the waves.

Substance Use. As indicated in Table 3, age effects were significant for each of the four substances. In the total sample, cigarette use, alcohol use, and binge drinking increased significantly with age, and these increases were primarily linear. For 12-month marijuana use, the age effect was primarily quadratic, increasing between Waves 1 and 2 and then decreasing between Waves 2 and 3. Nevertheless, these total sample findings are qualified to a large extent by the cohort by age interactions discussed in the following section on cohort comparisons.

Phase 2. Cohort Comparisons

The second phase of the analysis was to determine whether the courses of well-being and substance use during the transition to young adulthood just described varied across Cohort 1 (1976–81 senior year cohorts), Cohort 2 (1982–86 cohorts), and Cohort 3 (1987–92 cohorts).

Well-Being. In terms of overall cohort main effects (averaged across age), the first row in Table 3 reveals no such effects for well-being. But as revealed in the second set of rows in the "within-subjects effects" section in Table 3, the cohort by age interaction was significant for both self-efficacy and fatalism, indicating that age-related linear changes in these two measures varied as a function of cohort. The age-change coefficients for the three cohorts were compared to determine significant differences among the cohorts. As shown in the self-efficacy column in Table 4, the linear change coefficient for the total sample for self-efficacy was significant and positive, indicating a significant increase with age (as revealed previously in Figure 1). The pairwise comparisons of linear change coefficients in the three cohorts revealed that the age-related increase was significantly greater in Cohort 1 than in Cohorts 2 and 3 and was similar in Cohorts 2 and 3. For fatalism, which decreased significantly with age in the total sample, the decrease was similar for Cohorts 1 and 2 and was significantly greater in Cohorts 1 and 2 than in Cohort 3. Thus, the increase in self-efficacy and the decrease in fatalism that accompany the transition to young adulthood were less pronounced in recent cohorts compared with earlier ones. Increases in other aspects of well-being during the transition, however, have remained constant over the past two decades.

Substance Use. As indicated in the top row of Table 3, there was a significant overall cohort main effect for each substance use measure. The use of all four substances was significantly greater in Cohort 1 than Cohorts 2 and 3 and, except for cigarette use, significantly greater in Cohort 2 than Cohort 3.

Table 4. *Summary of significant cohort by age interactions:*
Age–change coefficients.

Age and cohort effects	Age–change coefficients					
	Self-efficacy	Fatalism	30-day cigarette	30-day alcohol	Binge drinking	12-month marijuama
Linear effects:						
Age effects[a]	.11***	−.13***	.14***	.27***	.06***	−.02*
Cohort by age interactions[b]						
1 v 2	.05*	−.04	.04*	–	.00	.11***
2 v 3	.03	−.08*	.03	–	−.05*	−.08**
1 v 3	.08**	−.13***	.07***	–	−.05*	.03
Quadratic effects:						
Age effects[a]	.02	.00	−.03***	−.02*	.00	−.05***
Cohort by age interactions[b]						
1 v 2	–	–	–	−.01	−.03	−.06**
2 v 3	–	–	–	−.10***	−.03	−.02
1 v 3	–	–	–	−.10***	−.06**	−.08***

Notes: Cohort 1 = 1976–81; Cohort 2 = 1982–86; Cohort 3 = 1987–92.
*** = $p < .001$, ** = $p < .01$, * = $p < .05$.
[a]These change coefficients are for the total sample. Significant positive and negative linear effects refer to linear-shaped increase and decrease over time, respectively; significant positive and negative quadratic effects refer to U-shaped and inverted U-shaped patterns over time, respectively.
[b]These change coefficients represent pairwise comparisons of change in each cohort over time. Significant positive and negative linear coefficients refer to significantly more positive and negative linear change, respectively, in the first cohort in the comparison versus the second; significant positive and negative quadratic coefficients refer to significantly more positive and negative quadratic effects, respectively, in the first cohort in the comparison versus the second.

On the basis of the significant cohort by time interactions summarized in Table 3, the age-related course of each substance use measure varied as a function of cohort membership, and this variation took the form of linear change differences (for all but 30-day alcohol) and of quadratic change differences (for all but 30-day cigarette use). These variations are illustrated in Figures 2 and 3 and also revealed in the comparisons of age-change coefficients in Table 4. The linear age-related increase in cigarette use was significantly greater for Cohort 1 than for the other two cohorts. Although the linear increase in 30-day alcohol use was similar for the three cohorts, the negative quadratic effect (i.e., inverted U-shape) was significantly greater in Cohorts 1 and 2 than in Cohort 3 (i.e., the increase leveled off between Waves 2 and 3 for Cohorts 1 and 2 but not for Cohort 3). Likewise, the linear increase in binge drinking was significantly greater in Cohort 3 than in Cohorts 1 and 2, and the leveling-off between Waves 2 and 3 was significantly less in Cohort 3 than in Cohort 1. There was a slight overall age-related decrease in marijuana use, and this decrease was significantly greater for Cohort 2 than for Cohorts 1 and 3; the negative quadratic effect was significantly greater for Cohort 1 than for Cohorts 2 and 3.

In summary, cigarette use was more prevalent and increased more rapidly during the transition in Cohort 1 than in Cohorts 2 and 3. In contrast, whereas overall levels

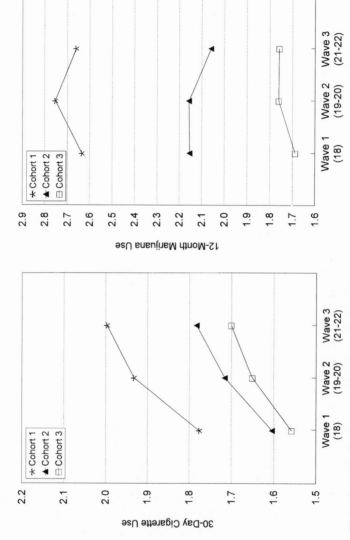

Figure 2. Cohort differences in substance use during the transition to young adulthood: cigarette and marijuana use. *Note:* Cohort 1 = 1976–81 senior year cohorts, Cohort 2 = 1982–86 cohorts, and Cohort 3 = 1987–92 cohorts (see Table 2 for description of measures).

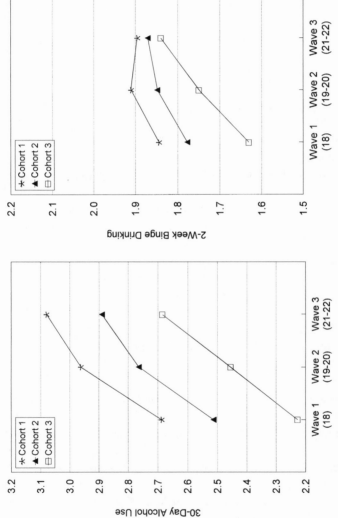

Figure 3. Cohort differences in substance use during the transition to young adulthood: alcohol use and binge drinking. *Note:* Cohort 1 = 1976–81 senior year cohorts, Cohort 2 = 1982–86 cohorts, and Cohort 3 = 1987–92 cohorts (see Table 2 for description of measures).

of alcohol use, binge drinking, and marijuana use were lower for each succeeding cohort group, alcohol and marijuana use, and especially binge drinking, appeared to increase more rapidly for Cohort 3 compared with Cohorts 1 and 2. It is important to reiterate here that the analytic strategy, although useful and appropriate given the purposes of this chapter, served to confound period effects with age and cohort effects. For example, the lack of increase in marijuana use between Waves 1 and 2 for Cohort 2 may be due in part to all of the Wave 2 measures having occurred between 1983 and 1988, a period when there were significant declines in marijuana use among young Americans generally.

Phase 3. Gender Comparisons

Well-Being. Overall, it was found that (averaged across age) men were significantly higher in self-esteem and self-efficacy and significantly lower in self-derogation, social support, and loneliness than were women (the general lack of gender by cohort interactions indicates that these overall gender differences have remained relatively constant over the past few decades; see Table 3). With regard to gender differences in the course of well-being during the transition (see Table 3), the findings indicate that self-efficacy and social support increased more rapidly for men than for women (see Schulenberg et al., 1998, for more detail). For the remaining measures of well-being, age-related changes during the transition were similar for men and women. There were no significant gender by cohort by time interactions, indicating that these gender differences and similarities in change in well-being during the transition did not vary by cohort over the past few decades.

Substance Use. Overall, averaged across the three waves, women were significantly higher in cigarette use and lower in alcohol use, binge drinking, and marijuana use compared with men (see Table 3). In two cases, these overall gender differences were modified slightly by the significant cohort by gender interactions: for binge drinking and marijuana use, gender differences decreased with succeeding cohorts. With regard to gender differences in the course of substance use during the transition, the findings revealed that the linear age-related increase in the use of each substance was significantly greater for men than for women. For cigarette use, men started lower but increased more rapidly than women, but the two converged by Wave 3. For the other three substances, men started higher than women, and these gender differences became amplified during the transition. There were no significant cohort by gender by age interactions, indicating that these gender differences in the course of substance use have not varied over the past few decades.

Phase 4. Life-Path Comparisons

In the final phase of the analysis, the courses of well-being and substance use during the transition for the 11 life-path groups (see Table 1) are compared, and interactions involving cohort and gender are examined. The relevant findings, which are extensive, are summarized in this section (see Schulenberg et al., 1998, for a detailed description of findings).

Well-Being. There were overall (averaged across age) life-path differences in all well-being measures except for social support (see Table 3). One of the most striking patterns is that in nearly all comparisons, the college-away group was found to exhibit significantly greater than average well-being, whereas the uncommitted and single-parent groups significantly lower than average well-being. In addition, the three college groups showed significantly greater than average self-efficacy and significantly less than average fatalism. These overall life-path differences have remained relatively constant over the past few decades and were similar for men and women.

With regard to life-path differences in the course of well-being, the life path by age interaction was significant for life satisfaction and loneliness. For life satisfaction, compared with the total group, the married–no children group showed a significantly greater linear increase with age, the uncommitted group a significantly greater linear decrease with age, and the married-parent group a significant negative quadratic trend. These differential changes are illustrated in Figure 4. Also, as illustrated in Figure 4, loneliness decreased during the transition at a significantly faster than average rate for the college-away group and decreased at a significantly slower than average rate for the uncommitted group.

For the remaining five indices of well-being, change during the transition to young adulthood did not vary by life path. However, for both self-esteem and self-derogation, there was a slight but significant life path by cohort by time interaction (post hoc analyses revealed that, with successive cohorts, the uncommitted group showed progressively less pronounced increases in self-esteem and decreases in self-derogation during the transition). Otherwise, similarities and differences in changes in well-being across the life-path groups did not vary by cohort or by gender.

Substance Use. Overall (averaged over time), life-path differences in all substance use measures were evident. All forms of substance use tended to be significantly greater than average among the employed groups and significantly less than average among the married groups. The three college groups were significantly lower than average in cigarette use; with regard to alcohol use and binge drinking, the college-away group indulged at a significantly greater than average rate, whereas the college-home group indulged at a significantly lower than average rate. Both the single-parent and uncommitted groups had higher than average cigarette and marijuana use.

As shown in the top portion of Table 3, these overall life-path differences for each measure of substance use were qualified by significant cohort and gender interactions (see Schulenberg et al., 1998, for description of these findings). For example,

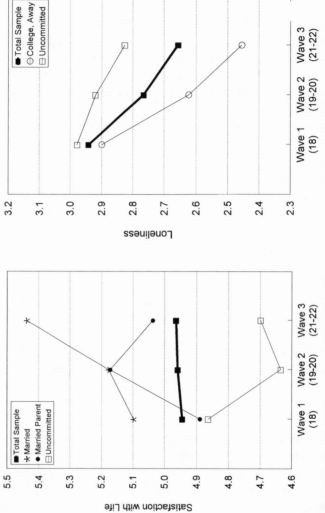

Figure 4. Life path differences in well-being during the transition to young adulthood: life satisfaction and loneliness. *Note:* See Table 1 for description of life path groups and Table 2 for description of measures.

242

cohort differences in cigarette and alcohol use were significantly less than average among the college students, suggesting the importance of considering intracohort variation when making intercohort comparisons. In addition, gender differences were less pronounced for alcohol use among college students and for marijuana use among those employed full time, illustrating the importance of considering gender differences in substance use in the context of life experiences during the transition to young adulthood.

The findings revealed significant life-path differences in age-related changes in all forms of substance use during the transition (see Table 3). As illustrated in Figure 5, the age-related linear increase in cigarette use was significantly more rapid than average for the employed-away, employed-home and away, single-parent, and uncommitted groups; and it was significantly slower than average for the college–home and two married groups. On the basis of the quadratic effects, the pattern of more rapid increase between Waves 1 and 2 than between Waves 2 and 3 was more pronounced than average for the employed-away group and less than average for the college-away group. There was a significant gender by life path by time interaction, indicating that, in the married-parent and single-parent groups, men were more likely to increase cigarette use over time than were women.

As illustrated in Figure 6, the linear increase in alcohol use during the transition was significantly greater for the college-away and college–home and away groups and significantly less for the employed-home and two married groups. On the basis of the quadratic effects, the change over time was more rapid between Waves 1 and 2 than between Waves 2 and 3 for the college-away and employed-away groups, whereas an opposite pattern was found for the employed-home, employed-home then away, single-parent, and uncommitted groups. There was a significant gender by life path by time interaction, and, based on post hoc analyses, it was found that, in the married-parent and single-parent groups, women were more likely to decrease alcohol use than were men.

The findings for binge drinking and marijuana use were quite similar to those just described for 30-day alcohol use (see Schulenberg et al., 1998). For example, both increased significantly more rapidly for the college-away and college–home and away groups and decreased for the two married groups. One notable difference in the findings for marijuana use was that it increased significantly faster than average for the uncommitted group.

To summarize some of the more compelling evidence for differential change in substance use as a function of life path, all forms of substance use increased less rapidly during the transition (or even decreased) for the two married groups, alcohol and marijuana use and binge drinking increased more rapidly for the college-away and college–home and away groups, cigarette and marijuana use increased more rapidly for the uncommitted group, and for the two groups that left home immediately following high school (college-away and employed-away), the increase in

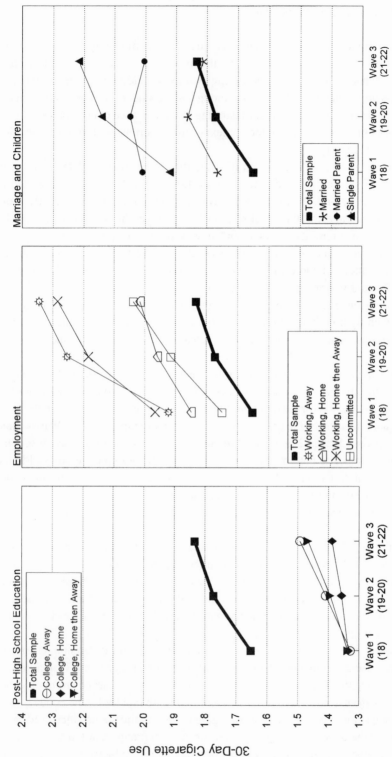

Figure 5. Life path differences in cigarette use during the transition to young adulthood. *Note:* See Table 1 for description of life-path groups and Table 2 for description of measure.

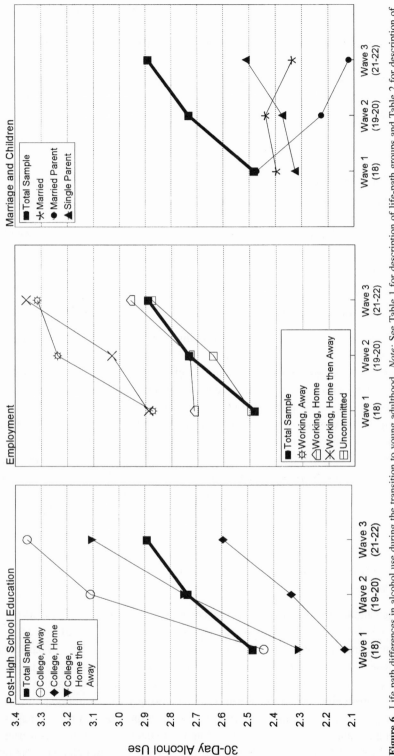

Figure 6. Life path differences in alcohol use during the transition to young adulthood. *Note:* See Table 1 for description of life-path groups and Table 2 for description of measure.

alcohol use and binge drinking was especially rapid between Waves 1 and 2. None of these differential changes among the life paths varied as a function of cohort, indicating that the differences among life paths in terms of rate and direction of change in substance use during the transition to young adulthood have remained steady over the past two decades.

Summary and Conclusions

Moving from high school into young adulthood is a critical developmental transition, a time of continuity and discontinuity in health and well-being. As we have shown in this chapter, how well one negotiates this transition, as evidenced by one's course of well-being and substance use, depends in part on historical cohort, gender, and life path.

1. Overall Changes in Well-Being and Substance Use During the Transition to Young Adulthood

In the total sample, we found that well-being increased significantly during the transition to young adulthood (i.e., self-esteem, self-efficacy, and social support increased; self-derogation, fatalism, and loneliness decreased), which is a finding consistent with previous studies (e.g., Aseltine & Gore, 1993; O'Malley & Bachman, 1979, 1983). Substance use (i.e., cigarette, alcohol, and marijuana use; binge drinking) was also found to increase significantly during the transition, although, as discussed below, these findings were qualified to a large degree by cohort differences. It is likely that the increases in well-being and substance use have a common origin in terms of leaving behind the constraints of the high school role and entering new roles and contexts that provide more freedom and opportunities (e.g., Bachman et al., 1997; Brook, Balka, Gursen, & Brook, 1997; Kandel & Davies, 1986).

2. Cohort Group Differences and Similarities in the Course of Well-Being and Substance Use

Although there were no overall differences (averaged across age) in well-being among the three cohort groups, it was found that the course of self-efficacy and fatalism during the transition differed somewhat among the cohorts. In particular, self-efficacy did not increase as much, and fatalism did not decrease as much in the more recent cohorts compared with the earlier ones, indicating that the "boost" in efficacious feelings one typically gets upon entering young adulthood may have become less powerful among recent cohorts. This phenomenon may reflect changing demographic and economic forces, resulting in the perception of more constricted job markets and future prospects that perhaps represents a popular view among members of "Generation X" that their career and economic success will fall short of that of their parents (Holtz, 1995). Nevertheless, it would be unwise to make too much of this finding given the small effects and the lack of cohort-based differential changes in the other measures of well-being. Indeed, the more general conclusion is that, overall, the course of well-being during the transition to young adulthood has been quite similar across the past two decades.

In contrast, the course of substance use during the transition varied considerably by cohort group, and to the extent that substance use poses health risks, there is both good news and bad news. The good news is that, consistent with previous findings from the MtF study (e.g., Bachman, Johnston, O'Malley, & Schulenberg, 1996; Johnston et al., 1998; O'Malley, Bachman, & Johnston, 1988), overall cohort differences (averaged across age) in substance use were found; substance use was higher in Cohort 1 (1976–81) than in Cohort 2 (1982–86), and, except for cigarette use, higher in Cohort 2 than in Cohort 3 (1987–92). To a large extent, these differences between cohorts represent period effects, for substance use generally declined among young people during the 1980s and early 1990s. These period effects reflect greater disapproval of substance use among young people as well as increased perceptions that substance use is risky (e.g., Bachman et al., 1996; Johnston et al., 1998) and thus represent a typical course of drug epidemics (Johnston, 1991). Cigarette and alcohol use are also influenced by changes in legal and economic sanctions, and the lower rates of alcohol use at ages 18–20 among more recent cohorts reflect to some extent the increase in the federal legal drinking age from 18 to 21 between 1984 and 1987 (O'Malley & Wagenaar, 1991).

The bad news is that alcohol and marijuana use, and especially binge drinking, increased more rapidly during the transition for Cohort 3 than for the two earlier cohorts. To the extent that a more rapid increase in substance use reflects difficulties with the transition (either as a contributor or consequence), this more rapid increase among more recent cohorts is troubling. In contrast, it may reflect a lengthening of the transition period to provide more "free time" before the more recent cohorts assume adulthood roles.

3. Gender Differences and Similarities in the Courses of Well-Being and Substance Use

For nearly all measures, men reported higher levels of well-being compared with women, and in the two cases of differential age-related change in well-being as a function of gender (i.e., for self-efficacy and social support), the increase was greater for men than for women. There was little evidence that these gender differences varied by cohort. These findings are consistent with the literature that men report greater well-being than women beginning in adolescence (e.g., Ge, Lorenz, Conger, Elder, & Simons, 1994; Petersen et al., 1993) and indicate that these differences remain intact even during the transition to young adulthood, when well-being tends to increase for all (e.g., Gore et al., 1997; Hankin et al., 1998; Kandel & Davies, 1986).

Men also reported higher levels of substance use (except for cigarettes) than women, and during the transition, substance use increased more rapidly for men than for women. These findings are in accord with the wealth of evidence (discussed previously) that men are more likely to indulge in psychoactive substances, and the findings are also consistent with the differential rates of entry into such adulthood roles as marriage and parenthood (both occur earlier for women than for men). Nevertheless, there was some evidence (i.e., gender by cohort interactions) to indicate that gender differences are eroding: For both binge drinking and marijuana use overall, gender differences across the transition decreased with successive cohorts, perhaps reflecting the increased ages of first marriage and first pregnancy over the past few decades.

4. Life-Path Differences in the Courses of Well-Being and Substance Use

The life-path analyses revealed a wealth of findings. Overall differences (averaged across age) in well-being were found across the life paths; those in the college-away group manifested higher than average levels of well-being, and those in the uncommitted group evidenced lower than average levels. These overall differences varied little by gender or cohort. There were life-path differences in the course of well-being. Life satisfaction increased for those who became married and decreased for those in the uncommitted group. Similarly, loneliness decreased at a slower than average rate for the uncommitted group, and, in contrast, decreased at a faster than average rate for the college-away group. The uncommitted and college-away groups appear to represent opposite extremes in terms of well-being during the transition to young adulthood, and although there was evidence to indicate that these two groups were initially different in well-being, there was also evidence to indicate increased divergences in well-being between these two groups as a function of young adulthood opportunities and experiences. It is important to recognize, however, that for five of the seven indices of well-being, age-related change did not vary by life path, indicating that initial differences between life paths remained intact during the transition. These life-path differences varied little by cohort and gender.

There were many overall differences (averaged over age) in substance use among the life paths, namely, the employed groups showed higher levels of substance use, and the married groups showed lower levels, which is a set of findings consistent with other analyses of the MtF data (e.g., Bachman et al., 1997). These overall life path differences were qualified to some extent by cohort interactions and gender interactions. For example, cohort and gender differences in alcohol use were less pronounced among the college groups, reflecting the consistently high levels of alcohol use on college campuses across the past two decades among men and women.

The age-related course of substance use varied by life path; that is, substance use typically increased more rapidly for those who left home to go to college and for those in the uncommitted group and increased less rapidly (or even decreased) for those who married. Although these life-path differences in the course of substance use during the transition varied somewhat by gender (e.g., parenthood is associated with a greater decrease in substance use for women than for men), they did not vary by cohort group, suggesting that social change influences on the course of substance use during the transition have been rather uniform.

Limitations and Future Directions

An important strength of this investigation was the use of national, multiple-cohort panel data spanning a 4-year period between late adolescence and young adulthood. In particular, the use of multicohort national panel data to construct and study life paths over time represents a powerful approach to understanding change that is possible only through large-scale survey research (e.g., Jackson & Antonucci, 1994; Schulenberg, Wadsworth, et al., 1996). Of course, such large-scale efforts must be complemented with smaller-scale, more intensive efforts to provide a fuller understanding of health and well-being during the transition to young adulthood.

Because the sample included only those who graduated from high school, generalizability of the findings to the noncollege population may be limited. Future research could improve on the study by starting earlier in adolescence to gain a better "before" picture as well as a more representative sample. Caution in interpreting the findings is needed because age, period, and cohort effects remain confounded. In particular, it is likely that the differential patterns of change over time found for marijuana use reflect more of a secular trend than a cohort effect, for marijuana use generally declined for all cohorts during the mid- to late-1980s (see Johnston et al., 1998; O'Malley et al., 1988). Because we do not have direct measures of social changes (or perceptions of social changes), any attempts to explain cohort group differences must rely on inferred social changes.

Although the use of multiple waves of panel data represents an important strength, the 2-year lag between the waves limits precision in specifying the life paths and in charting the course of well-being and substance use. In addition, the well-being measures available in the project lack some depth, which is perhaps a forgivable limitation of secondary analyses of national panel data (Brooks-Gunn, Phelps, & Elder, 1991). Corroboration based on other studies that include more intensive measurements of health and well-being would be useful in this regard.

There were sufficiently clear patterns in our statistically significant findings to indicate their substantive significance. Still, most of the effects were small to moderate. The transition to young adulthood is multifaceted – a quality not fully captured in the characteristics we selected to reflect experiences typical of this transition. A more comprehensive consideration of normative and nonnormative transitional experiences may yield more powerful links between the experiences and changes in well-being and substance use. Future research in this area would do well to consider the reciprocal influences between life paths and health and well-being.

Conclusions

The transition out of high school and into young adulthood is associated with an increased sense of well-being. Although the present study showed that the post–high school upturn in some aspects of well-being varied somewhat by cohort, gender, and life path, it is clear that, for the most part, launching into young adulthood is associated with increases in self-esteem, self-efficacy, and social support. Is the high school experience, especially the end of it, really that bad? Or is the post–high school experience really that good? In all likelihood, the findings reflect some of each, and thus the transition out of high school contributes to a better match between one's developmental needs and one's contexts and experiences, which in turn contributes to increased well-being (see Schulenberg et al., 1997). Indeed, the only exception to this widespread increase in well-being is for those who appear not to connect with post–high school experiences, that is, the uncommitted group that is not progressing in terms of educational, occupational, or family pursuits.

The transition out of high school is also associated with increased substance use. But the increase in substance use is not as widespread as the increase in well-being, and substance use appears more influenced by social change. The extent of increase, or even whether substance use increases, depends considerably on one's life path; greater increases are associated with leaving the home, and lesser increases (or even decreases) with getting married (see Bachman et al., 1997). Although few would argue that this upturn in substance use is healthy for young people, a period of experimentation and even excess with drugs, especially alcohol, appears to be normative during the transition to young adulthood (e.g., Schulenberg, O'Malley, Bachman, Wadsworth, & Johnston, 1996); such experimentation may even be viewed by young people as assisting in their negotiation of developmental transitions (e.g., Maggs, 1997; Silbereisen & Reitzle, 1992). Clearly, those who indulge too often and too much place themselves and others at risk for health and psychosocial difficulties, but these risks typically subside when (and if) individuals progress into adulthood roles and reduce substance use. The important exception is cigarette use. Nicotine dependence makes the stakes of young adult experimentation quite high indeed, because the majority of those who smoked regularly in their teens retained the habit throughout their 20s and beyond (Bachman et al., 1997).

Has the transition to young adulthood become more difficult over the past two decades? Perhaps, but the evidence is not at all overwhelming. It does appear that the increase in self-efficacy (and the concomitant decrease in fatalism) that accompanies the transition has been somewhat less pronounced among recent cohorts compared with earlier ones. And for those in the uncommitted group in particular, it appears that the boost in self-esteem has diminished among more recent cohorts. Although the more recent cohorts have lower initial levels of alcohol and marijuana use, the findings indicate that the increase during the transition is greater for the more recent cohorts. The relatively rapid increase in binge drinking among the recent cohorts is especially noteworthy (see Figure 3).

The findings provide evidence for both continuity and change in the adolescent experience over the past two decades; well-being represents the former and substance use the latter. Absolute levels of well-being have changed little, and the same is true for gender and life-path differences in well-being. The absolute levels of substance use have changed considerably over the past two decades, as have gender differences in substance use (e.g., gender differences in binge drinking and marijuana use have diminished with successive cohorts) and life-path differences in substance use (e.g., cohort differences in cigarette use, alcohol use, and binge drinking were less pronounced among college students). (Note, however, that life-path differences in age-related changes in substance use during the transition did not vary by cohort groups.) There are several possible explanations for the distinction between the findings for well-being and substance use, including the possibility that substance use is more of a social behavior and is perhaps more swayed by changes in the social context, whereas well-being represents more in terms of personality characteristics that may be less influenced by social change (cf. Nesselroade & Baltes, 1974; Reese & McCluskey, 1984).

The final set of conclusions pertains to how we study change over time. Studying change over time, at either the individual or societal level, is among the most difficult tasks facing developmental scientists. Studying both levels simultaneously to determine how social change may influence the course of individuals' lives is challenging at best and profoundly frustrating at the very least (cf. Cairns & Cairns, 1995; Elder, 1998). Rarely is social change sufficiently discrete to make meaningful demarcations possible or sufficiently pervasive that widespread effects can be observed. One exception was the Great Depression in the United States in 1929, and a more recent one was the fall of the Berlin Wall in Germany in 1989. And even in these rare instances, there may be little forewarning of the impending monumental social change. Instead, social change is typically an accumulation of major and more often minor events that are caused by the confluence of social, political, demographic, technological, and economic forces and whose importance is determined after the fact.

By all means, for those rare exceptions when monumental and discrete social change occurs, developmental scientists should be standing by (ideally with pretest data already in hand) to examine the interconnections between social and individual change. Otherwise, at least two interdependent approaches are available to the interested developmental scientist (e.g., Noack & Kracke, 1997; Schaie, 1984). The first, as exemplified by the IYFP in the United States (e.g., Conger & Conger, this volume; Elder, Hagell, Rudkin, & Conger, 1995) and the

Leipzig–Mannheim study in Germany (e.g., Noack & Kracke, 1997; Noack, Hofer, Kracke, & Klein-Allermann, 1995), is to focus on a segment of society that is experiencing fundamental social change with sufficient depth to track the movement of social change through communities and families and to examine its influence on how individuals negotiate various developmental transitions. The second, as exemplified by the present study, and more generally by the MtF project, is to monitor successive cohorts as they pass through the various developmental transitions to determine inter- and intracohort variation in the markers of the course of health and well-being. The former approach can offer needed insight into how social change translates into differential change at the individual level, and it can provide testable hypotheses for the latter approach. The second approach provides valuable information on variation and constancy in the adolescent experience over historical time that can offer testable hypotheses for the first approach; the second approach provides the "big picture" that can serve as the requisite backdrop to the first approach and stands ready as social change unfolds. More dialogue between these two approaches is needed.

References

Aseltine, R. H., Jr., & Gore, S. (1993). Mental health and social adaptation following the transition from high school. *Journal of Research on Adolescence, 3,* 247–270.

Bachman, J. G., Johnston, L. D., O'Malley, P. M., & Schulenberg, J. (1996). Transitions in alcohol and other drug use and abuse during late adolescence and young adulthood. In J. A. Graber, J. Brooks-Gunn, & A. C. Petersen (Eds.), *Transitions through adolescence: Interpersonal domains and contexts* (pp. 111–140). Mahwah, NJ: Lawrence Erlbaum Associates.

Bachman, J. G., O'Malley, P. M., & Johnston, L. D. (1978). *Youth in transition: Vol. 6. Adolescence to adulthood: A study of change and stability in the lives of young men.* Ann Arbor, MI: Institute for Social Research.

Bachman, J. G., O'Malley, P. M., & Johnston, L. D. (1984). Drug use among young adults: The impacts of role status and social environments. *Journal of Personality and Social Psychology, 47,* 629–645.

Bachman, J. G., Wadsworth, K. N., O'Malley, P. M., Johnston, L. D., & Schulenberg, J. (1997). *Smoking, drinking, and drug use in young adulthood: The impact of new freedoms and new responsibilities.* Mahwah, NJ: Lawrence Erlbaum Associates.

Brook, J. S., Balka, E. B., Gursen, M. D., & Brook, D. W. (1997). Young adults' drug use: A 17-year inquiry of antecedents. *Psychological Reports, 80,* 1235–1251.

Brooks-Gunn, J., Phelps, E., & Elder, G. H., Jr. (1991). Studying lives through time: Secondary data analyses in developmental psychology. *Developmental Psychology, 27,* 899–910.

Cairns, R. B., & Cairns, B. D. (1995). Social ecology over time and space. In P. Moen, G. H. Elder, & K. Luscher (Eds.), *Examining lives in context: Perspectives on the ecology of human development* (pp. 397–421). Washington, DC: American Psychological Association.

Clausen, J. A. (1991). Adolescent competence and the shaping of the life course. *American Journal of Sociology, 96,* 805–842.

Crockett, L. J. (1997). Cultural, historical, and subcultural contexts of adolescence: Implications for health and development. In J. Schulenberg, J. Maggs, & K. Hurrelmann (Eds.), *Health risks and developmental transitions during adolescence* (pp. 23–53). New York: Cambridge University Press.

Eccles, J. S., Lord, S. E., Roeser, R. W., Barber, B. L., & Jozefowicz, D. M. H. (1997). The association of school transitions in early adolescence with developmental trajectories through high school. In J. Schulenberg, J. Maggs, & K. Hurrelmann (Eds.), *Health risks and developmental transitions during adolescence* (pp. 283–320). New York: Cambridge University Press.

Elder, G. H., Jr. (1974). *Children of the Great Depression: Social change in life experience.* Chicago: University of Chicago Press.

Elder, G. H., Jr. (1986). Military times and turning points in men's lives. *Developmental Psychology, 22,* 233–245.

Elder, G. H., Jr. (1995). The life course paradigm: Social change and individual development. In P. Moen, G. H. Elder, Jr., and K. Luscher (Eds.), *Examining lives in context: Perspectives on the ecology of human development* (pp. 101–140). Washington, DC: American Psychological Association.

Elder, G. H., Jr. (1998). The life course and human development. In W. Damon (General Ed.) & R. Lerner (Vol. Ed.), *Handbook of child psychology, Vol. 1. Theoretical models of human development* (pp. 939–991). New York: Wiley.

Elder, G. H., Jr., Hagell, A., Rudkin, L., & Conger, R. (1995). Looking forward in troubled times: The influence of social context on adolescent plans and orientations. In R. K. Silbereisen & E. Todt (Eds.), *Adolescence in context: The interplay of family, school, peers, and work in adjustment* (pp. 244–265). New York: Springer-Verlag.

Elder, G. H., Jr., Modell, J., & Parke, R. D. (Eds.) (1993). *Children in time and place: Developmental and historical insights.* New York: Cambridge University Press.

Elliott, D. S., Huizinga, D., & Menard, S. (1989). *Multiple problem youth: Delinquency, substance use, and mental health problems.* New York: Springer-Verlag.

Flanagan, C., Schulenberg, J., & Fuligni, A. (1993). Residential setting and parent-adolescent relationships during the college years. *Journal of Youth and Adolescence, 22,* 171–189.

Ge, X., Lorenz, F. O., Conger, R. D., Elder, G. H., Jr., & Simons, R. L. (1994). Trajectories of stressful life events and depressive symptoms during adolescence. *Developmental Psychology, 30,* 467–483.

Gore, S., Aseltine, R., Colten, M. E., & Lin, B. (1997). Life after high school: Development, stress, & well-being. In I. H. Gotlib (Ed.), *Stress and adversity over the life course: Trajectories and turning points* (pp. 197–214). New York: Cambridge University Press.

Graber, J. A., & Dubas, J. S. (Eds.) (1996). *Leaving home: Understanding the transition to adulthood.* San Francisco: Jossey-Bass.

Hamilton, S. F. (1990). *Apprenticeship for adulthood: Preparing youth for the future.* New York: Free Press.

Hankin, B., Abramson, L. Y., Moffitt, T. E., Silva, P. A., McGee, R., & Angell, K. E. (1998). Development of depression from preadolescence to young adulthood: Emerging gender differences in a 10-year longitudinal study. *Journal of Abnormal Psychology, 107,* 128–140.

Holtz, G. T. (1995). *Welcome to the jungle: The why behind "Generation X".* New York: St. Martin's Press.

Hurrelmann, K. (1990). Health promotion for adolescents: Preventive and corrective strategies against problem behavior. *Journal of Adolescence, 13,* 231–250.

Jackson, J. S., & Antonucci, T. C. (1994). Survey methodology in life-span human development research. In S. H. Cohen, & H. W. Reese (Eds.), *Life-span developmental psychology: Methodological contributions* (pp. 65–94). Hillsdale, NJ: Lawrence Erlbaum Associates.

Johnston, L. D. (1991). Toward a theory of drug epidemics. In R. L. Donohew, H. Sypher, & W. Bukoski (Eds.), *Persuasive communication and drug abuse prevention* (pp. 93–132). Hillsdale, NJ: Lawrence Erlbaum Associates.

Johnston, L. D., Bachman, J. G., & O'Malley, P. M. (1995). *Monitoring the Future: Questionnaire responses from the nation's high school seniors, 1993.* Ann Arbor, MI: ISR.

Johnston, L. D., & O'Malley, P. M. (1985). Issues of validity and population coverage in student surveys of drug use. In B. A. Rouse, N. J. Kozel, and L. G. Richards (Eds.), *Self-report methods of estimating drug use: Meeting current challenges to validity* (NIDA Research Monograph No. 57) (pp. 31–54). Washington, DC: National Institute on Drug Abuse.

Johnston, L. D., O'Malley, P. M., & Bachman, J. G. (1998). *National survey results on drug use from the Monitoring the Future study, 1975–97.* Rockville, MD: National Institute on Drug Abuse.

Johnston, L. D., O'Malley, P. M., Schulenberg, J., & Bachman, J. G. (1996). *Aims and objectives of the Monitoring the Future study* (Monitoring the Future Occasional Paper No. 34, revised). Ann Arbor, MI: Institute for Social Research.

Kandel, D. B., & Davies, M. (1986). Adult sequelae of adolescent depressive symptoms. *Archives of General Psychiatry, 43,* 255–262.

Lerner, R. M. (1982). Children and adolescents as producers of their own development. *Developmental Review, 2,* 342–370.

Maggs, J. L. (1997). Alcohol use and binge drinking as goal directed action during the transition to post-secondary education. In J. Schulenberg, J. Maggs, & K. Hurrelmann (Eds.), *Health risks and developmental transitions during adolescence* (pp. 321–344). New York: Cambridge University Press.

Magnusson, D. (1995). Individual development: A holistic, integrated model. In P. Moen, G. H. Elder, Jr., and K. Luscher (Eds.), *Examining lives in context: Perspectives on the ecology of human development* (pp. 19–60). Washington, DC: American Psychological Association.

Modell, J., Furstenberg, F. F., Jr., & Hershberg, T. (1976). Social change and the transition to adulthood in historical perspective. *Journal of Family History, 1,* 7–32.

Mortimer, J. T. (1992). Adulthood. In M. L. Borgatta (Ed.), *Encyclopedia of sociology* (pp. 189–211), New York: Macmillan.

Nesselroade, J. R., & Baltes, P. B. (1974). Adolescent personality development and historical change: 1970–72. *Monographs of the Society for Research in Child Development, 39.* 1–79.

Noack, P., Hofer, M., Kracke, B., & Klein-Allermann, E. (1995). Adolescents and their parents facing social change: Families in East and West Germany after unification. In P. Noack, M. Hofer., & J. Youniss (Eds.), *Psychological responses to social change: Human development in changing environments* (pp. 129–148). Berlin: Walter de Gruyter.

Noack, P., Hofer, M., & Youniss, J. (Eds.) (1994), *Psychological responses to social change: Human development in changing environments.* Berlin: Aldine de Gruyter.

Noack, P., & Kracke, B. (1997). Social change and adolescent well-being: Healthy country, healthy teens. In J. Schulenberg, J. Maggs, & K. Hurrelmann (Eds.), *Health risks and developmental transitions during adolescence* (pp. 54–84). New York: Cambridge University Press.

Nowicki, S., & Strickland, B. R. (1973). A locus of control scale for children. *Journal of Consulting and Clinical Psychology, 40,* 148–154.

O'Malley, P. M., & Bachman, J. G. (1979). Self-esteem and education: Sex and cohort comparisons among high school seniors. *Journal of Personality and Social Psychology, 37,* 1153–1159.

O'Malley, P. M., & Bachman, J. G. (1983). Self-esteem: Change and stability between ages 13 and 23. *Developmental Psychology, 19,* 257–268.

O'Malley, P. M., Bachman, J. G., & Johnston, L. D. (1983). Reliability and consistency of self-reports of drug use. *International Journal of the Addictions, 18,* 805–824.

O'Malley, P. M., Bachman, J. G., & Johnston, L. D. (1988). Period, age, and cohort effects on substance use among young Americans: A decade of change, 1976–1986. *American Journal of Public Health, 78,* 1315–1321.

O'Malley, P. M., & Wagenaar, A. C. (1991). Effects of minimum drinking age laws on alcohol use, related behaviors, and traffic crash involvement among American youth: 1976–1987. *Journal of Studies on Alcohol, 52,* 478–491.

Petersen, A. C. (1993). Creating adolescents: The role of context and process in developmental trajectories. *Journal of Research on Adolescence, 3,* 1–18.

Petersen, A. C., Compas, B., Brooks-Gunn, J., Stemmler, M., Ey, S., & Grant, K. (1993). Depression in adolescence. *American Psychologist, 48,* 155–168.

Reese, H. W., & McCluskey, K. A. (1984). Dimensions of historical constancy and change. In K. A. McCluskey & H. W. Reese (Eds.), *Life-span developmental psychology: Historical and generational effects* (pp. 17–45). New York: Academic Press.

Rosenberg, M. (1965). *Society and the adolescent self-image.* Princeton, NJ: Princeton University Press.

Ryder, N. B. (1965). The cohort as a concept in the study of social change. *American Sociological Review, 30,* 843–861.

Schaie, K. W. (1984). Historical time and cohort effects. In K. A. McCluskey & H. W. Reese (Eds.), *Life-span developmental psychology: Historical and generational effects* (pp. 1–15). New York: Academic Press.

Schulenberg, J., Bachman, J. G., Johnston, L. D., & O'Malley, P. M. (1995). American adolescents' views on family and work: Historical trends from 1976–1992. In P. Noack, M. Hofer, & J. Youniss (Eds.), *Psychological responses to social change: Human development in changing environments* (pp. 37–64). Berlin: Walter de Gruyter.

Schulenberg, J., Bachman, J. G., O'Malley, P. M., & Johnston, L. D. (1994). High school educational success and subsequent substance use: A panel analysis following adolescents into young adulthood. *Journal of Health and Social Behavior, 35,* 45–62.

Schulenberg, J., Maggs, J., & Hurrelmann, K. (Eds.), (1997). *Health risks and developmental transitions during adolescence.* New York: Cambridge University Press.

Schulenberg, J., O'Malley, P. M., Bachman, J. G., & Johnston, L. D. (1998). Life-paths into young adulthood and the course of substance use and well-being: Inter- and intra-cohort comparisons (Monitoring the Future Occasional Paper No. 43). Ann Arbor, MI: Institute for Social Research.

Schulenberg, J., O'Malley, P. M., Bachman, J. G., Wadsworth, K. N., & Johnston, L. D. (1996). Getting drunk and growing up: Trajectories of frequent binge drinking during the transition to young adulthood. *Journal of Studies on Alcohol, 57,* 289–304.

Schulenberg, J., Wadsworth, K. N., O'Malley, P. M., Bachman, J. G., & Johnston, L. D. (1996). Adolescent risk factors for binge drinking during the transition to young adulthood: Variable- and pattern-centered approaches to change. *Developmental Psychology, 32,* 659–674.

Schuman, H., & Scott, J. (1989). Generations and collective memories. *American Sociological Review, 54,* 359–381,

Sherrod, L. R., Haggerty, R. J., & Featherman, D. L. (1993). Introduction: Late adolescence and the transition to adulthood. *Journal of Research on Adolescence, 3,* 217–226.

Silbereisen, R. K., & Reitzle, M. (1992). On the constructive role of problem behavior in adolescence: Further evidence on alcohol use. In L. P. Lipsitt & L. L. Midnick (Eds.), *Self-regulation, impulsivitiy, and risk-taking behavior: Causes or consequences* (pp. 199–217). Norwood, NJ: Ablex.

Stevens, J. (1986). *Applied multivariate statistics for the social sciences.* Hillsdale, NJ: Lawrence Erlbaum.

15 What Is a Cohort and Why? – An Old Question Revisited

Klaus Boehnke

In this chapter I will endeavor to discuss the two preceding chapters by Schulenberg, O'Malley, Bachman, and Johnston and by Conger, Rueter, and Conger. This is a task of honor indeed. Both chapters report evidence from studies that are among the most ambitious, well-designed empirical studies of youth in the world. The Monitoring the Future Study (MtF) conducted at the University of Michigan and the Iowa Youth and Families Project conducted at Iowa State University have acquired a paradigmatic standing in the realm of youth studies in the social sciences.

What do these studies have in common beyond their concern with the same or at least a similar life phase, the years 13+ in the chapter by Conger et al. and the years 17+ in the Schulenberg et al. case? Let me try to point to similarities and differences by rereporting the two studies through my personal looking glass.

The study by Schulenberg et al. is descriptive in its focus. Its aim is to document and analyze changes in substance use and well-being during the passage from late adolescence to young adulthood (a) at different historic times and (b) under different forms of living arrangements. Schulenberg et al. address their question by offering impressive nationally representative multicohort panel data of U.S. high school graduates whom they surveyed during the senior year in high school and twice thereafter. This in itself is an accomplishment as yet unmatched. The findings were that well-being and substance use both went up during the transition from late adolescence to young adulthood, that overall levels of substance use decreased from the mid-1970s to the early 1990s, and that substantial differences in change gradients for substance use and well-being levels were found for young people in different life circumstances. Level and change-gradient differences also varied by cohort and gender.

This chapter was prepared while the author was a visiting professor at the Department of Sociology and the Institute for Human Development, Life Course and Aging of the University of Toronto. It has greatly benefited from discussions with Victor Marshall, the Director of the Institute. The author's visit to the Institute was facilitated through grants from the German Academic Exchange Service and the German–American Academic Council Foundation.

The study by Conger et al. focuses on testing a conceptual model. Its aim is to show that economic pressure influences adolescent adjustment primarily by putting the parental relationship at risk. Conger et al. address their topic by offering questionnaire and observational panel data of some 450 families from central Iowa, a region severely struck by an agricultural crisis that occurred in the Midwest of the United States in the 1980s. The findings were that objective economic hardship (as measured, for example, by the debt-to-asset ratio) and subjective economic pressure (measured, for example, by self-reports of having made downward adjustments in spending) are indeed related (though only moderately); that economic pressure, through eliciting parental emotional distress, is an important source of marital conflict; and that marital conflict and marital instability lead to less nurturant parenting, which in turn results in adolescent maladjustment.

An obvious commonality of the two studies is that they offer panel data, a prerequisite for making any scientifically sound statements about change phenomena. Also, they are, in principle, concerned with the same outcome variables, namely, various aspects of well-being and delinquency. Beyond that, commonalities may at first glance appear scarce. The MtF study offers nationally representative multicohort data from surveys conducted between 1976 and 1992, whereas the Iowa Youth and Families Study, in principle, is a quantitative case study from a crisis-stricken area in one U.S. state at the end of the historic period covered in the MtF Study. Nevertheless, both studies let me ask the same question, the question posed in the title of this chapter, namely, What is a cohort and why? The question was first posed by Rosow (1978) in a rarely cited paper. This is why I call it an old question revisited.

The Iowa Youth and Families Project: Questions to Be Asked

The questions to pose concerning the Conger et al. study pertain to aspects of generalizability. Specifically, would the same findings (of economic pressure influencing adolescent adjustment via marital conflict and changes in parental nurturance arising from marital instability) have been obtained in an area with, for example, a dying heavy industry? Would the same findings have emerged during other historic times that have also seen agricultural crises? Would marital conflict have played such an important role in less individualized cultures than the U.S.? Does the model apply to sociopolitically induced economic hardship only, or does it also hold for families in a "self-made" economic crisis (e.g., families of brokers who went bankrupt)?

One can see all these questions as addressing the theme of generalizability, but one can also reframe them. Besides addressing the generalizability issue they also put on the table the question of whether the experience of Iowa farm families is peculiar to a certain cohort of farm dwellers only. According to Glenn (1977), a cohort denotes "those people within a geographically or otherwise delineated population who experienced the same significant life event within a given period

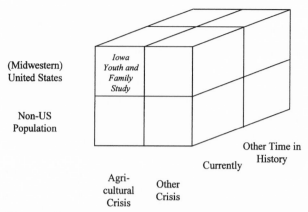

Figure 1. Cohort-sensitive study series supplementing the Iowa Youth and Families Project.

of time" (p. 8). In the Conger et al. study the population is the inhabitants of the rural Midwest of the United States, the significant event is the farm crisis, and the given period of time is the late 1980s.

There is no way to reject the cohort-specificity allegation from within the Iowa Youth and Family Study: The *tertium comparationis* is missing. Studies that systematically vary the three components of Glenn's definition of a cohort need to be undertaken to free the Iowa study of the presumption that it is indeed merely a case study bearing little generalizability beyond the Plains. Figure 1 presents amendments that would immunize the Iowa Youth and Families Project against the criticism of merely reporting about the lives of "The Anglo Peasant in Middle America in the 1980s."

The figure proposes that, in accordance with Glenn's definition of a cohort, a supplementary series of seven additional cohort-sensitive studies into the consequences of economic hardship for adolescent adjustment need to be undertaken. Studies in regions of the United States stricken by crises other than the farm crisis, both currently and at a different time in history, are equally necessary as are farm and nonfarm studies in other parts of the world now and at a different historic time.

Some of the evidence sought in such a study series may already be available. The consequences of rapid social change for adolescent adjustment are the focus of numerous ongoing studies in Germany after unification. Some explicitly draw on the model forwarded by Conger, Rueter, and Conger (e.g., Noack, Hofer, Kracke, & Klein-Allermann, 1995; Butz & Boehnke, 1997). Earlier accounts of responses to agricultural and other crises in the United States are cited in the Conger et al. chapter and are well known (e.g., Elder, 1974, Angell, 1965; Komarovsky, 1940). What seems to be widely lacking is studies into consequences of agricultural crises – current and prior – outside of North America that allow a test of the generalizability model proposed by Conger et al.

In summary, the Iowa Youth and Family Project employs a paradigmatic approach to linking sociopolitical events to adolescent well-being; it wants, however, for replication, for cohort-sensitivity, as I would call it.

The Monitoring the Future Study: Questions to Be Asked

Questions to pose regarding the MtF study do not pertain to generalizability unless one asks for generalizability to more than just the United States or across an even longer historic period. The study's multiple cohort design can only be applauded wholeheartedly. What does, however, elicit questions is the study's concept of cohort and what the study calls a "life path." The term *cohort* is first introduced in the sense of a single-year birth cohort. A bit later Schulenberg et al. go on to divide the 17 single-year birth cohorts they analyze into three multiyear cohorts of approximately equal length. They support this division in part by noting that the office terms of presidents of the United States coincide with their grouping of birth cohorts. Schulenberg et al. follow the tradition of social scientific research in which census data are used (see Maddox & Campbell, 1985), yet their conceptualization of what is a cohort seems post hoc and rather technical. To cite Marshall (1983), "It is a way to organize data" (p. 32), not a theoretical concept. To point again to Glenn's (1977) definition, a significant life event experienced at a given time in life is needed to distinguish one cohort from another cohort. Office terms of presidents seem unlikely to "create" cohorts. In accordance with Marshall (1983), I am convinced that the clustering of adjacent-birth cohorts into multiyear groups has to be based on either theory or data indicating when an important shift in orientation has occurred; it cannot be done post hoc on the basis of prima facie evidence. Grouping cohorts according to theory or empirical evidence will rarely result in equal-length intervals that are so handy for analyses of variance.

How can the clustering of birth cohorts into multiyear groups be based on data? Later in this chapter I will give an example from my own work, but let me first elaborate on the theme within the confines of the Schulenberg et al. chapter. Schulenberg et al. analyzed their data in accordance with a three-factorial repeated-measures multivariate analysis of variance (MANOVA) design. Cohort (their technical clustering of single-year birth cohorts into three multiyear groups), life path, and gender were the three fixed (independent) factors. Their findings show numerous interactions of cohort, life path, and gender that are difficult to interpret. Readers will recall that life paths are defined by Schulenberg et al. as mutually exclusive life circumstances of young adults. Categories are built on dwelling localities (at or away from parental home), work situation (full-time employment vs. full-time student), marital status, and parenthood. But, one is inclined to ask, are cohort and life path really independent concepts? Is there not a qualitative difference between being a single parent in the late 1970s and in the early 1990s? Could not different prevalences of the various life paths over time even be definitive for different cohorts? A certain time in history may be a time of single parenthood, a time of low employment rates, or a time of being uncommitted (the label Schulenberg et al. chose for young people in their late teens and early 20s who are unmarried, have no children, and are neither full-time employees nor full-time students). Life-path prevalences are not static over time and should thus not be seen as a concept independent from the cohort concept.

The matter becomes trickier yet. Even the dependent variables of the Schulenberg et al. study can, in principle, define cohorts. With regard to substance use, a certain time in history can be an age of personal freedom; another time may be a time of repression. For example, to find cohort differences in alcohol consumption before, during, and after prohibition would be an outright tautology.

To summarize, the MtF study cannot be commended enough for employing a multiple cohort panel design, but to use cohort as an explanatory concept, a more elaborated theoretical understanding of what constitutes a cohort is needed. As with the Iowa Youth and Families Project – though very different in what precisely may be seen as lacking – more cohort sensitivity is needed.

The East–West Youth Study

Let me conclude by suggesting a way to delineate cohorts on the grounds of empirical data. Doing so adds to the sociological discussion on what constitutes a generation. Marshall (1983), in the tradition of Mannheim (1952), prefers the term generation over that of a cohort when he remarks that "the term to use for non-arbitrary clusters of single-year birth cohorts which can be shown to be qualitatively different on some social variable is the term 'generation'" (p. 53). Glenn (1977) – preferring the term "cohort" over "generation" – points out that "the term generation is sometimes used synonymously with birth cohort, or it may refer to a birth cohort with 'natural' rather than arbitrary boundaries" (p. 8).

In German postunification research the question has been raised as to whether the fall of the Wall constitutes a cohort- or generation-defining event. To be more precise, the question is whether people who have experienced the fall of the Wall in their middle to late teens (according to Mannheim, 1952, the "sensitive phase" for generation founding) have to be seen as a new generation distinct from people born earlier.

We have previously addressed this question (Boehnke, Merkens, Steiner, & Wenzke, 1998). The essence of what we have suggested is as follows: Take data from multiple birth cohorts (as was done in the MtF study). Dummy-code different conceptualizations of cohort splits on the basis of the year of measurement (see the following discussion). Enter all different dummy-coded conceptualizations of cohort splits into a stepwise multiple regression and let them predict the dependent variable(s) at stake. The outcome will be that the "best" dummy-coded conceptualization of a cohort split will come out as the strongest predictor of variation in the dependent variable(s), thereby suggesting the most plausible boundary of a cohort or generation.

Let me elaborate by way of example. Our research group is in the rare position of being able to offer data that have been gathered from ninth graders in 1977, 1979, 1980, 1983, early 1989, early 1990, 1991, 1992, 1993, 1994, and 1995 in East Germany. Adolescents from various regions of the former German Democratic Republic (GDR) were surveyed in all these years *using the same items*.

Ninth graders in East Germany are 15 1/2 years of age on average. The aim of our data analyses is to *test statistically* the impact of certain conceptualizations of a cohort, or, in Rosow's (1978) words, to test the validity of certain "drawings of the line" between cohorts. To do so we used all data available across all 18 years as variables to be predicted, grouping them into family-related, household, school-related, and society-related variables. As predictors we used, on the one hand, gender and region (of origin within East Germany). On the other hand, we used – in this case eight – different conceptualizations of cohort as *competing* predictors of the outcome variables. Three conceptualizations are technical in principle, namely, year of measurement, decade, and cycle of study[1]. The other five are discrete formulations of possible cohort boundaries as follows:

1. Before and after 1980 (sometimes said to be the final year of positive identification of GDR citizens with their state).
2. Before and after 1983 (sometimes mentioned as the year after which the political development of the GDR started to deteriorate).
3. Before and after the fall of the Wall in 1989.
4. Before and after unification in 1990.
5. Before and after the restructuring of the East German school system in 1991.

Data analyses were conducted using a multiple regression approach. Predictors were gender, region (Berlin vs. other regions), and time. The central question addressed was in which year(s) there were historic breaks in the value orientations and the psychosocial well-being of East German adolescents, or, in other words, which birth cohorts (years) can be collapsed into one meaningful historic cohort or generation.

Of all variables (gender, region, the eight conceptualizations of time, and the various multiplicative interaction terms of gender, region, and time) only gender and region were "forcefully" entered into the regression equation to partial time-related results for possible gender and regional influences. After that, only *one* more step was allowed in regression calculations. That rule ensured that *only the strongest time-related predictor* entered the regression. By enforcing this rule we hoped to isolate the most decisive "cohort-defining" conceptualization of historic time in

Table 1. *Substantial time-related ß-coefficients for various conceptualizations of cohort splits.*

Topics		Time-related variation
Family-related variables	ß	Substantive change over time
Subjective justice in the family	−.16	Subjective feeling of justice *lower* after unification
Authoritarian restrictiveness	−	
Monitoring	.11	Degree of parental monitoring *higher* after unification
Smoking	−.26	Freedom to smoke *increased* for girls after 1980
Household variables		
Availability of high-price consumer goods (e.g., automobiles)	.35	High-price consumer goods *more readily available* after 1980
Availability of high prestige consumer goods (e.g., musical instruments)	.15	High-prestige consumer goods *more readily available* after 1980
School-related variables		
Class climate	−	
Subjective justice in school	−	
Academic performance	−.28	Academic performance *worse among girls* after the change of the school system
Society-related variables and values		
Subjective justice in public	−.10	Subjective feeling of justice *lower* after unification
Emphasis on intact social relations	−.19	Emphasis on intact social relations *higher* after unification
Anomic life views	.27	Anomic life views *generally higher* from study cycle to study cycle
Centrality of work	−.15	Centrality of work *lower* from decade to decade

the lives of East German adolescents between 1977 and 1995. Also this strategy rules out multicollinearity problems that might arise if more than one time-related predictor were included.

Table 1 documents results of the pertinent three-step regression analyses. For the sake of brevity, it only reports the standardized ß-coefficients for the time-related variable whenever they are above .10, a threshold chosen because of the large overall sample size of $N = 6264$. Results on gender and region have to be omitted as well as detailed descriptions of our samples and our dependent measures.

When we look at time-related variation in our dependent variables, we see that three of our conceptualizations of time never appear as substantial predictors, namely, the fall of the Wall, pre- and post-1983, and the (simple) year of measurement. This result should be highlighted: In no single case can the most substantial time-related difference in outcome variables be found between the years before and after the fall of the Wall. Obviously it is not *the* critical historical event for East German midadolescents. The same is true for the partition into the time before and after 1983. Furthermore, no monotonic trends seem to be defined, so-to-speak, by the year of measurement.

Most changes in adolescents' values and psychosocial well-being seem to have taken place *after* unification and in the late 1970s at the beginning of our study series. Although our selection of dependent variables is by no means representative or comprehensive, we are inclined to read our data in a way that suggests the existence of three distinct cohorts. If one takes into consideration again that the average ninth grader in Germany is between 15 and 16, those born before 1965 form the first cohort, those born from 1966 to 1976 form the second, and those born after 1976 form the third cohort.

Summary and Conclusions

In summary, this discussion calls for greater cohort or generational sensitivity in youth research. The Iowa Youth and Families Study is paradigmatic in its way of documenting the impact a socioeconomic crisis has on adolescent adjustment. The MtF study is unique in its multiple cohort panel design. The pivotal position the two studies hold in the realm of youth research could, however, be strengthened even further if more emphasis were put on the impact of historic time and place.

It would be exciting to see studies that match the import of the Iowa study undertaken in other cultural contexts, at different historic times (looking forward or backward), and in the context of other types of crises (socioeconomic as well as more private). It would also add to the remarkable accomplishments of the MtF study if its understanding of what a cohort is would become somewhat more theoretical and less technical.

A very imperfect way to reconcile theory and data in an attempt to sharpen the understanding of what a cohort – or if need be a generation – is, was briefly brought forward in the last part of this discussion. It suggested using different conceptualizations of what a cohort could be – grounded in an analysis of (current) history – as technical predictors of variation in dependent variables and thereby determining the "best" conceptualization of breaks between cohorts. This approach still needs considerable thought and work but could add more conceptually sound cohort sensitivity to long-term, multicohort youth research.

References

Angell, R. C. (1965). *The family encounters the depression*. Gloucester, MA: Peter Smith.

Boehnke, K., Merkens, H., Steiner, I., & Wenzke, G. (1998). Gibt es eine Generation der 89er? Versuch einer empirischen Antwort anhand von Studien zu Werthaltungen und psychosozialer Befindlichkeit ostdeutscher Jugendlicher von 1977 bis 1995 [Is there a generation of 1989? An attempt at an empirical answer based on studies of values and the psychosocial state of East German adolescents between 1977 and 1995]. *Zeitschrift für und Soziologie der Erziehung Sozialisation Beiheft.* 103–120.

Butz, P., & Boehnke, K. (1997). Auswirkungen von ökonomischen Druck auf die psychosoziale Befindlichkeit von Jugendlichen [Consequences of economic pressure for the psychosocial well-being of adolescents]. *Zeitschrift für Pädagogik, 43,* 79–92.

Elder, G. (1974). *Children of the Great Depression: Social change in life experience*. Chicago: University of Chicago Press.

Glenn, N. D. (1977). *Cohort analysis*. Beverly Hills: Sage.

Komarovsky, M. (1940). *The unemployed man and his family*. New York: Octagon Books.

Maddox, G. I., & Campbell, R. T. (1985). Scope, concepts and methods in the study of aging. In R. H. Binstock & E. Shanas (Eds.), *Handbook of aging and the social sciences* (pp. 3–31). New York: Van Nostrand Reinhold Co.

Mannheim, K. (1952). The problem of generations. In D. Kecskemeti (Ed.), *Essays on the sociology of knowledge* (pp. 276–320). London: Routledge and Kegan Paul.

Marshall, V. W. (1983). Generations, age groups and cohorts: Conceptual distinctions. *Canadian Journal of Aging, 2,* 51–62.

Noack, P., Hofer, M., Kracke, B., & Klein-Allermann, E. (1995). Adolescents and their parents facing social change: Families in East and West Germany after unification. In P. Noack, M. Hofer, & J. Youniss (Eds.), *Psychological responses to social change* (pp. 129–148). Berlin: de Gruyter.

Rosow, I. (1978). What is a cohort and why? *Human Development, 21,* 65–75.

Part v

**Interventions: Promoting Healthy Development
in Times of Social Change**

16   Research, Intervention, and Social Change: Improving Adolescents' Career Opportunities

Stephen F. Hamilton and Mary Agnes Hamilton

Adolescents are peculiarly sensitive to social change. Their attitudes and beliefs are more labile than those of adults. Furthermore, they may carry into adult life the stamp of events that transpired as they were forming attitudes and making life choices and ideological commitments (Elder, 1974).

Adults who try to intervene on behalf of adolescents confronted by social change never know for sure what changes will actually occur, what their consequences will be, and what intervention might ameliorate their negative consequences. Social science research can reduce but never eliminate these uncertainties. The following are three contributions research can make to interventions to help adolescents cope with social change, provided that the change is slow enough:

1. Research can serve as an early warning system, identifying changes that might not otherwise be visible and, ideally, identifying their sources as well.
2. Research can discover responses, for example, by comparing the incidence and consequences of changes – historically, cross-nationally, and in different locations – and drawing attention to desirable conditions or effective interventions.
3. Research can test interventions to help shape them and determine their effectiveness.

Social change is too vast, inchoate, and protean to be grasped at once. However, like a fishing net, once it is grasped by a single knot, everything proves to be connected, however tangled and unmanageable the whole. We will take hold of one knot in the net of social changes affecting contemporary adolescents in the United States, treating it as a useful starting point that necessarily leads to other changes. That knot is the constricted employment prospects of young people who have not graduated from college.

We will review research that has identified some of the crucial changes in the labor market that have affected youth and then turn to studies suggesting responses.

Craig Nicholls conducted essential statistical analyses for this study. Colleagues and students too numerous to mention also contributed to various aspects of the larger project. The research reported here was supported by a grant from The Pew Charitable Trusts. The opinions expressed in this report are those of the authors and do not necessarily reflect the views of The Pew Charitable Trusts.

The largest section of this chapter describes a research and demonstration project that illustrates one approach to testing interventions. We conclude with reflections on the contributions of research to intervention.

The Changing Youth Labor Market

Young people today have unprecedented access to bad jobs. Participation of youth in the labor market is quite high, but the quality of their jobs in terms of real earnings, benefits, security, and career ladders is not.[1] The growing service sector has opened millions of part-time jobs for teenagers that are easily combined with school enrollment, especially as retail trade has moved out of center cities into the suburbs, where many teenagers live. The service jobs most teenagers have provide them with spending money and teach such "workplace basics," as punctuality, reliability, and customer relations. Although evidence on the effects of such employment is mixed, there is little empirical basis for the fear that it is seriously harmful to large numbers of young people.

Greenberger and Steinberg's (1986) pioneering study of adolescent employment raised concern that high school students working half time (20 hours or more per week) might turn their attention away from school and do less well academically as a result. In addition, these researchers pointed to some less obvious negative consequences of employment, including increased stress (indicated by greater use of alcohol and marijuana) and new opportunities for engaging in unethical and illegal behavior (stealing from the workplace, lying to the boss). (See also Steinberg & Dornbusch, 1991; Steinberg, Fegley, & Dornbusch, 1993; Schulenberg & Bachman, 1993.) However, other research has failed to replicate the negative findings on the impact of employment on education (e.g., Mortimer, Finch, Ryu, Shanahan, & Call, 1993). One limitation to this line of research is the difficulty of eliminating selection effects; there is evidence that adolescents who reject school and indicate other negative behaviors may be the same ones who choose to work longer hours (Bachman & Schulenberg, 1993). Another limitation is that work hours by themselves do not capture important differences in adolescents' work experience. Recent studies find that the quality of adolescents' work experience is more important than previously thought. Key components of quality are the opportunity to develop and use skills and work's relation to schooling (Stern, Stone, Hopkins, & McMillion, 1990; Schulenberg & Bachman, 1993; Finch, Mortimer, & Ryu, 1994).

The current structure of the youth labor market has some serious consequences for young people. "Youth jobs" can become a trap, offering earnings and other rewards of employment at an early age but failing to provide career ladders by which young people can move incrementally into more responsible, more secure, and more lucrative positions as adults. There is no reason to expect a 10–15 hour per week job in a grocery store to be harmful to most young people; in fact, the lessons learned may be quite valuable, and the income earned may boost feelings of autonomy and self-confidence. However, many young people who do not continue their education after high school discover that such jobs are the best they can find for several years after graduation (Hamilton & Levine-Powers, 1990).

Low wages are the most serious constraint on young people's post–high school employment prospects. Median real wages fell overall by 6% between 1973 and 1993. Workers with a high school education or less have been most severely affected by this decline. For male high school graduates, real wages fell 20% over those two decades (from $14.02 per hour in 1973 to $11.19 in 1993, in 1993 dollars). Wages for male high school dropouts fell by 27% (from $11.85 to $8.64) (*Economic Report of the President*, 1995). Ironically, although most high school students can easily find part-time jobs, high school graduates have increasing difficulty finding jobs that pay a living wage.

Early Warning

A few studies noted these changes at an early stage, calling attention to a newly emerging relationship between youth and work that is now well established. Barton (1975) coined the term, "youth labor market" and identified some of the special challenges facing young people in gaining employment. Osterman (1980) empirically characterized the youth labor market, raising concern about the employment prospects of young people who are not poor but who lack advanced educational credentials. He explored the place of youth in the "secondary labor market," which is characterized by low-skill, low-wage jobs with little security, no benefits, and few prospects for advancement into the "primary labor market" of jobs with the opposite characteristics. And he revived the term, "floundering period," from 1930s sources to describe the typical experience of young workers without college degrees. More recently Osterman has cited as evidence for "floundering" the remarkable finding that by age 30 less than half of U.S. workers with no more than a high school education had held their current job for 2 years or more (Osterman & Iannozzi, 1993).[2]

Osterman's initial research is noteworthy for its combination of survey data analysis that established the generality of the phenomenon with case studies of working-class youth illustrating vividly how the phenomenon plays out in their lives. The case studies challenge the optimistic interpretation of "churning" (i.e., changing jobs frequently) as a career exploration process by demonstrating that the sequence of jobs held by young people had no coherence and that the "real jobs" (i.e., in the primary labor market) that some of his subjects finally found were more attributable to luck than to anything that can be described as a search strategy. Essentially, Osterman saw young people moving randomly from job to job until they found a job with high enough pay, regular enough hours, and sufficient longevity to settle into. It may be that middle-class youth choose careers; working-class youth find jobs.

Discovering Responses

Labor economists with great faith in free markets acknowledge the "churning" that youth experience when they enter the labor market but characterize it as a largely constructive phenomenon that eventually sorts people into jobs and occupations that match their educational levels and personal preferences (e.g., Klerman & Karoly, 1995). However, cross-national studies, notably those by Reubens and colleagues (1983), challenge the assumption that a prolonged period of marginal employment, moving in and out of low-skilled jobs before beginning a coherent career, is a benign phenomenon reflecting the inability of young people to make career choices and their limited capacity for serious employment. She noted that, in contrast to all other nations studied, in which youth unemployment normally exceeded adult unemployment, Germany and Japan protect young people's entry into the labor market, though she also noted that some young adults in those countries experience difficulties once the protective mechanisms are withdrawn.[3] Reubens' study illustrated the use of cross-national research in identifying potential means of dealing with emerging social change; it demonstrated that the employment behavior Americans attribute to youthfulness results from the labor market rather than from inherent qualities of young people.

The William T. Grant Foundation Commission on Work, Family and Citizenship issued an interim and a final report in 1988, both titled *The Forgotten Half*. These reports challenged the conventional wisdom that "everyone" goes to college and exposed the absurdity of the assumption that the country would be better off if everyone really did (an assumption that gained prominence in the 1996 elections). The reports gave currency to concerns based in research about the school-to-work transition and offered policy responses that were eventually incorporated in one of the Clinton administration's major initiatives, the School-to-Work Opportunities Act of 1994. Another source of that legislation was the report *America's Choice: High Skills or Low Wages!* (National Center on Education and the Economy, 1990), a report that drew heavily on both domestic and cross-national research. It is certainly significant that Hillary Rodham Clinton was an active member of both commissions and that, as governor, Bill Clinton supported pioneer "youth apprenticeship" efforts in Arkansas.

One of the recommendations of *The Forgotten Half* that received wide public attention was that the United States look to German apprenticeship for ideas about ways to meet the needs of young people who do not complete 4 years of college. German apprenticeship was one of many exemplary practices noted in *America's Choice*, and it was highlighted in other reports and news media (e.g., Lerman & Pouncy, 1990, Nothdurft & Jobs for the Future, 1990). The Bush Administration proposed a test of this idea in a bill that died in Congress before the election of 1992. One of the first initiatives of the new Clinton Administration was securing bipartisan sponsorship and passage of the School-to-Work Opportunities Act of 1994.[4]

Testing

As the President noted in signing the School-to-Work Opportunities Act, the ideas in it were already being tested in several locations, a fact manifested by the phalanx of participants from demonstration programs on the dais as he spoke. He even signed the bill on a portable desk that had been designed and built in a week by one group of youth. That testing was supported by a mixture of federal, state, and foundation funds. Recently published results have demonstrated that practices inspired by German apprenticeship fit into the American system and have had a generally positive impact on youth (U.S. Department of Labor, 1994; Pauly, Kopp, & Haimson, 1994; Kopp & Kazis, 1995). Testing has also demonstrated just how ambitious the interventions that the act prescribes are.

Unlike most interventions, which create new *programs* in response to specific problems, the act called for the invention of new *systems* that would weld current programs and institutions into a more coherent and more effective mechanism for moving young people from education into careers (*America's Choice*, 1990; Hamilton, 1990). A small-scale demonstration project cannot test a system; it can only try out components, which will necessarily function differently when they become part of a whole. Nevertheless, the studies of early demonstration projects (cited in the preceding paragraphs) and of related approaches already in operation (Bailey & Merritt, 1993) have affirmed that the basic ideas of using workplaces as learning environments for youth and linking schooling more closely to careers are feasible and powerful. The investigations have also highlighted the challenge of implementing these ideas on a large scale, which requires substantial changes in schools and workplaces and a level of commitment and investment in human resources that employers in the United States have never made before. These studies illustrate the third function of social science in relation to interventions to help youth cope with social change, which is to assess the effectiveness of various responses to social change and to guide them.

The 1994 legislation identifies three key components of a school-to-work opportunities system: school-based learning organized around a career major, work-based learning leading to an industry-recognized credential, and strong connections between work-based learning and school-based learning. The inspiration of German apprenticeship may be seen in these components, especially work-based learning, but the legislation allows for a wide variety of approaches, including apprenticeship and similar types of work-based learning (e.g., cooperative education), but also less intensive types of work-based learning such as job shadowing and unpaid community service.

A Research and Demonstration Project

In 1990 we began planning a demonstration of European-style apprenticeship in the United States. Our goal was to try out some of the ideas in *Apprenticeship for Adulthood* (Hamilton, 1990), especially learning in the workplace, which we viewed as the most challenging component of what later became known as "school-to-work". The project was located in the Binghamton, NY, metropolitan area. From September 1991, when the first cohort began, to June 1995, when we turned over

Table 1. *Program enrollment, 1990–1996.*

Apprentices	11th grade		12th grade		13th (college)[a]		14th (college)	
	Started	Finished	Started	Finished	Started	Finished	Started	Finished
Class of 1993	22	20	20	20	2	2	2	2
Class of 1994	21	19	17	16	3	2	2	2
Class of 1995	28	26	25	23	4	3	–	–
Class of 1996	29	28	27	26	–[b]	–	–	–
Totals	100	93	89	85	9	7	4	4

[a] The number enrolled in college is the number of youth who continued the apprenticeship program while enrolled in college.
[b] Dashes indicate that no information was available at the time of the report.

the project to our local partners, it involved 7 high schools, 11 employers, and 100 young people (see Table 1). Working closely with employers, we developed apprenticeships in three occupational areas: administration and office technology, health care, and manufacturing and engineering technology. These occupations were chosen because they were predicted to grow and because they offer rewarding employment for substantial numbers of people with less than 4 years of college education. High school sophomores were recruited for the program every spring. Those who were interested applied for positions in specific firms. Following a screening process, employers hired apprentices based on interviews, recommendations, and school records. We had envisioned a 4-year program that continued through 2 years of community college, but very few graduating apprentices formally remained in the program. Some chose new career paths. Others left the community to enroll in college. In a few cases, apprentices enrolled in health-related programs at the community college that had separate fieldwork components instead of participating in the apprenticeship.

Of the 100 juniors who enrolled in the program over the 4 years, 85 continued through high school graduation. Seven dropped out during the first year, four over the summer, and four as seniors. Nine of the 15 dropouts changed career plans. Two moved. Four dropouts were unable to maintain both their apprenticeship and their school grades, sometimes because they also had a second job in addition to the apprenticeship.

We strongly believe all young people can benefit from apprenticeship. However, we advocated the recruitment of "middle students" into the program because those already bound for 4-year colleges do not need apprenticeship as much, and those with severe problems are much more costly to employers. Youth with multiple problems would benefit from extensive preapprenticeship experiences designed to prepare them to perform well in, and take advantage of, apprenticeship. Entering grade point averages (GPAs) of apprentices were in the C+ to B− range, indicating that employers chose young people who fit our criteria. The first and fourth cohorts

Table 2. *Education level attained by apprentices'*
parents.

Highest level of either parent[a]	No.
4 years of college or more	18
2 years of college	25
High school diploma	52
No high school diploma	2
No information	3
Total	100[b]

[a]Based on 70 parent reports and 27 child reports. (Child reports
were used when parent reports were not available.)
[b]Because $n = 100$, numbers are identical to percentages.

included students with GPAs of A, whereas the second, third, and fourth cohorts
included D and F students. Inclusion of students with a wide range of GPAs helped
to avoid the stigma often attached to targeted programs.

The majority of apprentices had parents with less than 2 years of college education. A high school diploma or less stands as the highest education level attained
by either parent in 54% of the families. Forty-three percent of the families have a
parent with 2 or more years of college (see Table 2).

Young people from minority groups constituted only 6% of 15- to 19-year-olds in
Broome County, where all but one school and one firm are located. Thirteen percent
of apprentices were minority youth. The overrepresentation of minorities reflected
employers' commitment to affirmative action and their view of apprenticeship as
a means of "filling the pipeline" with qualified potential applicants. We strongly
believe disadvantaged youth have the most to gain from opportunities like this,
but we chose to concentrate initially on designing and testing a program nearby
rather than in a more diverse large city. Now that several urban areas have school-
to-work grants, we hope to learn more about the challenges of race and of large
cities. The response of employers in the Binghamton area was encouraging in this
regard.

Young people responded eagerly to the program. We had to limit the number of
schools we worked with and to recruit carefully because it was easy to generate
hundreds of applications for each apprenticeship place. In an ideal world we might
have assigned applicants randomly to treatment and control groups. We did not
attempt to do this because it would have violated the employers' right to hire their
own apprentices and because we believed a controlled experiment was premature.
We first had to learn more about how to design and operate an American-style youth
apprenticeship system and about what kinds and levels of effects we could expect to
measure. We did arrange to administer a questionnaire to an unmatched comparison
group of students enrolled in Regents (i.e., college preparatory) English classes in
participating schools and to examine their grades and course enrollment patterns

in parallel with the apprentices'. As will be seen, the comparison students' initial status as college-bound students clouded the comparison of school achievement.

Although 11 employers were willing to participate and the number of places increased yearly, employer participation was the most serious limitation on the size of the program. We would have preferred a larger number of employers, each enrolling larger numbers of apprentices. Employers generally felt unable to take on more apprentices because of the resources required, especially in the face of actual or potential downsizing. Money to pay apprentices was not the key resource required of employers. Most employers found that apprentices became productive enough to earn their wages within 6 weeks or less. As apprentices became more competent, their productivity substantially exceeded their earnings. Far more serious than wage costs were the costs of adult employees' time for

1. Supervising apprentices (managing, coaching and mentoring);
2. Designing a learning plan and assessing performance;
3. Orienting, training, and supporting coaches and mentors;
4. Planning and coordinating, within and across firms; and
5. Communicating with school and parents.

These costs are not easily quantified, but they were real and substantial. They surely varied considerably among employers.[5] Economies of scale will result from employers' taking larger numbers of apprentices, and some costs to employers can be reduced by collaboration within a regional partnership, a state, or an industry.

Impacts on Youth

The most obvious question to ask in any test of an intervention is whether it has its intended effects. To secure political support and the enthusiastic cooperation of professionals, parents, and youth, interventions must have broad and multifaceted aims, making the question of effects much easier to ask than to answer. Measurement is also a challenge. There is an inverse relation between the significance of an effect and the ease of its measurement. The following paragraphs present some indicators that we collected of impact in three domains: work-based learning, academic achievement, and continuation in the occupational area.

Work-Based Learning. The strongest and most direct impact of apprenticeship on participating youth was that they acquired work-related competencies. In collaboration with employers, we classified competencies as technical (how to perform tasks) and personal and social (how to behave appropriately at work). We asked supervisors to rate apprentices using two checklists, one of technical competencies, the other (which applied equally to all three occupational areas) of personal and social competencies. Apprentices also testified to their learning when they were interviewed at the end of each year beginning with an open-ended question: Looking back over the past year, what stands out for you in your experience as an apprentice at (firm name)? Without any further prompting, apprentices answered predominantly in terms of what they had learned. Fifty of 59 senior apprentices[6] responded to this question by describing the acquisition of technical competence. In response to the same question, 55 seniors also talked about gaining personal or social competence, or both. Personal competence included career planning, self-confidence, initiative, responsibility, motivation, and continuous improvement. Social competence included understanding the workplace as a system, following rules and norms (e.g., professional ethics, maintaining schedules), communication, and teamwork. Learning to act like an adult was a common theme associated for many with growing self-confidence and often contrasted with behavior in school. Apprentices' self-reports are corroborated by supervisors' written evaluations, testimony in interviews with supervisors and parents, observations in workplaces, and demonstrations of work-related competence given as part of apprentices' "senior projects."

Comparing apprentices and nonapprentices in terms of their acquisition of technical competencies would have been pointless. Only an apprentice in a hospital's pathology laboratory had the chance to learn how to perform tests on blood and tissue samples in that laboratory. However, we did use some items on a questionnaire having to do with work experience to compare the responses of apprentices with those of comparison group members who had been employed during the school year. Apprentices were statistically significantly more likely than employed nonapprentices to say that what they were learning at work would help them find employment in the future and that the work they did was meaningful. Although students in the comparison group who were employed also learned from their work experience, the apprentices appeared to see their work as more educational.

Academic achievement. Part of the rationale for youth apprenticeship is that young people who see the uses of academic knowledge at work will learn better both at work and in school, partly from the motivation provided and partly from the real-world context. We looked for this effect in apprentices' grades and in the courses they took. The results were mixed.

We calculated GPAs for apprentices, including only academic courses. Their mean GPA began at the B- to C+ level in grade 10. It moved slightly downward in grade 11 and then moved upward in grade 12 (see Figure 1). However, GPAs calculated for comparison students showed a similar pattern. Changes in both groups' grade levels from one year to the next were statistically significant, but differences between apprentices and the comparison group were not (with GPAs in grade 10 controlled).

Grades are one indicator of academic achievement; course enrollment is another. Social studies and English courses are required in all four years of high school. The critical question for apprentices is whether to enroll in optional science and mathematics courses in grades 11 and 12. Apprentices in all three occupational areas need mathematics. Those in health care and in manufacturing and engineering

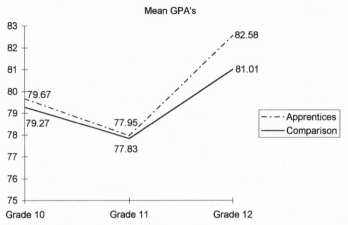

Figure 1. Mean GPAs of apprentices and comparison students.

technology also need science. Among the three cohorts that had completed their senior year when these analyses were done, 28 of 59 apprentices (47.5%) enrolled in mathematics courses during their senior year, but only 18 of 59 (30.5%) enrolled in science courses. Proportionately more members of the comparison group enrolled in mathematics courses (64.2%), and about the same proportion (36.5%) enrolled in science courses. Although the college-bound comparison students should be expected to take higher-level courses, the small proportion of apprentices who did so was a particularly distressing finding, indicating a major weakness in the program.

The consequences of poor grades and of failure to take nonrequired courses have surfaced as we have contacted former apprentices periodically to ask about their postsecondary education and employment. Too many of them have found their career prospects limited or their plans slowed by the need to take remedial courses before enrolling in courses that are part of college degree programs leading to desired occupations. Lacking the academic knowledge and skills taught in those courses, young people are at a severe disadvantage in today's labor market. Requiring high school apprentices to enroll in advanced mathematics and science courses appropriate to their occupational area would help to avert this problem.

Continuation in the Occupational Area. Another indicator of the program's impact is the inclination of apprentices who graduated from high school to remain in a related occupational area, either as students or employees. One year after graduating from high school, 67% of apprentices in the demonstration project were either enrolled in postsecondary education related to their apprenticeship or employed in a related occupation. Fifty-six percent continued along a related career path 2 years after graduation (see Table 3).

The graduates who enrolled in postsecondary education related to their apprenticeship most closely match our expectations for the program (58% 1 year after

Table 3. *Continuation of apprenticeship*
career path through education and work after
high school for the classes of 1993 and 1994.

	n	Related		Not related	
1 year after high school	36	24	67%	12	33%
2 years after high school	36	20	56%	16	44%

high school, 50% 2 years after high school). Those employed in related work but
not enrolled in postsecondary education (8% 1 year after high school, 6% 2 years
after high school) have poorer long-term career prospects, but their prospects are
better than those of most recent high school graduates because we included in that
category only apprentices in positions that their apprenticeships qualified them for.
For example, we counted work as a cashier as unrelated even though a former
apprentice might see it as related to administration and office technology because
recent high school graduates without apprentice training are often hired as cashiers.

Apprentices who made a conscious decision to follow an unrelated career path
via further education are not failures; they simply found the occupational area of
their apprenticeship unsuitable (19% at both 1 year and 2 years after high school).
The 14 and 25% of apprentices (after years 1 and 2, respectively) who were neither
enrolled nor employed in a related field fit the typical pattern of "floundering"
found among recent high school graduates; they showed no sign of having been
aided immediately by their apprenticeships.

Conclusions About the Impact of the Demonstration Project

The clearest impact indicators we assessed were of work-related competence and
academic achievement. The former were strongly positive; the latter were not.
Apprentices' post–high school career paths, the third impact indicator, seemed more
directed than those of the young people Osterman (1980) described, but the absence
of comparative data and the short time period render any conclusions tentative. As
program operators, we are not satisfied with either the academic achievement or
the number of apprentices who continued in related career paths after high school.

One conclusion to be drawn from this initial assessment of impact is that a
program must be designed specifically to affect the outcomes that will be used
to evaluate its effectiveness. The strongest impact we found was also the most
direct. We arranged for young people to be placed in workplaces where they could
learn work-related skills, and they succeeded. We hoped they would work harder
in school and choose to take more rigorous courses because they could see at
work why academic achievement is important. We learned from this effort that
teachers, counselors, parents, and workplace mentors need to understand and to

communicate to apprentices the vital importance of academic achievement. This did happen in a few cases with positive results for individual apprentices. However, we also discovered to our dismay that some counselors actually advised apprentices to withdraw from upper-level science courses to make room in their schedules for work experience.

A parallel lesson emerged regarding the critical importance of preapprenticeship activities. In Europe, young people anticipating apprenticeship receive formal advice and career education and, perhaps more important, a plethora of informal information and advice from family and friends and the opportunity to observe and try out apprenticeships in multiple occupations (practica or "sniffing apprenticeships"). The absence of such activities in the program surely led some participants to use their apprenticeship as a form of career exploration, which was useful to them but expensive for their employers.

In our project, apprenticeship did not improve academic achievement by itself. Apprenticeship should be incorporated into a system that includes high academic standards and comprehensive advising. Apprenticeships should be preceded by exploratory work-based learning experiences, career information, and advice to prepare youth to make a well-grounded choice. The School-to-Work Opportunities Act envisions a system with all of these elements. By emphasizing work-based learning, we unintentionally neglected school-based learning, which is also essential to opening career opportunities. Confirmation of the importance of the systemic approach is an important finding from the demonstration project.

Implications for School-to-Work as an Intervention

Our demonstration project did not attempt to test all the elements that were later incorporated into the School-to-Work Opportunities Act. However, it served as an early test of some of the central ideas. Evaluation data from our project are generally consistent with those cited in the preceding paragraphs from other early trials. Some programs reported more positive academic outcomes than ours. Most reported strikingly high postsecondary enrollments when one considers that they recruited students who were not considered college-bound. To our knowledge, no other studies have followed graduates' post–high school career paths past initial enrollment.

Other studies have also found that employer participation remains a serious limiting factor. A survey finding that employers generally express willingness to work with youth is encouraging (Lynn & Wills, 1994), but the true test will come with current efforts to implement School-to-Work on a large scale. President Clinton has convened a National Employer Leadership Council with leaders of major corporations who are committed to implementing their own programs and encouraging others to do the same.

Many of the adults who supervise youth apprentices ("coaches and mentors" in our terminology) told us in interviews that participation had been very beneficial for them, as well as for the youth. They, and sometimes their supervisors, said explaining things to an apprentice had forced them to rethink many practices and that dealing with the range of issues involved had enhanced their supervisory skills. The functions of adult coaches and mentors are central to work-based learning. One direction we are now pursuing will lead to more formal training and support for workplace teachers. It may be that providing such support, which is part of the German system, will increase the impact of work-based learning in this country.

We have come to believe that youth apprenticeship will thrive only in firms that treat it as one component of a broader effort to become "learning organizations." That, in turn, suggests a selective rather than a blanket approach to involving employers. It may well be that youth apprenticeship will make economic sense only in particular sectors of the labor market, notably those occupational areas with rapidly increasing skill demands and, perhaps, with massive impending retirements. We consciously chose relatively prestigious occupational areas to make our demonstration project attractive and to avoid stigmatizing participants. On a larger scale, some less prestigious occupational areas such as hospitality and tourism, food service, and retail trade should be included. The McDonalds Corporation has made a major commitment to youth apprenticeship and has initiated its efforts with minority youth in inner cities. This is an encouraging development because it has the potential of involving massive numbers of youth and because, if the epitome of all secondary labor market employers can succeed in creating serious work-based learning opportunities tied to academic achievement and career ladders, then fewer employers will be able to claim that their niche in the economy makes participation inappropriate.

Recent developments in German apprenticeship are relevant to these considerations. Unification and heightened global competition have led to serious reductions in the magnitude of the German system. Learning from their U.S. competitors that profits can be boosted by reducing the work force and minimizing investments in human resources, some leading firms have stopped training apprentices, and others have cut back their numbers. Lagging economic development in the former East Germany coupled with a near absence of small and medium-sized firms (which tend to benefit financially from apprentices' cheap labor) and a dearth of service occupations have severely constrained apprenticeship opportunities there. Although some foresee the death of apprenticeship in Germany, it seems more likely that it may become less universal and will continue to thrive in those regions, occupations, and economic sectors where it serves employers' self-interest. The availability of apprenticeship places for "only" half of all youth in the appropriate age group is considered a crisis in Germany but would be a miraculous achievement in the United States. (See Lempert, 1995, for an historical perspective on "the perpetual decline of the dual system.")

We believe the mixed results in our program confirm the necessity of systemic reform. Persistence along career paths was respectable but could have been improved if prospective apprentices had known more about occupational choices by grade 10. A range of career education, career exploration, and opportunities for advice preceding apprenticeship would be preferable. We found the link with post-secondary education unexpectedly difficult to forge. Apprentices needed far more advising than they received about course selection in high school and financial aid for postsecondary education. Poverty was a formidable barrier to some youth; they lacked money for college tuition and transportation. We were also struck by the power of life events such as illness, family turmoil, childbirth, and death in the family to disrupt career paths in ways that no program could completely over-come.

Michael Rutter (1994) has pointed out that when assessing the impact of a pro-gram on participants, one must think in terms of comparisons with other "treat-ments" that might have been offered instead, not only with no treatment. Although there is no obvious single comparative treatment, it would be worth comparing the impact (using the same indicators) of a year of full-time postsecondary vocational education, of participation in the Job Corps, of military training, and of related programs such as cooperative education.

Implications for Research in Support of Interventions

Another set of implications has to do with the nature and functions of research in interventions like this one. We have had the unusual and sobering experience of participating in research both at the stage of discovering responses and testing interventions. Discovery is more enjoyable and less risky than testing!

More rigorous research designs would provide better tests. Our comparison group was useful as a reality check, preventing us from claiming credit for a general up-ward trend in apprentices' grades. However, it was merely a convenience sample, not a matched comparison; the members' initial orientation to college may have resulted in underestimations of the effect of apprenticeship on academic achieve-ment. Furthermore, we have not yet analyzed post–high school graduation data from comparison students, which will give us a better sense of whether the majority of apprentices' post–high school activities are distinctive in the apprentices' orien-tation toward careers or whether the comparison students look similar. Random assignment would be even better in some ways but would introduce issues of dif-ferential sample attrition. (Heckman and Smith, 1995, have rigorously argued that randomized experiments are not necessarily preferable to matched comparisons in social policy research, partly because of attrition.)

The challenges continue well past design issues. Timing is a major one. In passing the School-to-Work Opportunities Act Congress mandated that an evaluation report be submitted by 1998, expecting, of course, to read in that report about the impact on youth of programs funded by the legislation. But the first programs were funded in 1995; few will be established in less than a year. Six years after our program began, only two cohorts had the chance to complete the program as we envisioned it. We can point to some former apprentices who are now gainfully employed by their training firms in positions that are ordinarily reserved for people 5–10 years older. Other apprentices are still students in 4-year colleges. Some have not yet completed 2 years of postsecondary education because they have been enrolled less than full time, sporadically, or both. Definitive information on the impact of participation is still not available. Communities that begin building systems with young people earlier than grade 11 will take even longer to demonstrate postgraduation impacts. Furthermore, employment and educational attainment 5–10 years after completion would be a better measure of impact than measures made just after high school graduation.

Especially if the mandate to build new systems is taken seriously, the changes required by the School-to-Work Opportunities Act will take years to be implemented, and participants must be involved for years before its effectiveness can be fairly tried. Yet political realities and fiscal prudence dictate early evaluation. Under these circumstances, proximal indicators are the best we can hope to provide, despite the distal goals of the legislation. This adds urgency to improving practices that boost academic achievement because it is an early indicator that is clearly relevant and easily understood.

We emerge from 4 years as researcher-practitioners with a strengthened commitment to an approach the Germans call "scientific accompaniment" (*wissenschaftliche Begleitung*). We contrast this approach with the more conventional role for researchers in experimentation and evaluation. In a social experiment, the researcher specifies the conditions of treatment. In both experiments and evaluations, researchers collect data to substantiate their judgments about the effectiveness of practice–judgments offered from a safe distance. We hope in the future to establish collaborative relationships with practitioners in which we will share what we have learned in the past and conduct new research to help answer questions that arise in the settings, both our own and the practitioners' and policymakers'. We do not believe social science research has yet achieved the power to decide questions of effectiveness and viability unaided by other considerations, but it can contribute a needed voice to deliberation about these issues (Cohen & Garet, 1975).

References

Bachman, J. G., & Schulenberg, J. (1993). How part-time work intensity relates to drug use, problem behavior, time use, and satisfaction among high school seniors: Are these consequences or merely correlates? *Developmental Psychology, 29,* 220–235.

Bailey, T., & Merritt, D. (1993). *The school-to-work transition and youth apprenticeship: Lessons from the U.S. experience.* New York: Manpower Demonstration Research Corporation.

Barton, P. (1975). Youth unemployment and career entry. In S. Wolfbein (Ed.), *Labor market information for youth.* Philadelphia: Temple University Press.

Cohen, D. K., & Garet, M. S. (1975). Reforming educational policy with applied social research. *Harvard Educational Review, 45*, 17–43.

Elder, G. (1974). *Children of the Great Depression.* Chicago: University of Chicago Press.

Finch, M. D., Mortimer, J. T., & Ryu, S. (1994, March). *Work intensity and the academic achievement of high school students: A test of three behavioral models.* Paper presented at the biennial meeting of the Society for Research on Adolescence, San Diego, CA.

Greenberger, E., & Steinberg, L. (1986). *When teenagers work: The psychological and social costs of adolescent employment.* New York: Basic Books.

Hamilton, S. F. (1987). Apprenticeship as a transition to adulthood in West Germany. *American Journal of Education, 95*, 314–345.

Hamilton, S. F. (1990). *Apprenticeship for adulthood: Preparing youth for the future.* New York: Free Press.

Hamilton, S. F., & Levine-Powers, J. (1990). Failed expectations: Working-class girls' transition from school to work. *Youth and Society, 22*, 241–262.

Heckman, J., & Smith, J. (1995). Assessing the case for social experiments. *Journal of Economic Perspectives, 9*, 85–110.

Klerman, J. A., & Karoly, L. A. (1995). *The transition to stable employment: The experience of U.S. youth in their early labor market career.* Santa Monica, CA: RAND.

Kopp, H., & Kazis, R. (with Churchill, A.) (1995). *Promising practices: A study of ten school-to-career programs.* Boston: Jobs for the Future.

Lempert, W. (1995). Das Märchen vom unaufhaltsamen Niedergang des "dualen Systems" [The fairy tale of the perpetual decline of the "dual systems"]. *Zeitschrift für Berufs- und Wirtschaftspädagogik, 91*, 225–231.

Lerman, R. I., & Pouncy, H. (1990). The compelling case for youth apprenticeships. *The Public Interest, 90*, 62–77.

Levitan, S. A., & Gallo, F. (1991). *Got to learn to earn: Preparing Americans for work* (Occasional paper 1991-3). Washington, DC: Center for Social Policy Studies.

Lynn, I., & Wills, J. (1994). *School lessons, work lessons: Recruiting and sustaining employer involvement in School-to-Work programs.* Washington, DC: Institute for Educational Leadership.

Mortimer, J. T., Finch, M. D., Ryu, S., Shanahan, M. J., & Call, K. T. (1993, March). *The effects of work intensity on adolescent mental health, achievement and behavioral adjustment: New evidence from a prospective study.* Paper presented at the biennial meeting of the Society for Research in Child Development, New Orleans, LA.

National Center on Education and the Economy. (1990). *America's choice: High skills or low wages!* Rochester, NY: Author.

Nothdurft, W. E., & Jobs for the Future. (1990). *Youth apprenticeship, American style: Report of a conference held on December 7, 1990.* Cambridge, MA: Consortium on Youth Apprenticeship.

Office of Managemant & Budget. (1995). *Economic report of the President.* Washington, DC: U.S. Government Printing Office.

Osterman, P. (1980). *Getting started: The youth labor market.* Cambridge, MA: MIT Press.

Osterman, P., & Iannozzi, M. (1993). *Youth apprenticeships and School-to-Work transition: Current knowledge and legislative strategy.* Philadelphia: National Center on the Educational Quality of the Workforce, University of Pennsylvania.

Pauly, E., Kopp, H., & Haimson, J. (1994). *Home-grown lessons: Innovative programs linking work and high school.* New York: Manpower Demonstration Research Corporation.

Reubens, B. G. (Ed.). (1983). *Youth at work: An international survey.* Totowa, NJ: Rowman & Allanheld.

Rosenbaum, J. E., Kariya, T., Settersten, R., & Maier, T. (1990). Market and network theories of the transition from school to work: Their application to industrialized societies. *Annual Review of Sociology, 16*, 263–299.

Rutter, M. (1994). Concepts of causation, tests of causal mechanisms, and implications for intervention. In A. C. Petersen & J. T. Mortimer (Eds.), *Youth unemployment and society.* Cambridge, England: Cambridge University Press.

Schulenberg, J., & Bachman, J. G. (1993, March). *Long hours on the job? Not so bad for some adolescents in some types of jobs: The quality of work and substance use, affect, and stress.* Paper presented at the biennial meeting of the Society for Research in Child Development, New Orleans, LA.

Soskice, D. (1994). The German training system: Reconciling markets and institutions. In L. M. Lynch (Ed.), *Training and the private sector: International comparisons*. Chicago: University of Chicago Press.

Steinberg, L., & Dornbusch, S. M. (1991). Negative correlates of part-time employment during adolescence: Replication and elaboration. *Developmental Psychology, 27*, 304–313.

Steinberg, L., Fegley, S., & Dornbusch, S. M. (1993). Negative impact of part-time work on adolescent adjustment: Evidence from a longitudinal study. *Developmental Psychology, 29*, 171–180.

Stern, D., Stone, J. R., Hopkins, C., & McMillion, M. (1990). Quality of students' work experience and orientation toward work. *Youth and Society, 22*, 263–282.

U.S. Department of Labor (1994). *The School-to-Work/Youth Apprenticeship Demonstration: Preliminary findings* (Research and Evaluation Report Series 94-E). Washington, DC: Author.

17 Preparing Adolescents for Social Change: Designing Generic Social Interventions

Ruby Takanishi

Current social interventions aimed at adolescents rarely seek to prepare them for living under conditions of rapid, often unpredicted social change. Instead, interventions tend to target single problems, such as the prevention of teenage pregnancy, substance abuse, school dropout, HIV, and violence. Some of these approaches (Botvin, Baker, Dusenbury, Botvin, & Diaz, 1995) incorporate social or life skills that are more generic in nature and aim to increase a young person's capacity to deal with stress, uncertainty, and conflict. The irony of these targeted interventions, however, is that the psychosocial disorders they seek to prevent or treat are likely to be responses to the very strains of social change experienced by contemporary adolescents (Chisholm & Hurrelmann, 1995; Rutter & Smith, 1995).

The school-to-work area (Hamilton and Hamilton, this volume; Marshall, 1997) is an exception to targeted interventions that do not typically concern themselves with future life challenges for adolescents. Yet even in the work preparation area, some labor economists admit to limits in forecasting the requirements of the future workplace (Nadel, 1997).

The nature of future changes in work, family life, communities, and nations is not easily predicted. Often these changes, such as recent political and economic developments in central and Eastern Europe, occur unexpectedly (Ringen & Wallace, 1994). Forecasts of a global economy (Reich, 1991) with its political and social ramifications (Schwab & Smajda, 1996) are abundant. Adolescents must be prepared to compete in a worldwide labor market and must have the skills to understand and appreciate cultures other than their own. For those who will become part of the business and financial sector, such appreciation must also translate into behaviors that reflect intergroup cultural competence. Rarely are these forecasts, which may not materialize, incorporated or considered in the design of social interventions for adolescents. Researchers themselves also bear responsibility in this area: Their research on the effects of social change does not address the implications of their

My thanks to Elliott Milhollin for his research assistance and preparation of the reference section of this paper.

findings for social interventions to prepare and support adolescents for times of social upheaval (see, for example, Moen, Elder, & Luscher, 1995).

All this being said, it is important to remember that the human species has remarkable adaptive qualities and is the product of a long, slow process of biosocial evolution. The capacity to learn, innovate, and respond to environmental and social change is quintessentially (but not uniquely) part of being human. Some individuals are more likely to develop and to mobilize these adaptive qualities than others. What body of research addresses why these individual differences exist? How can social policies and environments be organized to make it more likely that individuals flourish, rather than falter or succumb, under conditions of rapid change?

From a psychosocial view, social interventions should attempt to develop individuals who are able to deal productively with uncertainty; who can identify, analyze, and solve problems; who understand that some human conditions are complex and not amenable to problem-solving modes; and who behave ethically in their personal and institutional relationships. Thus education in life or social skills should be seriously considered as part of social interventions to prepare young people for rapid social change (Hamburg, 1997).

But the responsibility for coping with such change is not only a matter for individuals. Social policies, including public systems, must be formed and implemented to support individuals caught up by economic and political events (Ringen & Wallace, 1994). Traditional socializing institutions in a society, by definition, are not accustomed to dealing with change. Most often, they seek to replicate themselves, particularly along gender and class lines, even in the face of change. Yet they can play a crucial, constructive role in facilitating the development of young people for the future (Carnegie Council on Adolescent Development, 1995). Fortunately, social conditions change, and individuals are not merely passive but rather agents that shape their own development. These factors provide an essential counterforce to what might be disastrous, complete societal reproduction.

The central thesis of this chapter is that the design of social interventions to prepare young people for social change must identify what are basic or enduring developmental tasks and what are new skills that enable young people to be successful when faced by changing conditions. The crucial role of social institutions – families, schools, health care agencies, community organizations, media, and business – in supporting this preparation must be articulated with the relevant and supportive social policies.

Essential Requirements for Healthy Development

In *Great Transitions: Preparing Adolescents for a New Century*, the Carnegie Council on Adolescent Development (1995), based on syntheses of research on the second decade of life, argued that although new social circumstances have vastly altered the landscape for adolescent development, all adolescents continue to have fundamental human requirements that must be met if they are to grow up into healthy, constructive adults. All run the risk of diminished lives if these requirements are not met (p. 49).

The Council argued that if these requirements are met by society's key institutions, adolescents are more likely to emerge healthy, well-educated, and prepared for living in a new century. The Council also addressed changing cognitive and social tasks for adolescents given the transition to what is called a global economy driven by telecommunications technology and easy transfer of capital across national borders.

In *Great Transitions*, two categories of essential requirements for healthy adolescent development were identified. The first category encompasses universal, enduring requirements (what some call "basic survival skills") for adolescents to make a successful transition into adulthood regardless of the conditions of their lives, including the following:

1. Experience of sustained, caring relationships with at least one or a few adults (Werner & Smith, 1992).
2. Social support systems, starting with families and including schools, community institutions, and health care systems (Gottlieb, 1991).
3. Development of social competence and life skills that enable adolescents to have a sense of self-worth and make informed choices about, and plan for, their education, occupation, relationships, and health (Clausen, 1995).
4. Preparation to become active, contributing members of their communities and nations as workers, citizens, and parents (Takanishi, Mortimer, & McGourthy, 1995).
5. Belief in a promising future with real economic and social opportunities to lead a decent life (Wilson, 1987).

The second category of requirements include those that are at a premium given the growing globalization of the economy and related political and social changes (Schwab & Smajda, 1996). These requirements include the following:

1. Technical and analytic capabilities to participate in a high-technology, knowledge-rich international economy (Reich, 1991).
2. Motivation for lifelong learning and flexibility regarding work responsibilities and skills.
3. Values to live peacefully and respectfully in the community with an array of ethnic, religious, and cultural groups.
4. Ability to live with uncertainty and change. As *Great Transitions* noted, "Indeed, an important part of preparation for adulthood today is preparation for change itself" (p. 49).

A Comprehensive, Generic Approach

The Carnegie Council's approach was to deal directly with the underlying factors that predispose adolescents to engage in high-risk or problem behaviors by providing social environments that research indicates are related to positive outcomes. Such an approach is generic, comprehensive, and preventive in its orientation. At its heart is the restoration and strengthening of social supports that were once available to adolescents within their families and communities but that can no longer be taken for granted.

Such a generic approach focuses not just on problem behaviors after they occur but on their common antecedents, including school difficulties, family problems, and economic disadvantage. It emphasizes the positive possibilities inherent in the adolescent transition – possibilities for educating and motivating adolescents to pursue healthful lifestyles, for fostering social and decision-making skills to help adolescents choose alternatives to very risky behavior, and for providing them with reasons and tools to build constructive lives.

A comprehensive, generic approach includes the following elements:

Life-Skills Development

If adolescents are to address enduring dilemmas of human relations, develop healthful lifestyles, cultivate intellectual curiosity, access the social systems they need, and meet the demands of the workplace, they must learn certain basic skills for everyday life. The development of interpersonal, decision-making, and coping skills can help students resist pressures from peers, from irresponsible adults, or from the media to engage in risky behaviors. Such skills can increase their self-control, help reduce stress and anxiety, and teach them ways to make friends if they are isolated. Young people can acquire these skills through instruction and practice as well as through role playing and group problem solving. When combined with a life sciences curriculum in the middle schools, life skills development can be a potent force in motivating adolescents to adopt healthy practices throughout their lives.

Adult Mentoring

A fundamental need of young people is for a few stable, supportive relationships with caring, mature adults who can help them access resources, encourage them to persist in difficult situations such as schooling, and provide support and ethical guidance. Elder citizens can contribute substantially as mentors to adolescents, bringing new meaning into their lives while helping the younger generation grow up. It is important that mentoring programs be linked with other resources in the community, including education, health, and social services.

The health-promoting and preventive power of a sustained relationship with a caring adult in the lives of young people has strong support in the research and program literatures. The caring relationship has achieved the status of a mantra in the child and youth development field. Two critical caveats must be highlighted: First, such a relationship is not necessarily a natural act; not all adults can be effective mentors, tutors, and guides. Even those who are reasonably effective need an infrastructure, including support for volunteering, opportunities to reflect and meet with other mentors and tutors, skills to deal with difficult issues, and so on. Second, these relationships do not occur in a vacuum; social and institutional supports are important to nurture and sustain them.

Both caveats point to the necessity for paid staff to provide the needed infrastructure for voluntary activity. Creating a long-term relationship with a caring adult requires paid staff for monitoring, training, and supporting adult mentors and a support system for young people involved in these efforts. These activities require more than technical assistance; they require ongoing, committed, and skilled staff people.

Social Support Systems: Strengthening Families and Reengaging Them with Adolescents

A substantial body of research now attests to the critical contribution of well-functioning families to positive adolescent outcomes. Research is also showing that it is during times of social change, particularly economic dislocations, that the strength of family–adolescent relations can make an important difference in how adults and adolescents cope with economic hardships and in their ability to weather difficult times (Conger & Elder, 1994).

Social policies and interventions that support and strengthen families and their capacity to guide their adolescent children are likely to have beneficial effects. Public and workplace policies can make a difference in the time parents of adolescents have to spend with their children. Employers, such as corporations and public agencies, should extend to parents of adolescents the workplace policies now available for those with young children, including parental leave, flextime, job sharing, telecommuting, and part-time work with benefits. Such family-friendly workplace policies would allow parents to become more involved in middle and high schools, serve as volunteers in community organizations, and spend more time with their adolescents. These policies enjoy, for the most part, support across the ideological spectrum.

Economic hardship is affecting increasing numbers of families throughout the world owing to corporate downsizing, advances in telecommunications, economic globalization, and rapid political change (Ringen & Wallace, 1994). Studies of economically stressed families in rural America (Conger & Elder, 1994) suggest ways in which families can better cope with or recover from economic hardship, including job retraining, employment and placement services, and governmental assistance. Family counseling, including family support to maintain effective child-rearing practices, may be necessary for families who experience emotional distress.

Economic strains on families are only likely to increase in the United States because many of the jobs created and filled in recent years are in low-wage, largely service sectors (Rosenthal, 1995). The global economy has resulted in growing income inequality, especially in the United States. The economic and social consequences, as they are perceived by adolescents and influence their investment in their education and health, are frightening. No government in the industrialized world has yet addressed the implications of this potentially destabilizing economic fact of life (Schwab & Smajda, 1996), which is one that has profound effects for adolescents and for the larger society.

Social Support Systems: Developmentally Appropriate Schools

Every modern nation must strive to develop the talents of its entire population if it is to have any chance of being economically competitive and socially cohesive. An adolescent who is doing well in school is unlikely to become involved in the juvenile justice system and to become an adolescent parent. Therefore, social policies and interventions that enable adolescents to be fully engaged in learning in schools and that meet their developmental requirements are a critical element of a comprehensive, generic approach to healthy development (Carnegie Task Force on Education of Young Adolescents, 1989).

The eight principles for *Turning Points* schools are as follows:

1. Large middle grade schools are divided into smaller communities for learning.
2. Middle grade schools transmit a core of common knowledge to all students.
3. Middle grade schools are organized to ensure success for all students.
4. Teachers and principals have the major responsibility and power to transform middle grade schools.
5. Teachers for the middle grades are specifically prepared to teach young adolescents.
6. Schools promote good health; the education and health of young adolescents are inextricably linked.
7. Families are allied with school staff through mutual respect, trust, and communication.
8. Schools and communities are partners in educating young adolescents.

Research on *Turning Points* principles in schools in Illinois indicates that comprehensive implementation of these principles is related to higher student achievement and improved student behavior conducive to learning. These promising results indicate that young adolescents can be better educated than they now are and can have a better chance at personal success in the future than many now do.

Social Support Systems: Health Promotion and Preventive Services

Under conditions of rapid social change, adolescents are likely to be affected emotionally and to have psychosomatic symptoms precipitated by stress (Chisholm & Hurrelmann, 1995; Rutter & Smith, 1995). A generic approach addresses such stress by health promotion strategies that include the cooperation of families, schools, communities, and local media in fostering healthy practices for life. Schools are conceived as health-promoting environments – from a life sciences curriculum (integrated life sciences and health education) in the classroom to good nutrition in the cafeteria and smoke-free policies for students and adults. Life-skills development, described earlier, is also part of the package.

Social Support Systems: Community and Youth Organizations

The experience of growing up in communities in most industrialized nations has changed significantly in recent decades. The sense of belonging to a community that offers mutual aid and a sense of common purpose, whether it is found in families, schools, neighborhoods, religious places, or youth organizations, has been compromised.

The entry of women into the workforce – an economic imperative for most women and families in the United States – has led to increases in the time many adolescents spend alone. The out-of-school hours constitute a time of increased vulnerability for high-risk behavior. Analyses of several national data sets on adolescents show that those left on their own or only with peers stand a significantly greater chance of becoming involved in substance abuse, sexual activity leading to unintended pregnancy and sexually transmitted diseases, and crime and violence than their peers who are engaged in activities with good adult supervision (Zill, Nord, & Loomis, 1995).

Thus, adolescents from all economic strata often find themselves alone in communities where there are few adults to turn to and no places to go. Young people from low-income families are especially affected by lack of constructive and safe places. Time spent alone, however, is not the crucial contributor to high risk. What adolescents do during that time, where they do it, and with whom leads to either positive or negative results (Zill, Nord, & Loomis, 1995). The potential of youth and community organizations, in partnerships with schools and other community agencies, to turn the now-lost opportunities of the out-of-school hours into attractive, growth-promoting settings is great.

Programs for youth can extend the school's responsibility for education and facilitate the transition from school to work into the out-of-school hours. Such programs can reinforce the family's responsibility for teaching enduring values and building character during the hours when parents are working. Ideally, community programs can create meaningful opportunities for parents and schools to become involved in fostering and recognizing young people's accomplishments. Community service should be an integral part of these programs, enabling adolescents to learn about the civic life of communities as well as how to provide tangible services to others.

The Pervasive Media Environment

One aspect of social change experienced by all adolescents is the powerful, pervasive, and rapidly changing multimedia environment at the end of the 20th century.

Television is no longer the sole source of information and entertainment. Adolescents are increasingly part of cyberspace; indeed, many are more adept on the World Wide Web than their parents. The potential emerging technologies have to transform education, health care, entertainment, consumption, and social life itself is enormous.

Given the media's pervasiveness, social interventions must include the fostering of critical media literacy beyond the printed page to the multimedia capacity of current computer technology. A major policy issue is the potential disparity in access to, and skills in, leading edge technologies by adolescents from different income backgrounds. It is clear that individuals who are not knowledgeable about telecommunications technology and who cannot keep pace with rapid developments will be seriously disadvantaged in a competitive economy.

The preceding generic approaches have the potential to prevent major problems during adolescence because they address fundamental requirements that all adolescents have for optimal development. These approaches can be implemented in a wide array of institutions concerned with offering adolescents a decent chance in life. Ensuring the healthy growth and development of adolescents requires the combined commitment of all the institutions that have a profound impact on youth. No single influence – adult or institutional – can be responsible for a young person's successful journey from adolescence into adulthood.

From families, the Carnegie Council asked that they take the time to reengage with their adolescent children within the home, in their schools, and beyond, supported by appropriate workplace and employment policies. From schools, the Council asked that they understand and meet the unique developmental needs of adolescents. From health care institutions, the Council asked that they recognize opportunities to promote good lifelong health practices. From community organizations, the Council asked that they form partnerships with other organizations to provide safe places and high-quality programs for all adolescents during the out-of-school hours. From the media, the Council asked that they redirect their pervasive power toward becoming a more positive force in the lives of the young. More detailed recommendations for these pivotal institutions are offered in *Great Transitions* (Carnegie Council on Adolescent Development, 1995).

Social Policies to Support Social Interventions

Generic social interventions, as described in the preceding sections, are the building blocks for preparing young people for a future we adults cannot completely predict or necessarily control. But describing such interventions is not sufficient because their very feasibility, implementation, and effectiveness are inextricably linked with the macrosocial and economic policies of a nation. This approach is a variant of one that links individual development to proximal institutions (such as families, schools, and community agencies) and to distal ones (such as government and workplaces).

I am no expert in industrial, trade, and labor market policies. However, what is clear is that much of our policy energies must be focused on the widening income disparity in the United States (Rosenthal, 1995), its causes, and its implications for the well-being of adolescents and their families. This economic disparity caused by the global economy is creating major change and anxiety in the American workforce. Although schools and human service agencies, particularly those serving very low-income groups, have borne the brunt of criticism and the decline of public funds, corporate social responsibility has escaped similar examination. Yet underemployment and the lack of decent wage jobs, even for the well-educated and prepared, and the displacement caused by downsizing are having major economic and social effects on many American families and their children. These are clearly areas where the business sector is a major player and contributor.

Linked to these changes are volatile policy issues of immigration, race relations, and the sustained viability of intergenerational support systems such as Social Security and other "safety net" or welfare provisions. Taken together, these issues form the critical context for generic social interventions that must include national economic and social policies, including family support.

Conclusion

I am not a historian. Thus I find it difficult to draw conclusions about whether the nature and rates of social change in the last three decades are different and present more difficulties to young people today than those created by earlier periods of change such as the Industrial Revolution. What I do conclude is that neither researchers nor policymakers are adequately addressing what social interventions make the most sense given our current state of relevant knowledge. Equally important, policymakers and elected leaders are not attending to interrelated economic and social issues that influence the effectiveness of social interventions on adolescents and their families.

We live in a time of great opportunity and great risk. I hope that the ideas presented in this chapter will contribute to urgently needed scientific, policy, and public conversations about how we prepare all young people throughout the world to face the uncertainties of the coming century (Takanishi & Hamburg, 1997). Although these uncertainties and their social ramifications may not be more disruptive than ones in the past, we do have the comparative advantage of a body of relevant scientific knowledge and community-based experience. Whether we can now do better than our predecessors have will be fascinating to watch as we enter another century.

References

Botvin, G. J., Baker, E., Dusenbury, L., Botvin, E. M., & Diaz, T. (1995). Long-term follow-up results of a randomized drug abuse prevention trial in a white middle-class population. *Journal of the American Medical Association, 273,* 1106–1112.

Carnegie Council on Adolescent Development. (1995). *Great transitions: Preparing adolescents for a new century.* Washington, DC: Author.

Carnegie Task Force on Education of Young Adolescents. (1989). *Turning points: Preparing American youth for the twenty-first century.* Washington, DC: Carnegie Council on Adolescent Development.

Chisholm, L., & Hurrelmann, K. (1995). Adolescence in modern Europe: Pluralized transition patterns and their implications for personal and social risks. *Journal of Adolescence, 18,* 129–158.

Clausen, J. A. (1995). Gender, context, and turning points in adults' lives. In P. Moen, G. H. Elder, Jr., & K. Luscher (Eds.), *Examining lives in context: Perspectives on the ecology of human development* (pp. 365–389). Washington, DC: American Psychological Association.

Conger, R. D., & Elder, G. H., Jr. (Eds.). (1994). *Families in troubled times: Adapting to change in rural America.* Hawthorne, NY: Aldine de Gruyter.

Gottlieb, B. H. (1991). Social support in adolescence. In M. E. Colten & S. Gore (Eds.), *Adolescent stress: Causes and consequences* (pp. 281–306). Hawthorne, NY: Aldine de Gruyter.

Hamburg, D. A. (1997). Meeting the essential requirements for healthy adolescent development in a transforming world. In R. Takanishi & D. A. Hamburg (Eds.), *Preparing adolescents for the 21st century: Challenges facing Europe and the United States.* New York: Cambridge University Press.

Marshall, R. (1997). School-to-work processes in the United States. In R. Takanishi & D. A. Hamburg (Eds.), *Preparing adolescents for the 21st century: Challenges facing Europe and the United States.* New York: Cambridge University Press.

Moen, P., Elder, G. H., Jr., & Luscher, K. (1995). *Examining lives in context: Perspectives on the ecology of human development.* Washington, DC: American Psychological Association.

Nadel, H. (1997). The economics of education and training in the face of changing production and employment structures. In R. Takanishi & D. A. Hamburg (Eds.), *Preparing adolescents for the 21st century: Challenges facing Europe and the United States.* New York: Cambridge University Press.

Reich, R. B. (1991). *The work of nations: Preparing ourselves for 21st century capitalism.* New York: Alfred A. Knopf.

Ringen, S., & Wallace, C. (Eds.). (1994). *Societies in transitions: East-Central Europe today* (Vol. 1). Brookfield, VT: Ashgate Publishing Company.

Rosenthal, N. H. (1995). The nature of occupational employment growth: 1983–93. *Monthly Labor Review, 18* (6), 45–54.

Rutter, M., & Smith, D. J. (Eds.). (1995). *Psychosocial disorders in young people: Time trends and their causes.* West Sussex, England: John Wiley & Sons Ltd.

Schwab, K., & Smajda, C. (1996, February 1). Start taking the backlash against globalization seriously. *International Herald Tribune,* p. 8.

Takanishi, R., & Hamburg, D. A. (Eds.). (1997). *Preparing adolescents for the 21st century: Challenges facing Europe and the United States.* New York: Cambridge University Press.

Takanishi, R., Mortimer, A. M., & McGourthy, T. J. (1995). Positive indicators of adolescent development: Redressing the negative image of American adolescents. In *Indicators of children's well-being: Conference papers, Volume III: Cross-cutting issues: Population, family, and neighborhood: Social development and problem behaviors.* Madison, WI: University of Wisconsin-Madison, Institute for Research on Poverty.

Werner, E. E., & Smith, R. S. (1992). *Overcoming the odds: High risk children from birth to adulthood.* Ithaca, NY: Cornell University Press.

Wilson, W. J. (1987). *The truly disadvantaged: The inner city, the underclass, and public policy.* Chicago: University of Chicago Press.

Zill, N., Nord, C. W., & Loomis, L. S. (1995). *Adolescent time use, risky behavior, and outcomes: An analysis of national data.* Rockville, MD: Westat, Inc.

18   Adolescents in the 21st Century: Preparing for an Uncertain Future

Anne C. Petersen

These are very interesting times because many aspects of life are in flux. As the authors of the two preceding chapters contend, an important responsibility of adults in a society is to prepare adolescents for the future, and yet no one can predict exactly what the future will bring. This uncertainty is not lost on young people, who reflect this ambiguity. What can guide us in these times? Is it best to assume that the future will not be so different from the past? Or is it best to prepare for ambiguity by attaining basic skills adaptable to most any future? What are the basics of preparation and the constants in life? How can research add to our knowledge of these issues?

In this commentary on the two previous chapters, I shall attempt to address these questions, taking a global perspective to the extent possible for me. I first review what I regard as the central points of the two chapters in addressing the questions together with some other interesting perspectives on the issues. I then attempt to provide a holistic perspective on what we might do in these uncertain times.

The two preceding chapters identify important issues in preparing adolescents in the current times, at least in the United States. As Takanishi (this volume) notes, current interventions rarely prepare adolescents for tremendous social change. At the same time, she notes that humans are remarkably adaptable – at least over evolutionary time. What can we learn from research about individual adaptability, particularly over the shorter term? We know that some individuals are more adaptive than others (e.g., Levine & Wiener, 1989) and that individual and contextual factors seem to aid or hinder effective coping during adolescence (e.g., Petersen, Susman, & Beard, 1989). But we know relatively little about what societal factors make it more likely that adolescents, relative to other groups, will flourish rather than falter or succumb during periods of rapid social change. This question could be addressed with existing data to at least identify what interventions might be attempted to enhance the likelihood of young people's flourishing. Such work seems to be very high priority.

Drawing from the Carnegie Council on Adolescent Development report (1995), Takanishi (this volume) identified the following "basic survival skills" for adolescents to "make a successful transition into adulthood regardless of the conditions of their lives" (p. 286):

1. A sustained caring relationship with at least one adult.
2. Social support systems (including families, schools, community institutions, and health care systems).
3. Development of social competence and life skills.
4. Preparation to become active, contributing members of communities and nations.
5. Belief in a promising future with real economic and social opportunities.

Individual qualities especially needed in the light of current social changes in the United States include the following:

1. Technical and analytic capabilities to participate in a technologically knowledge-rich international economy.
2. Motivation for life-long learning.
3. Values to live peacefully in a diverse society.
4. A capacity to live with uncertainty and change.

Although the report Takanishi cites focused primarily on the United States, she notes the importance of addressing the needs of young people across the globe for the coming century. This indeed is an important issue because most nations of the world have some form of elected democracy as well as at least partly capitalistic economies. The need to identify opportunities for young people in capitalistic, democratic societies is tremendous.

Hamilton and Hamilton (this volume) strike similar chords but from the perspective of the specific issue of the transition to productive adult work roles. As they note (p. 267), "adolescents are peculiarly sensitive to social change." Because young people understand the need to prepare for the future, they are especially attuned to change in society. But as the Hamiltons also note, we "never know for sure what changes will actually occur, what their negative consequences will be, and what interventions might ameliorate their negative consequences."

The biggest change in the U.S. economy, like many others, is the dramatic increase in the service sector. Because this sector is growing so rapidly, it makes sense that it would be a primary source of jobs for youth. The dead-end nature of many of these jobs has been noted by many, for such employment lacks career ladders with which to move into more demanding, secure, and lucrative positions. Initially, scholars linked these characteristics with youth jobs. Increasingly, however, it has become clear that those with less privilege, and especially less education, have few options but these sorts of jobs, whatever their age. The manufacturing jobs of the industrial era as well as jobs involving extraction of resources (e.g., mining) have been declining in view of increased manufacturing efficiency and the dearth of resources to extract.

Although apprentice programs provide the extremely important facilitation of the transition from school to adult work roles, it is imperative to consider whether the model fits with current jobs and especially with likely future jobs for young people.

As Hamilton (1994) noted it is more difficult to map apprenticeships onto service jobs because of the lack of guilds monitoring entry of new workers, the lack of clearly identifiable skills that are difficult to gain through other routes, and general employer indifference to the business need for apprenticeships. When apprentice-ships have been adopted in service areas in the United States, the motivation has likely been the altruistic one of facilitating this important youth transition rather than the more conventional motivations stemming from the need to attract skilled workers. It will continue to be important to examine trends in apprentice programs, especially in Europe, as economies shift more to the service sector. If my specula-tion is correct, we will see less use of apprentice models, except when the employer recognizes the importance of facilitating the transition from school to work for the development of young people.

An entirely different approach to preparing adolescents for an uncertain future is taken by Rutter and Smith (1995a). They posed the question of what could be learned about likely trends in the new century, in the light of the past century's history in psychosocial disorders of youth. Some have assumed that psychosocial disorders result from an inability to cope with difficult conditions, including condi-tions involving uncertainty. Smith and Rutter (1995) concluded that rates of various psychosocial disorders, including crime, suicide, depression, and substance abuse, have increased, particularly over the past 50 years among youth. Typically, the rates for young men and women have increasingly converged.

The authors in the Rutter and Smith (1995a) volume pursued various causal ex-planations for these time trends. Rutter and Smith (1995b) concluded that, although social disadvantage is associated with psychosocial disorders at any one point in time, worsening living conditions do not account for the rising levels of disorder. Similarly, unemployment creates psychosocial risks, but high unemployment does not explain the observed increases. Conversely, increasing affluence does not ac-count for the increases in disorder but plays some role in the opportunities for crime and for alcohol and drug abuse. Increasing affluence may also have effects through increased expectations on youth. Much research has demonstrated the pos-itive effects on student achievement and occupational outcomes of appropriately high expectation, but when expectations are unrealistically high, they can make young people feel like failures. Poor physical health creates mental hazards, but the historical increases in psychosocial disorder were accompanied by trends to-ward improved health. Thus, no simple explanation for the increase in psychosocial disorders was supported. Additionally, no clear evidence emerged supporting more complex hypotheses, perhaps because few researchers have attempted to examine them.

Turning to specific potential causes of disorder in social contexts, Rutter and Smith (1995) concluded that, although increasing levels of family discord and breakup are linked to psychosocial disorder at the individual and community levels, the risks appear to be based on marital discord rather than breakup of marriage.

Although media are unlikely to be the cause of the increase in psychosocial disorder, they may augment the effects of societal change and affect individual behavior. Increased faith in individual behavior, as compared with faith in community or societal control, may be linked to increases in psychosocial disorders, particularly when individuals are not able to handle pressures or changes themselves.

The very nature of adolescence was also examined in this volume as a potential cause for the increase in psychosocial disorders. The increased duration of adolescence began well before the increases in disorder were observed and therefore is unlikely to be the cause. Rutter and Smith (1995) found some evidence, though, for increased risks of disorder associated with youth culture (e.g., youth-created music), isolation of youth from adults, financial dependence combined with autonomy from parents in other respects, earlier sexual experience, increased psychosocial stressors, increased peer influence, and increased breakdown of cohabiting relationships. All of these factors can be construed as reflecting societal change and as supporting the hypothesis that societal change increases psychosocial disorders among youth.

None of the accounts just discussed generates confidence in our will or even ability to support young people to have better lives in the future. What should we do differently? What can we learn from the current status to enable adolescents to become effective and fulfilled adults?

Many of the factors identified by Takanishi (this volume) would address the problematic issues cited by Rutter and Smith (1995). Supportive and enabling adult relationships with adolescents are essential throughout most of this decade of life (Leffert & Petersen, 1995; Petersen & Leffert, 1995) to reduce excessive and destructive peer influences, including youth culture. In a recent national study of adolescents, having connections to parents, family, and school was found to be protective against almost every health risk behavior examined (Resnick et al., 1997). The breakdown of important social groups, especially the family, has created more stress on young people and has frequently left them without socializing and supportive guidance as well as without parents or other adults who love and care for them. The now legion cases of angry, destructive adolescents who were neglected or abused as children provide stark testimony to the costs of our failures as adults and the failings of the "advanced technological societies" we have created. Repairing the social fabric where it is torn or thin must be a high priority. Where communities are yet intact, as is the case in some "less developed" regions of the world, we must preserve the strengths of family and community but at the same time enable them to prepare their young people to compete in the world ahead by using information technology where possible to permit them to stay in villages that provide important nurturance.

Whatever interventions we develop to produce the kind of young people described by Takanishi (this volume), we also must take care to identify from the outset how they can become self-sustaining. Short-lived programs that create hope and then disappoint can ultimately be more destructive than no programs at all. Increased accountability to at least do no harm is clearly important. Self-sustaining programs, conversely, provide cumulative learning and strength and benefit adolescents as well as their families and communities. Fortunately, examples of these sorts of programs already exist and can be replicated and improved.

In closing, I quote from Federico Mayor (1995), Director General of UNESCO, who said; "What matters in the end is not the world we will leave to our children, but the children we will leave to the world."

References

Carnegie Council on Adolescent Development. (1995). *Great transitions: Preparing adolescents for a new century*. Washington, DC: Author.

Hamilton, S. F. (1994). Social roles for youth: Interventions in unemployment. In A. C. Petersen & J. T. Mortimer (Eds.), *Youth unemployment and society* (pp. 248–269). New York: Cambridge University Press.

Leffert, N., & Petersen, A. C. (1995). Patterns of development in adolescence. In M. Rutter & D. Smith (Eds.), *Psychosocial disorders of young people: Time trends and their causes* (pp. 67–103). Chichester, England: Wiley.

Levine, S., & Wiener, S. G. (1989). Coping with uncertainty: A paradox. In D. S. Palermo (Ed.), *Coping with uncertainty: Behavioral and developmental perspectives* (pp. 1–16). Hillsdale, NJ: Lawrence Erlbaum.

Mayor, F. (1995). Address launching the United Nations Year for Tolerance, New York.

Petersen, A. C., & Leffert, N. (1995). What is special about adolescence? In M. Rutter (Ed.), *Psychosocial disturbances in young people: Challenges for prevention* (pp. 3–36). Cambridge, England: Cambridge University Press.

Petersen, A. C., Susman, E. J., & Beard, J. L. (1989). The development of coping responses during adolescence: Endocrine and behavioral aspects. In D. S. Palermo (Ed.), *Coping with uncertainty: Behavioral and developmental perspectives* (pp. 151–172). Hillsdale, NJ: Lawrence Erlbaum.

Resnick, M. D., Bearman, P. S., Blum, R. W., Bauman, K. E., Harris, K. E., Jones, J., Tabor, J., Beuhring, T., Sieving, R. E., Shew, M., Ireland, M., Bearingger, L. H., & Udry, J. R. (1997). Protecting adolescents from harm: Findings from the National Longitudinal Study on Adolescent Health. *Journal of the American Medical Association, 278*, 823–832.

Rutter, M., & Smith, D. (Eds.) (1995a). *Psychosocial disturbance in young people: Time trends and their causes*. Cambridge, England: Cambridge University Press.

Rutter, M., & Smith, D. (1995b). Towards causal explanations of time trends in psychosocial disorders of young people. In M. Rutter & D. Smith (Eds.), *Psychosocial disturbance in young people: Time trends and their causes* (pp. 782–808). Cambridge, England: Cambridge University Press.

Smith, D., & Rutter, M. (1995). Time trends in psychosocial disorders of youth. In M. Rutter & D. Smith (Eds.), *Psychosocial disturbance in young people: Time trends and their causes* (pp. 763–781). Cambridge, England: Cambridge University Press.

Endnotes

Chapter 1

1 Adolescents are in the process of forming personal values that will guide their goals and choices in adulthood. Because adolescents' values appear to be more malleable than those of adults and more affected by social change, the adolescent years have been characterized as "impressionable years" (Alwin, 1994).

Chapter 3

1 In the Baltimore Study of Teenage Motherhood, several factors were predictive of the mother's economic dependence in 1984: level of education of the teenage mothers' parents, their own educational aspirations, whether they were at grade level, and whether they had two or more children. Over 40% of young mothers whose parents did not have at least a 10th-grade level of education were on welfare in 1984 (compared with about 16% of those with more educated parents); about 37% of those who had low educational aspirations were on welfare (compared with less than 11% of those with high educational aspirations), as were almost 45% of those who were not at grade level themselves (compared with about 17% of those at grade level) and over 40% of those who had at least two children (versus 20% of those with fewer or no children) (see Figure 6.1, p. 134, from Furstenberg, Brooks-Gunn, & Morgan, 1987). It is likely that the second generation of young mothers, given their high rates of grade failure (compared with their mothers) and school graduation rates (compared with their peers) will have difficulties in the labor market.

2 Because the girls who are being compared differed in mother's age of childbearing and their own timing of childbearing, we cannot attribute these differences to maternal effects alone.

Chapter 5

1 A youth stage is characteristic of modern societies, but it also existed in many others, including medieval Europe (for boys of noble families), England in the 16th century, ancient Greece, and African age-graded societies like the Swazi and Zulus.

2 The term *cultural capital* has been used to designate a family's or other group's assemblage of goods, especially prestige goods, and knowledge that are deemed to be of cultural significance. In general, it covers the less tangible elements in the acquisition or maintenance of high status. A difficulty in this term is that *capital* usually refers to elements in the process

of production, including means to production and control over the output. A better term is *cultural stock*, a supply of tangible or intangible goods that can be stored, exchanged, or given way. Capital is not given away; stock, however, is often distributed as a reward or in order to accrue honor through generosity. The appropriate model is that of redistributive economies, not capitalistic ones. Adolescents, like adults, distribute their cultural stock through judicious sharing or exchange of goods and knowledge.

3 Parents, too, are anticipating the disruption of the family when their adolescent children leave home in the near future at the same time that they may be looking forward to the greater leisure and free time they will have once the children are on their own. For adolescent children and their parents in modern society, adolescence is a time of ambivalent feelings about the near future and ambiguity about present roles and relationships.

4 This material comes from discussions with Joanna Dankowska and from Dankowska (1996).

5 This material comes from Davis (1995) and Davis and Davis (1989).

Chapter 6

1 The research was sponsored by the Anglo German Foundation for Studies in Industrial Society.

Chapter 10

1 Dahrendorf (1994, pp. 424–425) here refers to classical authors interpreting modernity, especially de Tocqueville and Marx. In Jonestown, a mass suicide of 916 American fellows of Father Jones occurred.

2 These investigations were sponsored by the Federal Ministry for Family.

3 All the results reported here were tested on the basis of log-linear models by means of the system JMP (SAS Institute 1996). The data were first published in Bertram (1995).

4 The most path-breaking study in this context is still the investigation by Rossi and Rossi (1990).

5 With respect to Kaufmann and Leisering, the terms "generational interactions" and "generational relations" are differentiated as follows: Generational interaction is taken within the context of the social interaction of family members of different generations, whereas generational relations refer to the social systems in the organization of time, which may not be experienced by the single person. See Leisering (1992, pp. 44ff.), cited in Kaufmann, in Lüscher & Schultheiß (1993, p. 97). See also Mannheim (1964) and Matthes (1985).

6 Examples for this discussion are Clausen (1995), Conger & Elder (1995), and Vaillant (1995).

Chapter 11

1 For respondents who were unsure, a middle category ("neither likely nor unlikely") was added as a response, resulting in a final 5-point ordinal scale ranging from very unlikely through very likely.

2 For consistency, the stability measures were reverse coded so that, in the final scale, high values correspond to *instability*.

3 Because the number of individual cases used to create the aggregate measures varied slightly by community, the variance of the residuals is not constant. Therefore, weighted least-squares (WLS) regression was used to induce homoscedasticity of error variances: Each

case was weighted by the square root of the unweighted sample size (Hanushek & Jackson 1977, pp. 143, 152), giving more weight to areas with a larger respondent sample.
4 These data reflect the location of incidents known to the police – not arrests. Incident data are thus a good proximate measure of the actual distribution of crime by geographical location. I gratefully acknowledge the assistance of Richard Block, Chip Coldren, and Jeffrey Morenoff in obtaining, cleaning, and aggregating these incident data to the neighborhood cluster level.

Chapter 14

1 Because respondents with more frequent senior year illicit drug use were oversampled by a factor of 3 for follow-up, corrective weighting of .333 was required for those individuals. All analyses were conducted using the weighted sample.
2 Preliminary analyses indicated that shifting the cohort groupings by 1 or 2 years would not yield findings substantially different from those presented in this chapter.
3 We conducted preliminary analyses to determine if it would be possible to combine some of these groups (e.g., the employed-away and the employed–home and away), but found that such combinations would result in the loss of some important information.
4 Although we were unable to avoid violating some assumptions of using repeated-measures ANOVAs (i.e., MANOVAs), we decided to use this procedure for two reasons: (1) MANOVAs tend to be robust to the violations we encountered; and (2) the clarity of the correspondence between the pattern of statistically significant findings and the several illustrations of the means argued for the validity of the inferential statistics. Moreover, among the various analytic options, the MANOVA strategy provided the most straightforward way to address the purposes of this study. Because of the unbalanced design (i.e., independent variables are not orthogonal), order of entry of independent variables was a concern (e.g., Stevens, 1986); the selected order (i.e., cohort, gender, life paths) reflected the extent to which the variables were exogenous, and preliminary analyses (in which the order was reversed) revealed that order of entry had little impact on significant findings. Although there were moderate intercorrelations among many of the dependent variables, we decided against the use of doubly multivariate ANOVAs (i.e., repeated-measures MANOVAs) because there was some amplification of relationships among the well-being variables with age and some disintegration of relationships among the substance use variables with age as well as because of an already complex analytic design. (See Schulenberg et al., 1998, for details on assumption violations.)
5 There was an initial concern with the potential for small-cell difficulties in these four-way MANOVAs for the well-being analyses (66 cells, with $n = 3, 586$). Thus, after the four-way MANOVAs were conducted, two sets of three-way MANOVAs (i.e., Cohort by Gender by Age; Life Paths by Gender by Age) were conducted only for the well-being measures. With very few minor exceptions, these analyses yielded conclusions consistent with those from the four-way analyses.

Chapter 16

1 Labor force participation of students in high school and college has grown substantially since 1950 (Levitan & Gallo, 1991), and participation rates of females have converged with those of males. However, employment-to-population ratios for Black males have substantially worsened. Although those ratios varied around 50 for White males ages 16–19 from 1954 to 1994 and above 20 for Black females of the same age, they increased from 37 to 48 for White

females and decreased from 52 to 25 for Black males (*Economic Report of the President,* 1995, Table B-39, p. 319). Part of this decline for Black males reflects higher rates of school enrollment, but it also indicates that Black males are much less able to combine enrollment with employment than White males or females and that they face much higher unemployment rates after graduation.

2 The percentage of 29- to 31-year-olds who had been employed in their current job more than 2 years in 1988 was 54.8 for male high school graduates, 31.7 for female high school graduates, 27.7 for male high school dropouts, and 19.4 for female high school dropouts (*Economic Report of the President,* 1995, Table 2, p. 5). For a competing analysis, see Klerman and Karoly (1995).

3 Germany provides this protection with apprenticeship, as discussed later. Japan does so primarily through close relations with high schools whereby schools recommend their best students for employment, which motivates students who do not compete for college entrance to perform well in school. See Rosenbaum, Kariya, Settersten, and Maier (1990).

4 The first author drafted some sections of the interim *Forgotten Half* report, which cites his 1987 article. His book was published in 1990 with a jacket blurb by then Governor Clinton. The author spoke at the December 1990 conference and communicated his opinions about some aspects of the School-to-Work Opportunities Act while it was in draft form. Marc Tucker, President of the National Center on Education and the Economy, and Ira Magaziner, his co-chair on the Commission on the Skills of the American Workplace, both spoke at the 1990 conference and were important advisors to President Clinton. Hilary Pennington, President of Jobs for the Future, and Bob Schwartz, Education Program Director for the Pew Charitable Trusts, were both members of the new administration's transition team and were active in drafting the legislation. Jobs for the Future has provided the most significant support to states and communities developing youth apprenticeship and related approaches. Sam Halperin, Executive Director of the William T. Grant Foundation Commission on Work, Family and Citizenship was very active in stimulating and shaping the legislation. The German Marshall Fund and especially Anne Heald helped lay the groundwork by sending numerous delegations to observe apprenticeship firsthand in Europe.

5 A compelling analysis of German apprenticeship concludes that small firms receive a net gain by training apprentices because they contribute more to production than they cost, whereas large firms invest more in training apprentices and recoup their costs only by retaining apprentices as regular employees for several years after their training has been completed (Soskice, 1994).

6 The first three cohorts at the end of their senior year of high school. The members of the fourth cohort had not completed their senior year at this writing. Apprentices who dropped out or completed only one year are excluded.

Index